Luminos is the open access monograph publishing program from UC Press. Luminos provides a framework for preserving and reinvigorating monograph publishing for the future and increases the reach and visibility of important scholarly work. Titles published in the UC Press Luminos model are published with the same high standards for selection, peer review, production, and marketing as those in our traditional program. www.luminosoa.org

SCALE

SCALE

Discourse and Dimensions of Social Life

———

Edited by

E. Summerson Carr and Michael Lempert

UNIVERSITY OF CALIFORNIA PRESS

University of California Press, one of the most distinguished university presses in the United States, enriches lives around the world by advancing scholarship in the humanities, social sciences, and natural sciences. Its activities are supported by the UC Press Foundation and by philanthropic contributions from individuals and institutions. For more information, visit www.ucpress.edu.

University of California Press
Oakland, California

© 2016 by E. Summerson Carr and Michael Lempert

This work is licensed under a Creative Commons CC-BY-NC-ND license. To view a copy of the license, visit http://creativecommons.org/licenses.

Suggested citation: Carr, E. Summerson and Lempert, Michael (eds.) *Scale: Discourse and Dimensions of Social Life*. Oakland: University of California Press, 2016. DOI: http://doi.org/10.1525/luminos.15

Library of Congress Cataloging-in-Publication Data

Names: Carr, E. Summerson, editor. | Lempert, Michael, editor.
Title: Scale : discourse and dimensions of social life / edited by
E. Summerson Carr and Michael Lempert.
Description: Oakland, California : University of California Press, [2016]
|Includes bibliographical references and index.
Identifiers: LCCN 2016015688| ISBN 9780520291799 (pbk. : alk. paper) |
ISBN 9780520965430 (electronic)
Subjects: LCSH: Scaling (Social sciences)
Classification: LCC H61.27 .S325 2016 | DDC 300.72—dc23
LC record available at https://lccn.loc.gov/2016015688

25 24 23 22 21 20 19 18 17 16
10 9 8 7 6 5 4 3 2 1

To Michicagoan participants, past and present

CONTENTS

List of Illustrations   ix
List of Tables   xi

Introduction: Pragmatics of Scale   1
E. Summerson Carr and Michael Lempert

PART ONE. SCALAR PROJECTS: PROMISES AND PRECARITIES

1. Projecting Presence: Aura and Oratory in William Jennings Bryan's Presidential Races   25
   Richard Bauman

2. Interaction Rescaled: How Buddhist Debate Became a Diasporic Pedagogy   52
   Michael Lempert

3. Shrinking Indigenous Language in the Yukon   70
   Barbra A. Meek

PART TWO. INTERSCALARITY: IMAGINATION AND INSTITUTION

4. Scale-Making: Comparison and Perspective as Ideological Projects   91
   Susan Gal

5. Balancing the Scales of Justice in Tonga   112
   Susan U. Philips

6. Interscaling Awe, De-escalating Disaster 133
   E. Summerson Carr and Brooke Fisher

PART THREE. PREDATORY SCALES: ENCOMPASSMENT AND EVALUATION

7. Scaling Red and the Horror of Trademark 159
   Constantine V. Nakassis

8. Semiotic Vinification and the Scaling of Taste 185
   Michael Silverstein

9. Going Upscale: Scales and Scale-Climbing as Ideological Projects 213
   Judith T. Irvine

Acknowledgments 233
References Cited 235
Contributors 251
Index 255

ILLUSTRATIONS

1.1. William Jennings Bryan, 1896   *27*
1.2. Bryan campaign poster, 1896, "Cross of Gold" speech   *28*
1.3. "Blowing Himself around the Country," political cartoon from *Puck*, 1896   *31*
1.4. Bryan's whistle-stop speech in Wellsville, Ohio, 1896   *34*
1.5. National Phonograph Company advertisement   *41*
1.6a. Suggestions to record dealers for a "Bryan Window"   *45*
1.6b. William Jennings Bryan windows   *45*
3.1. Census data on language in Canada from 1996, 2001, and 2006   *73*
3.2. Aboriginal language endangerment in the Yukon Territory, Canada   *77*
3.3. Languages spoken by Kaska First Nations populations   *81*
3.4. Speaker competence in relation to potential role as aboriginal language instructor   *84*
3.5. Individuals who could potentially gain fluency in Kaska quickly   *84*
3.6. Fluency scaled in relation to potential to learn   *85*
4.1. Fractal recursions in Gábor and Galasi's argument   *108*
6.1. "Monolith"   *137*
6.2. Scaling the monolith, still from *2001: A Space Odyssey*   *141*
6.3a. Docking relations   *150*
6.3b. Docking relations   *150*
6.4. Scaling disaster: head of the Tsunami Evacuation Interpretive Trail   *151*
7.1. Christian Louboutin's registered trademark for "a lacquered red sole on footwear"   *160*
7.2. Yves Saint Laurent's "DNA of the Brand—YSL Colors"   *161*

7.3. Au-Tomotive Gold keychain, VW registered trademark, and VW key chain   *176*
8.1. Evaluative dimensions of the serial phases of the aesthetic encounter with wine   *190*
8.2. The "eucharistic" semiotics of aesthetic evaluative discourse   *197*
8.3. The "aroma wheel"   *200*
8.4. Advertisement for Colombian coffee growers   *205*

TABLES

8.1. A Wine-Tasting Note by Sir Michael Broadbent, Formerly of Christie's   *189*
8.2. Genre Structure of the Wine-Tasting Note of Table 8.1, Exemplifying Register Usage   *191*
8.3. Tasting Notes on 2007 Puligny Montrachet, Folatieres   *193*
8.4. Genre Structure of the *Wine Advocate* Wine-Tasting Note of Table 8.3, Exemplifying Register Usage   *193*
8.5. Genre Structure of the Stephen Tanzer Wine-Tasting Note of Table 8.3, Exemplifying Register Usage   *193*
8.6. Wine-Note-Like Coffee-Tasting Notes from a 1991 Starbucks Customer Flyer   *204*
8.7. Starbucks' Explanation of "Barista Talk" for Its Retail Customers   *206*
8.8. Barista "Rant" about an Encounter with a Noncompliant Customer   *207*

INTRODUCTION

Pragmatics of Scale

E. Summerson Carr and Michael Lempert

In the first place, I wish to lay before you a particular, plain statement, touching the living bulk of this leviathan, whose skeleton we are briefly to exhibit. Such a statement may prove useful here.

According to a careful calculation I have made, and which I partly base upon Captain Scoresby's estimate, of seventy tons for the largest sized Greenland whale of sixty feet in length; according to my careful calculation, I say, a Sperm Whale of the largest magnitude, between eighty-five and ninety feet in length, and something less than forty feet in its fullest circumference, such a whale will weigh at least ninety tons; so that, reckoning thirteen men to a ton, he would considerably outweigh the combined population of a whole village of one thousand one hundred inhabitants.

Think you not then that brains, like yoked cattle, should be put to this leviathan, to make him at all budge to any landsman's imagination?

—HERMAN MELVILLE, MOBY-DICK

How can one man fathom the sheer magnitude of a sperm whale when all that lie before him are skeletal remains? Melville forewarns that landsmen are not equipped to imagine something so great, their brains being yoked like cattle when it comes to matters of scale. Thus, he assigns his narrator, Ishmael, a daunting task—that is, to *communicate* the leviathan to those who cannot see, nor even imagine it for themselves.

To that end, Ishmael is intent on producing a "particular, plain statement" that "touch[es] the living bulk." At first, he resorts to measurement. He makes a "careful calculation" of the whale's length and circumference, converting what one could measure of the bones with certain equipment on hand to the weight of the behemoth's past flesh in tons. Ishmael grows the whale by way of numbers, thus relying on the authority of quantification. Still, this quantification is apparently not enough, since Ishmael exploits professional allegiance as well as arithmetic to do his scalar work. His calculations are based on citing, and relying upon, Captain Scoresby, whose surname not so subtly suggests that quantifications must be socially qualified. In this, Ishmael concedes that the problem of scale eludes any hope of unadorned description. He finds that he must rely on rhetoric to make big and render real both the bygone "living bulk" and the actual skeletal remains that now stand before him.

Sensing that neither the appeal to maritime expertise nor the cool, authoritative objectivity of measurement can transport the innumerate landsmen, Ishmael offers a poignant analogy so as to better apprehend the whale's greatness. He scales the whale in reference to the human body: one ton, he reckons, equals thirteen men, which means that the whale "considerably outweigh[s]" a whole village. Through this calculus, he zooms out from the most immediate comparable unit, the whaler's own body, until he reaches that of a village, thereby offering a palpable sense of enormity. Ishmael thereby dwarfs, in aggregate, the members of his audience, just as he once had been dwarfed by the towering beast in the awesome event of the still unanalyzed encounter. In other words, his exercise in scale is a lesson in perspective, an attempt to get his land-bound audience to see what and how the whaler has seen. After all, if the leviathan is to be made myth out of a single man's phantasm, the whaler's calculations must be collectively apprehended.

In describing the whale, he goes on to suggest that there is something enduring, if not eternal, about its qualities, thereby further enriching a statement that once promised to be simple, empirical, plain. Scaling, it turns out, may organize not only spatial relations but spatio*temporal* ones as well. Indeed, when one tries to apprehend things and their qualities, a present moment may be linked to and authorized by a moment figured far back or projected forward in time. In order to determine when and where we are, we may evoke a grand continuity, if not an evolution. The scaling of the whale in temporal terms is evident as Ishmael continues:

> There are forty and odd vertebrae in all, which in the skeleton are not locked together. They mostly lie like the great knobbed blocks on a Gothic spire, forming solid courses of heavy masonry. The largest, a middle one, is in width something less than three feet, and in depth more than four. The smallest, where the spine tapers away into the tail, is only two inches in width, and looks something like a white billiard-ball. I was told that there were still smaller ones, but they had been lost by some little cannibal urchins, the priest's children, who had stolen them to play marbles with. Thus we see how that the spine of even the hugest of living things tapers off at last into simple child's play.

Here we see that a ready sign of frailty, of death—a creature's very skeleton—is represented as that which endures like heavy masonry. Indeed, Ishmael begins this passage implying there is something mighty, if not godly, in the Gothic construction of the whale. However remote to the imagination the creature may at first have seemed, note that the leviathan is ultimately rendered approachable by even the most ungodly among us, from pool sharks to cannibal urchins.

Note further how Ishmael offers this gift of perspective to his audience by way of explicit comparisons, reminding us that scaling not only involves manipulating standardized measures but deploying metaphor as well. In tracing the vertebrae, Ishmael moves analogically from spirelike majesty to childlike play, and from the solid, heavy greatness of the past to a highly malleable, quotidian present. He sets before the mind's eye an array of things whose qualities and relations give both the impression of a great spatial and temporal scale, and a vantage from which to study it, a view from *somewhere*. The passage thereby reminds us that, as human beings, we are uniquely endowed with the powers of perspective, which unyoke the imagination and allow us to steal, play with, and ultimately manage even the most initially awesome spectacles of our worlds. After all, we can see that the huge is but a marble or a pool ball if we look at it in a certain way. When we *scale*, we orient, compare, connect, and position ourselves so that "even the hugest of living things tapers off at last into simple child's play."

. . .

Like Melville's account of one eloquent oarsman, this volume demonstrates that the scales that social actors rely upon to organize, interpret, orient, and act in their worlds are not given but made—and rather laboriously so. For *to scale* is not simply to assume or assert "bigness" or "smallness" by way of a ready-made calculus. Rather, and as we have seen above, people use language to scale the world around them. Indeed, even the greatness of whales must be discursively forged out of comparisons and distinctions among potentially scalable entities (bones, men, villages, spires, billiard balls) and qualities (weight, height, length, circumference, and structural integrity). Although things can be made big though analogy, scale-making always also entails drawing distinctions between the bigness of a whale's rib and the smallness of a marble, for instance. As an inherently relational and comparative endeavor, scaling may thus connect and even conflate what is geographically, geopolitically, temporally, or morally "near" while simultaneously distinguishing that nearness from that which is "far." Similarly, scaled hierarchies are the effects of efforts to sort, group, and categorize many things, people, and qualities in terms of relative degrees of elevation or centrality. Think, for example, of the way one entity or domain seems to encompass another, as with maps that subordinate localities within higher order administrative units, or of the way nation-states are commonly thought to hover "above" communities.

The fact that scaling involves vantage points and the positioning of actors with respect to such vantage points means that there are no ideologically neutral scales, and people and institutions that come out "on top" of scalar exercises often reinforce the distinctions that so ordained them. In other words, the scales that seem most natural to us are intensively institutionalized, and that is why collectives readily accept that the leviathan of the State or God hovers above landsmen, or that one realm of political or ritual authority encompasses another. Yet people are not simply subject to preestablished scales; they develop scalar projects and perspectives that anchor and (re)orient themselves. Working from the premise that scale is process before it is product, this volume is dedicated to explaining how, why, and to what ends people and institutions scale their worlds.

THE PROBLEMS OF SCALE

Over the last several decades, a diverse group of scholars across a range of disciplines have suggested that scholarly analysis is yoked by limited understandings of scale.[1] For instance, the problem of scale has been taken up concertedly in cultural geography so as to liberate "procrustean research that attempts to fit complex spatial politics within the narrow confines of a handful of conceptually given scales such as the local, national or global" (Moore 2008, 211; see also Marston 2000; Taylor 1982). Critical geographers, like Erik Swyngedouw, have underscored that "scalar configurations [are] the outcome of socio-spatial processes that regulate and organise social power relations" (2004, 26). And, in an effort to capture the manifold ways in which actors can in turn manipulate and sometimes defy the scalar formations they confront in social life, geographer Neil Smith wrote a set of influential essays on scale-"jumping" (1992) and scale-"bending" (2004).

Critical theorizations of scale can be found in a number of other disciplines, if far too rarely. In gender studies, the division of the "private" and "personal" versus the "public" and "political" has been addressed as a problem of scale, with scholars working to add empirical and theoretical weight to the feminist adage that the personal *is* political (e.g., Berlant 1997, 2008; Gal 2002; Steedman 1987). Many in science studies have insisted that in order to theorize the travels and translations of forms of knowledge, informants' scalar distinctions, like "bench-to-bedside," must be interrogated rather than simply adopted (Sunder Rajan, and Leonelli 2013; see also Lynch 1985; Yaneva 2005). And in sociology, the enduring methodological standoff between the "macro" and the "micro" has led to a number of recent proposals, perhaps most prominent and compelling of which is Michel Callon and Bruno Latour's Actor Network Theory, which begins with the assertion that there are no intrinsic differences between these so-called domains of sociological study (Callon and Latour 1981; Callon 1986; 2013; Latour 2005; see also Knorr-Cetina and Cicourel 1981). The task of the analyst, they further suggest, is to leave behind a priori scalar distinctions and instead empirically track how social actors carve and cleave—or *scale*—their worlds.

The problem of scale has long been a concern in anthropology as well, as we ot to connect what we conceive as events with the *longue durée,* fleeting face-to-face interaction with durable social institutions, or the long arm of global media with discrete points of its putative reception. In a sense, anthropology from its inception has been preoccupied with matters of scale, focused as we have been on questions about what is particular to the places and peoples we study, and what, if anything, is shared by humanity as a whole. For over two decades now, ethnographies of globalization have complicated cartographies that break the world into discrete nation-states and exposed networks and flows that may intersect with such official geographies of power but are often orthogonal to them (for example, Appadurai 1996; Clifford 1997; Chu 2010; Helmreich 2009). For instance, Arjun Appadurai's (2006) *Fear of Small Numbers* reflects on the manner in which "cellular globalization," whether that of "terror" networks or transnational activists, threatens to dispense with the nation-state, for ill and for good. Similarly, in *Alien Oceans*, Stefan Helmreich underscores that the "local and global are effects—not preconditions of how genome science [that he studies] is narrated" (2009, 173).

A few anthropologists have concertedly and critically examined the scalar habits of the discipline. For instance, Marilyn Strathern, who defines scale as "the organization of perspectives on objects of knowledge and enquiry" (2004, xvi), suggests that anthropological analysis is, in its very essence, a scale-making endeavor. It is so because ethnographers must find ways to cope with cultural complexity so as to make it legible, and to do so, we tack back and forth between different ways of looking at the same things, whether through different sets of eyes, with different degrees of focus, or with different ways of relating to our object, as distinctive, singular, composite, or metonymic.

Anthropologist Anna Tsing, who originally took up the notion of scale in her 2008 book *Friction*, worries that "*scale* has become a verb that requires precision; to scale well is to develop the quality called *scalability*, that is, the ability to expand—and expand, and expand—without rethinking basic elements" (2012, 505; see also 2015). What is lost, she asks, when we continue to think in metonyms, as if the corporation is just a "bigger" version of the individual, for instance? In light of these questions, Tsing urges anthropologists to interrogate "ideologies of scale" (2000, 347) and attend to "scale making" projects (2000, 2012, 2015). Along similar lines, James Ferguson (2006) has written about how stubborn "topographies of power"—that is, conceptual scales that project that the international, national, and civil stand in tiered relationship—make it difficult if not impossible for analysts to track how contemporary African politics actually unfold, as nongovernmental organizations use state letterhead and guerilla armies fight having been trained in China and funded by American right-wing churches. Like Latour and Callon, he suggests that social analysts should be prepared to travel analytically on a "flatter" terrain in order to appreciate how scales are produced and used knowledge and social relations.

Indeed, anthropologists have grown increasingly impatient about scale as a heuristic, though alternative analytics have been hard to come by. Consider an essay in the journal *Cultural Anthropology*, in which one young anthropologist notes that many in the Occupy Movement have been captivated by the scalar antinomies of "the local" and "global," geopolitical categories that they then ethically elaborate into a narrative of the corrupt "They" of global finance versus the communal, democratic, activist "We" (Glück 2013). He urges anthropologists to follow the lead of the most sophisticated of the Occupy activists, who have jettisoned such seductive scalar tropes and refocused their energies on reimagining and erecting alternative scalar formations like "interurban" networks and "Inter-Occupy." This pragmatic approach to questions of scale can be found in a handful of recent ethnographies, such as Timothy Choy's (2011) account of how Hong Kong environmentalists build scalar analytics through which they can project various forms of "specificity," and Stefan Helmreich's (2009) ethnography of marine biologists' fascinating attempts to scale the sea. This important work notwithstanding, even those of us anthropologists who document scale-making projects still regularly slip back into assuming that scales are ontological givens, suggesting their stubborn grip on our thinking.

In linguistic anthropology, more specifically, a critical interest in scale began to emerge as the spatiotemporal boundaries of its objects of analysis—such as "language," "discourse," "interaction," and the "speech event"—were questioned rather than assumed. The rediscovery of Mikhail Bakhtin's writings encouraged attention to the pervasive presence of other voices in what apparently single speakers say and made it difficult to maintain that speech is ever anchored in any one place and time. Accordingly, research in the past decade on "interdiscursivity" and "intertextuality" has stressed just how porous the spatial and temporal boundaries of communicative events can be. Rather than treat episodes of communication as if they were always already neatly circumscribed, linguistic anthropologists have instead effectively explored how event boundaries and interevent relations are forged by actors through discursive practice itself (see especially Agha 2005). Indeed, the actors we study habitually point to, cite, reanimate, and repurpose text and talk that they understand to be located "elsewhere" in time and space, thereby troubling our very sense of where they stand. In taking seriously actors' busy event-linking, relation-making labor, one acquires a keen sensitivity both to process and practice, a sensitivity that we, in this volume, share.[2]

In sociolinguistics, some scholars have turned to scale to expose how languages under globalization are "organized on different, layered (i.e., vertical rather than horizontal) scale-levels" (Blommaert 2010, 5), an insight indebted in part to Wallersteinian world-system theory. Indeed, standard languages are frequently imagined and institutionally positioned as translocal compared to other language varieties, which has obvious consequences for the perpetuation of social and political inequities, given that competence in a standard language is unevenly distributed in multilingual nation-states. In this sense, language is seen as a resource that enables or inhibits scalar mobility. Sociolinguistic research also considers how actors negotiate and sometimes help reproduce preexisting scalar formations with the aid of language. For instance, Jan Blommaert (2007, 6) offers this elegant little illustration:

> Student: "I'll start my dissertation with a chapter reporting on my fieldwork."
> Tutor: "We start our dissertations with a literature review chapter here."

The tutor, explains Blommaert, (2007, 6), performs what he and others call a "scale-jump" "in which s/he moves from the local and situated to the translocal and general, invoking practices that have validity beyond the here-and-now."

A sensitivity to language, combined with an attention to the capacity of actors to negotiate scalar distinctions, is notable in Charles and Clara Mantini-Briggs's (2004) ethnography of conspiracy narratives in the 1992–1994 cholera epidemics of eastern Venezuela. They describe how health officials racialized indigenous victims, blaming their indigeneity for their failure to distinguish natural from cultural causes of disease and their habit of turning to traditional healers when they should have chosen biomedical care. Assumed by the state to be trapped by this dense locality, indigenes responded defiantly. Specifically, they hatched conspiratorial narratives, which "involve impressive leaps of scale, as they connected the deaths of relatives and neighbors with racial conflicts, national policies, international relations, and transnational corporations" (Briggs 2004, 175). Not only did their stories about cholera seem to "leap" between what was already understood to be local and global (a common feature of conspiracy reasoning, as Fredric Jameson [1992] and others have remarked [Marcus 1999]), but they often did so with such force that they pierced that scalar imaginary itself, "making the notion that members of 'traditional' communities cannot see beyond local horizons or rigid cognitive patterns and fixed points of reference seem ludicrous" (Briggs 2004, 175). The question remains as to whether the now common trope of "leaping" or "jumping" scales (see also Smith 1992) denaturalizes or reifies the scalar divides being crossed.

In pursuing the ethnography of scale, we will inevitably find that tropes like scalar "leaps" or "jumps," or the often-used idea of scaling "up" or "down" do not mean any one thing across cases and should not be treated as stable analytic terms. Furthermore, these tropes hardly exhaust the dynamics of scale but rather invite us to recognize that there is much more drama to scale—plot and character, stakes and consequences—than generic, analytical scalar distinctions suggest. In all these cases, we want to remain critical when actors or analysts naturalize what they claim to cross, bend, or leap over, as if such scales were always already there, waiting to be inhabited, manipulated, or traversed.

SIGN ACTIVITY AND THE (UN)MAKING OF "MICRO" AND "MACRO"

Despite all these thoughtful interventions, the problem of scale persists in anthropology and beyond. Think, for instance, of the continued adherence to the macro-micro distinction and tendency to assign political economy to the former, face-to-face interaction to the latter. Think, too, how we continue to divvy up academic labor accordingly and not uncommonly with a lack of respect "as when anthropologists alternate between accusing one another now of myopia, now of panoptics" (Strathern 2004, xv). This disrespect stems in part from a conviction that scalar perspectives in scholarship, institutionalized as they are in our disciplines (e.g., micro versus macro sociology or history or economics), limit what and how we can see and know. Disciplinary scaling is felt to have epistemological and, by extension, ethicopolitical consequences. Ignore, say, the capitalist world-economy, and we will fail to see the real, systemic causes of inequality, making our research not just blinkered but complacent. Alternatively, humanist critics typically complain, for instance, "that analysis in terms of the world-system entails a fatal disrespect for culture, or subjectivity, or difference, or agency, or the local" (Palumbo-Liu, Robbins, and Tanoukhi 2011, 5).

Again and again, we find ourselves intellectually stymied in micro-macro standoff. While many of us feel that such a priori scaling of social and intellectual life is unproductive, even obfuscating—and have had plenty of reminders that this is so—we continue to rely upon categories such as macro and micro as if they were something other than the products of our own or others' classifying activities (cf. Barnes 2001). We ontologize scalar perspectives, rather than ask how they were forged and so focused. Indeed, it is all too easy to proceed with our analyses as if the oft-critiqued but still-convenient tiers of macro, meso, and micro were the ready-made platforms for social practice, as if social life simply unfolded in more or less intimate, proximate, local, grounded, or contained situations.

How might we open up analyses beyond these stubborn scalar distinctions so that we are then in a position to understand the scalar practices of social life? This volume responds by paying special attention to the semiotic means by which social actors and analysts scale our worlds. In doing this, we circumvent familiar prejudices about the purportedly inherent micro scale of signs, including the widespread assertion that the origin of language is in the minds of discrete individuals, or that face-to-face "interaction" is inescapably local. After all, such a view scales language use before our investigation can even begin. Nor do we assert that sign behavior is somehow foundational—a view that would risk smuggling back in the idea that semiosis is somehow underneath other, more macro orders of existence, perhaps even generative of them.

Rather, we take a semiotic approach because we regard it as an especially powerful ethnographic strategy for showing how scale is a practice and process before it is product. Inclined to explore how event-boundaries and social relations are forged, figured, and sorted by actors through their discursive practice, we can elucidate the *process* of scaling with marked clarity. Ethnographically, the chapters that follow document the complexities of scale as it is produced and experienced in the social worlds we study, challenging the presumed fixity of ready-made analytic scale(s). Embarking from the conviction that social analysis should resist the urge to "settle scale in advance" (Latour 2005, 220), we are especially interested in elaborating the work required to bring scale into being and make it matter in social and cultural life. Accordingly, we do not wish to pin down the definition of scale or list all possible scalar distinctions, nor even to catalogue the ways it is made in the fields that we study. Instead, we encourage an empirical and theoretical openness to learn about social life and action by examining the diverse ways that scales are conceived, cultivated, practiced, and institutionalized.

THE PRAGMATICS OF SCALE

To attend to the *pragmatics of scale* means—most fundamentally—to take a critical distance from given scalar distinctions, whether our own or others', and focus instead on the social circumstances, dynamics, and consequences of scale-making as social practice and project. Since scales are the more or less stable effect of people's conceptual and practical labor, we begin with an inquiry into how the fields we study have been scaled as they have, whether in relation to the bigness of a whale, the intimacy and efficacy of a communal here and now, or the qualities of some media that prompt people to call it "mass." We assume that the scales we encounter in our studies have been built—that is conceptualized and materialized—for the convenience of scale-makers, as pragmatists in their own right. But since scale-making projects are also often institutionalizing projects, in which a particular way of seeing and being is socially enforced (Gal this volume; Irvine this volume), we are especially careful to attend to power in the pragmatics of scale—that is, how some positions and perspectives are privileged at the expense of others as scales are institutionalized.

If in one way our approach to scale is pragmatic in the most colloquial sense of analytically prioritizing situated practical matters over general principles, readers may also find evidence of an affinity with, if not an allegiance to, the early American pragmatism of writers such as Peirce, James, and Dewey. Along these lines, this volume examines not just how scale materializes but also how and why scale matters. Indeed, the chapters that follow ask what scalar distinctions illuminate for social actors, empirically speaking, and how these distinctions serve as the basis of practical action. After all, scales are useful, in part, because they help people orient their actions, organize their experience, and make determinations about who and what is valuable. As we will see, scaling can allow us to imagine some things, encounters, or events as status elevating, as Silverstein (this volume) shows for wine and wine talk, or democratizing and intimate, as Bauman (this volume) shows as he chronicles William Jennings Bryan's populist speaking tour in 1896. Communities can be constituted in part by scalar regimes, as when a nation-state engaged in a politics of recognition uses scalar methods to monitor and "respect" the health of its minority citizens (Meek this volume). To be sure, scales are ways of seeing and standing in the world, and as such, they are also instruments for political, ritual, professional, and everyday action. Consider that the whole field of American social work education has been organized into subfields of micro-, meso-, and macro-level practice. To study scale, then, is to examine how the ideals of social life stand in tension with notions of what is practically achievable. In this sense, we treat scale as a problem that social actors, as pragmatists in their own right, seek to solve.

Last but not least, we speak of a *pragmatics* of scale to signal our interest in sign behavior as an especially effective material for scale-making. Yet whereas pragmatics, as a branch of linguistics, is perhaps best known as a method for demonstrating the influence of social context on meaningfulness, we do not wish to assume context in advance, but instead look at how contextual boundaries are discursively drawn by social actors who differentiate one place, time, social position, or experience from another. In other words, we are centrally interested in how scales are assembled, made recognizable, and stabilized through various communicative practices. For if it seems obvious that a whale is huge, we must remember the semiotic labor of one whaler stitching together a mass of bones with so many discursive threads.

This is not to say that scaling work is made up simply or exclusively of human sign activity: after all, there are actual skeletons of sperm whales on beaches, even if they have to be *made big* by the semiotic work of scaffolding bones, tons, men, masonry, village, and spire. Accordingly, this volume insists that the study of scale ought to be expansive in what it considers, since scaling projects typically rely on complex, heterogeneous, and sometimes far-flung assemblages that include extra-discursive forms. For instance, think of the multiparty enactment of that mass sporting ritual which makes what appears to be a single wave ripple sequentially across the surface of a teeming crowd. This is scaling-as-sign activity, par excellence. Nevertheless, the wave is impossible, or at least unrecognizable, without the contributions of the ovoid structure of the stadium, the seats arranged in columns and rows, not to mention the moveable limbs of the human participants. In the pages that follow, we give empirical attention to how bodies, technologies, commodities, communities, ecologies, and built environments afford scalar practices and impose limits on those who try to scale them, while nevertheless appreciating that anything can be made big, brought near, or perched atop a hierarchy. Thus, the point of our semiotically oriented pragmatics of scale is neither to cordon off matter from media, nor to collapse the two. Rather it is to take seriously how scaling reaches across and draws together many kinds of participants.

Scholars of all stripes find tempests in teacups, cosmologies in landscapes, social orders in an architectural motif, race or gender or class in an accent. Aren't we all sometimes guilty of feats of scalar magic that depend on our assumptions about the natural scale of things? In promoting a pragmatics of scale, the authors convened in this volume have become keenly aware of how the division of academic labor can prescale our objects of knowledge, thereby supplying us with such assumptions. Methodologically, we therefore engage the study of scale as a reflexive endeavor. For only when we keep careful track of the scalar dimensions embedded in our own habits of analysis can we identify the degree of congruence and tension between our own and others' uses of scale. And ultimately, if we are to show how scales are made evident and effective in social life, we need more inductive, empirically grounded studies of how *scalar projects* socially and ideologically unfold and to what effect.

SCALAR PROJECTS

Social actors not only construct and feel their worlds in scalar terms but also conduct themselves—and try to affect others—accordingly. They have scalar projects, which they engage with varying degrees of reflection. Some of the essays in this volume highlight instances in which social actors take for granted the scalar categories that they build and by which they abide, treating them as if they were always already grounded in nature, inscribed by law, or endowed by the divine. Other chapters focus on instances of scalar innovation: political projects, religious rituals, legal rulings, or marketing strategies that centrally involve manipulating accepted relations of scale so as to achieve particular ends. Richard Bauman's chapter illustrates this well. He chronicles the pioneering scaling-making effort of two-time Democratic presidential candidate William Jennings Bryan, who turned to trains in 1896 and the phonograph in 1908 in a "Herculean" effort to build a voting public. We see serial aggregation at play as the politician takes to the tracks, travels the rails from town to town, and collects as many voters as possible. Yet readers will note that Bryan also aggregates with his words, as when he mentions to audiences at one stop where he has been and where he will go, thereby inviting his immediate audience to locate themselves within a projected "mass." As in the scalar calculus of Ishmael, aggregation is aided by other forms of arithmetic: Bryan shortens his speeches to reach more stops and more people. The frantic pace of the tour is itself communicative of the populist principle of equation, demonstrating that no one stop is more important than another, that he speaks to the "people" and not especially to elites. He benefits from the multiplying effect of newspapers, word of mouth, and his radiating charisma. Through this scalar project, Bryan performs the very principles of democracy.

Michael Lempert's chapter also chronicles an ambitious scalar project, with an eye on the sentiments of those who encounter it and the principles it performs and seeks to produce. Since his exile to India in 1959, the Dalai Lama and like-minded diasporic Buddhist reformers have tried to "expand" the practice of debate—a brash face-to-face argumentation in which monks wrangle twice daily about philosophical doctrine—that has long been central to the curriculum of monasteries of the dominant Geluk sect of Tibetan Buddhism. This practice, its reformers argue, helps inculcate a certain critical rationality—an attribute claimed to be at once Buddhist in origin and consistent with the hallowed faculty of reason celebrated by the European Enlightenment. As Lempert argues in his chapter, reformers promote Tibetan Buddhist debate as a diasporic pedagogy with "universal" relevance, therefore capable of reaching new categories of subjects. Yet despite the aspirations of this scalar project, most Tibetan refugees find the project backward, forever tied to a premodern Tibet.

Indeed, scales can fail, or at least fail to achieve their purposes. After all, Bryan was never elected president. And the diasporic ambitions of Tibetan debate were undermined by a counterdirectional temporal scaling that dragged the practice back in time. With such examples in mind, we would do well to recall the vulnerabilities of scalar projects and the communicative labor needed to make them plausible and sustainable.

INTERSCALAR RELATIONS AND INSTITUTIONS

With the pragmatics of scale put front and center, several challenges in understanding scale come into sharper focus, the most obvious and unsettling of which is that "scale" never means one thing. It is not only that many aspects of social life can be and are scaled (space, time, politics, publics, and interactions of all types); it is also that people employ different *senses of scale* when they engage in scalar practice.

The chapters that follow highlight several distinct analytics of scale commonly used in both social and scholarly life. Mensural scales, for example, are commonplace in the social and applied sciences and include all sorts of methods for measuring and ordering attributes, whether quantitatively and ordinally—as with Likert scales that ask respondents to rank how much they agree or disagree—or qualitatively and nominally, using scales that assign categorical values to numbers without ranking them (i.e., male = 1, female = 2; or blood type A = 1, B = 2, AB = 3, O = 4). Arguably, exercises in quantification are quintessentially scalar to the extent that they claim to capture phenomena in the most "general" terms, implying that qualitative accounts simply fill in the details of the outlines that quantification provides. As Barbra Meek's chapter shows, government-funded Kaska language revitalization efforts in Canada's Yukon Territory centrally involve mensural scaling, through which bureaucrats monitor the health of indigenous languages and allocate resources accordingly. For this they need language experts, who are motivated by and help feed an "acute awareness of the shrinking numbers of speakers" (Meek, this volume) while finding ways for their numbers to speak for themselves. However cool, interest-free, and "objective" their scalar measurements may seem—and *must* seem, insofar as administrative and governmental parties demand both accountability from their experts and an assurance that they won't meddle (Porter 1995, 2006)—the labor involved in scaling must be obscured.

Consider, too, cartographic senses of scale. These include the geometric notion of "uniform scaling" in which the identity and proportionality of some feature is preserved despite transformations that make it smaller or larger. We may extend this notion to consider anxieties about how best to preserve (or destroy) the identity of some thing, practice, or kind of person. For instance, Meek's chapter goes on to show that as bureaucrats count and plot linguistic competence and morbidity, scaling is not strictly a matter of quantitatively tracking, plotting, and remedying decline in linguistic competence per se. At the same time, there are also efforts to examine the proportion of declining speakers in relation to speakers of other dialects, especially with respect to a heteroglot whole—that is, the "larger" imagined community of the territory that ought to be recognizing, and respecting, its indigenous members. Indeed, native language endangerment projects are caught up in a multilingual politics of recognition in which a part-to-whole logic—and the slice-of-the-proverbial-pie distributions that follow from that logic—matters critically.

Some senses of scale imply vertical, hierarchical integration in which one spatiotemporally delimited domain is imagined to be nested "within" another, like tiered concentric circles or embedded matryoshka dolls. The micro, within the meso, within the macro. The local, within the national, within the global. While this sense of scale is especially prominent in ecological models of the social (see, for example, Broffenbrenner 1979), which seek to show how different levels of social activity are part of a whole, we also see it appear in cases where some people or things are figured as more *central* or *encompassing* than others. Indeed, as an inherently comparative or relational endeavor, scaling involves not only standardized measures but also metaphorical practices that are often not recognized by scholars to be scaling at all.

Some try to tease and hold apart various senses of scale as if they could be sorted out typologically. The authors convened here resist this tendency. After all, social actors also frequently combine and strategically shift between distinct senses of scale in ways that demand our attention. For instance, in Ishmael's attempt to persuade, he moves surely between measurements of length and weight to a part-whole, social-geographic scale in which individual bodies are set within a village. So it is not simply that scales are discursively forged as people distinguish, compare, analogize, categorize, and evaluate. It is also that one kind of scale so established can be made to build on and relate to another, resulting in novel *interscalar* assemblages, a configuration of scalar effects that exceeds any one scalar distinction within it.

In her study of "higher" and "lower" court levels in Tonga, Susan Philips sheds light on precisely this issue by explaining how a variety of scalar dimensions reinforce each other, allowing groups of social actors to agree that a wedding is "big," a court is "high," or an infraction is "serious." Her chapter is a study of the powerful effects of *interscalabilty*—that is, the way different potentially scalable qualities or dimensions can be made to reinforce each other, almost like a kind of scaffolding on which people rely but take for granted. Tongans scale courts by way of overlapping distinctions, rather than simply balance or compare what is near in terms of what is far, or what is central in terms of what is peripheral. Philips asserts that there is a totalizing coherence of the overlapping scalar dimensions, a mutual propping up of each other.

For instance, the distinction between a "high" court and a "low" court can be taken for granted by those in their jurisdictions, given that this distinction is sealed by the homologies drawn among aspects of the built environment, levels of "seriousness," scope of jurisdiction, and linguistic conventions, including what language is spoken in which court and when. In contrast to the lower courts, the higher courts enjoy wider geographic jurisdiction; they encompass the lower courts in administrative and legal authority; they handle the more serious cases; they boast larger, more elaborate courthouses—and so on. Many, many mutually reinforcing scalar relations and distinctions conspire to make Tonga's courts into a neatly tiered system whose touted scalar qualities of "high" and "low" seem perfectly natural to those who abide by it. This demonstrates that *interscalar relations* may be stabilized and naturalized to the point that we may no longer even notice these relations *as* relations.

To be sure, scaling projects frequently disavow if not erase their own communicative labor, personnel, and material supports, naturalizing the scalar distinctions they produce. How else could differentially situated actors so frequently agree on what is near and what is far, what is high and what is low, what is local and what is universal? Indeed, Ishmael is not alone in assuming that the scale of the life around him can be "plainly" seen and stated. A pragmatics of scale responds by assuming that scale is always a matter (and a materialization) of a carefully fashioned perspective that orients actors in particular ways.

Interested in why, how, and under what circumstances particular scalar distinctions become salient in certain domains of social practice, this book examines how different and sometimes competing *scalar orientations* are negotiated in the flow of social life. In other words, we show how people make sense of their lives and orient their activities through the scalar distinctions available to them. Along these lines, Summerson Carr and Brooke Fisher consider the intensive scaling work that accompanied the 2012 landing of a dock from Misawa—a tsunami-struck town in northern Japan—on Agate Beach, Oregon. Their chapter examines how various parties—from ecologists to public officials, marine biologists to local tourists—interscaled the dock as "monolithic," "awesome," and "alien" and to what interested ends. For instance, city and state officials seized upon the dock, so scaled, to project a future natural disaster too big to either centrally manage or individually ignore, thereby enacting a form of risk management central to neoliberal governance. At the same time, the story of the dock illustrates how intimate connections can be forged between the human senses and that which has been scaled as awesome and alien, a dynamic Carr and Fisher call *de-escalation*. Documenting the many socialities emerging from the prolifically scaled dock, their chapter shows that there is more than one pragmatics of scale, and that scaling is a practice that can—among other things—spawn a sense of intimacy and an ethic of interrelatedness at the same time that it serves projects that differentially authorize, individuate, and alienate.

On the question of scalar orientation, the volume theorizes the inherently *perspectival* nature of scale, asking of our material "whose scale is it," "what does *this* scale allow one to see and know," and "what does it achieve and for whom"? This is especially clear in Susan Gal's chapter, which explores a clash of scalar perspectives. Gal shows us how serious scalar tensions can surface and be addressed in seemingly mundane places, such as a kitchen conversation in the German-speaking Hungarian town Bóly. In Bóly, most speak German, and all also speak Hungarian, the language of the state and of the larger, nearby county seat, Pécs. Administratively, Bóly is stuck in a subordinate relationship to Pécs, which sometimes troubles townsfolk. People from Bóly can't escape this positioning from within the strictures of this entrenched classification, but they can and sometimes do defy this positioning by deploying *different* comparative models. In one conversation, Bóly speakers invoke a well-known opposition between "farmers" and "artisans," each side of which has its own bank of valued, contrastively defined qualities (e.g., plain versus elaborate, rooted in place versus worldly, etc.). Crucially, these two categories of person are not hierarchically ordered. What makes this model different from the administrative classification is that the artisan-farmer opposition is routinely projected ("fractally," Gal argues) onto other things and levels of organization, which enables perspective shifting. Farmers can metaphorically identify artisan-like people within their ranks or playfully act artisan-like themselves, for instance, and vice-versa. The farmer-artisan divide can also be projected onto places, allowing people from Bóly to recast their relationship to Pécs as reciprocal, not hierarchical.

Importantly, Gal also illustrates how rigid classifications can block such perspective shifting. A bilingual German-Hungarian woman is reduced to tears as she feels the crush of a linguistic taxonomy that forces her to "choose" between the national languages German and Hungarian, when she in fact is attached to both. Indeed, once we acknowledge the ideological nature of scaling, the next step is to examine how certain scalar orientations take hold and exert influence, benefiting some and frustrating others.

PREDATORY SCALING

How do we understand the *institutionalization* of scalar perspectives that ensure that some scalar projects are relatively more effective and durable in the first place? This volume shows that institutions of various sorts—including academic disciplines—are in the business of selectively stabilizing and naturalizing scalar perspectives into *scalar logics:* that is, explicit or implicit rules for seeing relations from a particular point of view.

This is taken up concertedly in Judith Irvine's chapter, which begins with a discussion of Malinowski's now renowned conceit that "primitives" cannot see the "big picture" of their practices, the same big picture that the ethnographer goes on to explain for his readers. Irvine details how scalar projects strive to impose epistemological constraints, allowing participants and subjects—including social scientists—to see and know some things and not others. She goes on to ask critically and provocatively about the ends and effects of such efforts. Certain scalar perspectives—in this case the ethnographer's claim to see the "big picture"—require ignoring or erasing others' perspectives. Turning then to various census practices, both in the United States and in colonial Africa, Irvine's chapter addresses one central aspect of the micro-macro problem: that is, the ways that some scalar logics claim a sovereign vision.

As Irvine points out, construing a big picture—or a "type"—often involves the claim of encompassment, wherein other entities come to be seen as (mere) tokens, that which fills in the general outline. This, she underscores, is an ideological move par excellence. Yet depending on the project at hand, "big pictures" may be dismantled to refocus attention on the particular, local, and individual—scaling work that is no less ideological. Consider how people's attempts to be recognized as political or social groups are stymied as their *collective* claims are rescaled as assortments of *individual* ones. For instance, Carr (2009, 2011) describes a case in which an administrative body charged with running "client-sensitive" social service programs in the midwestern United States insulates itself from clients' claims that services are inadequate, misguided, and substandard. Administrators borrow quasi-clinical terms such as *denial* and *codependency* from program therapists so as to frame these collective claims as evidence of embodied pathologies. Once administrators can rescale collective critique as individual symptom, they can also return to business as usual. In such cases, we see the potential violence of some scalar projects, but not because there are some things and qualities that are *immune* to scale (Tsing 2012, 2015). Rather, we might more productively worry about the relative degree of control that people have over how their claims, identities, and very lives are scaled, since scaling is critical to whom and what is politically and socially recognized (Meek this volume).

When thinking about the institutionalization and rationalization of scale, instances when institutions aspire to figure out and stick to rules about what scale is, or should be, are especially enlightening. Along these lines, Constantine Nakassis's chapter focuses on how trademark law tries to control a seemingly unscalable quality—that is, the red color of a particularly fashionable shoe. Nakassis describes a striking confrontation between competing scalar logics, which have little to do with the scalability of the object in question and far more to do with the political and ontological commitments of relevant scaling agents. One court rules that a red-colored outsole is protectable only when its distinction from the coloring of the rest the shoe is acknowledged, as if the shoe form itself offers up the only possible perspective. Other legal arguments focus on the recognizability of red as a token of a type of person who designed the shoe. For the central actors involved, the highest stake of these efforts to legally institutionalize a scalar logic are whether the red sole productively indexes brand. And while "source" may be read as the product of a scalar dynamic of vertical encompassment, Nakassis's analysis ultimately suggests that the millennial market is composed of semiotically managed comparability and copying.

SCALAR VALUE AND EVALUATION

To illustrate her thesis that scaling is central to cultural value-production, economic anthropologist Jane Guyer (2004) asks us to picture a kind of scale we have yet to mention. The *balance scale* is an apparatus that compares the mass of two objects by evaluating the relative force of gravity, a relation then translated and quantified in standardized units of "weight." Through this imagery, we are reminded not only that scale is inherently *comparative* but also that it allows those who use it to make determinations about the relative *value* of two or more things, which need not be readily quantifiable, and which are, in fact, only quantifiable *by* the act of scaling. That the balance scale is iconic of the British-derived American justice system may give us some pause, given that such a scale promises to compare ad infinitum, without reference to any attribute other than *weight*. Indeed, to analytically engage in the pragmatics of scale, then, is to track how forms of social life are differentiated using various metrics and metaphors, endowed with relative weight or dimension, and valued accordingly.

The evaluative nature of scale-making, and its role in value production, is highlighted in Michael Silverstein's examination of what is commonly understood to be the simultaneous "rise" and "spread" of wine culture. Silverstein shows us how once-humble comestibles like coffee, chocolate, and beer have been "elevated" to the lofty heights of wine through the extension of florid wine-talk to them, almost as if they, like their consumers, were also capable of upward mobility through self-refinement. What he calls "vinification" clearly relies on analogic work, and not simply by registering that beer and coffee are like wine because they are said to share certain distinguishable qualities. Wine talk motivates and stabilizes an even more productive chain of associations: a type of person who is endowed with the cultivated sensibilities of taste. Silverstein thus elaborates on Bourdieu's (1984, xxix) famous argument that taste "classifies the classifer," by showing exactly how it is that distinguished drinks confer distinction upon the consumer. And while consumers and comestibles are elevated through wine talk, a vision of an encompassing marketplace that responds to, rather than produces, elite sensibilities is simultaneously projected. In other words, by way of a scripted set of analogies and associations, markets themselves are scaled as the circuitry for the "flow" of elite goods and people.

As with Ishmael's rhetorical exercise, Silverstein's chapter reminds us that scaling is socially productive precisely to the degree it is successfully relational. Recall that the distinction between higher and lower Tongan courts depends on how scalar dimensions are made to lean on each other in practice. Like scaffolding, the integrity of one dimension appears dependent on the integrity of the others, or so promise the workers who constructed it so that their colleagues might safely move around, picture what they are doing from various angles, and build, even if not necessarily from the ground up. But of course scaffolding is taken apart far more easily than it is put together, suggesting that the dimensions of the structure on which so many depend are not necessarily or naturally related and will likely be put together elsewhere in an entirely different way. Indeed, scales taken individually can allow us to rank and classify, but they are frequently combined in practice in all sorts of ways through the selective construction of scalar interdependencies. Though the trope of the scaffold, we recognize scale as relationally built and therefore precarious.

RADICAL SCALABILITY

In pointing to the sheer diversity of scalar practices and projects, this volume suggests that social existence is *radically scalable*. There isn't anything that cannot be scaled, nor is there any scale that is inviolable. We need only call to mind the optical illusions of "forced perspective" in the cinematography of old, or in what is now a small, playful online industry of tourism pics: a man seems to grasp the Eiffel Tower between thumb and forefinger, a woman kisses the profile of the sphinx (cf. Doane 2003). Collapsing near and far, small and large, this scalar magic may alert us to the very work of (re)scaling, to the idea that there is nothing all that rare or peculiar about all this. The pragmatics of scale remind us of an episteme that Foucault (1973) famously attributed to premodern Europe, where sympathies spanned impossible distances, defied categories, allowed for a thousand occult influences; no distance was too great, nothing too remote for there not to be *some* relation.

In arguing that our lives are radically scaled and scalable, we should pause to reconsider Anna Tsing's claim that scaling can blind us to forms of life, ways of being that might otherwise be readily evident. More specifically, she calls upon anthropologists to attend to the "mounting piles of ruins that scalability leaves behind" and "show how scalability uses articulations with nonscalable forms even as it denies or erases them" (2012, 56). In her most recent work, she claims that "scalability banishes meaningful diversity, that is, diversity that might change things" (2015, 38). To be sure, scales can problematically fix our view, add weight to some dimensions of cultural life and not others, and propel some social projects at others' expense. But what exactly is a "nonscalable" form, and why should we assume that value lies not only outside scale but also in its very wreckage? Indeed, there is a tendency to discern something dehumanizing—even violent—about scale, perhaps because of its association with measurement and ordination, on the one hand, and vertical power arrangements, on the other. But as we have seen, qualities are as scalable as things that are readily quantified, and scaling projects can flatten hierarchies as well as construct and maintain them. And if hierarchies, elites, and market ideologies are products of scaling projects, so are morality, sensory experience, community, ritual, and our very sense of who, where, and what we are. So while we must be ever alert to the ways that scalar logics limit our imagination of passable human terrain, we should remember that precisely because scaling is inherently perspectival and relational, it is also potentially transformative and humane.

. . .

Scaling may be how social actors orient themselves to their worlds, but it has nevertheless proved disorienting for social analysts. From the micro-macro debates to the efforts to reconcile storied antinomies like "individual and society," notions of scale have animated and vexed so many of us, in part, perhaps, because those notions are freighted with political and ontological commitments (Alexander 1987). In the face of these impasses, the past few decades have seen renewed attempts—many imaginative—to resolve the alleged antinomies by trying to "link" (Alexander 1987) and think "across" scales (e.g., Collins 2013; Ganapathy 2013). Linking, bridging, jumping, bending, finding "dialectics" and "relations" between scales—all this effort continues to take for granted the givenness of scalar distinctions.

Some of those who address the problem of scale think that we should find finer and empirically better-motivated scalar distinctions, suggesting that the scalar categories that actors and analysts abide by are simply too coarse. Given the view that scalar practices have epistemological implications, enabling and limiting what we can know, many scholars have asked such methodological questions as: how many spatial units should be identified in order to define some thing or happening as "local" (Moore 2008)? Or, how many temporal scales must we distinguish in order to explain the causes of an event—as many as twenty-four (Lemke 2000), or as few as two or three (Wortham 2006)? Would an exact combinatorics of scale pin down, once and for all, the things and qualities we study, allowing us to say positively what counts as, say, the "here and now"? Is studying scale simply a matter of discovering and cataloguing "different levels of empirical reality" (Alexander et al. 1987, 2), and should we follow the ambitious few who aspire to draw all scales together into one comprehensive vision of the world?

In addition to those who devote themselves to seeking out and delimiting scales in the social and natural world, other scholars emphasize the epistemological aspects of scale, that scale is a matter of perspective, a way of looking at some worldly entity that differentially emphasizes some of its dimensions at the expense of others. This scholarship recognizes that scaling is not simply a scholarly practice but also a way that social actors orient themselves to other people, things, and situations. To be sure, the study of scaling reveals the multidimensionality of cultural life, the idea that the *same things* can be approached and understood in many different ways. However, we should not take this to mean that scaling is simply a way of *seeing* something from afar that distorts, to a greater or lesser degree, its "object status" (Matsutake Worlds Research Group 2009, 381). The scaling projects detailed in this book richly demonstrate that ways of seeing are entwined with ways of doing, making, and being. Tongan courts are *made* high, indigenous speakers *become* communities, craft beer is *elevated* into a status commodity, because of the way they are scaled. Rather than focusing on whether our analyses "interrupt [the] object status" of the things we study (Matsutake Worlds Research Group 2009, 381), as if the status of objects were or should be set in stone, we should keep careful track of how things change and to what effect as they are rescaled by actors and institutions.

By treating the problem of scale pragmatically, this volume both avoids the seduction of stabilizing our objects of analysis and abandons the quest for an epistemological high ground—a perfectly comprehensive or synoptic view of scale that could encompass and exhaust all relevant spatial and temporal distinctions. Here again, we draw inspiration from Melville, who, in portraying the discursive work of one eloquent scale-maker, reminds us of a passage in the Book of Job. Of the leviathan, it is written: "any hope of subduing it is false; the mere sight of it is overpowering" (Job 41:9). Accordingly, the point of a *pragmatics of scale* is not to reduce scale, to pin it down and subdue it by a superordinate form of analysis. Nor is it to simply take different perspectives on the same object, as if that object could or should be stable. Rather, the study of scale requires an openness, a pragmatic sensibility that allows us to track and narrate, rather than capture and catalogue, the many ways that social life is scaled.

To study scale is surely not easy. In reference to the actual body of the beast it was written in the Old Testament: "His scales are his pride, shut up together as with a close seal.... They are joined one to another, they stick together, that they cannot be sundered" (Job 41:15, 17)—but this is true, too, of the scales that people make out of potentially relatable, felt qualities in the world, including the leviathan of the State, as Hobbes would have it. This volume attempts to pry apart these seals in order to have us appreciate the labor, especially the semiotic labor, that presses scales together so as to obscure their interdependence. In doing so, we hope to reveal, again, how something as seemingly "plain" as the greatness of a whale is a pragmatic achievement.

NOTES

1. In cultural anthropology, see, for example, Barnes 1962; Briggs 2004; Choy 2011; Ferguson 2006; Gupta and Ferguson 1992; Helmreich 2007, 2009; Maurer 2005; Matsutake Worlds Research Group 2009; Matthews 2009; Strathern 2004; Tsing 2000, 2005, 2012, 2015. In cultural geography, see Brenner 2004; Lefebvre 1991; Manson 2008; Marston 2000; Marston, Jones, and Woodward 2005; Moore 2008; Smith 1996, 2004; Springer 2014; Swyngedouw 1997, 2004, 2010. In economic anthropology, see Guyer 2004; Riles 1998. In gender studies, see Mountz and Hyndman 2006; Roberts 2004; Safri and Graham 2010; Steedman 1987. In literary, film, and art historical studies, see, for example, Bakhtin 1986; Doane 2003. In philosophy, see Rotman 1993. In science studies, see Choy 2011; Lampland and Star 2009; Latour 1999; Sunder Rajan and Leonelli 2013; Yaneva 2005. In sociology, see Barnes 2001; Brubaker 2002, 2005; Brubaker and Cooper 2000; Callon 1986; Callon and Latour 1981; Goffman 1983; Latour 2005.

2. The problematic of "scale" has been important in many language-centered works of late, both in linguistic anthropology (e.g., Wortham 2012; Agha 2007; Silverstein 2003; Irvine and Gal 2000; Kuipers 1998) and in related fields such as sociolinguistics (see, for example, Lemke 2000; Collins and Slembrouck 2005; Collins, Slembrouck, and Baynham 2009; Blommaert 2007, 2010; Collins 2013).

PART ONE

SCALAR PROJECTS

Promises and Precarities

1

PROJECTING PRESENCE

Aura and Oratory in William Jennings
Bryan's Presidential Races

Richard Bauman

The metaphysics of presence bedevils social analysis in myriad ways, not least in the comprehension of problems of scale. To the extent that we privilege—or even prioritize—"being there" as the methodological foundation of ethnographic discovery, or "the interaction order" as the primordial locus of sociality, or the situational context as the bedrock of social meaning, or any other like rubric founded on immediacy, we encounter difficulties in extending our findings or our purview to social formations that are temporally or spatially distant from the ecology of copresence. Nowhere is this truer than in the study of performance. Notwithstanding efforts to problematize presence as an ontological category, or to challenge the salience of liveness in a mediatized society, or to insist on the always already inscribed nature of all signifying practice, conceptions of performance keep coming back to the immediacy of copresence and to the auratic power of "being there." Then, whether one is concerned with performance as artful communication in focused interaction, as in sociable storytelling or fireside singing, or with performance as platform event, as in oratory or theater, the fetishization of presence makes it difficult to explore the relations that link performance forms and practices to society and culture more generally.

Part of the problem in the analysis of scale, whether in relation to performance or any other situated activity, is that what we preconceive as the larger-scale units, whatever they may be (the institution, the tribe, the nation-state), are then considered in polar opposition to the domain of presence in a classic macro-micro relation. In this chapter, I want to try out an alternative perspective. Rather than taking the micro or the macro as presupposed, I propose to explore scale as a practical problem for participants in performance—that is, how participants produce and align their performances with an eye toward extending their reach beyond the interaction order. I draw the term *interaction order* from Erving Goffman to designate the social-ecological space in which participants "are physically in one another's response presence" (1983, 2). I am concerned here with the ecology of interaction, without any implication of boundedness or a priori assumptions about scale (cf. Lempert this volume). Specifically, I offer a preliminary exploration of two related historical case studies involving a performer's efforts to carry the interaction order to what is conventionally understood to be the macro level of the nation-state. My cases in point are provided by William Jennings Bryan's pioneering whistle-stop campaign tours as the Democratic Party candidate in the presidential election campaign of 1896 and his recordings of campaign speeches in the presidential campaign of 1908.

WILLIAM JENNINGS BRYAN, ORATOR

Bryan (figure 1.1) was one of the most prominent public figures in the United States from the 1890s until his death in 1925, as a member of Congress, three-time Democratic candidate for president, secretary of state, and hugely popular speaker on the commercial lecture circuit.[1] He was a staunch populist and champion of working people, and a vigorous campaigner against the forces of economic inequality in American society. Bryan was also a lifelong evangelical Christian, best remembered today, to the detriment of his reputation, as a lawyer for the prosecution in the 1925 Scopes trial against a young Tennessee teacher for teaching evolution.

Oratory, together with preaching, was the preeminent public form of oral performance in late nineteenth-century America. William Jennings Bryan cultivated this art form from early childhood, and especially strongly during his years as a college student, as he sought and won honors in public speaking contests (Bryan and Bryan 1925, 85–89; Springen 1991). Shortly after moving from his native Illinois to Nebraska in 1887, Bryan became active in Democratic Party politics and began to attract favorable notice for his energy and oratorical skill. As recorded in his memoirs, he experienced an epiphany at the age of twenty-seven concerning his oratorical powers. Mary Bryan recounts the mythic moment:

> An epoch in his career as a speaker came at the age of twenty-seven, shortly after we went to Nebraska. He had spoken in a town in the western part of the state, came home on a night train, and arrived at daybreak. I was sleeping when he came in, and he awakened me. Sitting on the edge of the bed, he began: "Mary, I have had a strange

FIGURE 1.1. William Jennings Bryan, 1896. (Source: Library of Congress.)

experience. Last night I found that I had power over the audience. I could move them as I chose. I have more than usual power as a speaker. I know it. God grant I may use it wisely." (Bryan and Bryan 1925, 249)

And use it he certainly did. From at least that revelatory moment, and throughout the rest of his life, Bryan's public career rested on his power as a speaker and his readiness to exploit it.

In his first campaign for office, as a Democratic candidate for Congress, Bryan delivered more than eighty speeches (Leinwand 2007, 29); his prowess on the stump as a youthful Nebraska politico earned him the nickname "the Boy Orator of the Platte." Within months of taking his seat in Congress in the fall of 1891, Bryan began to attract national notice for his skills as an orator. An article in

FIGURE 1.2. Bryan campaign poster, 1896, "Cross of Gold" speech. Note the appeal to the farmer *(lower left)* and the factory worker *(lower right)*, Bryan's primary constituents. (Source: Library of Congress.)

the *New York Times* observed, "His voice is clear and strong, his language plain, but not lacking in grace. He uses illustrations effectively and he employs humor and sarcasm with admirable facility."[2] He quickly became one of the Democratic Party's most popular speakers and received invitations to address civic and political groups all over the country (Kazin 2006, 34). By the end of Bryan's second term in Congress, his celebrity as an orator was well established, and, as a leading figure in the Democratic Party, he traveled widely as a political speaker. It was during this period that he also began to capitalize on his celebrity by delivering paid speeches, promoted by professional lecture bureaus (Kazin 2006, 47–48). So, by the time Bryan arrived at the 1896 Democratic National Convention in Chicago, he was widely renowned for his ability to move and excite political audiences, and expectations were high in anticipation of his address. His electrifying speech at the convention, late on July 9, with its ringing, poetic peroration—"You shall not press down upon the brow of labor this crown of thorns. You shall not crucify mankind upon a cross of gold"—secured him the Democratic nomination for president at the age of thirty-six and became a part of American political mythology (see figure 1.2).

THE WHISTLE-STOP: ORATORICAL SCALING AND THE PRESIDENTIAL CAMPAIGN OF 1896

Bryan faced a number of formidable obstacles in his quest for the presidency.[3] There was a significant split within the Democratic Party over monetary policy, the leading issue of the campaign, with the "gold Democrats" remaining in favor of the gold standard in the face of Bryan's ardent "free silver" platform, which sought to establish a parallel silver standard in the interest of expanding the money supply to alleviate the economic pressures facing the farmers and workers. This opposition within the party not only undermined the efficiency of the pro-Bryan party leadership, but it also led to a debilitating lack of support from the Democratic newspapers, which could normally be counted upon to endorse the party's candidate. Finally, Bryan's constituency, primarily farmers and working people, lacked the resources to offset the considerable financial advantages of the Republican Party, which attracted ample campaign funds from the wealthier classes, whose interests the party represented.

Bryan's response, in the face of these difficulties, was to place his faith in his proven and widely celebrated skill as an orator and carry his campaign directly to the people, in both a figurative and a literal sense. His decision to go "among the people" represented a considerable departure from the established conventions of presidential campaigning,[4] in which the long-entrenched ideology dictated that as in the case of George Washington, the office should seek the man, not the man the office (Dinkin 1989, 67). In a theme that Bryan repeated over and over again in his speeches during the long campaign season, he had "departed somewhat from precedent and . . . gone over the country myself," because "I do not know where a candidate is going to go if you do not allow him to meet the people."[5] This is the canonical populist strategy. By "the people," Bryan was invoking the fundamental populist opposition between the farmers and laborers who were his core constituents—"men who labor, men who toil . . . the great common people of this country" (*Indianapolis Journal,* October 8, 1896, 5, quoted in Kelly 1969, 91)—and the moneyed, privileged elite (Canovan 1999, 5). He was determined to carry the Democratic message directly to the people, to reach as many constituents as he could on a series of campaign tours in which he would deliver as many speeches as humanly possible. "He will set the prairies of the west and south on fire with a wave of enthusiasm that will sweep far toward the east," proclaimed one newspaper account (Glad 1964, 173). That is to say, in the service of conducting a national-level political campaign, Bryan proposed to extend the reach of copresence to the maximal extent of which he—and it—was capable. The physical arduousness of his campaign, the sheer effort of delivering an unprecedented number of speeches across broad reaches of the country, would also make manifest his capacity for hard work, in symbolic alignment with his farmer-labor constituency.

To be sure, Bryan anticipated a multiplier effect—that is, a still further extension of his audience from newspaper coverage of his speeches, which made them accessible to dispersed publics beyond those who heard him speak directly, even if the newspapers were only local or regional in distribution. Bryan's celebrity and the heightened mood of a presidential campaign ensured that his appearances were eminently reportable, even in newspapers that were opposed to his candidacy (Harpine 2005, 19). It is important to recognize as well that Bryan's quest to maximize his contact with the people was enabled by that other burgeoning communicative technology of the day, the railroad. His campaign tours would not have been possible without the expanded rail networks then newly available, reaching far and wide into the hinterlands, and the establishment of reliable train schedules that allowed him to maximize his personal appearances (see figure 1.3) (Dinkin 1989, 103). Still, he relied principally on the medium of his own resonant voice and the affecting power of his presence.

To understand the dynamics of Bryan's ambitious campaign speaking tour, it is necessary to recognize the nature of his oratorical performances. Certainly, to his constituents among "the producing classes" (Glad 1960, 5), his position on the "burning issues" of the day produced a great part of his political appeal. But political sympathies alone could not sufficiently warrant Bryan's depending centrally and powerfully on his abilities as an orator. Issues alone did not evoke the support he needed. More important to the success of his campaign trips were his virtuosity and celebrity as a performer.

Perhaps foremost among Bryan's resources as an orator was his splendid voice. Observers were effusive in their descriptions: "sonorous and melodious," "deep and powerfully musical," "soothing but penetrating," "free, bold, picturesque," "clear as a cathedral bell" (quoted in Kazin 2006, 48). Not only was Bryan's voice rich in tone, clarity, and timbre, but it also had great projecting power, especially important in an age before mechanical amplification, and well suited in sheer

FIGURE 1.3. "Blowing Himself around the Country," political cartoon from *Puck*, September 16, 1896. Bryan speaking from the platform at the end of the train to a wildly enthusiastic audience of farmers as newspaper reporters following the campaign take careful notes. (Source: Library of Congress.)

physical terms to Bryan's goal of extending the reach of the interaction order. "It is strong enough to be heard by thousands," observed one newspaper account on the threshold of the 1896 campaign (*Indianapolis Journal*, July 11, 1896, 5, quoted in Kelly 1969, 96). In an oft-cited passage, Mary Bryan recalls an occasion on which she could hear her husband clearly from a hotel room three blocks from the site of his speech (Bryan and Bryan 1925, 253). Observers also noted his skill at varying his voice for emotional, dramatic, and rhetorical effect: "It is so modulated as not to vex the ear with monotony, and can be stern and pathetic, fierce or gentle, serious or humorous, with the varying emotions of its master" (*Indianapolis Journal*, July 11, 1896, 5; quoted in Kelly 1969, 96). In tone, it was "sometimes familiar as if in personal conversation, at other times ringing out like a trumpet" (Kazin 2006, 48) to reach a larger assembly. Bryan was also a master of the oratorical gesture, never more so than in the spectacular finale of his "Cross of Gold" speech at the nominating convention. As described by biographer Paolo E. Coletta,

> When he voiced the first metaphor his two hands, raised to the sides of his head, the fingers spread inward, moved slowly down and close to his temples, so that the spectators were almost hypnotized into seeing the thorns piercing the brow and the blood trickling from the wounds. "You shall not crucify mankind upon a cross of gold."

Here his hands left his head and followed his arms out at right angles to the body. There he stood, the crucified man in the flesh! He retained his position for about five seconds. Then he placed his arms at his side and took a step backwards. The delegates sat as if transfixed. (Coletta 1964, 1:141)

Then pandemonium broke loose among the crowd, and Bryan's place in American political mythology was assured.

While the extravagant gesture and the ringing peroration were the most striking and memorable displays of Bryan's oratorical virtuosity, he drew attention as well for his mastery of a range of valued oratorical techniques. Consider the following passage from the early congressional speech that catapulted Bryan to national attention and prompted the admiring account in the *New York Times* cited earlier. Bryan is speaking against tariffs as causing undue hardship for working people and addressing the Republican proponents of tariffs:

> And I am willing that you, our friends on the other side, shall have what consolation you may gain from the protection of those "home industries" which have crowned with palatial residences the hills of New England, if you will simply give us the credit of being the champions of the homes of this land. It would seem that if any appeal could find a listening ear in this legislative hall it ought to be the appeal that comes from those co-tenants of earth's only paradise; but your party has neglected them; more, it has spurned and spit upon them. When they asked for bread, you gave them a stone, and when they asked for a fish you gave them a serpent. You have laid upon them burdens grievous to be borne. You have filled their days with toil and their nights with anxious care, and when they cried aloud for relief you were deaf to their entreaties. (Bryan 1911, 1:69–70)

In these few lines, Bryan attacks his opponents with sarcasm for how their professed concern for humble "home industries" had provided mansions for the wealthy, and he inserts learned references to Michael Drayton's classic poem "Ode to the Virginian Voyage" ("earth's only paradise"), Shakespeare's *Merchant of Venice* ("spurned and spit upon them"), and the Bible, with its parallel cadences ("When they asked for bread, you gave them a stone, and when they asked for a fish you gave them a serpent" [Matthew 7:9]; "have filled their days with toil and their nights with anxious care" [2 Corinthians 11:27]). Perhaps a bit florid for contemporary tastes, this kind of artful embellishment was the height of oratorical virtuosity by the performance standards of the day.

The oratorical skills by which Bryan made his name as a performer were characteristically showcased in extended, formal speeches in ceremonialized settings: the floor of Congress, lecture halls, political conventions, and the like. These were heightened platform events, in Goffman's term, in which the speaker stands on a raised platform before an assembled audience, elicits the gaze and participative attention of its members, and delivers an extended, essentially monologic utterance (Goffman 1981, 7; 1983). Moreover, the extended speeches were customarily embedded in what Goffman (1983, 7) calls celebrative social occasions, scheduled, bounded, participative public events that featured parades, framing speeches by others, musical performances, flags, bunting, fireworks, and other forms of festive hoopla that amounted to cultural performances, events in which the most resonant meanings and values of a community are placed on display before an audience for reflexive contemplation. Performance events of this kind and scope were certainly part of Bryan's 1896 campaign tours, attracting large audiences—up to tens of thousands—and providing occasions for local dignitaries to share the limelight.

The problem, however, was that the very length and elaborateness of these events worked against Bryan's agenda of achieving direct, immediate engagement with as many people as possible, including especially farmers and other rural people, away from the more densely populated urban areas. Not only were the events themselves unduly time-consuming, but also the sheer process of getting in and out of them in the face of the adoring crowds that greeted him along the way absorbed even more of his precious time and energy. This is a problem in the logistics of scale: the more time and energy Bryan spent in any given appearance, the less he had available for additional speeches down the line. "It has been a great pleasure to note the interest which the people of this State are taking in the campaign," Bryan told an audience in Raleigh, North Carolina, but "their demonstrations of affection and interest sometimes come near keeping me from getting into the place of speaking and out of it." Still, he acknowledged that "while it is rather hard to bear up under all the affection that is bestowed upon a candidate, it is a great deal easier to get along with it than it would be to get along without it."[6]

Bryan's great oratorical innovation for the 1896 campaign, to counterbalance the formal speeches and maximize the reach of his voice and his presence, was the development of the whistle-stop speech: brief, succinct, delivered from a temporary platform at the depot or—as he came to prefer—the back of the train itself. The title of a newspaper account of Bryan's travels through Iowa underscores the extreme brevity of the campaign stops: "Story of Four-Minute Stops at Small Cities."[7] And the following description, from Bryan's account of his 1896 campaign, highlights the emphasis on economy and efficiency that drove the tours, an emphasis on managing time as a means of expanding space:

> I soon found that it was necessary to stand upon the rear platform of the last car in order to avoid danger to those who crowded about the train. I also found that it was much easier to speak from the platform of the car than to go to a stand, no matter how close. Much valuable time was wasted by going even a short distance, because in passing through a crowd it was always necessary to do more or less of handshaking, and this occupied time. Moreover, to push one's way through a dense crowd is more fatiguing than talking. (Bryan 1896, 19)

It is noteworthy here that Bryan saw physical contact as a hindrance to the kind of copresence he wished to achieve; far more efficient to touch people with his voice

FIGURE 1.4. Bryan's whistle-stop speech in Wellsville, Ohio, 1896. (Source: Wikipedia/Wikimedia Commons.)

than with his hand. Whistle-stop speeches approached the minimal end of the platform format, the *einfache Form* of political oratory. Audiences could still enjoy the festive exuberance of the occasion—with its bands, bunting, flags, and other enhancements—while they waited for the train to appear and after it left, but Bryan did not need to be bogged down in time-consuming spectacle (see figure 1.4).

ORATORY AND AURA ON THE CAMPAIGN TRAIL

While these quick in-and-out speeches were not without touches of the oratorical virtuosity for which Bryan was acclaimed—note, for example, the parallelism of "get along with it / get along without it" in the above quote from Bryan's Raleigh speech—their effectiveness depended on another order of performance, what we might call *auratic* performance, drawing on Walter Benjamin's notion of aura, as developed in his seminal essay "The Work of Art in the Age of Mechanical Reproduction" ([1936] 1969) and Cormac Power's discussion of "auratic presence" (2008, 47–85). I draw also on Robert Plant Armstrong's phenomenological aesthetics, especially on his notion of *affecting presence,* things or events that are endowed with or exercise potency, heightened emotion, and value—in a word, aura—by their very presence (1971, 1975, 1981). Armstrong distinguishes two grounds for affecting power: formal excellence or skilled execution on the one hand, and possession of special power—whether identified as aura, charisma, indexical resonance, talent, or celebrity (Armstrong 1981, 7)—on the other. The former, he terms an aesthetic of virtuosity, the latter an aesthetic of invocation (Armstrong 1981, 10). I suggest that the thrust of Bryan's exhaustive effort to interact with the largest possible number of constituents during the 1896 campaign, and the potential efficacy of his whistle-stop performance format, depended heavily on an aesthetic of invocation, on auratic performance.

There can be no doubt that Bryan was a powerfully charismatic figure. The *Washington Post*'s hyperbolic account of Bryan's appearance at the 1896 Democratic Convention conveys well the affecting power that he was capable of exercising over audiences:

> This young man Bryan suddenly appeared, tall, shapely, handsome as a Greek demigod, classic of outline, impassioned of address, thrilling with his tremendous message to the people—appeared like a fairy upon a dull and lifeless stage, and in one moment threw 20,000 human beings into a fever of indescribable exaltation. He called back from the vanished past the witchery of Orpheus, the magic of Demosthenes, the irresistible forces of the great Napoleon. He stood there, and with a dozen fiery phrases he converted thoughtful men into fanatics; he changed them as utterly as the wizard changes the toys he plays with on the stage. In all the annals of politics there was never such a scene.[8]

That Bryan was considered a handsome and imposing figure of a man by the standards of the day didn't at all harm his appeal, but what comes to the fore in this effusive description is the vocabulary of magic, enchantment, "irresistible forces" that Bryan evokes in this writer and in his audience. Indeed, references to magic recur in accounts of Bryan's speeches and his ability to "intoxicate his listeners" (*Saint Louis Republic*, May 28, 1895; quoted in Melder 1965, 70). This effect is the hallmark of a charismatic personality, precisely the quality that Armstrong identifies as the touchstone of an invocational presence. And by the same token, populist movements tend to select for charismatic leaders as a focus of the heightened emotion that energizes their engagement in the political arena (Canovan 1999, 6).

The evangelical tenor of Bryan's religious faith, his frequent resort to a scriptural register in his oratory, and his fervent advocacy for the downtrodden, coupled with his magnetic personality, led many to view him as divinely inspired, a prophet, a savior. One early associate was convinced that Bryan possessed "some Supernatural power" (Kazin 2006, 30). Kazin cites letters from many quarters that testify to such identifications on the part of Bryan's supporters: "In all times of great peril to the people, God has raised up a leader to save them from their errors and lead them up to a higher plane of height"; "God has brought you forth, and ordained you, to lead the people out of this state of oppression and despondency into the Canaan of peace and prosperity"; "I look upon you as almost a prophet sent from God" (75, 82). One correspondent gives Bryan's biblical mandate an explicitly contemporary twist, identifying him as "a Moses destined to lead the chosen people out of their bondage of trusts, tariff abuse and unnatural taxation" (quoted in Melder 1965, 60). An observer of the 1896 campaign recorded that he "has seen the poor, the weak, the humble, the aged, the infirm, rush forward by hundreds, at the close of Mr. Bryan's speeches, and hold up hard and wrinkled hands with crooked fingers and cracked knuckles to the young, great orator, as if he were in very truth their promised redeemer from bondage" (Kazin 2006, 73).

These testimonials make clear that Bryan's great popular appeal was not grounded solely in the formal virtuosity of his speechmaking but drew powerfully on his celebrity and charismatic personality. It was sufficient simply to be in his presence to be deeply affected, whether or not he exercised his oratorical artistry (cf. Gamson 1994, 189). Thus, he could make a very brief appearance from the rear platform of his train, greet the assembled crowd, make a few remarks, and quickly move on to the next whistle-stop while leaving behind him large numbers of ecstatic admirers who never forgot the experience.[9] Here, under the headline, "Vast Crowds Cheer," is the transcript of a speech that Bryan made in Clarksburg, West Virginia, which must closely approach the minimal level that the whistle-stop speech could attain. In fact, it disclaims its own status as a speech: "I am not going to make a speech here because I believe I have an appointment at the fair grounds and we must hasten there in order to catch the next train. As the people are not in good financial condition it is not an easy thing to come all the way to Nebraska to call on me. (Applause.) As they are not able to get out there, I am reversing the process and I will come to see the people."[10] This is a speech about not giving a speech in order to catch the train for the next scheduled speech—a scaling device in its own right. Note that there is a rhetorical as well as a mechanical component to this aggregative process of addressing larger and larger numbers of "the people" over wider and wider spaces. By reminding his hearers that he had other speeches to make in other places, Bryan was able to build up in any given audience member's mind the sense that he or she—and the surrounding crowd—were part of a burgeoning public, an ever-growing mass of listeners to his inimitable voice and celebrants of his affecting presence. Brief though it was, this speech also makes the point that Bryan is determined "to see the people," and in making this brief stop he is doing just that. It was the piling up of large numbers of such auratic performances, coupled with the lesser numbers of full-blown formal speeches, that allowed Bryan to stretch the spatial and social limits of the interaction order—that is, the kind of physically copresent communication that he took to be especially powerful and efficacious—as far as he was able.

While the presentational thrust of these whistle-stop speeches was brevity, and the merest appearance would suffice as an auratic performance, the genre displayed other formal and functional characteristics that served Bryan's strategic goals in engaging directly with his public. One prominent feature of the whistle-stop speeches is the reflexive attention that Bryan devoted to the importance of interactional contact with the people who had come to see and hear him. "I thank you for this opportunity of meeting you," he said, or "I thank you for this opportunity of greeting so many of you,"[11] or "I thank you, my friends, for this opportunity to speak to you" (Bryan 1896, 52–53). Note first the pronominal deictics ("I," "you") and vocative forms ("my friends") that index the participants in the immediate event.[12] Moreover, meeting, greeting, speaking to "the people" all emphasize the interactional access and direct communication that undergirded his strategy of building his campaign by relying on the interaction order. We might compare the more distanced stance of Bryan's more formal speeches, in which he speaks of the local constituents in objective terms rather than as direct addressees. In Canton, Ohio, for example, home of his opponent, William McKinley, Bryan asserted, "I am glad to meet the people of this city, the home of my distinguished opponent, and am glad in their presence to testify to his high character" (Bryan 1896, 305).

Presentation of a political argument, central to the longer, more formal speeches, was far less important to the whistle-stop speeches than contact. Bryan noted explicitly that the brevity of the genre did not lend itself to complex argumentation: "My friends, the short stop that we are giving here does not permit of any elaborate discussion of any question" (*Columbus Daily Herald,* October 6, 1896, 1; quoted in Kelly 1969, 76). In any event, most of the crowds that Bryan addressed already knew the issues and were familiar with his political positions from newspaper accounts and local political discussions.

What efforts Bryan made at argumentation and persuasion in the whistle-stop speeches, consistent with his emphasis on direct engagement with his audiences, tended to be more dialogic and interactional than the longer, more formal speeches allowed him to be. In the latter, audiences were largely restricted to back-channel responses, however enthusiastic, such as applauding, cheering, or stamping their feet. The closer physical engagement with crowds at the train depot, and the greater proportional attention to the personal contact that Bryan wanted his auratic performances to highlight, opened the way to greater conversational engagement with individuals in the audience (Baskerville 1979, 133). According to a newspaper account of a speech in New London, Connecticut, attacking the Republican monetary policy for its susceptibility to foreign influence, Bryan asserted,

> And that is what the Republican platform means.
> (A voice: "Where will we be when we get free silver?")
> Are you in favor of a gold standard?
> (The voice: "Yes.")
> Tell me why?

(The voice: "Because I believe it is best for the country. Every nation will accept a dollar for a dollar.")

Why? I will tell you. Because of its value. The reason why our gold dollar and gold bullion are worth the same is because the law says that you can convert bullion into a dollar at the mint.

(The voice: "Well, how about silver?")

When the laws are so, under the free coinage of silver, that the holder of silver bullion can convert his silver bullion into dollars at the mint that will fix a mint price for silver then, as we have a mint price for gold now, and silver dollars will be worth as much abroad as our gold dollars. (Great applause and cheering.)[13]

In such instances, of course, a dyadic conversational interaction could be heard by the rest of the assembled crowd, as ratified overhearers. Moreover, exchanges of this kind with ordinary members of the audience—potentially, anyone who cared to speak up—fostered a sense on the part of audience members that they were, in effect, equal participants in the political process with immediate access to the great man himself.

A speech that Bryan delivered at Lexington, Kentucky, illustrates further his openness to dialogic engagement with his interlocutors. In the midst of his speech, the proceedings were interrupted by a parade of supporters on horseback carrying signs and banners in endorsement of the Democratic Party principles. When he was able to resume his talk, Bryan observed of the riders:

They bore banners and presented mottoes which make any further speaking unnecessary. If I were to talk to you from now until night, I could not more than emphasize the mottoes which have passed in procession before you. (Applause.) I noticed one motto, which, though written in letter not altogether according to the latest pattern, presented a truth which ought to find a lodgment in the memories of all. It was 'High money—Low times.'

I challenge you to find in any of the speeches that will be made this year by the opponents of free silver, a single sentence which contains as much of political economy and common sense as is contained in that phrase, "High money—Low times."[14]

And so on, through several other mottos. These interdiscursive gestures to the immediate situation at hand made the members of the community cocreators of Bryan's oratory. What greater honor than to join in the creation of a speech by the greatest living orator of the day?

These examples make clear one of Bryan's most effective rhetorical techniques for expanding the horizons of his very local whistle-stop speeches: seizing upon an element from the immediate situational context and upscaling it to national-level relevance by assigning it broader meaning with respect to the political issues of the day and identifying local actors as representatives of nationally salient social types. Note, too, the contextualizing work accomplished by deictics of person ("I," "you"), place ("before you"), time ("now," "this year"), and demonstration ("that phrase"), which index the immediate social and discursive context of the speech. The speeches are replete with deictic references of this kind. To cite but one more suggestive example, Bryan told the crowd at the depot in Flint, Michigan, the following story:

> My attention has been called to an incident which occurred in this town and which illustrates how well the farmer understands the money question and how ignorant the average financier often is on the subject. One of your bankers called a farmer into his room and said to him, "If Bryan is elected President, I shall foreclose the mortgage on your farm." The farmer replied, "If McKinley is elected you can have the farm, because I will not be able to pay it, but if Bryan is elected you cannot foreclose the mortgage because under bimetallism I will be able to pay it off." Who understood the money question, the farmer or the banker? (Bryan 1896, 562)

Thus, an anecdote recounting an interaction "in *this* town," involving "one of *your* bankers," aptly indexes the key issue of the campaign, "the money question."

In the end, though he lost the election, the brevity and efficiency of Bryan's whistle-stop speeches had made it possible for him to interact with and move astonishing numbers of people. These auratic performances allowed him to maximize the reach of the interaction order by giving large numbers of speeches day after day. Near the close of the campaign, he made some seventy speeches in four days, with about fourteen hundred miles of travel in Michigan alone (Melder 1965, 74). In one day in western Michigan, he gave a total of twenty-five speeches in nineteen different communities, finishing up in Lansing near midnight, only to pick up the round of speeches again early the next morning (Bryan 1896, 561). Bryan himself said of some of his crowds that they could be "measured by the acre rather than the head" (Williams 2010, 105). In some areas, the penetration of his efforts was especially broad: for example, newspapers estimated that at one time or another he spoke to fully half the voters in West Virginia (Williams 2010, 105). All told, he traveled approximately eighteen thousand miles, delivered nearly six hundred speeches, and addressed, by some estimates, something approaching five million people. Even allowing for some exaggeration in the figures, and considering that Bryan's crowds included women and children while only adult men could vote, and that some nonsupporters were attracted by his celebrity with no intention of voting for him, his achievement in projecting his presence onto the national stage was prodigious. Kazin suggests, "It is quite possible that a majority of the men who voted for Bryan in November had heard him speak that fall" (2006, 68). In a very real sense, the aggregate crowds that Bryan gathered on his speaking tours constituted an embodied, material actualization of "the people" as the core of the national polity he set out to engage (Tambar 2009, 532).

ENTERING THE NATION'S LIVING ROOMS: PHONOGRAPHIC SCALING IN THE CAMPAIGN OF 1908

In the 1896 campaign, Bryan maximized what he could accomplish single-handedly in engaging an immediate public on a national scale. He went on to mount similar campaign tours in his two other losing campaigns for the presidency in 1900 and 1908, but he could never again match the strength and vigor that he brought to his first national effort at the age of thirty-six. In 1908, however, he had one more opportunity to extend the reach of his oratorical voice beyond the immediate contexts of his long speeches and his quick whistle-stop addresses. Beginning with Edison's National Phonograph Company, followed by Victor and Columbia, Bryan made a series of phonograph recordings keyed to the presidential campaign, believing that "it would be advantageous to get the Democratic campaign arguments before the people of the country in that form"—that is, in a form that conveyed not only his words but also his voice.[15]

Notwithstanding the central linkage of the recordings to the presidential campaign, two of Bryan's ten recorded speeches were oratorical display pieces lifted from earlier speeches. "An Ideal Republic," the stirring peroration of Bryan's speech accepting the presidential nomination in 1900, was billed as illustrating "the wonderful store-house of his imagination" and his mastery of "the difficult dual art of conceiving ideal conditions and finding suitable language for describing them," not as addressing a past or present political situation. "Immortality," excerpted from Bryan's most popular and frequently delivered Chautauqua lecture, titled "The Prince of Peace" (Canning 2005, 158; Springen 1991, 73), concerned life after death and was advertised as "an example of fervent American oratory" demonstrating that Bryan was "as profound a thinker upon such questions as upon those affecting the country's political welfare."[16] It was reportedly "the best seller of them all."[17] The large majority of the speeches, however, addressed "the leading political questions of the day" and were closely keyed to the principal issues with which Bryan had long been publicly identified, to major planks in the Democratic platform. Of "Imperialism," for example, the *Edison Phonograph Monthly* notes, "This is a subject on which Mr. Bryan never fails to delight his hearers."[18] While the eight issue-oriented speeches dealt with matters that Bryan had addressed in longer speeches on numerous other occasions, the recorded texts were all composed specifically for the recording process.

According to the National Phonograph Company, the idea of recording Bryan in connection with the campaign originated with an Edison dealer in Bryan's hometown of Lincoln, Nebraska (Brooks 1999, 60, citing *Talking Machine World*, August 15, 1908, 37), but there was certainly a precedent that might plausibly have influenced Bryan's willing participation in the project. In the 1906 New York gubernatorial campaign, William Randolph Hearst, ever the mass-media innovator, had been the candidate of the Independence League, running against

Magazine Advertising

Fourteen of the highest class and most widely circulated monthly and weekly periodicals will carry our advertising for July. The advertisement, of which a reduction is shown here, will occupy full pages in Ainslie's, Cosmopolitan, Delineator (200 lines), Everybody's, Munsey's, Review of Reviews, Success, Sunset and World's Work. It will also occupy half-pages in Collier's Weekly and Saturday Evening Post and quarter-pages in Associated Sunday Magazines, Puck and Youth's Companion.

This means that some twenty-five million people will read another very interesting story of what an Edison Phonograph will do for their homes in the way of music and entertainment.

The illustration is from a drawing by Hitchcock, one of the cleverest artists in the country. It has the true vacation atmosphere and it is not at all likely that any magazine reader could pass it by even if he were so inclined. Notice also, the reference to the Bryan Records.

It is a very good plan for Dealers to do an extra amount of local newspaper advertising at the time the magazines containing our advertising are circulated. The first come out about the middle of the month. From then until the first of the next month is a good time to go doubly strong on your newspaper advertising and window displays.

Our national magazine publicity creates a desire for the Edison Phonograph and Records, but the dealer should supplement this with reminders to the readers in his town that his store is the place to secure the goods.

Newspaper Advertising

The advertisement above is a reduced duplicate of one devoted to the William J. Bryan Records that we ran in a list of 146 daily newspapers throughout the country. The announcement occupied a space of six inches, double column—12 inches altogether.

The combined circulation of the newspapers is over eight millions. There are supposed to be about 18,000,000 homes in the entire country, so is is safe to say that our advertisement was read in a large majority of the homes that can afford to pay for a Phonograph.

This same advertisement could be used by Dealers with the last few lines changed to give the Dealers' name and address, and an invitation to come in and hear the Bryan Records.

Don't miss the golden opportunity offered by these Records to double your summer business.

FIGURE 1.5. National Phonograph Company advertisement, "Bryan Speaks to Millions through the Edison Phonograph." (Source: *Edison Phonograph Monthly* 6, no. 7 [1908]: 18.)

the Republican candidate, Charles Evans Hughes. To aid in his campaign effort, Hearst had recorded twelve cylinders of campaign speeches for distribution to "hamlets and villages in remote sections of the State which he either will not have time to visit or which his luxuriously appointed special train cannot reach for the reason that there is no railroad leading to them." Hearst's plan was to send agents to "the out-of-the-way places, where a real campaign speech is rarely heard, even in a Presidential year," to play the recordings in local halls or other venues, like the corner grocery store, that classic site of male sociability in American small towns and rural areas.[19] Hearst had been one of the few newspaper publishers to support Bryan in 1896 and 1900, and his effort to expand the spatial reach of his own campaign oratory by means of the phonograph was very likely known to Bryan.

In 1908, producers and commentators on the campaign recordings conceived the expansion of scale in similar terms, envisioning that the recordings would reach "persons who otherwise never could get anywhere near the men to have them speak."[20] Or they would reach constituents "in other parts of the country where the people will not have the opportunity of hearing Bryan in person."[21] The potential reach of the records was envisioned not only in terms of broader space but also in terms of greater numbers. At the beginning, projections were simply a matter of speculation. A National Phonograph Company advertisement proclaimed, "Bryan Speaks to Millions through the Edison Phonograph"[22] (see figure 1.5). A newspaper editorial was more modest, suggesting that the use of the phonograph would "enable thousands of people to hear with ease and comfort . . . Mr. Bryan" who could not hear him in any other way.[23] In the end, the recorded speeches sold fairly well, judging from one industry representative's comments about the market: "To date we have sold more than 600,000 records of Mr. Bryan's speeches. . . . We knew that the sales would be big, but the demand for the Bryan speeches has far surpassed our expectations."[24] Sales figures alone, of course, do not tell the whole story, since they cannot indicate how many listeners each recording may have reached. We can, however, gain some idea concerning multiplier effects by consulting other sources. I'll return to this question below.

The project of extending the reach of Bryan's speeches—his most potent campaign resource—by disseminating them on phonograph records introduced an explicit and inevitable element of institutional and technological mediation into the oratorical process that undercut the power of presence that Bryan was able to achieve in his extensive campaign tours. The medium of the phonograph, dependent on sound alone, deprived the recorded speeches of the semiotic density that intensified Bryan's live performances. The record companies' implicit answer to this problem was to foreground the capacity of the recordings to convey the speaker's "real" or "actual" *voice*, the quintessential instrument of human presence. "These records are remarkably successful, faithfully reproducing not only Mr. Bryan's voice but every mannerism and inflection," proclaims the *Edison Phonograph*

Monthly.[25] The purported mimetic fidelity of the recordings became a strong selling point in naturalizing the speaker's recorded voice: "They are among the plainest and most natural Records we have ever turned out."[26] The companies' focus on voice found a public echo in the observations of journalists on this new campaign phenomenon. An editorial in the *Kansas City Star*, for example, marvels at the ability of the recordings to convey "the full round voice of the . . . orator, accompanied with all the distinctness and shades of intonation that we heard from the flesh and blood . . . orator," and thus to present the "real personality" of the performer.[27] In the absence of the living performer, the record companies and commentators fell back on an imputed quality of liveness that resided in the voice issuing from the phonograph.

One important characteristic of the recorded performances is their brevity. The adaptation of campaign speeches to the temporal affordances of phonographic technology restricted them drastically, to two to four minutes in duration. Commentators made a point of the condensed form of the speeches on the recordings. In this, the recorded speeches resembled the whistle-stop speeches of Bryan's railroad campaign tours, but they represented yet another innovation in genre. One trade journal referred to the recorded speeches as "tabloid addresses," which, in then-contemporary usage, highlighted their brevity, concision, and concentration of expression.[28] An especially revealing newspaper account observes, "The records are short and directly to the point. They deal with the conspicuous issues discussed by the candidates in a simple and straightforward manner. Nobody wearies of listening to them. The different appeals are completed within the brief space of three minutes, and they make a strong and lasting impression on the mind. On any of the single questions treated by the phonograph records one gains as clear an idea as if he listened to a speech an hour or two in length covering all of the issues of the campaign."[29] Brevity is here tied to rhetorical efficiency: short speeches get the point across without tiring or boring the listener.

Bryan's issue-oriented speeches are rhetorically tight. They begin characteristically by defining the principal elements of the problem at issue or identifying an existing condition that serves as a frame of reference for the delineation of his own position. Following this framing section is generally a statement of what is required to answer or remedy the problem; next follows Bryan's or the party's policy, to provide the necessary corrective and the moral grounds for doing so. The speeches are predominantly expository and deliberative, even didactic; one journalistic observer suggested that "the new use to which the phonograph has been put gives it a respectable rank as an educator."[30] Poetic devices and virtuosic flourishes are conspicuously minimized. There are occasional instances of grammatical parallelism, rhetorical figures, or measured cadences—Bryan, being Bryan, could not avoid at least some slight virtuosic display—but overall, by contrast with the two display speeches, "An Ideal Republic" and "Immortality," the speeches are surprisingly unadorned. Here, by way of example, are the opening and closing sections of Bryan's recorded speech "The Trust Question."

> A trust may be defined as a corporation which controls so large a proportion of the supply of a given article as to be able to fix the price of the same. Opposition to trusts does not, however, mean opposition to private monopoly. A private monopoly is indefensible and intolerable. We cannot afford to allow any person or group of persons to establish arbitrarily the price which all must pay for a necessary of life.
>
> ... The only remedy for private monopoly is extermination, but the dissolution of a monopoly does not mean the destruction of industry, but just the reverse. When a monopoly is dissolved, the factories formerly owned by the trust become independent factories, and competition between them will prevent extortion in price, and a reduction in price will increase the number of factories and give employment to more labor in production.[31]

RECORDED ORATORY AND AURATIC PRESENCE

If the recorded speeches are far from full-blown virtuosic displays, they are also, by their mediated and semiotically reduced nature, restricted in their capacity to invoke the strong affect that auratic performances might achieve. For one thing, while the recorded speeches evince intertextual links to Bryan's longer campaign speeches, from both the current and the earlier campaigns, they are conspicuously free of other contextualization cues: no vocatives of address to hearers, no deictic anchorings in time or place, no indexing of situational contexts of production or reception. In the entire corpus of issue-oriented recordings, Bryan employs a grand total of two deictic constructions, or, rather, one deictic construction used twice: the emphatic device "I may add," which indexes both the speaker and the antecedent discourse, now to be supplemented by what follows.[32] That's it. The absence of contextualization cues, to be sure, rendered the speeches maximally open to insertion into new contexts. The companies made an energetic effort to provide contextual frames of reference by which prospective listeners might imagine—and then actualize—their engagement with the recorded speeches.

An early point of contact between recordings and consumers was the newspaper advertisement, such as the ad that proposed that "Mr. William Jennings Bryan Wants to Talk to You Personally," thus setting up a virtual reactivation of the interaction order in the form of a dialogue between the candidate and the reader, cast by the ad as Bryan's direct addressee (from *The Commoner* [Lincoln, NE], August 21, 1908, quoted in Kazin 2006, 158). The mass medium here appears as a vehicle of intimate interpersonal contact. Advertising copy was an important site of metacultural construction on the part of the record producers and the dealers. Indeed the dealers' stores were the first physical sites in the chain of consumption at which customers might hear the campaign records. Accordingly, the advertising

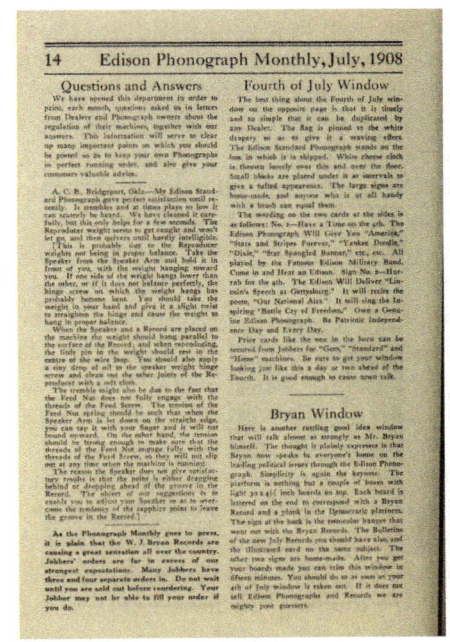

FIGURE 1.6A. Suggestions to record dealers for a "Bryan Window." (Source: *Edison Phonograph Monthly* 6, no. 7 [1908]: 14.)

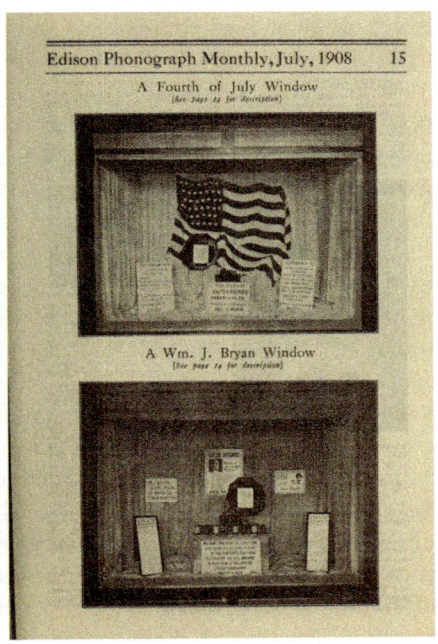

FIGURE 1.6B. Two examples of William Jennings Bryan windows. (Source: *Edison Phonograph Monthly* 6, no. 7 [1908]: 15.)

texts the company prepared for its local dealers aimed at grounding the speeches in place and time, as in: "Bryan Speaks Today / William Jennings Bryan delivers choice passages from his best orations at our store today."[33] The records were, after all, commercial products. "It is the easiest thing you know," urged the *Edison Phonograph Monthly*, "getting almost anybody to pay 35 cents to own one of Bryan's speeches, delivered by Bryan himself."[34] Indeed, the house organ for Edison dealers kept up a constant barrage of sales promotion ideas from June to December of 1908 (see figure 1.6).

Perhaps the most radical recontextualization of the recorded speeches centered on the record companies' promotion of the phonograph as a technology of home entertainment. Hearing political campaign speeches in one's own home amounted to nothing less than a shift of political oratory from public to private space. Moreover, this spatial reorientation had temporal correlates as well: one could hear the speeches at the time of one's choosing rather than being subject to the external scheduling imperatives of the speaker and the campaign machinery. Record company advertising proclaimed the shift, as in: "You can now hear William Jennings

Bryan speak at your convenience and in your own home."[35] And what a privilege that would be. A model advertising letter offered in the *Edison Phonograph Monthly* in July 1908 sets up an intriguing virtual scenario that exploits the invocational power of Bryan's presence: "If William Jennings Bryan offered to deliver his favorite orations in your home, you would consider you had a very great privilege, would you not? Well, we make you an offer that practically amounts to the same thing."[36]

Unfortunately, it is hard to assess how and to what extent purchasers actually used the campaign recordings in the privacy of their homes. We can find only sporadic references to them being played during private social entertainments, as for instance: "Mr. and Mrs. John Henry Lynch entertained a small company of friends at their home on North Buchanan street [in Edwardsville, Illinois] last night. Refreshments were served and a social time enjoyed. The particular feature of the evening was the rendering of the . . . campaign records on the graphaphone [sic]."[37]

In one sense, the recontextualization of Bryan's speeches to private homes amounted to a certain form of downscaling. His live performances drew crowds, up to tens of thousands. Played on a phonograph in domestic space, the recorded speeches could reach only a few listeners at a time. Yet in another sense, the goal of extending the spatial and social reach of the campaign by means of recorded speeches depended on the sale of the records to many households, on their penetration into areas where Bryan did not appear in person, and on their appeal to constituents who might not wish to attend one of his live performances—perhaps members of "polite" society or women who wanted to avoid the press of boisterous crowds but who could afford a phonograph.

Beyond the focused interaction of the household sociable gathering, the campaign recordings were employed as a substitute for the live speaker at platform gatherings. Dealers were urged to target local political organizations as potential customers for campaign recordings.[38] One of the most frequently reported sites for the recorded speeches turned out to be the political club meeting.

An article in an Ohio newspaper constructs a virtual scenario for such an event, highlighting again how Bryan's voice is the agent of immediacy in a mediated situation and how the recordings are meant to work in the interest of increasing the reach of Bryan's presence:

> "Gentlemen, we will now listen to the voice of our Peerless Leader," remarks the chairman of the entertainment committee of the Blank Democratic Club, and turns a crank.
>
> Then from the phonograph issue the well-known tones of the once Boy Orator of the Platte, speaking in tabloid form on some of the subjects which Mr. Bryan conceives to be vital issues. . . . The political clubs have taken very kindly to the record scheme and they have a serious purpose of getting them before the persons who otherwise never could get anywhere near the [candidates] to have them speak.[39]

Bryan's recordings were played at meetings of Democratic organizations around the country.[40] But of course, it was not merely a voice that meeting participants were hearing; it was a voice engaged in making a speech. What the phonograph offered to participants at political club meetings was oratorical performance, in which the mediated nature of the performance might be bracketed in an effort to simulate a copresent performance event. Consider this account from the *Washington Post*:

> Two hundred and fifty Washington Democrats listened last night in the local club's quarters . . . to a number of speeches by Mr. Bryan, delivered through the medium of the phonograph. . . . Much enthusiasm was displayed, but no applause interrupted the speech of Mr. Bryan. All of it came after the speech was finished.
> The topics on which Mr. Bryan addressed the audience were "The railroad question," "The trust question," "The Guarantee of bank deposits," and "Immortality."[41]

At the beginning of the account, the mediation of the phonograph is explicit, but in the second paragraph the mediating technology drops out and it appears that "Mr. Bryan addressed the audience" directly. This report is also interesting in what it suggests about audience responses to the recorded speeches. The default expectation for live speechmaking was that audience members had license to interrupt the orator with applause, whereas this audience, at least, saved its applause—however enthusiastic—for the end. This shift in response patterns may have been a consequence of the lack of obvious applause lines in the recorded speeches. Recall the excerpts we considered earlier from "The Trust Question," one of the recorded speeches played at the Washington meeting. Where would one feel enthusiastic enough to interrupt this expository and didactic disquisition, especially since the speaker would not pause but speak right through the applause?

While the substitutive oratorical performances furnished by Bryan's recordings might elicit "enthusiastic" responses from audiences at Democratic political clubs, they apparently had the potential as well of evoking the wild enthusiasm of his personal appearances.[42] The recordings could function as stand-ins for the principal himself not only at club meetings but also at the fullest reach of the interaction order, in the spectacle of celebrative events. Playing again on the virtual/actual ambiguity of the above account of a Democratic club meeting in Washington, D.C., at which the organizers played Bryan recordings, the following newspaper account of the use of the records at the New York State Democratic Convention, with its complement of festive paraphernalia, demonstrates how effective the records could be in triggering the excitement of the crowd:

> Shortly after the convention convened William J. Bryan was called upon to speak in the person of a phonograph.
> The announcement caused the large auditorium to tremble from the cheers which arose from the delegates.

Then the phonograph started.
The words came clear and distinct and were audible throughout the hall.
The convention was a waving riot of color, every delegate having been presented a small flag which he waved at the slightest opportunity.[43]

Thus it appears that even while delivering unadorned expository speeches, mediated by the technology of the phonograph, Bryan's voice had the capacity after all to convey his auratic appeal. Remediated from the live speech, reframed by the metacultural constructions of the record producers, and reinserted into platform events, Bryan's recorded speeches retained at least some of their invocational power.

CONCLUSION

For William Jennings Bryan, the calibration of scale in the presidential elections of 1896 and 1908 was a practical problem. His challenge was to extend his active quest for votes as far as possible within a broadly dispersed national electorate while exploiting his strongest campaign resource—namely, his ability to move copresent audiences with the power of his oratory. His task, then, as he saw it, was "to go to the people," to bring the immediacy of his oratorical performances to the voters of the nation-state. The question, then, is how Bryan conceived his task and how he attempted to extend the reach of the interaction in order to encompass a national public.

In Bryan's understanding, his scaling problem as a presidential candidate was essentially a matter of adapting performance as a mode of political discourse in such ways as to extend the power of his presence to what were taken to be ever-larger social and political formations. Oratory was a platform performance form, often a component of celebrative or ceremonial performance events, and Bryan, for whom his skill as an orator and his ability to move audiences by his speech were fundamental to his conception of himself as a person and as a politician, depended upon copresent audiences for his personal and political success. During his earlier campaigns for Congress, he had been able to reach his constituents quite readily, and the speeches on the floor of the House of Representatives that won him celebrity took place in a well-established venue for political oratory. When he decided to run for president, however, the perceived scale of the polity and the size of the territory it encompassed demanded new measures to stretch the reach of the interaction order. The problem he faced was this: how can a performer encompass an expansive national polity while preserving the tried-and-true features and qualities of performance that moved traditional gathered audiences?

Two of Bryan's projects to extend the reach of his voice by upscaling his oratorical performances demonstrate how he attempted to solve this problem. Both projects involved new ways of exploiting communicative technologies: the expansion of railroad networks allowed him to multiply beyond any precedent the number of speeches he delivered and the number of constituents he faced in his whistle-stop tours; and the emergence of the phonograph as a commercial medium made it possible to project his voice into areas that he couldn't reach in person. Likewise, both projects depended upon innovations in genre: the whistle-stop speech in 1896, and the stripped-down expository speeches tailored to the phonograph in 1908.

Both efforts at extending the power of his presence by maximizing the reach of his voice among "the people" involved not only the exploitation of new communicative technologies and the development of new oratorical genres but also the recalibration of performance modes, from the virtuosic performances by which Bryan made a name for himself as an orator to the auratic performances of the whistle-stop tours and the recordings. To be sure, the framing of the recorded speeches as auratic performances required the metadiscursive collaboration of the record producers, journalists, vendors, and organizers of political gatherings, since the recordings themselves are stripped of all contextualization cues and the mediation of the recording technology actually distanced audiences from Bryan's living voice and auratic presence. Catalog entries, advertisements, and introductory announcements at political meetings assimilated the sonic icons issuing from the phonograph to Bryan's "real," "actual," "life-like" voice and invited listeners to re-create in virtual, imaginary form the platform events that remained the default contexts for political oratory. Party functionaries attempted to re-create those cultural performances in more concrete form, using the phonograph as a stand-in for Bryan himself in gatherings that also included other accoutrements of celebrative display and elicited the same kinds of enthusiastic responses (applause, cheers) as the flesh-and-blood auratic performances that thrilled Bryan's live audiences.

The contrast between Bryan's upscaling projects of 1896 and 1908 marks a critical juncture in American political history. His 1896 whistle-stop campaign was a herculean effort to stretch copresent interaction as far as he was able by the superaddition of as many platform performances as possible. While whistle-stop tours have remained a part of the American campaign tool kit, candidates could never again hope even to approximate the scale of Bryan's 1896 campaign in terms of the sheer numbers affected by the great man's presence among them. The resort to commercial sound recordings in 1908, however, marked the beginning of political campaigns as mediatized marketing efforts, a first step in the trend toward what Richard Jensen (1969) terms the "merchandising style" of presidential campaigns. It was also a formative moment, to which Habermas alerts us, in the development of a process by which "private enterprises evoke in their customers the idea that in their consumption decisions they act in their capacity as citizens" ([1962] 1989, 195). From that point on, it has been marketing and media all the way down, first in the United States and now throughout the world.

NOTES

I thank the members of the Michicagoan Faculty Seminar on Linguistic Anthropology, especially Susan Gal and Summerson Carr, for their helpful comments in the development of this essay. Thanks also to Patrick Feaster, my collaborator in earlier work on the campaign recordings of 1908 (Bauman and Feaster 2004).

1. The biographical literature on Bryan is extensive. Useful works include Coletta (1964), Glad (1960), Kazin (2006), and Leinwand (2007).

2. "Tariff-Reform Champion, Nebraska Furnishes a Fine Democratic Fighter," *New York Times*, March 17, 1892, 5.

3. On the campaign of 1896, see Barnes (1947), Bryan (1896), Harpine (2005), Melder (1965), and Whicher (1953). An extremely useful source for Bryan's campaign speeches is the Railroads and the Making of Modern America website, http://railroads.unl.edu/documents/view_document.php?views[0]=Bryan&yearStart=1896&yearStop=1896&addrLine[0]=CT&id=rail.wjb.18960928.02.

4. "Speech by William Jennings Bryan," *Lincoln (NE) Evening News*, October 15, 1896, 8.

5. Ibid.

6. "Stops in the Capitol City, Nominee Bryan Reaches Raleigh and Addresses an Audience in Nash Square," *Omaha World Herald*, September 18, 1896, 1.

7. "Across the State, Story of Four-Minute Stops at Small Cities," *Omaha World-Herald*, August 8, 1896, 1.

8. "William Jennings Bryan," *Washington Post*, July 11, 1896, 6.

9. Concerning this campaign stop, see Kazin (2006: 159). The memory of a personal encounter with Bryan during one of his campaign tours lives on in some families. My next-door neighbor told me that his father, a baby at the time, was kissed by Bryan during a campaign visit to Poseyville, Indiana, in 1908.

10. "Vast Crowds Cheer, Swarms of Humanity Pack the Streets of Whiting to Greet the Leader," *Omaha World-Herald*, October 2, 1896, 2.

11. "Mr. Bryan Averts a Panic, Coolness of the Democratic Leader Prevents a Disaster at Delphos, Ohio," *Omaha World-Herald*, October 11, 1896, 5.

12. Deictics are lexical or grammatical forms, the meanings of which are derived from their situational context of utterance, such as person deictics (e.g., I, you), spatial deictics (e.g., here, there), and temporal deictics (e.g., now, then). Vocatives are terms of direct address.

13. "All Sections Interested, Mr. Bryan Explains the Need of Bimetallism by People Everywhere," *Omaha World-Herald*, September 29, 1896, 5.

14. "TWENTY THOUSAND PEOPLE, They Stand Ankle Deep in Mud to Hear Mr. Bryan," *Omaha World-Herald*, September 16, 1896, morning edition; "The First Battle: A Story of the Campaign of 1896," *Omaha World-Herald*, September 16, 1896.

15. The 1908 Edison campaign recordings have been compiled on a CD by Archeophone Records, accompanied by excellent historical notes by Patrick Feaster and transcriptions of the recorded speeches. See *Debate '08: Taft and Bryan Campaign on the Edison Phonograph*, Archeophone CD-1008 (Champaign, IL, 2008). The parallel recordings issued by Victor are available on the first CD of the two-CD set *In Their Own Voices: The U.S. Presidential Elections of 1908 and 1912*, Marston CD-52028-2 (West Chester, PA, 2000), with historical notes by Kathleen Hall Jamieson and Ward Marston.

16. "Ten Edison Records by William Jennings Bryan," *Edison Phonograph Monthly* 6, no. 6 (June 1908): 7.

17. "Phonographs in Politics," *Elyria (OH) Evening Telegram*, November 27, 1908, 6.

18. "Ten Edison Records by William Jennings Bryan," 7.

19. "Hearst Speech 'Canned' for Up-State Farmers: He Talks It and Gestures It into Phonograph and Camera; a 12-Cylinder Harangue; the Absent-Treatment Candidate Will Be Projected in Sound and Shadow before the Voters of the Remoter Regions," *New York Times*, October 10, 1906, 1.

20. "Phonographs in Politics," 6.

21. "Democrats Listen to 'Master's Voice,'" *Trenton (NJ) Evening Times*, August 24, 1908, 2.

22. *Edison Phonograph Monthly* 6, no. 7 (July 1908), 18.

23. "As to 'Canned' Oratory," *Kansas City Star*, in *Washington Post*, September 8, 1908, 6.

24. "Denial Came Too Late," *Bedford (PA) Gazette*, October 16, 1908, 3.

25. "Bryan Speaks to Millions through the Edison Phonograph, *Edison Phonograph Monthly* 6, no. 7 (July 1908): 18.

26. "Ten Edison Records by William Jennings Bryan," 6.

27. "As to "Canned" Oratory," 6.

28. "Ten Edison Records by William Jennings Bryan," 6.

29. "As to 'Canned' Oratory," 6.

30. Ibid.

31. "The Trust Question," Edison 9917, *Debate '08: Taft and Bryan Campaign on the Edison Phonograph*, 42–43.

32. Ibid., 43; and from the same collection, "Popular Election of Senators," Edison 9919, 67.

33. "Window Talk," *Edison Phonography Monthly* 6, no. 10 (October 1908): 15.

34. "Push the Bryan Records," *Edison Phonography Monthly* 6, no. 7 (July 1908): 9.

35. "Bryan Speaks to Millions through the Edison Phonograph," 18.

36. "Push the Bryan Records," 9.

37. "What Society Is Doing," *Edwardsville (IL) Intelligencer*, September 5, 1908, 1.

38. "Making the Most of the Political Situation," *Edison Phonograph Monthly* 6, no. 10 (October 1908): 5; see also "The Phonograph as a Political Factor," *Edison Phonograph Monthly* 6, no. 11 (November 1908): 7.

39. "Phonographs in Politics," 6.

40. "Mere Mention," *Nebraska State Journal* (Lincoln), September 11, 1908, 8; "Hear 'Peerless' Voice," *Los Angeles Times*, October 7, 1908, I12; "Democratic Club Event," *Williamsport (PA) Daily Gazette and Bulletin*, June 24, 1908, 5; "Talks on Politics," *Oshkosh (WI) Daily Northwestern*, August 25. 1908, 5; "Canastota: Have Issued a Call," *Syracuse (NY) Herald*, October 10, 1908, 3; "Advertises Bryan Records," *Edison Phonograph Monthly* 6, no. 7 (July 1908): 19.

41. "Listen to Bryan Records; District Democrats Supplement Real Speeches by 'Canned' Ones," *Washington Post*, September 4, 1896, 3.

42. "Hear 'Peerless' Voice," 12.

43. "Johnson Renominated," *Syracuse (NY) Herald*, August 20, 1908, 1.

2

INTERACTION RESCALED

How Buddhist Debate Became a Diasporic Pedagogy

Michael Lempert

There is a damning phrase Erving Goffman used in the twilight of his career that confirmed, for his critics at least, just how blinkered his whole project was. That phrase, "the interaction order," was the title of his 1982 presidential address to the American Sociological Association and was proposed as a distillation of decades of writing on face-to-face encounters, encounters that transpire in "environments in which two or more individuals are physically in one another's response presence" (Goffman 1983, 3). In this deliberately cribbed microsociology, scale was used conceptually and rhetorically to separate interaction from mainstream sociology, to constitute it as an object—not unlike the way many disciplines have tried to carve out a distinctive domain by purifying their object of knowledge from competing disciplinary logics (cf. Latour 1993; recall, for example, Ferdinand de Saussure's [1983] efforts to establish a science of linguistics by defining and walling off an irreducible core of language that encroaching fields such as psychology, history, and sociology couldn't touch). Whatever disciplinary motivations may have inspired the scalar segregation of interaction—this was, after all, an address to his field in his role as president—and apart from any analytic purchase this rhetoric of scaling may have had for audiences in the early 1980s, it is now clear that "the interaction order" has had some unfortunate consequences, both conceptual and empirical.

While it is still common to speak of and even celebrate the "local," "situated" nature of face-to-face interaction, many have troubled these qualities and are no longer content to treat "the interaction order" as if it were some watertight chamber of activity insulated from macrosocial dynamics and pressures. They spotlight and marvel at what they take to be the scalar hybridity and heterogeneity of discursive interaction, like the way resources and materials associated with distinct spatial and temporal scales converge and are even melded in the crucible of face-to-face encounters. In interaction they discover "larger" things—Discourses, language ideologies, categories of identity, master tropes, and narratives. Interaction so imagined is a nexus, not a matrix. Yes, interaction may have "a life of its own," as Goffman (1957, 47) famously wrote; it may be "a little social system with its own boundary-maintaining tendencies," "a little patch of commitment and loyalty with its own heroes and its own villains" (1957, 47), but many later found this system to be porous if not enmeshed and therefore not so little after all. In that essay on the interaction order, Goffman (1983, 3) doubled down on the intrinsic scale of interaction but allowed for a "loose coupling" with respect to the "macrosocial," a minor concession, compared to the opening of the proverbial floodgates that would follow.

Other interactionists, working more from inside out than from outside in, accept that interaction is micro but find ways to aggregate it, charting "larger scale" trajectories of interaction—like the way identity seems to crystallize and sediment longitudinally over lots of discrete, situated events. Still others have tired of the coarse "micro-macro" distinction and propose what they believe to be finer, middle-range—"meso"-level—distinctions. And when writers of all dispositions try to link the levels or scales they construct, moving from the relatively small to the relatively large, they rely on remarkably few connection types, all rather wooden. There is, for instance, the methodological commonplace that interaction should be set "in" some larger context (institutional site, sociocultural matrix, state regime, global flows) that ferries in contextual information to participants, making their encounter meaningful and pragmatically consequential in some enriched way. Some, unsure of the precise directionality of these relations (whether uni- or bidirectional, whether one level causally influences the other more), throw up their hands and declare the whole micro-macro relationship a "dialectic," which often just means that no side is responsible and that no further explanation is needed.

All the moves inherit the sense of interaction's diminutive scale.

Bruno Latour (2005) takes apart this axiom. "People are only too ready to accept that . . . abstractions like structure, context, or society should be criticized," writes Latour, but they are convinced that there is something concrete and local and micro about the abstraction called interaction. In a characteristically mischievous exercise, a series of "gymnastics," as he puts it, Latour picks apart our intuitions about the scale of interaction until we aren't sure how small or large, local or nonlocal, micro or macro, interaction is.

No interaction is "isotopic," because "what is acting at the same moment in any place is coming from many other places, many distant materials, and many far-away actors" (Latour 2005, 200). No interaction is "synchronic," because the pieces it comprises did not all begin at the same time. Interactions are not "synoptic" either, says Latour, in the sense that only some participants are visible and focal at any given point. Those who inhabit participant roles like "speaker" and "hearer" make up only the official roster of actors present. Nor are interactions "homogenous," his fourth and related gymnastic. The kinds of agents that make up interactions are not necessarily the same type, and some aren't even human. The "relays through which action is carried out," he writes, "do not have the same material quality all along," but instead there is a "crowd of non-human, non-subjective, non-local participants who gather to help carry out the course of action." Interactions are not, finally, "isobaric"—a meteorological trope, Latour's attempt to speak of the varied "pressures" exerted by the manifold agents of action. Taken together, these gymnastics suggest that it is "impossible to start anywhere that can be said to be 'local'" (Latour 2005, 200–202).

Latour would have us be "indifferent" to the scale of interaction, not because scale is illusory, but because he does not want to "settle scale in advance"; he wants to provide actors "enough space," he writes, "to deploy their own contradictory gerunds: scaling, zooming, embedding, 'panoraming,' individualizing, and so on" (2005, 220). His negative propositions about interaction are meant as theoretical "clamps" to prevent one from prematurely jumping scale, so that the scale-jumping virtuosity of participants can become an object of empirical investigation (cf. Oppenheim 2007).

All the varied approaches to interaction have been illuminating in their own way, but what if we want to appreciate practices and projects that operate *on* scale, that seem preoccupied with interaction's dimensionalities? How might we explore an interactional ritual that looks as if it has been painstakingly modularized, limited in scope to specific times and places and people, its participants corralled spatially through the brute materiality of, say, a perimeter, be it wall or fence? And, conversely, how might we capture the communicative labor and human drama involved in trying to undo those seemingly settled, institutionalized dimensionalities, such as by aspiring to "expand" or "curtail" such a practice? It is true, as the ethologically minded will point out, that even the most ordinary forms of discursive interaction exhibit some measure of spatial and temporal boundary-making, but such boundary-making is an artifact of communicative practice itself. There is labor involved in creating and maintaining an "eye-to-eye ecological huddle" (Goffman 1966, 95) when we talk, through restrictive posture and gaze and spatial orientation, just as there is labor in temporally delimiting a conversation, such as through the bookendings of verbal greetings and leave-takings. The intuition that interaction is micro is no "mere" disciplinary invention, then, because this intuition is nurtured daily through routine semiotic practice. Yet to naturalize these scalar qualities and forget that these are precarious effects of communicative labor would make it difficult to study the pragmatics of scale. Most of the time, the scalar dimensionalities of interaction may not matter enough to merit a pragmatics. They may be sensed tacitly but not be relevant socially in any gross sense. But when these dimensionalities do matter, we need ethnographies of scale that take care not to settle scale in advance.

It is in this spirit, of exploring the (re)scaling of interaction, that I turn to the troubled production of persons at Tibetan Buddhist monasteries in India. I focus on a form of face-to-face argumentation, Buddhist "debate" (*rtsod pa*). Debate is strongly modularized and anchored in a spatiotemporal here and now; but as an educational "rite of institution" (Bourdieu 1996, 102–115), it is meant to gird the whole monastery from below and ensure its continuity over time. It does this through serving as a site for a certain routinized interscalar performativity, where qualities acted out in the here-and-now envelope of this interaction are meant to exemplify comparable qualities of something "larger," something beyond debate's self-drawn perimeter. This potential, typical of ritual, may seem to lie within the event's boundaries, as if we could find this interscalar potency *in* the practice, perhaps in communicative behavior that can be revealed through the science of recording, transcription, and analysis: a "close reading." However, the scaling potential of debate would be wildly unstable were it not for debate's institutional "placement," its embeddedness within a highly distributed assemblage of practices that is designed to serve as a kind of scalar infrastructure or "backing" for debate. This backing both makes plausible and narrows down what participants are likely to "see" dramatized in this interactional practice. This backing helps entrain associations that may otherwise spin off this way and that, so that practitioners and spectators can learn to recognize what this ritual "really" exemplifies and does. The more one inspects this heterogeneous, far-flung assemblage, which includes but exceeds the debating courtyard, the more indistinct the edges of "the interaction order" grow. Yet the point of the exercise that follows is not to dwell on this fact but to inspect the preparation, the conditioning, and the labor involved in scaling debate as a rite of institution and, as we shall later see, in rescaling debate into something new: a diasporic pedagogy that aspires to remake Tibetans in exile.

DEBATE'S DIMENSIONS

At first glance, debate has clear, unmistakable edges at places like Sera monastery in India, where it is the premier educational practice. Founded in the early 1970s in Bylakuppe, Karnataka State, Sera is one of the largest exile monasteries of the dominant Geluk sect and is renowned for its rigorous debate-based philosophical curriculum. India's Sera presents itself as an avatar and legitimate heir of its namesake, Tibet's Sera, founded in 1419 on Lhasa's outskirts. (Tibet's Sera still exists, but as Sera monks in India have often insisted, its curriculum pales compared to India's Sera.) Stylistically, debate grates on the senses. It is loud, brash, and agonistic, and I came to Sera for fieldwork in part to explore the fate of this style of wrangling in a period in which liberal-democratic principles were being used by agents like the Dalai Lama to reimagine exile governance and Tibet's religious patrimony, Buddhism. Asking about a single discursive practice may prime us to see debate as a discrete object of analysis with clear boundaries. Nevertheless, debate itself does much to encourage this impression.

Debate does everything to distinguish itself from its surround. Sensorially, it does not look or sound anything like the way Tibetans ordinarily deliberate and argue. In debate, monks use a specialized lexical repertoire and a formal method of argumentation called "consequences" (*thal 'gyur*). More striking than debate's lexical register and method of reasoning is the comportment monks adopt when they wrangle. Monks playing the challenger role act in ways that would look boorish and even violent off the debating courtyard. When challengers make points, they shout and stomp their feet and fire piercing open-palmed claps that explode in the direction of the seated defendant's face. They hurl taunts, some of which—like "shame [on you]!" (*o tsha*)—belong to debate's lexical register. Debate is conspicuously *un*like quotidian communicative behavior among monks. The practice suspends—flouts, really—ordinary monastic etiquette. Noisy and visually arresting, debate steals attention and gathers crowds; it invites observers to think that everything of interest unfolds "within" its proscenium, as if debate had a clear inside and outside. If ever there were a neatly circumscribed "speech event" (see Agha and Wortham 2005), it would surely be found among the ranks of rituals like debate.

Spatially, debate is also heavily perimeterized. It cannot happen anywhere but in designated places, notably in each college's debating courtyard (*chos rwa*). Temporally, debate is scheduled, set to rhythm. At Sera Mey in south India—one of Sera monastery's two colleges, which served as my primary field site—twice-daily, two-hour-long debate sessions convene during fixed times, and then there are the innumerable formal debate "defenses" (*dam bca'*) that occur on set dates in the monastic calendar.

And so: a distinctive lexical register and mode of argumentation; a "violent" comportment exhibited by challengers that flouts ordinary monastic etiquette; the practice's spatial and temporal regimentation. All this, and more, digs a channel around the practice, giving it its sharp, unmistakable edges.

IN THE DEBATE COURTYARD

As circumscribed as debate seems, and is, it is a commonplace that rituals are also axiological (value-setting) sites of macrosocial relevance—thrumming engines of social and cultural "reproduction," as Durkheim and Mauss (1963, 11) once imagined.[1] How strange that a practice so bounded in one way should be so far reaching in another, capable of operating at a scale far beyond its self-styled immanence.

Before tracing debate's reach, let me describe in more detail what occurs within its perimeter. Debate features two speech-event roles that may be glossed as "challenger" and "defendant." The challenger, who stands while the defendant sits cross-legged before him, tries to induce inconsistencies in claims the defendant makes about Buddhist doctrine. He problematizes relentlessly, no matter what he may personally think about the philosophical issue at hand and no matter how he may feel about the defendant. The defendant is the challenger's mirror image, for he is expected to have a thesis and be committed to what he says, and his task is to defend doctrine against the challenger's attacks. The defendant is obliged to restore consistency among philosophical claims and is judged competent to the extent that he does this. Monks take turns playing these roles in daily courtyard debate. They spend some of the time as defendant, some as challenger.

As for debate's flow, it begins slowly and placidly. Placid, because the challenger—and it always begins with one challenger but ends up a many-on-one affair—can often seem helpful if not deferential. He leaves intact the assumption of doctrinal integrity and treats the defendant with a modicum of respect. By default the defendant is presumed to be knowledgeable, and he sits accordingly. In formal debate defenses, the defendant sits perched on the highest seat in the room. And in all debates, he sits cross-legged on a cushion and remains that way for the whole debate, while the challenger paces about frenetically. Rather than immediately challenge the presumption that the defendant knows doctrine well, the challenger asks seemingly innocent questions, questions that elicit things already known and shared between them—such as definitions and divisions found in doctrinal texts, material they have both committed to memory.

Debates thus begin with consensus building, and this can be seen most dramatically in formal debate defenses (*dam bca'*). After approaching the defendant and delivering an open-palmed hand clap—a clap that is muted relative to the claps fired when the debate really gets started, the challenger utters an auspicious line used to start all debates. The line invokes Mañjuśrī, a deity embodying Buddha's insight into the nature of reality. In the annual Sera Mey Rigchung preliminary debates I attended, for instance, the monk challenger, as was customary, would lob at the seated defendant a cryptic, trisyllabic fragment drawn from a line in a text.

The challenger selects the fragment beforehand and takes it from the chapter on which the debate will be focused. The defendant's memory is on trial, because his first task is to identify the line from which the three syllables were taken and then cite the whole source line flawlessly. Once the source line has been quoted, the challenger then asks the defendant to name the section title that houses that line, and once that is named, the defendant must name the other, lateral section titles (so that if there are four sections and he just named one, he would need to name the other three).

The challenger continues to drive the defendant "upward" through the book's hierarchically dense outline: "From where does [that] stem?" (*ga nas 'phros pa*), he asks repeatedly, goading the defendant "up" the textbook's scaffolding. The defendant names the superordinate section that houses those subsections, moves up to the next higher section, and so on, till he climbs up and out of the text, assuming a high ground, below which the original source quote that started the debate sits neatly in its place. The vista opened before them is that of a panorama of cohesive text, a corpus they both know well, having painstakingly memorized and studied its details off the courtyard.

In this first phase of debate, the challenger spurs the defendant and may taunt him gently when he delays or slips up. Still, he remains collegial and may even help the defendant a bit. The whole tenor of the interaction at the outset of debate differs from that of the argument phase, when consensus ends and debate truly begins. The first phase of debate, brief though it often is, is a test of memory in which challenger and defendant join hands in paying deference to what both should revere and accept: the college's textbook and its warren of definitions and divisions. The "textbook" (*yig cha*) literature consists of Tibetan sub-subcommentaries on canonical Indian Buddhist works but is enormously important in the Geluk curriculum (Cabezón 1994; Dreyfus 1997, 2003).

Once consensus is established, debate's plot takes a sudden, tragic turn. Tragic in the sense of peripety, the chiastic, counterdirectional turn that Aristotle counted as an ingredient of tragedy. The challenger turns against doctrine, shattering the picture of coherence he just helped create. He threatens doctrinal integrity and holds the defendant responsible for any harm done to it. As the defendant tries to mend text, the challenger does not extend a hand or encourage him. Instead, he hurls taunts and fires open-palmed hand claps that resemble stylized physical strikes. Deference never returns, and debates end without compromise or a return to consensus. Biphasic in structure, debates thus move from consensus to dissensus. In handling this tragedy, the defendant looks—or should look, anyway—majestically unflappable, a demeanor projected through such methods as a conspicuously nonresponsive uptake when provoked by the challenger. He is to act as unshakeable as the doctrine he defends. In demeanor and discourse he is to be the institution incarnate.

OFF THE COURTYARD: DEBATE REDISTRIBUTED

Debate's drama—its plotline of consensus building and deference toward doctrine and defendant, the way that collapses tragically, the defendant's unflappability—is reminiscent of certain tensions outside debate's perimeter. Debate's tensions may even feel as if they were a figurative condensation of tensions that concern attachments to college-based textbooks more generally—and hence attachments to Sera's colleges.

Sera has two "monastic colleges" (*grwa tshang*), Sera Jey and Sera Mey, and in many respects the two seem equal and solidary. If one takes the words for Sera's parts, the names for its major administrative units, the monastery may seem one neat hierarchically nested whole: Jey and Mey are both "colleges" (*grwa tshang*), colleges that fit within Sera, the "monastic seat" (*gdan sa*) that houses them, which makes it easy to think that the colleges are equivalent and get along well. Sera's visual landscape and built environment seemed to confirm this. During fieldwork I saw little signage distinguishing the two colleges and no conspicuous fences or walls separating them. The debating courtyards were not near each other, but many Jey and Mey structures did often neighbor each other and were hard to distinguish. A general assembly hall (*lha spyi*) accommodated monks of both colleges from time to time, and it was not as if monks broadcasted their ties to Jey or Mey through legible clothing or other emblems of identity. Plus, Sera had just one main circumambulation route, which monks of both colleges would follow, murmuring mantras while clicking off their prayer beads, accumulating merit as they walked along it.

The colleges could often seem like equal members of a single, harmonious corporate body, Sera, but the monastery is just as riven by division. Administratively, each college has its own abbot (*mkhan po*), disciplinarian (*dge skos*), financial officer (*phyag mdzod*), and so forth. Each has its own debating courtyard, assembly hall, set of regional hostels where monks live, library, publishing house, secular schoolhouse, general store, restaurant, and telephone center. As for consumption, food is to be eaten at one's own college's restaurant, goods purchased from one's own general store, and so on. Although under the same roof, the colleges strain to be autonomous, so much so that Dreyfus (2003) has suggested that the English gloss of *grwa tshang* as "college" is misleading, that it is better to call Jey and Mey "monasteries" in their own right.

Asked about the basis for Sera's corporate division into two colleges, the monks I spoke with—at least the well-socialized ones—invoked doctrine. Different colleges exist because doctrinal differences exist. Their differences are said to be enshrined in the textbooks of Jey's and Mey's respective curricula. Both colleges belong to the Geluk sect, which traces descent to Tsongkhapa (1357–1419), the sect's founder, but Sera Jey and Mey college uphold and teach monastic "textbooks" (*yig cha*) written by different authors who were contemporaries in the mid-fifteenth and early sixteenth centuries.[2] So each college rests on doctrinal foundations that are threatened by its neighbor.

Within each college and outside the debating courtyard, monks care for texts. In every modality they pay deference to the textbook literature as well as to the canon of authoritative Buddhist literature. In one assembly hall, the Buddhist canon and the collected works of Tsongkhapa were set at the furthest reaches of the room and on the highest ledges. As for bodily hexis, monks handle books of such caliber with delicacy. If the books are of the traditional, long, unbounded sort, they wrap them snugly in auspiciously colored fabrics—orange, yellow, gold, or red—when not in use. When in use, monks take care not to bend corners or mar pages, and if they must write in the pages to aid study, they prefer pencil and keep the marks faint.

This care of texts extends to content, which, as noted earlier, monks commit to memory and cite often in debate. The ability to quote texts fluently and accurately in debate is a valued skill, for should a monk's memory fail him—should he forget a key definition or distinction—it can be perilous. For training, mnemonic practices figure prominently. Most monks begin their day with memorization and end each day reciting what they've memorized, and memorization exams occur at all stages of the monastic curriculum.

So monks cultivate care for books, both in terms of embodied habits with respect to the books' materiality as text-artifacts and in terms of textual content. Expectedly, there is an official hermeneutics of retrieval that applies to the entire corpus of authoritative Buddhist works, a corpus that includes not only one's college's textbook literature but also doctrine attributed to the historical Buddha and to revered lineage masters like Tsongkhapa. All this propositional content is said to hang together. Superficial contradictions may exist, but these can be resolved and an underlying coherence discovered. This talk about textuality comprises more than just polite words said about doctrine. It affects debate, since one will not hear defendants blatantly contradict their textbooks in public—especially not in formal debate defenses—and one type of taunt hurled at defendants even thematizes their departure from what the texts say: "[You] contradict text, [you] contradict scripture"! (*dpe cha dang 'gal / phya dpe dang 'gal*; see Lempert [2012a]).

When it comes to the textbook literature, then—a literature that assumes enormous importance in each college—monks should accept what it says, though it is perfectly fine to poke at imperfections in the *neighboring* college's textbook. (The occasional maverick monk will risk being contrarian, but one can't overstate the level of commitment a monk is expected to have for his own college textbook.) These practices are by no means seamlessly integrated, yet all this care and cultivation of attachments toward text—through bodily hexis; through mnemonic practices, exams, and citation; and through an official hermeneutics that talks as if all authoritative books were cohesive—helps sediment a kind of "textual ideology," a caption we may use for a loose congeries of semiotic practices that overdetermine beliefs about text and textuality. These practices make it easy to feel as if received Buddhist doctrine had an aura of inviolable integrity and wholeness.

It is this very textual ideology that the monastery targets in debate. Curricular texts that anchor each college seem threatened by neighboring colleges that uphold a different textbook (and although I cannot delve into this here, this neighbor is a rival in respects other than doctrine, too). Which means that if the textual ideology is threatened during debate—and it is, because the challenger must problematize received doctrine—and if the defendant fails to save doctrine, the synecdochic shockwaves may be felt by the whole college. This explains why a defendant's poor performance not only is bad for him—as an individual whose career very much depends on his capacity to debate well—but also might even offend the college. "These scholars know," remarks Dreyfus (2003, 319), "that any doubt they express publicly about the orthodoxy of their school or even of their . . . [college's] . . . manuals will be taken as attacking the overall value of these institutions and their legitimacy."

If we draw these observations together and relate them back to debate's design, it would seem that the textual ideology and the institutionalized threat to it posed by the division into two colleges together set up debate's performativity as a rite of institution.[3] Sera has placed debate right at the center of fierce centripetal and centrifugal forces, those that try to bind the monastic college to its curricular texts, others that divide and rend the college and hence risk undermining the integrity of the monastery as a whole. Debate's storyline involves a movement from consensus to dissensus, which, in a way, seems to recapitulate "within" the ritual proscenium, at a smaller scale, tensions from debate's surround (though this is no simple case of homology or "reproduction," as I clarify below). By design, debate asks the defendant to act out "stability" in the midst of doctrinal division and dissension. In this respect, the defendant enacts in demeanor what he aspires to do in terms of text—that is, to present himself as doctrinal tradition *ought* to be: stable, immutable, whole. If successful, the defendant appears as a cross-modal figure (a figure made up of multiple semiotic modalities, not just of language) of and for doctrinal tradition's "stability" or, more dynamically, its "reunification."

Debate is thus a ritual site in which challengers threaten doctrinal integrity so that this integrity can be maintained. (In the ritual literature, this is a familiar irony. Recall Gluckman's [1954, 1963] classic notion of "rituals of rebellion," where ritual expressions of societal tension mitigate the risk that "real" outrage will erupt outside the ritual proscenium, ironically preserving societal cohesion.) Since the texts under debate are typically—at least during the early and middle stages of the curriculum—the college-textbook literature, a literature that the monastic college claims as its foundation, this stability has implications for the college. The defendant's unflappability spreads by default to the college, stabilizing it in turn.

SCALAR ASSEMBLAGES, SCALAR BACKING

What allows for this strange cross-scale cohesion, where the defendant's stability can seem to extend to doctrinal stability and in turn to the monastic college that subsumes him? In the Durkheimian imagination, the analytic steps upward were remarkably few and the movement effortless: a scalar leap of faith, perhaps, in the primacy of "the social." In *Primitive Classification*, for instance, Durkheim and Mauss (1963, 11) famously argued that the "classification of things reproduces ... [the] ... classification of men." They found cultural classifications that looked like diagrams of a group's structure (diagrams, wrote Peirce, "represent the relations ... of the parts of one thing by analogous relations in their own parts" [1932, 157]), and took this to be evidence of the social. As Needham recognized in his introduction to the English edition of *Primitive Classification*, there is no reason to assume a one-to-one correspondence between social morphology and cultural classification; and in stating that the "classification of non-social things 'reproduces' the classification of people," the term *reproduces* "immediately assumes that which is to be proved by the subsequent argument, viz. the primacy of society in classification" (1963, xix, xiv).

Nor did it help that Durkheim and Mauss neglected to examine the formal properties of signs, so that we are never quite sure what motivates the diagram at all—why *these* particular signs and not others? (Silverstein 1981; Urban 1991; Parmentier 1997). Contemporary scholarship on ritual in linguistic and semiotic anthropology has responded well to this last failing, often demonstrating how the formal patterning of signs in ritual events diagrammatically models features of context in a bid to reproduce or transform it.[4] The question remains open as to how such diagrammaticity could be registered and stabilized for a social domain of people, however. Rather than moving brusquely from the "close reading" of a ritual text to some analytic reconstruction of its "context," as if there were nothing in between, what if we were to slow down and trace out the labor and materials and practices within which this ritual-to-context projection is staged? While I cannot inventory here all the conditions that afford and stabilize debate's diagrammaticity, I have moved elliptically around the debating courtyard in order to identify a few prominent features of Sera's landscape without which debate would confer no cross-scale stability on defendants and the monastery at all.

By disaggregating the assemblage of discursive practices that make up Sera's landscape, one can better see just how distributed and heterogeneous the conditions and materials and practices that afford debate's interscalar performativity are. These range from materials like text-artifacts and built environments like courtyards, to practices like quotidian acts of deference to books and scheduled memorization exams. Debate does not scale itself. Debate's scalar effectiveness—its capacity both to stand apart and stand for something beyond itself, bolstering from below the monastery and its monks—depends on its intricate "placement." It is perimeterized and delicately set in relation to a congeries of other discursive practices that conspire to overdetermine its significance as a rite of institution. By *placement* I mean the varied efforts to set discursive practices off from and in relation to other practices, to array and coordinate them, the very effort of which invites us to imagine some overarching relational field *in which* these practices operate, and in relation *to which* it becomes natural to ask what some focal practice "does" with respect to this surround. Placement is as fraught an effort as any, and the results are rarely perfect. There is no guarantee of success, nor should we exaggerate the cohesiveness and integrity of the relational field that results.

This applies to the status of debate as a rite of institution. It may be tempting to imagine this as just another neat case of "reproduction" (as Durkheim and Mauss suggested) or fractal recursion, where one set of distinctions is reiterated at a higher or lower scalar order (Irvine and Gal 2000), like the rippling out of tiered concentric circles from a pebble tossed into a pond. But let us poke, instead, at imperfections that make debate's diagrammaticity a poor picture of its surround—or better, let us identify surplus materials that can alter a monk's sense of what debate does as a rite of institution. Consider the following:

- The challenger-defendant role-relation is not perfectly homologous with the Jey-Mey relationship (i.e., challenger : defendant :: Jey : Mey), because the colleges are *symmetrical* (they are structured similarly and share the same rights and obligations), while challenger and defendant are *asymmetrical* (or rather, they are symmetrical only in the way mirror-image opposites are).

- The threat posed by a neighboring college's doctrine is periodic, not constant; it has a calendrical metricality to it, spiking especially during events like scheduled, annual intercollegiate debates.

- Monks from each college do, indeed, cultivate attachment to their own college's textbook literature, especially during the foundational years of their philosophical training, but they *share* some literature with their neighbors, such as works by the sect's founder, Tsongkhapa.

- All the things that invite monks to see Sera as a solidary, corporate whole (the words for Sera's parts, the inconspicuous signage, the presence of a shared assembly hall and circumambulation route, etc.) do not necessarily exert the same force (they are not "isobaric" [Latour 2005]) as the things that incite division, which means that Sera does not feature some elegant equilibrium between unity and disunity.

- Not all forms of division at Sera are doctrinal, for some play out in terms of patronage and consumption, while others play out—literally—on the soccer field (quite a few monks engage in clandestine, prohibited soccer matches). Doctrinal grounds may be claimed by the well socialized as the foundation for all other intercollegiate divisions, but monks do not always and everywhere feel this way.

These relatively small "imperfections," which muddy any simple picture of ritual reproduction, could be multiplied. I list these not as exceptions to an otherwise snug fit between ritual and the institutional surround but rather as reminders that we need to distinguish the impossibly clean, sharp lines of scalar diagrammaticity as (potentially) experienced by participants and as reconstructed by analysts from the ragged, uneven, and far-flung assemblages of practices and materials that aspire to establish a place for interaction and make it a predictable rite of institution.[5]

In short, the cross-scalar work of ritual can't be explained by straining to see how a supposedly microevent articulates with some larger context, because those scalar distinctions are themselves effects—effects that are also highly distributed. The scalar diagrammaticity of this ritual, its capacity to buttress the monastery from below through the cross-scalar enactment of "stability," works only to the extent that it is backed. Which is another way of stressing that scale cannot be read directly off of communicative behavior in some focal event or site; scale is neither there in advance as an a priori dimension of social life, nor is it an effect of situated discourse. Institutional projects of scaling tend to distribute "scale" *across* parts of an assemblage. Discourse issued in one place is rarely enough to make scale compelling and consequential. How unconvincing it would be, for example, if this institution were merely to assert a symbolic equivalence between defendant and college. Instead, the scales projected by discourse "work"—that is, they are plausible, effective—only in relation to the (backgrounded) assemblages in which these discursively projected scales are staged (cf. Latour 2005, 183–190). Imagine how preposterously infelicitous it would be for the wrong personnel to address, say, "the American people" in a humble, untelevised domestic space. Without proper backing to serve as felicity conditions, the scalar work of this address would fail or just appear comedic or ironic or something else. What makes a tempest in a teacup—or in a transcript of face-to-face interaction, for that matter—feel overblown is not the scalar pretensions of discourse per se but the dissonance: the felt mismatch between scale as discursively projected and scale as pragmatically backed.

DEBATE RESCALED AS A DIASPORIC PEDAGOGY

Debate's scalar reach is no settled fact. Dramatic changes have accompanied this practice, offering a new kind of backing for debate. In the decades following the Dalai Lama's dramatic flight from Lhasa to India in 1959, debate has "expanded" in ways that suggest its involvement in a project of diasporic subject formation, a project informed by ethnonationalist concerns and globalizing liberal ideals. When I first studied the primers on logic and dialectics in Dharamsala, where the Dalai Lama resides, I did so as a layperson at Ganden Choeling nunnery; a basic course had started there, and I was granted permission to take it. I later discovered how extraordinary this was, for Geluk nuns had historically not pursued debate-based study. This, I learned, was part of a movement in which debate-based inquiry was being promoted to monasteries that had never had it before. For example, Namgyal Monastery, the Dalai Lama's personal monastery, founded by the Second Dalai Lama (1476–1542), was established anew in upper Dharamsala in Himachal Pradesh, next to the Dalai Lama's compound. Debate-based study was introduced for the first time in the early 1970s.

Asked about the spread of debate to a neighboring Nyingma monastery, a sect that has traditionally not privileged the practice, a Geluk lama from Mey credited the Dalai Lama: "Now, after that, after having arrived in India, the Precious Conqueror [the Dalai Lama] offered advice, right? At all monasteries, [monks] are [now] learning by studying philosophy a little bit, right?"[6] He continued: "The Exalted Presence [the Dalai Lama] is constantly offering [this] advice. [He says], 'These small monasteries need to study a bit of philosophy. The study of philosophy is not the responsibility of the monks of the [Geluk] monastic seats alone.'"[7] Since Geluk monks study philosophy through debate, invocations of philosophical study mean debate-based philosophical study by default. (The two are virtually inseparable for the Geluk sect, since debate in India has not been widely conceptualized as a "method" that can be abstracted and applied to non-Buddhist content.)

Monks credit the Dalai Lama for debate's expansion, and indeed, the spread of debate must be understood in relation to his refashioning of Buddhism into a religion of "reason" compatible with modern empirical science and distinct from religions, like Christianity and Hinduism, that are said to rely on faith alone (Lempert 2012a; see Lopez 1998, 2002, 2008). In public addresses to Tibetans in India, the Dalai Lama has argued repeatedly that Buddhism's path of reason cannot be limited to the clergy any more. As the Dalai Lama has acknowledged and harped on at times, few monasteries in Tibet taught doctrine well. Even in the renowned Geluk monastic seats of Sera, Drepung, and Ganden monasteries, rigorous philosophical training was pursued only by the few, perhaps as few as 10 percent of their monks. The Dalai Lama has tried to counter this in exile and expand the scope of this education. In an early talk to teachers delivered in Dharamsala on January 28, 1964 (Gyatso 2000, 67), for instance, he exhorted his audience to integrate religious and secular instruction. Religious instruction must mean more than parroting what scripture says. Students must think, and think critically: "In saying 'the Lama and Buddha are great sources [of truth]' and so forth, without stating any reasons whatsoever, there is the danger of stabbing ourselves at some point with our own knife."[8]

Buddhism is said to differ from religions like Christianity for the way it eschews "blind faith" (*rmong 'dad*); and Tibetans in exile must be especially vigilant to avoid blind faith, the Dalai Lama argues, because if challenged by those with competing truth claims—which presumably happens often in exile—Tibetan refugees would otherwise be left mute, unable to respond and vulnerable to losing their patrimony. They may even end up converting. The ability to defend Buddhism as if one were a defendant testing his mettle before a challenger is a capacity that all Tibetan refugees need to cultivate. For decades the Dalai Lama has argued that Tibetans cannot rely on religious habits inherited from their parents, popular religious practices like mantra recitation, prostrations, and the spinning of prayer wheels. In an address from 1964, for instance, he conceded that difficult works of Buddhist philosophy will remain opaque to all but scholars, but stated that elementary reasoning ought to be studied by all. The curricula of all Tibetan Buddhist centers of learning—monasteries and nunneries, and all sects, not just the Geluk—should offer at least *some* philosophical study; even secular Tibetans schools should introduce students to the rigors of Buddhist reasoning. Mass Buddhist philosophical education has not been realized in India, but the debate-based philosophical curriculum has spread to more Buddhist educational institutions than ever before (Lempert 2012a).

Debate has been rescaled to encompass, not quantitatively more of the same category of social actor, but a new, higher-order category: a Tibetan diasporic subject. Debate-based learning exemplifies Buddhism's commitment to reason and is promoted as a way to "stabilize" diasporic subjects against the challenges of exile. Debate is rescaled as a diasporic pedagogy.[9]

This does not mean that monks routinely experience debate as a diasporic pedagogy (any more than they routinely experience debate as a practice that stabilizes doctrinal tradition and in turn their monastic college). It means only that changes in debate's placement and distribution in India, along with new accompanying discourses about critical rationality in Buddhism, invite people to recognize a new upper limit for debate's performativity. These changes in debate's backing motivate an even "larger"-scale diagrammaticity in which debate can now be imagined to stabilize the defendant qua diasporic subject against the challenges of exile, steeling this subject's identity for an eventual return to the homeland. This reframing of debate builds on rather than replaces debate's desired effect of "stabilization"; debate still stabilizes, only now the subject stabilized is a generalized diasporic subject, not a monk associated with a particular monastery or monastic college. Debate's stabilizing, reproductive force is hence trained no longer exclusively on a college or monastery or sect but also on Tibetan Buddhism *tout court*, Tibet's patrimony.

This rescaling—the sense that debate now functions in a more expansive surround—is an achievement aided by discourses that talk in new ways about debate and the need for reason in exile, and, no less critically, by new regimes of placement that try to put debate in sites that have historically lacked it. To be convincing as a generalized diasporic pedagogy, debate must escape the orbit of the Geluk monastic seats of old (which positions the monastic seats as the fount of critical rationality in exile and thereby tries to restore the importance they enjoyed before exile). Debate must reach institutions such as Geluk tantric colleges, nunneries, small monasteries that had previously offered just training in prayers and rituals, and monasteries of other Tibetan Buddhist sects that tended to eschew debate. It should even enter nonmonastic schools. This attempt to cross old divides invites Tibetans to infer that this discursive practice must really be meant for a *broader* category of subject, a diasporic subject. The felt expansion in debate's placement figures a felt expansion in its scale.

Rescaling requires concerted reflexive activity (including but not limited to new ways of talking about debate) and the accompanying labor of placement (e.g., dissemination of debate to places that never had it before). Should the rescaling of debate succeed—and we should never assume success, just as we should never assume success to last—if, that is, Tibetans feel that debate *has* become a crucible in which a diasporic subject steels himself against the challenges of exile, then this alters (the sense of) what debate does. This explains the fluency with which a senior Mey monk I once interviewed, a renowned scholar and ex-abbot of the Mey college, told me that debate is invaluable because it makes a monk's knowledge of Buddhism "firm" (*gtan po*), and then added that the Dalai Lama had been promoting the practice in India precisely for this reason. Debate stabilizes knowledge under the unstable conditions of exile.

That rescaling is precarious can be appreciated by recalling how this rescaling of debate into a diasporic pedagogy has been more aspirational than actual. The very need to redefine debate's purpose and scope bespeaks the beleaguered status of the Geluk monasteries themselves, which have struggled to reassert their relevance in the field of education in India. Many Tibetans in India simply cannot see places like Sera as anything other than part of the old society, a world incompatible with modern, "secular" education in India and the opportunities that world offers. It is telling that in the early 1970s, India's Sera monastery had just a few hundred monks, and very few from the exile community in India wanted to join. There were no signs of Tibet's mass monasticism of old in the 1970s. Sera monastery changed dramatically in the early 1980s. The opening of the Tibet-Nepal border in 1980, coupled with liberalization in Tibet, made it possible for Tibetans to get visas. Refugees fresh from Tibet began to stream in. Sera grew exponentially, which led to a demographic shift: The monks that now constitute the vast majority at Sera monastery in India (and at the other major Geluk monasteries) are the post-1980 generation of new refugees, not the refugees who have been around longer.

. . .

I close with these notes about the troubled status of debate in a project of diasporic subject formation to underscore the vagaries of interaction's scale—all the more reason that scale should not be settled in advance. Against Goffman's scaling of interaction, which argued that "whatever is distinctive to face-to-face interaction is likely to be relatively circumscribed in space and most certainly in time" (Goffman 1983, 3), many have tried to escape the limits of "the interaction order" but often in ways that continue to presume rather than investigate what the scale of this abstraction called interaction is.

Approaching scale as an artifact of sociospatial and temporal practices does not mean that we should assume that every interaction *has* a scale (or scales), just one that is, say, "emergent" rather than given. Despite the inexhaustible scalar complexity that can (n.b., a potential) be discovered in interaction, there is no guarantee that scale matters—in the sense of being *registered* by interactants, if only tacitly, and of scale being pragmatically *consequential* in social life. In this sense, interaction may not have any scale at all.

Interaction analysts like to stress how the very definition of action and sense of "what is happening" in conversation is plastic and given shape locally and over time, and we could conceivably extend this to the way interactants scale their own interaction through discourse and even through the way they manage their bodies (see Blommaert 2007; Blommaert et al. 2015). Similarly, work on interdiscursivity and intertextuality in fields such as linguistic anthropology (e.g., Agha and Wortham 2005; Bauman 2004; Hanks 2000) has shown how participants can forge spatiotemporal links across events, at times scaling and rescaling themselves in the process. As important as such practices of scale can be, I have directed attention here to highly institutionalized scaling practices, or "projects of scaling." The projects described here involve enforced arrangements of materials and agents and practices, ranging from daily courtyard debates to regimes of formal testing and assessment. Such scaling projects cannot be illuminated by close readings of transcripts that are then placed in some reconstructed surround, because that would leave us where we started, stuck on a seesaw that alternates between event and context, ritual and the social, interaction and society. It would presume in advance interaction's diminutive size and modularity and fail to make its placement and scale objects of study. It would settle scale in advance.

NOTES

This chapter was adapted from *Anthropology and Education Quarterly* 43, no. 2 (June 2012): 138–156, and reproduced by permission of the American Anthropological Association. That original 2012 article arose from a conference session on scale, convened by Stanton Wortham, and was later published as part of a special issue of the *Anthropology and Education Quarterly*. For comments on this adapted chapter, I thank Summerson Carr and Robert Oppenheim.

1. On reproduction in schools, see, for example, Bourdieu and Passeron (1977), Willis (1977, 1981, 1983), and Levinson, Foley, and Holland (1996).

2. This commitment to different monastic textbooks is true of each of the three major Geluk monastic seats in south India—Sera, Drepung, and Ganden. Each monastic seat contains two colleges, and each of the two colleges follows different textbooks, even though some of these textbooks

are shared by colleges of *different* monasteries (e.g., Sera Jey uses the same textbook as Ganden's Jangtse-college, located in Mundgod, India).

3. By "rite of institution," Bourdieu meant rituals that tend to "consecrate and legitimate an *arbitrary boundary*, by fostering a misrecognition of the arbitrary nature of the limit and encouraging a recognition of it as legitimate" (Bourdieu 1991, 118; cf. Bourdieu 1996, 102–115). Bourdieu focused on elite schools in France and the reproduction of state nobility by means of rites like examination, training, isolation, and selection, all of which distinguished and naturalized stratified differences among categories of social actor. Debate does help distinguish monks from lay peers, and elite monks who study philosophy from those who do poorly in the philosophical curriculum and who end up doing monastic labor and service; but my concern here is with what debate does for the college and, in turn, for the monastic university.

4. See, for example, Stasch (2011), Silverstein (1981, 2004), Tambiah (1981), Urban (1990), Parmentier (1997), Keane (1997), Wortham (2001).

5. Compare with efforts to distinguish "text" from "text-artifact," "interactional text" from "discursive interaction," "intertextuality" from "interdiscursivity" (Silverstein and Urban 1996; Silverstein 1997, 2005).

6. *Da de nas rgya gar la slebs nas rgyal ba rin po che bka' gnang pa red pa / dgon pa sgang gar mtshan nyid blta yas tog tsam tog tsam sbyong gi 'dug ga.*

7. *Sku mdun gis ga dus yin na'i gnang gi yog red..bka' slob / dgon pa chung chung de tsho a ni mtshan nyid tog tsam sbyong dgos gi 'dug zer [/-s/] / mtshan nyid sbyang yas de gdan sa'i grwa pa gcig po'i las 'gan ma red zer [/-s/].*

8. *Rgyu mtshan gang yang ma brjod par bla ma dang / sangs rgyas rtsa ba chen po yin zer ba sogs byas pas nam zhig rang gri rang la 'dzugs nyen yod* (Gyatso 2000, 68).

9. This is not to suggest that this framing of debate is a direct effect of the Dalai Lama's discourse, as if this were merely a case of discourse "circulation"—even though this kind of unidirectional model of discourse circulation is what many Tibetans seem to suggest when they defer to the Dalai Lama as the prime mover in all modernizing reforms.

3

SHRINKING INDIGENOUS LANGUAGE IN THE YUKON

Barbra A. Meek

For people to care about and respond to a state of "language endangerment," they must first learn to see that a language is in decline; but how and with what effects does this awareness get produced? As it turns out, an awareness of endangerment happens through scale. By what semiotic means and for what ends is language endangerment (or its salubrious corollary, "language health") scaled, especially by the nation-state that claims to recognize and care for the indigenous languages within its borders? How do the very metrics used to scale indigenous languages and assess their "health" in the nation-state, condition present contexts and shape futures?

This chapter examines how a Canadian bureau, the Aboriginal Language Services in the Yukon Territory, scaled indigenous languages of First Nations peoples from the 1980s to the early twenty-first century. Though the assignment of endangered status to indigenous languages remained constant during this period, the metrics of scalar assessment changed. I demonstrate how these changes coincide with shifts both in the investments and ethical commitments of the nation-state and its bureaus and in the personnel involved in these scalar practices.

I take as my primary evidence intensively scalar bureaucratic texts. Bureaucratically, language endangerment policy and practice in the Yukon Territory has relied on sociolinguistic charts that render visible the putative state of indigenous languages and implicitly suggest courses of action. As we will see, the metrics featured on these charts—most notably age (generation), linguistic competence (fluency/health), and language varieties (dialects)—visually condense, mediate, and represent knowledge of indigenous languages. As these charts were modified over time, different scalar metrics became more or less prominent. Interestingly, the temporal directionality of bureaucratic scaling shifted as well. In early charts, the viewer was harkened to lament the decline or "shrinking" of indigenous languages within the compass of the nation-state with the help of metrics that calculated and visually demonstrated this historical decline. The overall current state of these languages seemed dire, since they were assessed in relation to a far more loquacious past.

Certain later charts, in contrast, were explicitly projective, scaling the present state of languages in relation to an imagined future. More specifically, these charts suggested future "potential" for expansion, more than imminent demise. The crafting of these latter charts coincided with a change in the management of First Nations' agendas through a policy commonly termed *devolution*—a process whereby First Nations gain (or regain) jurisdiction and management over certain bureaucratic domains (government programs), such as social services, local government and civil procedures, and, indeed, aboriginal language services themselves, which occurred finally in 2008. The rescaling of indigenous languages as capable of potential growth, thereby overcoming the threat of extinction, occurs at a time when increased autonomy is claimed to have been ceded to First Nation peoples. I contend, rather, that increased autonomy amounts to increased encompassment within and by the nation-state. More specifically, I show that the state project of scaling aboriginal languages coincides with a parallel politico-scalar project in which First Nation peoples are drawn into a regime of recognition and qualified reencompassment.

DIAGNOSING ENDANGERMENT

As with the formal assessment of any state or status by a socially licensed actor, some comparison is required. If we take a medical encounter as an example, the evaluation of a patient's condition by some medical professional is (at least) a twofold comparison, first with an individual's own previously healthy state and second with characteristics of other individuals' (un)healthy states. The assessment of language endangerment works similarly and even draws at times on medical tropes. Endangerment assumes a deviation from a previously healthy state. Symptoms of a language's poor health—its attrition, its loss of fluent speakers—are to be diagnosed and a remedy proposed. Although there are other ways to judge fluency, the key measure of health in the Yukon Territory, as elsewhere, is competence in grammar. Though implicit in the charts analyzed below, it is through grammar that fluency is assessed. A fluent speaker should have full knowledge of a language's grammar, and this fluency should be demonstrated empirically (and quantifiably) through speaking the language.

Long before this recent concern with the health of indigenous languages, settler-colonial experts were also focused, though for different reasons, on the seeming absence of grammar or language among native peoples. American Indian speech was often assessed as ungrammatical, unpatterned, unintelligible, and deficient. These assessments included both American Indian languages and the English spoken by American Indians and were informed by an overarching view of American Indians as less intelligent and less civilized than their benefactors, the nation-state and its entitled citizenry. Competence in grammar continues to be the primary measure of fluency by linguists and other language experts, most often demonstrated by people's abilities to produce utterances that conform to linguists' expectations of the grammatical structure of the aboriginal language and by aboriginal language speakers' abilities to generate novel forms. Competence is also assessed, to a lesser extent, through language experts' grammaticality judgments about whether some utterance (a sentence or word construction) conforms to their expectations of language structure.

While an assumption of grammatical knowledge is still embedded within the diagnostics used to assess language decline and allow for the enumeration of "speakers" and "nonspeakers," current bureaucratic studies of native language competence rely more on surveys and self-reports of linguistic practice rather than on expert assessments of performance. Self-reports of linguistic practices are then aggregated as evidence of language decline, which is then communicated through the enumerative imagery of the type of charts, tables, and graphs that I examine below.

The Canadian census, which has tracked demolinguistic factors since 1951, is the fodder of bureaucratic scalers' work. If we take an example from StatsCanada that compares the 1996, 2001, and 2006 censuses, the categories that get enumerated for the purpose of language scaling are several (see figure 3.1). This table aspires to be a "panorama" (Latour 2005), a constructed scalar model that purports to show everything, a whole multilingual nation in one glance (cf. Irvine this volume). The table also assumes the authority to define the nation's constituency demographically and linguistically. It distinguishes the two "official" languages, English and French, while lumping all "nonofficial" languages together in both the first major language category, "Mother tongue" (defined as that language which was first learned and is still spoken at home by the survey respondents at the time of the census), and the second major language category, "Language spoken most often at home." The last major category in figure 3.1 focuses on knowledge of Canada's two official languages.

These enumerative demonstrations—through surveys—provide some of the basic categories with which to assess language decline and provide evidence of

	Census year		
Subtopic	1996	2001	2006
Language			
% of population whose mother tongue is English only[24]	59.2	58.5	57.2
% of population whose mother tongue is French only[25]	23.3	22.6	21.8
% of the population whose mother tongue is a non-official language only[26]	16.1	17.6	19.7
% of the population who speak English and/or French most often at home[27]	91.0	90.3	88.9
% of the population who only speak a non-official language most often at home[28]	9.0	9.7	11.1
% of the population with knowledge of an official language[29]	98.3	98.5	98.3
% of the population with knowledge of both official languages[30]	17.0	17.7	17.4

FIGURE 3.1. Screenshot of census data on language in Canada from 1996, 2001, and 2006, www12.statcan.gc.ca/census-recensement/2006/dp-pd/92-596/P1-2.cfm?TID=600&Lang=eng&T=PR&PRCODE=01&GEOCODE=01.

crisis. They provide readers with scalar metrics—that is, the number of "mother tongue speakers." They also supply scalar logics—a decline of mother tongue speakers is equivalent to endangerment, if not the threat of linguistic extinction. For example, Dr. Barbara Burnaby, an aboriginal language advocate, scholar, and education consultant, discovered through a comparison of census data from 1951 to 2001 that mother tongue speakers of aboriginal languages have rapidly declined over the last fifty years, from 87.4 percent of the aboriginal population to 21 percent in 2001, thus demonstrating that "Aboriginal languages in Canada are at great risk (some much more than others)" (2008, 338).

RECOGNIZING "ABORIGINAL LANGUAGES"

Although the census lumps together aboriginal languages and makes few sociolinguistic distinctions, new forms of knowledge production helped intensify a sense of First Nation languages as endangered. Against the background of the Canadian Multiculturalism Act of 1988, new bureaucratic steps were taken to assess the state of aboriginal languages. That same year the Canada-Yukon Cooperation and Funding Agreement on the Preservation, Development and Enhancement of Aboriginal Languages was successfully negotiated in April followed by the adoption of the Yukon Languages Act in May (Meek 2009, 157–58; ALS 1991). Together these two legislative accomplishments provided funding and administrative support for the Yukon's aboriginal languages, including the establishment of the Yukon Native Language Centre for documenting grammar and developing pedagogical materials and the creation of Aboriginal Language Services (ALS) in February 1989, the government office tasked with administering the funding agreement. Both of these units have influenced the direction of aboriginal language documentation and revitalization in the territory and the ways in which these languages have been scaled. Most significantly, Aboriginal Language Services' first directive was to "design and conduct a survey to find out more about the state of native languages, and to report on the survey results" (1991, 4). This first survey and report set the standard and established the conventions for reporting on the state of aboriginal languages in the Yukon Territory, and the fact that scalar discourse pervades these conventions allows us to see how important scaling is in the work of bureaucratic governance on the one hand (see also Carr and Fisher this volume) and language revitalization projects on the other.

In the texts that ALS officials produced during this time, the aboriginal linguistic landscape appeared more complex than it had in the census. Unlike in the census, major varieties of aboriginal languages were now delineated, with eight officially recognized aboriginal languages named in the Yukon Territory. This expanded upon the census but still offered a narrow view of the sociolinguistic landscape, backgrounding local varieties of English, obscuring dialect differences, and aligning groups and languages in a strategically nationalistic way. Later, linguistic variation within communities and within the eight aboriginal languages came to be highlighted, complicating this compartmentalized view of these as discrete, monolithic languages and monolingual communities.

One might think that the disaggregation of languages once lumped together posed new challenges for those who sought to demonstrate the decline through a bifurcation of relatively healthy official languages and declining aboriginal ones. Given the new imperative to recognize indigenous languages within the nation-state, it is no surprise, then, that bureaucrats continued to speak of indigenous languages with reference to Canada's national linguistic scale, in which there were two "official" (and dominant) languages, English and French. There was no challenge to the relationship between aboriginal languages and the nation-state's official languages, English and French. Nor was one aboriginal language designated as the official language of the Yukon Territory, whether defined through historical narratives about origins or through an accounting of some majority, as in greatest numbers of speakers or populations.

Although the aboriginal-official dichotomy familiar from the census was left intact, so that aboriginal languages, by definition, could not also be national ones, efforts were made to elevate and respect native languages. A separate but equal philosophy was born with the aid of the bureaucrat's language scaling in conjunction with the passage of the Yukon Languages Act. For instance, the act legislated the linguistic accommodation of aboriginal language speakers in legal settings such that courtrooms would now accommodate First Nation peoples by supplying interpreters. Others insisted that discrimination against speakers of First Nation languages should not occur, so that they might feel more comfortable speaking their aboriginal languages in public contexts like stores and restaurants as well as at home and in their band offices. This rhetoric of linguistic recognition, respect, and accommodation worked in tandem with the rhetoric of First Nations' land claims' initiatives that laid out the process for aboriginal self-determination in the Yukon Territory. As if to anticipate future devolution of control, the 1991 ALS report begins by noting, not only that aboriginal languages "are in danger of being lost," but also that, "in recent years, native communities have shown that by keeping their language and culture alive and active, they can strengthen and unite the community. Children have a stronger sense of identity as a distinct people and take more pride in themselves. In this way, language is connected to economic and social well-being. With this kind of knowledge and with greater political awareness, native peoples have made language issues important to self-determination" (1991, 2).

This rhetoric characterized the Aboriginal languages of the Yukon as a nationalist diacritic of First Nation–hood and a step toward self-determination. Aboriginal languages were used to evaluate and define First Nation–hood, a move reminiscent of ethnolinguistic ventures in postcolonial contexts (Errington 2003; Irvine and Gal 2000; Silverstein 1998). The promotion of aboriginal languages in turn became an opportunity for advancing self-determination when the territory relinquished (devolved) control of Aboriginal language projects and services to the First Nations who had settled their land claims.

The elevation of aboriginal language status and the recognition of First Nation self-determination coalesced through the process of First Nations' land claims settlements. Signed into effect on May 29, 1993, the Umbrella Final Agreement established First Nations' governance, facilitated land claims negotiations, and negotiated devolution of certain government services. Part of the intent of the agreement was a response to the history of oppression and mistreatment suffered by the Yukon's aboriginal peoples, as well as to their general impoverishment. Very much in line with ALS's 1991 statement highlighted above, aboriginal languages were figured as one way to remediate and help devolve control.

This devolution did not happen immediately, nor was it applied everywhere all at once. The 1993 Umbrella Final Agreement aimed for First Nations' self-governance and self-determination and the creation of jobs for First Nations individuals within their own governments. The delineation of language as well as territory meant the expansion of language bureaucracy. Language positions such as translators, language program directors, and language resource personnel were created as part of this political and economic transformation. These language positions turned on the recognition of First Nations languages as central to the establishment of First Nations' (and tacitly the Canadian nation's) nationhood and as part of the expression of self-determination. However, to be able to incorporate aboriginal languages into self-governance would require several preliminary steps, from documentation to education. What was the then current state of aboriginal languages, though? New forms of knowledge about language were required, and reports were needed to publicize this knowledge.

CHARTING FLUENCY

Bureaucratic reports that supply language statistics are the most convincing and globally salient form of representation for motivating "elite" organizations such as governments, grant agencies, nongovernmental organizations, researchers, and so forth to take action against endangerment (Moore 2006, 303–5; Muehlmann 2012a). Such actions are typically accompanied by public discourse about the value of these endangered languages and a demand for funding in order to support their institutionalization (as either memorialization or regeneration, or perhaps both). Hill (2002) points out the hyperbolic quality of these public discourses, found on websites such as those of the nongovernmental organizations Terrafirma, UNESCO, and the Hans Rausing Endangered Languages Project, which emphasize the uniqueness, essentialness, and irreplaceability of endangered languages (Jaffe 2007, 60–61).

In conjunction with such hyperbolic flourishes, the style of representation, the forms used to present and forecast a language's dire situation, pattern similarly across texts. In an analysis of documentary forms used in corporate offices, Prentice notes that "aesthetic qualifications of form . . . , visual organization of information, meta-textual information, and pragmatic implicatures are inextricable dimensions of organization texts" (2015, 572; Hull 2012). I underscore here that a sense of an endangered language's scale relative to the nation-state depends in part on the aesthetics and the visual organization of the metrics used to measure it.

In the Yukon Territory, "taking action" against endangerment was a central part of the agenda of the government and its agencies, especially Aboriginal Language Services. They were also responsible for establishing the methods and bureaucratic categories for evaluating endangerment so as to ground and direct their interventions. The first representation of the sociolinguistic terrain for aboriginal languages in the Yukon appeared in the ALS publication discussed above, *A Profile of the Aboriginal Languages of the Yukon* (ALS 1991).

For over a decade, Aboriginal Language Services subcontracted out the evaluation to a consulting firm from British Columbia. The first survey in 1993 appeared to be derived from censuslike questions, asking about frequency of use in households, numbers of speakers, mother tongue affiliation, and so forth. The metrics relied on for scaling endangerment were seemingly straightforward assessment features based on categories derived from the academic and bureaucratic literatures (e.g., Joshua Fishman's *Reversing Language Shift* [1991] and the Canadian census). Charts were produced to represent the survey results.

Aesthetically, the charts, pie and bar, were severe black-and-white contrasts with some shades of gray (see figure 3.2). The starkness of the scenarios they intended to portray mirrored the starkness of the scenarios' color scheme, graphically displaying a dramatic shift in language use by generation (see Meek 2010, 141,

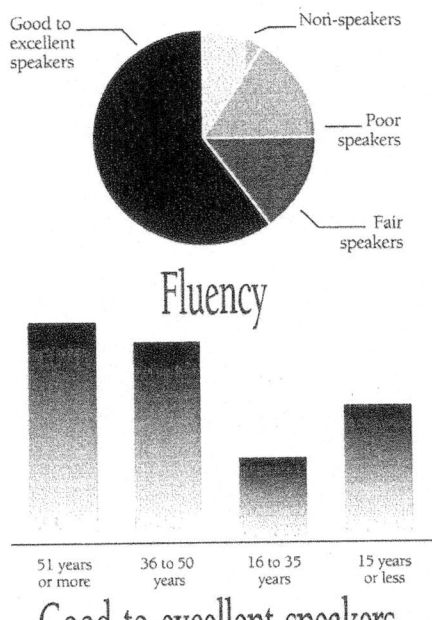

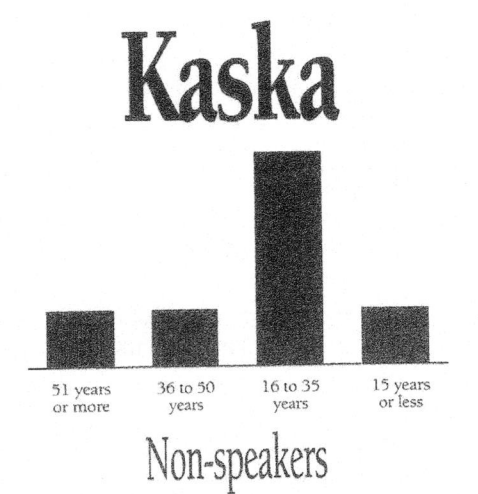

FIGURE 3.2. Early Aboriginal Language Services image portraying aboriginal language endangerment in the Yukon Territory, Canada (ALS 1991).

for illustration). In their attempt to scale fluency, the charts juxtaposed two categories of speaker: "good to excellent speakers" and "non-speakers." However, within the page, font size indexed a variety of scales embedded in the image itself. The most prominent (shown in boldface and the largest font size) is the name of the aboriginal language, in this case Kaska, a category of language—and people—contrasted implicitly here with "English." This tacit contrast suggests a scaling at the national level between nation and First Nation, and between English and Aboriginal languages such that the images construct the national scale as a purely presuppositional frame, indexed by the very use of English text. The national scale itself is not directly represented in the chart, but is taken as the default ideological vantage point through which most reader-viewers interpret the figures. That is, this style of image implicitly positions the reader-viewers as if they were peering down at the diversity of the nation from an unstated yet presumed national scale in which the default, national language is English.

In this panorama, endangerment is communicated through aggregating individuals into categories of age, speaker ability, fluency, and code (language) from the standpoint of an overarching nation. This view-from-above perspective suggests a social distance between the represented subject (aboriginal language speakers and nonspeakers) and the (English-speaking) viewer, reminiscent of the history of aboriginal-White interactions throughout Canada and, in turn, of paternalism. It is a panorama that presumes national authority and control rather than First Nations' self-determination and devolution.

Furthermore, from this top-down national perspective on endangerment, age is singled out. The "fluency" metric, most directly displayed by the pie chart at the top of the page, demarcates four categories of "speaker." The largest category within this scale is that of "good to excellent speakers," followed by "fair" and "poor" speakers. The smallest category is the "nonspeaker" category. As the eye moves down the page and zooms in (as suggested by font size) on details of the First Nations' landscape, the four categories of fluency are reduced to two, "good to excellent speakers," and "nonspeakers." Here the chart graphically eliminates all other categories and visually juxtaposes the "good" speakers with the (implicitly) "bad" nonspeakers. (Not surprisingly, the bars charting nonspeakers are in a grave, stark black unlike the shaded bars of the "good to excellent speakers" above.)

Who among the population is most at risk of language loss? The answer suggested here centers on age. This chart projects a moral narrative that favors older generations of speakers and faults those in the sixteen-to-thirty-five age range, while leaving some hope, perhaps, for the youngest cohort, those under fifteen years of age. The importance of age to the story of endangerment is made most apparent when the two categories of speakers are broken down further into four categories of age, ranging from "15 years or less" to "51 years or more." The cohort aged sixteen to thirty-five are shown to have the fewest number of good-to-excellent speakers and highest number of nonspeakers.

Although these charts represented certain differences in the aboriginal language landscape, they were not used to channel funding based on need. Funds at the time were distributed based on proposals from First Nations, often cowritten with ALS employees. Languages, and language communities, scaled and charted as being in dire straits (counting down to zero) were no more privileged than those communities with a speaker population of one hundred or more. Annual reports reflected this fact, revealing that the First Nations that received the most funding had *more projects* or were funding *more expensive* projects, and not fewer speakers, less fluency, and so on. Bureaucratically produced charts and graphs were aimed at securing funding and maintaining the Umbrella Final Agreement—yet it was not the numbers contained therein but the number of charts and graphs themselves that mattered. In other words, the number of documents a First Nation produced (surveys, reports, texts, genealogies, language lessons, etc.) was scaled as a sign of their commitment to language preservation and revitalization and of the degree to which they deserved support.

ALS seldom, if ever, turned down a proposal for funding.[1] Grant writers deployed charts and graphs to demonstrate a profound need for resources in order to develop programming that would support child language learners—that is, those precisely in the promising fifteen-year-old-and-younger category. The projects they funded ranged from Aboriginal Head Start initiatives, such as the play that was developed and performed during my fieldwork with Liard's Aboriginal Head Start program (Meek 2010), to the genealogical charts that documented people's Indian names and social histories. Such proposals were especially keen on creating immersion programs, in addition to enhancing the territory's aboriginal language curricula. In partnership, ALS and the First Nations were focused on the potential of children, rather than the intermediate cohorts, to acquire an aboriginal language (most notably the sixteen-to-thirty-five-year-old group), in part because language-shift research on Hawaiian and Maori languages had begun to show the success of immersion programs in the production of new speakers. Child speakers were also a concern for academic linguists because of a theoretical privileging of first-language speakers. The bell-curved trend of language shift across these age cohorts was a sign that if no intervention was instituted immediately, then the youngest generation, too, would "lose" the language and end up like the sixteen-to-thirty-five-year-olds.

These charts were also used to motivate elders to participate in language revitalization efforts and to motivate nonaboriginal citizens to privilege, and support, their participation. Hung on walls in government offices, the charts and graphs not only reminded visitors and employees of the ongoing decline of aboriginal language use but also highlighted the importance of the elderly aboriginal population as model speakers in the quest to revive aboriginal languages. These graphics subtly persuaded the viewer that the government should commit funds not only to aboriginal language projects but also to elder speakers in particular. At the same time, these images also decorated band office walls. In these contexts, elder speakers were reminded of their significant role in aboriginal language revival.

Interestingly, the sixteen-to-thirty-five-year-olds interpreted these charts differently. High school students, for example, viewed the charts as evidence that the best speakers were older and that the speaking of Kaska was, in particular, synonymous with being an "Elder." The fact that Elders became separated out as privileged carriers of indigenous language had many unintended consequences, such as a rift that was felt to be growing across generations (for details, see Meek 2007). So whereas bureaucrats scaled languages to garner support for young speakers, those speakers were primed to resist and resent precisely the kind of programs that might be instituted once funding was acquired.

CHANGING PANORAMAS, CHANGING PERSPECTIVES ON THE FUTURE

As regimes change, the metrics used to evaluate indigenous language change. For aboriginal language programming in the Yukon Territory, several shifts at the bureaucratic level coincided with transformations in the representational dimensions of aboriginal language endangerment. Later surveys and charts began to offer a slightly more nuanced portrait of endangerment that articulated a greater degree of variation, individually and linguistically. This was not just a matter of greater accuracy. For one, there was a dramatic perspective shift away from the top-down vantage point of the nation-state, as we shall see. This change in scalar perspective prefigured the upcoming devolution of aboriginal language services from under the direct jurisdiction of the territorial government to that of individual First Nations in accordance with the Umbrella Final Agreement.

In 2000, a new director of Aboriginal Language Services stepped in and worked toward developing a new diagnostic tool, hiring a young graduate student with a degree in education. Both the director and student worked for the territorial government at that time, one as director of Aboriginal Language Services and the other as an employee of the Yukon Territorial Government's Department of Education, with the government overseeing their efforts.[2] The figures below come from the 2004 report that was drafted by these two First Nations individuals.

Their efforts resulted in changes in the identification of language varieties and of language practices. Besides introducing a more elaborate framework for assessing language competence, they produced a new panorama and hence a new perspective. The perspective this panorama offered on endangerment was concertedly focused as a "view from within"—that is, from the First Nations'

Kaska Language Group: Overview

Total	1166
Mother Tongue: Ancestral Language	664
Mother Tongue: English	836
Speak or Understand Ancestral Language	758
Do not speak or understand AL at all	407

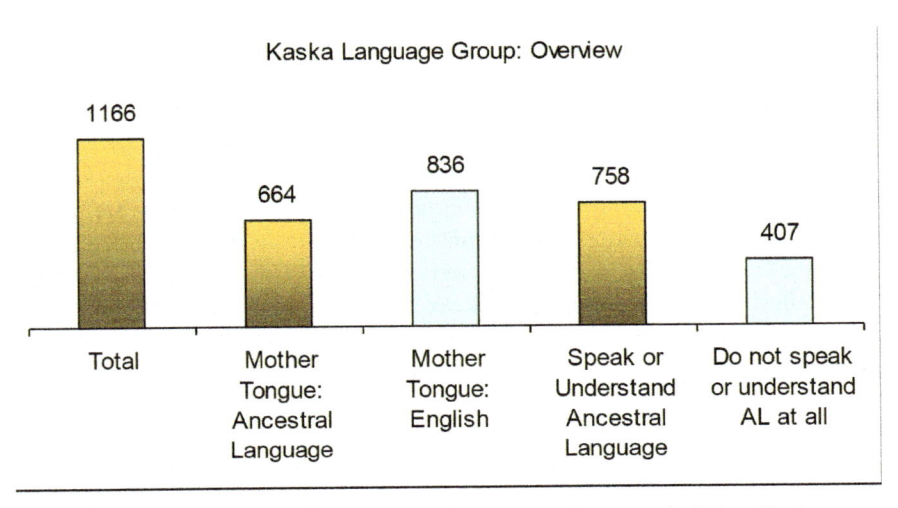

FIGURE 3.3. Languages spoken by Kaska First Nations populations in the Yukon Territory, Canada (ALS 2004, 57).

standpoint—rather than as a "view from above," or national scaling of aboriginal languages and speakers, as in the older approach.

In terms of improving how competence is assessed, a key change was introduced in terms of the critical metrics of mother tongue (language) and age. The graphic profile for Kaska begins by arranging groups of people in relation to two "mother tongue" categories—ancestral language (Kaska) and English—and two categories of "ancestral" language user: "Speak or understand ancestral language" and "Do not speak or understand AL at all" (see figure 3.3). Note that English is no longer the implicit vantage point in these visuo-discursive panoramas but instead becomes an explicit part of the linguistic profile of Kaska people *themselves*. They, too, are English speakers. First Nation speakers are reframed as bilinguals rather than as monolinguals subordinated within a dominant, nonindigenous nation-state that speaks an "official" language. This shift spotlights the linguistic diversity of the First Nation by foregrounding competence in English and Kaska *within* the aboriginal community, rather than treating English as the perspective from which the (linguistic) diversity of the Canadian nation is viewed. The presumed vantage point of the viewer-reader has shifted, no longer that of some generic English-speaking Canadian citizen but of an articulate, multilingual Canadian First Nations citizen.

While the earlier charts reflected a downward-looking view of First Nation peoples' lives from the high ground of the nation, these charts bring viewers into the sociolinguistic terrain. In particular the self-reported-fluency pie diagrams (see, for example, figure 3.4 below) represent the view of a new "we": First Nations people. In the charts presented in the self-reported-fluency section of these government documents, Kaska First Nations people appear to ask themselves: "How well do we say we speak? How well do we say we understand? How well do we say we read? How well do we say we write?" Not only is an aboriginal perspective indexed by the use of the first person plural pronoun in English (one that implicitly delimits the view as an exclusive aboriginal "we" rather than as a "we" inclusive of the Canadian nation; for a similar case, see Kroskrity 2014), but also the overt marking of the self-reportedness of the survey—"How well do *we say* we do X?"—reflects the sociolinguistic practice of grammatically indicating the origin of evidence. It corresponds with Kaska (and more broadly Athabaskan/Dene) colloquial speech and narrative conventions that linguistically mark the basis for what is being claimed, how we the speakers know what we are claiming. In this case, it is known firsthand through self-report rather than through observation, elicitation, or external report. Consider the differences in meaning across these phrases:

1. How well do we read?
2. How well do we say we read?
3. How well do we say they read?
4. How well do they say they read?
5. How well do they read?

Notice that the "we" in the list's first line is ambiguous, allowing a reading of inclusivity and exclusivity. The initial first-person pronoun in the list's second line narrows the scope of the second "we," allowing a reading of "we" exclusive to those who participated in the reporting. In the third line, "we" distinguishes the researcher-reporter from the participants of the study ("they"), an overt marking of research responsibility and authorship that seldom appears in this bureaucratic genre, as well as clearly differentiating the study participants from the study authors and readers. The phrase in the fourth line parallels the structure of the list's second line in that it grammatically marks the origin of the evidence (as with narrative uses of verbs of speaking, such as *éhdī géhdī*, "they said she/he said"), though a more precise translation would be something like: "It is said (reported) that they said that they read/write/do X (well)." Again, this phrase projects a vantage of the nation, of someone outside gazing down on the sociolinguistic situation of the Kaska language, of an English-dominant viewer more or less sympathizing with the plight of indigenous languages and people. It suggests an enduring paternalism and the dependent relationship of First Nations upon the nation. The phrase in the list's fifth line epitomizes this stance while at the same time erasing any explicit evidential base and any explicit attributions of responsibility for the assessment. This phrase captures the underlying orientation of the earlier reports, a generic question about some other group's competence.

Accompanying this perspectival shift in bureaucratic reports, First Nations began to claim more control of the direction and the methods used to preserve and revitalize their languages. More and more First Nations individuals attended national and international conferences and workshops on language teaching; some took the role of host of the 2011 Athabaskan languages conference. Moreover, the Kaska communities' collaboration with the University of British Columbia resulted in Kaska language classes offered for university credit in 2002. Locally, more individuals became involved in aboriginal language projects, learning how to operate video equipment to record narrative performances and creating online language resources such as the Kaska First Voices site. Kaska communities also began to organize and run their own language workshops rather than relying on the Yukon Native Language Centre's offerings. Most recently, the Kaska First Nations, in partnership with the Yukon Department of Education and the University of British Columbia, received a three-year grant from the Social Sciences and Humanities Research Council to develop an online "talking" dictionary and grammar.

The new panoramas offered a different perspective on endangerment in relation to the nation-state, yet they continued to use age as a scalar metric, if complicating this metric by way of more finely graded age-sets. The focus on generational cohorts in general is common in academic discourses about language loss (Suslak 2009),[3] and the earlier charts had highlighted age as the leitmotif of the narrative of endangerment. It is all the more interesting, then, that newer charts used the metric of age to suggest new forms of intervention and recruitment, to project a future rather than represent a decline. In the 2004 report, "potential instructors," for example, were identified in relation to personal assessments of "good to excellent" speaking, as presented in a pie chart by age cohort (see figure 3.4).

This scaling of language in terms of its future was also evident in a new discourse of potential fluency. In addition to the measures of actual fluency—that is, how people currently use language—metrics of age and "good-to-excellent understanding" were reframed as a profile of "potential fluency," which applied to those individuals who could understand Kaska but were currently "fair" speakers, "poor" speakers, or "nonspeakers." (See figure 3.5.)

Furthermore, while the older diagrams (such as figure 3.1) portrayed sixteen-to-thirty-five-year-olds as nonspeakers who were more the problem than the solution, this new profile redefined competence by adding comprehension to the equation, which in turn allowed for a reassessment of this age category in terms of language revitalization, suggesting their recruitability to the role of fluent speaker. Interestingly, this imagining of a fluent future relied upon rescaling age cohorts. Specifically, we see a category of twenty-five-to-forty-four-year-olds emerge in later charts, which crosscuts the largest earlier category of nonspeakers (sixteen to thirty-five years old). Scaled in this way, a new category of age-graded speaker (twenty-five-to-forty-four-year-olds)—one that, interestingly,

84 BARBRA A. MEEK

[Pie chart: Kaska Language Group: Potential Instructors — 65+ yrs: 11%, 45-64 yrs: 39%, 25-44 yrs: 25%, 15-24 yrs: 12%, 10-14 yrs: 13%]

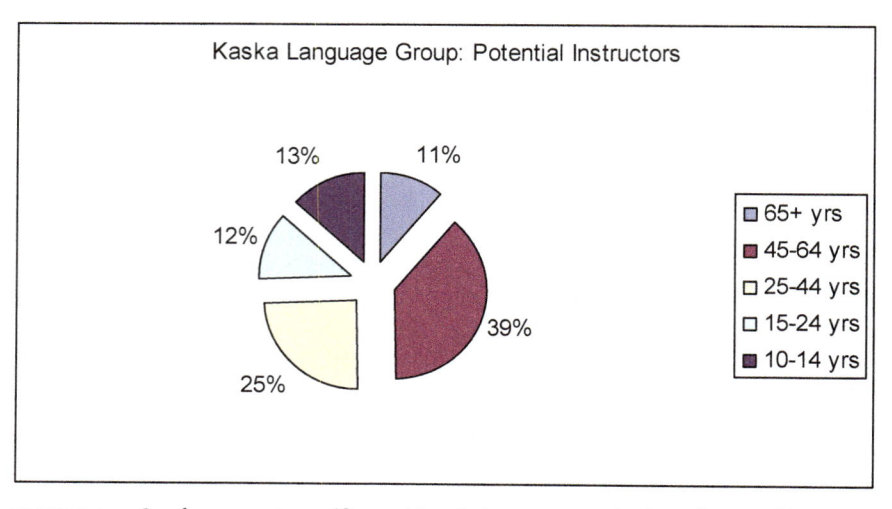

FIGURE 3.4. Speaker competence (fluency) in relation to potential role as aboriginal language instructor (ALS 2004, 66).

[Pie chart: Kaska Language Group: Potential Fluent Speakers — 65+ yrs: 15%, 45-64 yrs: 55%, 25-44 yrs: 17%, 15-24 yrs: 11%, 10-14 yrs: 2%]

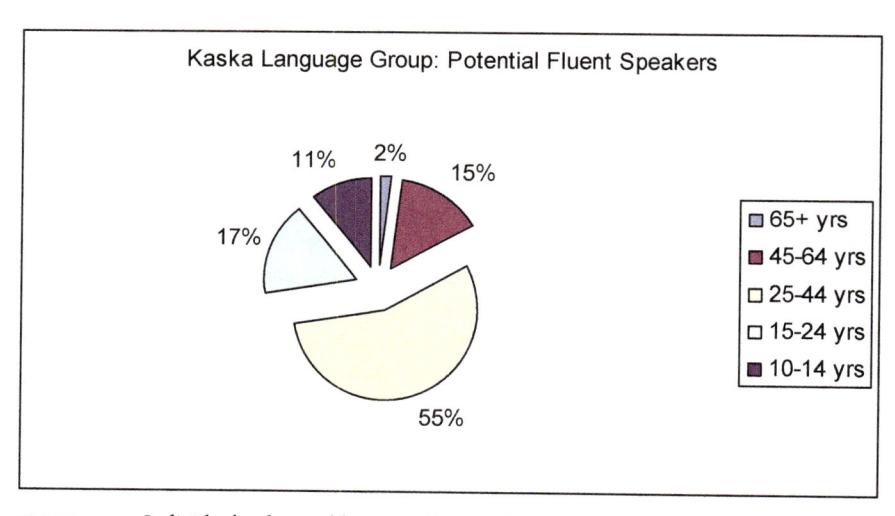

FIGURE 3.5. Individuals who could potentially gain fluency in Kaska quickly (ALS 2004, 67).

corresponds to those most likely to already be in professional and bureaucratic roles—now counts as the most likely to help revitalize the language.

Just as there is potential fluency for people with rudimentary skills, so there are "potential learners" (figure 3.6)—that is, those individuals "who do not speak nor understand the language at all." In figure 3.6, the two age categories of "25–44 yrs" and of "15–24 yrs" make up the greatest slice of the pie, 41 percent and 40 percent,

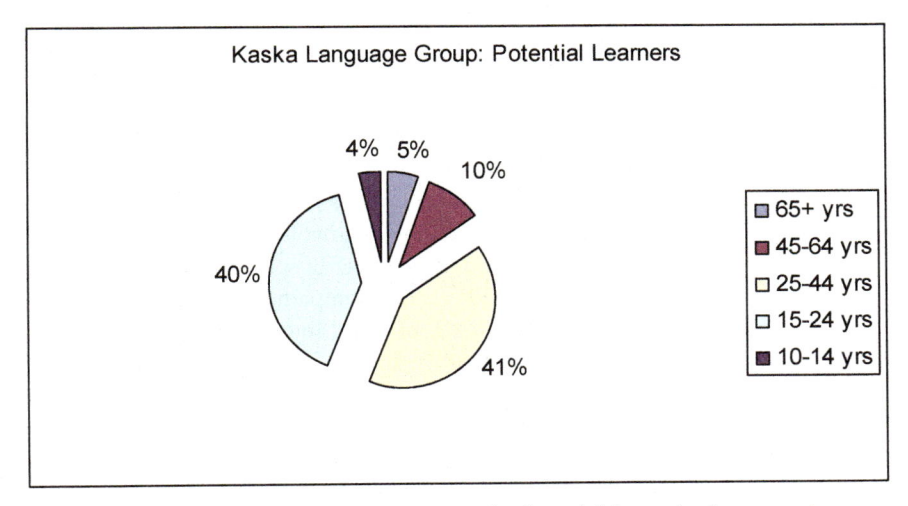

FIGURE 3.6. Fluency scaled in relation to potential to learn (of those who do not speak or understand Kaska; ALS 2004, 68).

respectively. However, rather than portraying these categories of (Kaska) individuals as incompetent, the authors redesigned the profile to suggest potential, the potential to acquire knowledge of the Kaska language and to develop skills for using Kaska (reading, writing, understanding, and speaking). While the earlier panoramas presented a more dire portrait of the Kaska language that emphasized its decline against a historical backdrop of widespread fluency and a national one of English dominance, these reconfigurations—though reliant on metrics similar to those used in the earlier versions—shift the interpretation to a future that recognizes, and invites, a range of potential roles across all ages. These shifts accompanied new partnerships (the University of British Columbia, for example) and new opportunities for using Kaska and participating in local language efforts. Younger people were hired by the band to work on developing the Kaska First Voices site. They were in charge of entering language data collected by older speakers into the band office's computers, they created sound files for current and future language learners to listen to and imitate, and they uploaded this information to the online site. Through these representational and practical changes, the old regime of language death was becoming reconfigured as a new linguistic future.

CONCLUSION: THE UNINTENDED PRAGMATICS OF SCALE

Unlike discourse, such graphic text-images render language endangerment, or any social change, strikingly visible. The aesthetics and visual organization of the information in these images, from a census table depicting a whole multilingual state to pie diagrams and bar charts illustrating the demolinguistic characteristics for one aboriginal language, provide linguistic portraits that set standards and expectations for social action and reform. Part and parcel with these panoramas is the question of address: for whom are they intended and to what end? In this case, the bureaucratic evaluation of language endangerment in Canada has served several goals, depending partly on the social actors involved.

For First Nations people, an increase in numbers of speakers is but one of the desired ends. Another end for First Nations and sympathetic language advocates is to raise awareness, and donations, nationally and internationally, whether for the purpose of linguistic diversity, biodiversity, or indigenous empowerment (Cameron 2007; Jaffe 2007; Muehlmann 2007). Yet another goal is to elevate a language's position within the nation-state *for* the nation-state, though not necessarily within or for the language communities associated with the endangered language. In her discussion of language endangerment discourse in a "linguistically politicized" Canada, Donna Patrick observes that "endangered language issues remain largely a matter for nation states" (2007, 35). For the Yukon First Nations, this has most certainly been the case where a national commitment to reconciliation frames contemporary Aboriginal-state interactions and discourses.

Whatever their intended purposes, the visuo-discursive panoramas meant to communicate knowledge about language endangerment and mobilize people to act have had many unanticipated effects. For instance, what are the consequences of foregrounding age as a metric for assessing fluency, rather than using some other variable (such as sex, genealogy, political faction, level of education, employment, etc.)? In the cases examined above, we saw that portraits of endangerment figured the most elderly individuals as the most fluent speakers of the territory's aboriginal languages, and their speech as the most grammatically "pure" or "authentic" forms of these languages. Only "Elders"—this being not just a neutral, analytic age category but also, by implication, a culturally valorized type of person in these communities (see, for example, Meek 2007)—were positioned as the authorities on and replicators of aboriginal languages.

This privileging of the variable of age is consistent with much of the scholarly literature on language endangerment (Fishman 1991, 2001; Krauss 1998) and may in part be due to the fact that discourses of language endangerment often draw on discourses of biodiversity in which participation is imposed in a top-down fashion.[4] While the academic literature has begun to criticize this approach (see Hill 2002; Moore 2006; Muehlmann 2012a; Walsh 2005), it has not examined how such metrics can enable certain forms of participation and foreclose others, how they can even increase tension across age cohorts who are differentially assessed in terms of linguistic competence. In the Yukon, assessment of fluency by age literally and figuratively marginalized younger individuals and aggravated their already thriving insecurity. Adults who had been raised in primarily monolingual Kaska households often lamented to me—during fieldwork I conducted there in 1998–2000—their own current lack of use and loss of knowledge, reflecting on their own language ability as substandard. Even adults who have worked on documenting Kaska often remarked on their uncertainty and requested that I mark items to check with other, older speakers. Rather than valuing their skill with and knowledge of the language, they would express frustration at not being equivalent to elders. This frustration was compounded by a worry that this older generation was rapidly aging, and that with their demise so goes the language.

There are other serious implications of the scaling projects I examine here. The reorganization of metrics represented in charts effectively repositions the previously marginalized categories of individuals: the younger nonspeakers. This enumerative change redefines the project of revitalization by including different social actors and, thus, expanding the participation framework. The enumerative devices and organizational aesthetics of panoramas supply perspectival frameworks for taking action in society. Changes in how age is represented, for example, chart a new course of action, a desired recuperation of individuals who may have previously felt excluded by their lack of fluency. By repositioning non-elders visuo-discursively as active participants in language rehabilitation, the hope was that this would have practical consequences. Certainly First Nations around the Yukon, not just the Kaska bands, are working toward their own immersion programs with the desire to one day have a First Nations immersion school that will involve all ages and be equal to the already existing French immersion school. As the metrics and aesthetics of language panoramas change in the Yukon, so the scales may begin to tip and once-endangered languages may begin to recover.

In recent years, Moore (2012) has compared the rhetoric of "loss" (of diversity) with Blommaert and Rampton's (2011) notion of "superdiversity," where the proliferation of linguistic varieties has resulted in an explosion of diversity. In part, the more recent call to recognize a broader range of linguistic acts and varieties within an endangered language community (as part of revitalization, re-creation, or regeneration) is a reorientation toward superdiversity rather than loss (e.g., Ahlers 2006; Field 2009; Goodfellow 2003; Leonard 2011; Meek 2010). The subtle changes in the categories used and the interpretations offered in the diagrams above suggest a shift in how language endangerment gets assessed, speaker competence evaluated, and participant roles framed. It is a shift away from endangerment and death to one of diversity and rejuvenation. It may also be an expression of the "empowerment" orientation that so often accompanies political projects of devolution. These shifts show that the metrics used to establish the scale of endangered languages within the nation-state can have complex social entailments, some prefigured by the charts themselves, and some unanticipated.

NOTES

Acknowledgements: A thousand thanks to Michael and Summerson for their incredible patience and editorial precision, and to the reviewer who waded through my imprecision. This research was sponsored in part by the University of Michigan, the Wenner-Gren Foundation, the Woodrow Wilson Foundation, and the National Endowment for the Humanities. I'm also deeply indebted to the Yukon Government, Liard First Nation, Ross River First Nation, Kaska Tribal Council, and most importantly the former Aboriginal Language Services crew. Without their commitment to language revitalization, none of this would have been possible.

1. In the 1998–2003 report on expenditures, ALS provided a breakdown of funding by language (2004, 61). The report noted that "every effort [was] made to ensure a fair and equitable distribution of funds." Differences in funding amounts were attributed to First Nations' varying capacities and stages of language revitalization.

2. With the devolution of certain Aboriginal services to First Nations as part of land claims' settlements, Aboriginal Language Services has since been disbanded. Now all First Nations have direct control over and responsibility for their own language revitalization efforts. The exceptions to this devolution process are those First Nations who have not settled, or refuse to settle, land claims, such as the two Kaska First Nations.

3. Recently, linguistic anthropologists have troubled the concept of "generation" within language endangerment discourses (Suslak 2009; see also Meek 2007). Henne-Ochoa and Bauman (2015) demonstrate how generational categories emerge in discourse rather than being a priori facts or attributes of an endangered-language situation.

4. For Moore (2006), this discourse emanated from a discourse of the "sublime," a discourse with medieval philosophical roots that continued (and continues) to resonate throughout the period of colonization captured in nineteenth-century American landscape paintings and early American fiction, a rhetoric of indigenous defeat and disappearance. For Duchêne and Heller (2007), discourses of endangerment, though often generically resonant with each other, emerge from the particular social-historical contexts of their articulation. For example, Jaffe (2007) shows how Corsican discourses have both essentializing elements and polynomic dimensions, which then complicate linguistic recognition, in part owing to ideologically homogenizing and economically pragmatic institutional needs. Muehlmann (2007) interrogates the concept of diversity, directly comparing its use for biological entities and for language(s).

PART TWO

INTERSCALARITY

Imagination and Institution

4

SCALE-MAKING

Comparison and Perspective as Ideological Projects

Susan Gal

Scenes of social life have innumerable qualities that can be measured. Matters of size, extent, encompassment, and degrees of interconnectedness have all been called "scale." But scalar visions are not ready-made platforms for action. Rather, scaling is a relational practice that relies on situated *comparisons* among events, persons, and activities. The results of comparison enable and justify action and institutional arrangements. My goal is to ask: How are social scales assembled (not always intentionally); how are they defended and challenged? In short, how do people *do* scale?[1]

To consider these questions, in this chapter I approach scale-making and scale-using as projects accomplished through semiotic processes. Also, I call these processes *ideological* in order to draw attention to the fact that frameworks of understanding constrain which aspects of social life deserve attention, which merit comparison with what, and how they are to be measured. Like any ideological project, scaling implies positioning and, hence, point of view: a perspective from which scales (modes of comparison) are constructed and from which aspects of the world are evaluated with respect to them. The focus on semiotic processes is crucial, because there is no single way of comparing. Instead, there are various models for doing comparison that differ in their logics and effects. Such models—used by observers as well as participants—are semiotic techniques that order phenomena with respect to each other. Thus, not only are there many qualities by which phenomena may be compared and scaled, but there are also different models by which this can be done. When invoked in real-time interaction, models for scaling contextualize experience, imaginatively placing the phenomena of experience in wider (and narrower) relational fields.[2]

The use of scales is a socially positioned activity that is also interactionally situated. Yet models of comparison—indispensable to scaling—differ strikingly in their presumptions about situatedness and perspective. Some create a single point of view from which to compare phenomena. They posit their own gaze as a "view from nowhere," as though the social interests and purposes for which phenomena are compared make no difference. Good examples of this are standard metrics and classificatory grids, which I discuss below. Both of these models are familiar and very widely distributed in the world. They are deeply embedded in routine activities, so that for many people their invocation no longer seems like measurement at all. They seem merely to signal the inherent, undeniable properties of the phenomena at issue. Such models therefore seem "a-perspectival," just as their authorizing ideology claims them to be. There are other models of comparison, however, that posit multiple points of view for characterizing and comparing phenomena.

Fractal recursivity is one such model that incorporates points of view. It is a way of bundling qualities into contrast sets and using them to characterize phenomena. As a semiotic process, it is best characterized as repeated application, by a positioned observer, of what is considered by participants the "same" qualitative distinction at many levels of inclusiveness, creating (roughly) self-similar categories of contrast. It is appropriately called *recursive* because the same distinction is applied again and again to a set of phenomena, creating subcategories and supercategories. It is called *fractal* because each distinction repeats a pattern within itself, as is the case with fractals in geometry. Irvine and I (Gal and Irvine 1995; Irvine and Gal 2000) have discussed this process as a semiotics of differentiation. Here I show how it operates as comparison and thus as a scaling technique: It creates, by analogy, more and less encompassing comparisons, where the degree of encompassment depends on the positioning of the evaluator. It accomplishes scaling in a different way than the more familiar a-perspectival models and therefore unsettles or outright challenges them.

Ideological agendas determine which of several possible models takes precedence in a situation and, thus, whether a model's perspective is acknowledged or not. Perspectival comparison and a-perspectival comparison can be taken up separately by those engaged in scaling projects. But they can also be made relevant simultaneously. Indeed, important scalar effects are achieved when models with disparate claims about perspective are juxtaposed: The social effects of perspectival models undermine models claiming to simply measure the way the world is. Conversely, perspectival models are themselves blocked by firmly institutionalized models purporting to be a-perspectival. Social struggles around alternative models are consequential because, as I will show, action based on models opens the way for the institutionalization of projects and the creation of real-time linkages among activities.

In what follows, I discuss in more detail the role of models in scaling and explicate the logic of fractal recursivity with examples from my fieldwork in Hungary. Examples are necessary to make clear the way this semiotic process operates. But like the practice of scaling itself, fractal recursivity is not specific to any world region or social group. It is a general process that organizes the specific ideological principles evident in particular ethnographic sites as it clashes with other models. Accordingly, I analyze particular interactional scenes that show how models claiming to be a-perspectival are contested by social actors through fractal logic. There are examples of (a) standardized (a-perspectival) metrics undermined with fractal recursivity, (b) fractal recursivity *blocked* by (a-perspectival) classificatory grids, and (c) extensions in participants' projects—increases in their scale—that result when fractal contrasts proposed in one situation are taken up in other situations and set into new relational fields. These ethnographic materials exemplify the role of the two kinds of models and their logics of comparison in scaling as a social practice.

The examples also underscore the centrality of communicative processes: Models are invoked and perspective (or its erasure) is achieved through situated talk or text. Thus, linguistic or broadly communicative practices of some kind always contribute to scaling. They allow us to see *how* participants "do" scale in different ways, how they invoke, switch, or collapse scalar models and sometimes try to contest them. Moreover, models that enable participants to compare and scale phenomena are not ephemeral, as talk is sometimes imagined to be. They are powerful semiotic tools in part because they are often embedded in sociolegal norms and routines. When institutionalized in this way, they can be used to defend existing social arrangements or to conceptualize and establish new ones. To illustrate this, I consider how one project, proposed in a powerful bureaucratic site, used mass communication and regulatory law to put into place a fractal model that undermined the taxonomy of the Cold War and reorganized a vast array of economic relationships.

TECHNIQUES OF COMPARISON: MODELS AND MEASURES

In semiotic terms, models—whether they are mappings, scenarios, or conceptual types—are diagrammatic icons that represent the relations among the parts of something by analogous relations in their own parts (Peirce 1955, 105). They have no *necessary* scale. Like maps, which can have diverse proportions with respect to what they represent, models defy commonsense differences of scale: A skyscraper can be a Peircean "sign," and so can a pointing finger or a thunderstorm; "musical chairs" has a relational logic as characteristic of international capital markets as of a children's game (Schelling 1978, 50). A model of some kind is indispensable for guiding comparisons. So is the process of making the model relevant in a situation, thereby creating an indexical relationship between the model and aspects of the social world in which it is invoked.[3] It is the combination of model-plus-situated-invocation that constructs comparison and thus the imagination of scale.

A *New York Times* article by Paul Krugman (2013) about competition among IT firms provides an example. He explicated Microsoft's failure to keep up with the ever-new iEverythings of Apple by invoking Ibn-Khaldūn's fourteenth-century analysis of North African empires. Rendered complacent by their success, agricultural elites (read: Microsoft) succumb to courageous desert tribesmen (read: Apple), who sweep in, conquer, and establish dynasties that eventually also become complacent and weak. Krugman's analogy works as (re)scaling. Ignoring many contrasting features of the two cases (differences in spatial extent, firepower, say, or organization), he instead identifies a few key relationships as the same in both. Using the gnomic present tense, Krugman frames the similarities as instances of a type of situation, a model. With these similarities, the juxtaposition *makes* unexpected, new scalar relations by invoking and then jumping across presumed, conventional scales: the temporal scale that would separate the fourteenth century and the present is collapsed, as is the supposed difference, on a presumed civilizational scalar dimension, between nomadic empires and capitalist firms. Analogies are often (re)scaling devices, as we will see with fractal recursivity. Krugman does all this in the situated textual event of a newspaper article, where the invocation of empire as a parallel to corporate competition is a political act in discussions of capitalism. When taken up by readers, the article contributed to multiple ideological projects: displaying the writer as well-read in history; pressing a point about the weaknesses of monopolies; even, perhaps, proposing economic policy.

In Krugman's article, the two scenarios were both taken to be instances/tokens of the same constructed type. The relation between types and tokens can itself be interpreted as a shift in scale, with types ideologized as "larger," in the sense of "more general," or as encompassing the instantiations. Even if not itself seen as a difference in scale, however, the token/type relation is important in comparisons. Because one focus of this chapter is on the way models are invoked in actual interaction, it is important to emphasize the work it takes to make a particular real-time event into an instance of some model. How a model is invoked, what counts as an instantiation, and what must be ignored (erased) in order to fit an instance into the invoked model are matters that *produce* the token/type relation, rather than being dependent on it (Goodman 1972). In other words, Krugman's story performatively created the specific similarities and scalarity it posited. In this way, models—like maps and other semiotic "infrastructures"—can be transformative. As many have argued, they alter social realities. When given political backing, they become models *for* ways of reorganizing relations, in order to match representations. Models of comparison—as in the scale-making I discuss below—are no exception.[4]

Krugman's scenario does not hide its perspective or its momentary and polemical point. I focus now on models that, in contrast, claim to be a-perspectival and are long-lasting, in order to compare them later with the perspectival technique of fractal recursivity. Classificatory grids deny perspective in a particular sense. They compare items by placing them in categories of a single domain. Some categories include other categories, encompassing or "standing over" them, so that the more encompassing ones are interpretable (in an ideological frame) as of greater scale. In state administration, for instance, counties are usually mutually exclusive, dividing up a province (in space) and reporting organizationally to provincial offices. In such a setup, the category of province is understood to incorporate county, spatially and administratively, in this way establishing a difference of scale. Taxonomies of language operate in a parallel way. A world of distinguishable, mutually exclusive kinds is presumed. Linguistic practices are assigned to one or another language. The language itself is assigned to mutually exclusive categories: for instance, it cannot be both Finno-Ugric and Indo-European. Such categorizations are based on a particular language ideology.[5] To be sure, there is often room in such systems for items that do not clearly belong in any rubric, thereby revealing that the model is necessarily "leaky" in practice (Garfinkel 1967). Nevertheless, the model fixes perspective: One might refuse to categorize, or demand more or different categories. But when users take up the model's perspective, the perspective also "takes" them, disallowing other frames, constraining their point of view on items to be classified (Bowker and Star 1999).

Another model of comparison that claims or presumes to be a-perspectival is that of standardized metrics: A magnitude of a property is used as a conventional unit for measurement of that property, in any situation. Any value of the property can be expressed as a simple multiple of the unit: meters as a metric of length, for example, where length is a dimension. Anything to be measured is first compared to the standard unit, and is then scalable (judged as more/less) with respect to other items also compared to the standard unit and thus measured in the same way. Prototypes of the standard unit are safeguarded for stability. In a similar way, ideologies of standard language rely on prototypes, safeguarded in dictionaries and grammars, as measures of the relative value—on a dimension of correctness—of linguistic usages.

In standard models—linguistic or other—there is often conflict about what can be measured at all, with what units (Espeland and Stevens 1998). But once in place, such systems are ideologized as a view from nowhere, an objective way of placing items on the predefined scale. Like the world of standardized languages, such systems are demonstrably the product of political conflict, bureaucratic imposition, and capitalist economy. Often they represent a state's-eye view (Kula 1986; Porter 1995; Scott 1998). Yet the prototypes are justified as natural forms, unaffected by human activities. For example, the authorizing narrative of the metric system, since its invention in the eighteenth century, has presented it as immune to social perspective (Alder 1995). In 1900, the physicist Max Planck declared, "With the help of fundamental constants we have the ability to establish units of length, time, mass and temperature which necessarily retain their significance for all cultures, even unearthly and non-human ones." By this logic, standard metrics and the scales they establish are ideologically positioned as free of human interests, part of the "structure of the world," merely displaying the inherent, real properties and dimensions of the phenomena compared (Planck cited in Crease 2011, 266).

CONTESTING SCALE: DIFFERENT LOGICS COMBINED

Fractal recursivity shares some features with both of these models, but contrasts with them in incorporating a difference of perspective within the model itself. Like those discussed earlier, it is an abstract scenario of comparison; it must be invoked in situated action. Unlike them, it is an organization of properties, as contrast sets, in an imagined quality space. Instead of creating a single point of view, it posits different perspectives on whatever phenomena are characterized, differentiated, and thus organized by those contrasting qualities. In order to understand how participants use fractal logics to contest and try to undermine taxonomic grids and standard measures, it is important to see how fractal recursivity itself is ideologically constructed. The illustrations are drawn from my fieldwork in Bóly, a town in southern Hungary inhabited in part by German-Hungarian bilinguals, who are descendants of eighteenth-century migrants from German lands.[6]

Constructing fractal recursivity. A first ideological move creates differentiation by proposing clusters of opposed and complementary qualities that are co-constitutive. One set of qualities is seen as what the other is not. Such axes of differentiation are contingent and open-ended, arising out of the historical experience of the group that presupposes them, and changing accordingly. Ideological frames define what practices display instantiations of the abstract qualities. The clusters of opposed qualities are summarized and labeled. In some cases these are political categories (e.g., public/private, populist/cosmopolitan; Gal 2002, 1991). More often, such *anchor categories* are person-types that are deemed the ideal locus of the contrasts.

In Bóly, these were "farmer" and "artisan," the pillars of social organization between about 1880 and 1950. These person-types were institutionalized in voluntary associations of artisans on the one hand and farmers on the other that functioned as reading circles, adult education, and centers of entertainment. Virtually all aspects of social life revolved around these formal, church-supported associations; artisans and farmers even held the office of mayor in alternating terms. The distinction remained important to townspeople throughout the twentieth century, despite the loss of farms and workshops to collectivization in the post–World War II communist period. Artisans were understood to display and value a cluster of qualities: elaboration, novelty, and worldliness in their sartorial, culinary, architectural and affective styles. They were expected to value skill in communication and familiarity with the world outside the town, acquired through apprenticeships in cities far and near. By contrast, farmers were typified as restrained, plain, austere, and valuing traditions and land; they were considered *echt,* authentic. Farmers, even rich ones, were imagined to eat the same, familiar menu every day, while (some) artisans famously varied their food and even collected recipes.[7]

Ways of speaking are usually privileged loci for the display of contrasting qualities in such models: the differences between linguistic forms are heard as embodiments of the qualitative contrasts. In Bóly, every German-speaker spoke Hungarian as well. However, two mutually intelligible registers of German—known as "artisan language" and "farmer language"—were emblematic of the qualitative differences posited between person-types. The artisan register was heard as elaborate and polished, in contrast to the farmer register, which was heard as austere and old. Artisans were thought to know Hungarian better and to borrow from it, in keeping with their emphasis on travel, variety, and communicative skills. Use of the two German registers enacted the stereotypes of farmer and artisan. In the heyday of the system—between the World Wars—the voluntary societies disciplined and reproduced these values and their distinct enactments. The farmer perspective valued austerity and criticized elaborate display; the typified artisan view was the opposite. Note that the qualities that distinguished the artisan figure from that of the farmer were *made* contrastive through ideological work; they would not necessarily contrast or cluster in other sociocultural formations. The qualities were seen as co-constitutive, the people types as codependent. Each view saw itself as best; neither accepted hierarchy between them. Importantly, both recognized the other as necessary because they contrastively defined each other.

A second ideological move projects the axis of differentiation to organize—by analogy—less-encompassing contrasts and more-encompassing ones. The recursions are relative judgments, creating categories of objects that are self-similar and nested. This is what makes the distinction fractal: each contrast repeats a distinction within itself, as geometric fractals do. Among any phenomena compared along an axis and found to contrast—say, house styles, person-types, and linguistic registers deemed either elaborate or authentic—those judged authentic could be compared to each other and a further distinction made among them, using the same criteria. This would create two sets or sides again, both encompassed as authentic from one comparative perspective, yet differentiated as "authentic versus elaborate" from a less encompassing perspective—that is, when comparing them only to each other. This process could be applied again and again, hence the term *recursive*. The fractal comparisons create scalar differences of encompassment. How any item is judged depends on the perspective that defines what it is contrasted to. The same practices, things, and people can count as instantiating one side of the axis when judged from one comparative perspective, and embodying the other side when judged from another. According to stereotype, farmers speaking to farmers use farmer language. But by using (some features of) the artisan register—as quotation, parody, or other voicing effects—farmers enacted recursions: a farmer could "be" the artisan among farmers. A farmer criticizing other farmers' practices as "elaborate" would be creating recursions, too; and so would artisans, if deriding each other as "authentic."

Finally, in a third ideological move, these analogical projections of the contrasts—both less and more encompassing—are framed as "the same" as the anchor contrast. The inevitable differences among the contrast sets are ignored, if only for the moment.

To emphasize the perspectival features of fractal recursivity, it is important to specify the way it differs from the two a-perspectival models I have discussed. First, it might appear that repeated contrasts simply construct taxonomies of categories, one set included in another. But this is not so: in taxonomies there is no relationship presumed among the categories at any one level. In a fractal system, a co-constitutive qualitative contrast among the superordinate categories is *repeated* in the relationship among subordinate categories. The two sets are analogous—they do display the same *contrast* of qualities—and in that sense are the same. Achieving this effect might well require ignoring many features. Second, it might appear that one can turn qualitative contrasts into gradients or continua. If so, fractal recursions would be merely a cumbersome way to represent an existing linear order. It is indeed sometimes possible to convert qualitative contrasts into linear degrees of difference. But note that such linearity is itself an ideological achievement: constructed not merely discovered. Such conversions (from contrast to continuum, from continuum to units) are practical moves with social consequences. We should ask: what projects do they serve; for whom; and how are they justified? Such transformations deserve analytical attention.[8]

Fractals and standard metrics, in practice. Whichever model we consider—taxonomies, standards, fractal recursions—it creates scalar relations when brought to bear in interactional scenes, while linking the comparison to positioned purposes. The situated communicative means by which this is done—with narratives, transpositions, quotations, and voicings—are fundamental in any study of interaction. Here, such devices are not considered for their own sakes but to show how participants use them to undermine the taken-for-granted, default (standard) scalar relations among the things they discuss. In this case, the comparison is between Bóly, which is the hometown of the speakers, and another settlement. By conventional (standard) metrics of population size and territorial extent, the town of Pécs, some kilometers north of Bóly, is decidedly bigger in scale: its population and territorial extent are many times larger than Bóly's. Pécs is also the administrative center to which Bóly reports, and one in which the national language (Hungarian), rather than minority German, is spoken. The names of the two towns are enough to invoke common knowledge of this undeniable scalar relation. Yet as the following segment shows, the natives of Bóly have another way of scaling that asserts their own relative significance in a quiet but enduring rivalry with Pécs (Gal 1994).

During a 1997 sojourn in Bóly, I was visiting an elderly husband and wife, both of them retired but from families that had been rich farmers before the Second World War. They were telling me (at this point in Hungarian) about a letter they had just received from a childhood friend, now living in Germany, whose family had been artisans, bakers. The letter writer ("he, Ferike" in the transcript) had been expelled from Hungary to West Germany after the Second World War, as were many of those who claimed German mother tongue.[9] The letter brought up the past and the artisan/farmer contrast. Mention of the letter was in part a response to what the couple knew about me: that I was a researcher from outside Hungary, a traveler, and a speaker of English, and was interested in learning about Bóly's history. The letter highlighted the couple's own extra-Hungary connections and their expertise in local history, while providing a topic through which we three could encounter each other. As it turned out, this short exchange relied on shifting perspectives to compare Bóly and Pécs in ways that undermined the purportedly a-perspectival measures of population, territory, and administrative hierarchy. The transcript starts as the letter writer is introduced.

The segment invokes the farmer/artisan distinction through labels—farmer bread and baker (artisan) bread. The husband and wife are not enacting the distinction, they are narrating someone else's past enactment. Presupposing that there is such a thing as farmers' bread (homemade) and bakers' bread (shop made), they typify a transaction that clinches the social complementarity between the two and their semiotic co-constitution: "The farmers liked the bakers' bread, and he [artisan] liked the farmers." The husband and wife cooperate in the juxtaposition of two brief vignettes. That juxtaposition creates, out of the farmer/artisan contrast, a more encompassing one by analogy. One scene takes place in Bóly in the distant past, the second (marked ◊) in Pécs in the more recent past.

Example 1. Transcript, Bóly, 1997, conversation with farmer couple; orthography standardized (97:2B:29:50):

Hu: His father was a baker [i.e., artisan], and then he says he always came and traded with the farmer kids, for the farmer bread [homemade], they—
Wi: Baker bread.
Hu: Baker bread [i.e., shop made]. The farmers liked the bakers' bread, and he liked the farmers' bread. He said, "Remember how we always traded, the bread, spread with chicken fat?"
Wi: And when Tibi [the couple's son] was a student, he went to Pécs
◊ everyday, I had to prepare bread with ham. A little butter on it thinly spread and then pieces of ham. Every day he traded that ham and bread for years, for—what do I know—for rolls or pretzels. But he never told us till later.
Hu: He never ate it; they always grabbed it. They came, the city folks, and begged it away from him and gave him something else that he did not have. Ferike [childhood friend] was like that: he always says, We traded.

Hu: *Az apja pék volt. és akkor mondja, mindig jött és cserélt a paraszt-gyerekekkel, paraszt kenyérért ők meg a—*
Wi: *Péki kenyeret.*
Hu: *Péki kenyeret. A parasztok szerették a péknek a kenyerét ő meg a parasztok kenyerét szerette. Azt mondta, emlékszel hogy cseréltünk mindig? a zsíros kenyeret.*
Wi: *És mikor a Tibi volt diák, az bejárt Pécsre minden nap. Sonkás*
◊ *kenyeret kellett készíteni. Kis vajat rá vékonyan, és sonka darabokat. Minden nap elcserélte évekig azt a sonkás kenyeret, nem tudom én zsemléér, vagy kifliér. De ezt nem mondta meg csak később.*
Hu: *Soha nem ette meg, de mindig harapták. Jöttek a városiak, elkuny-eráltak tőle, és adtak mást, ugye ami neki nem volt. A Ferike ilyen volt, mindig mondja hogy cseréltünk.*

The two vignettes are multiply linked to each other by the motif of bread exchange and by a series of parallelisms: The person categories in the two scenes are different, but the *contrast* is equated through juxtaposition: (farmer versus artisan in Bóly) = (Bóly student versus Pécs students in Pécs). The husband explicitly equates his childhood friend with the Pécs students and "city folks," noting, "Ferike was like that." In the qualities of bread too, the *contrast* is equated: (farmer bread versus baker bread) = (homemade-bread-with-ham versus pretzels, rolls). All these contrasts display the same farmer/artisan qualities: authentic, old fashioned (i.e., homemade) versus elaborate.

There is also a shift in the referents of deictics, through which the narrator takes up different perspectives. In the first vignette the husband, positioned as narrative *origo,* says the artisan boy "came" to the farmer kids, construing artisan kids as distal to proximate farmer kids. Later, the artisan friend is quoted as saying "we," creating a unified, first-person-plural Bóly of artisans-and-farmers. This is significant, because in the second vignette, the narrator takes up his son's position, making that the *origo,* now hearable as Bóly-in-Pécs, a figure to which "came" the "city folks." Artisans are distal to farmers in Bóly; and in a parallel way, all of Pécs is distal to a figure from Bóly, in Pécs. These transpositions and parallelisms constructed momentary fractal analogies. A distinction along the axis of differentiation anchored by the artisan/farmer categories was projected to distinguish Bóly from Pécs, by analogy. Viewed from Bóly, Bóly counted as farmer—that is, authentic/traditional/austere, when compared to Pécs.

Recall that hierarchy between the two people-types was denied. Hence, Bóly (farmer) was being claimed as the *equal* of Pécs (artisan), contradicting standard metrics and administrative hierarchies. The analogy rescaled the two towns and served the ideological project of rivalry I have mentioned. Bóly's leading families had a strong sense—some have called it arrogance—of their town's superiority to Pécs, despite Pécs's size. This scalar vision made imaginable, in Bóly, a variety of actions for linking the two towns. When seen as artisan-like, people in Pécs could be recognized as suited to reciprocity (as in the vignettes). Regional planning drew on such images. Alternatively, some in Bóly opposed political alignment with Pécs, justifying their position by dismissing Pécs as a bunch of artisans, with the predictable stereotypes of spending and ornamenting.

Taxonomic grids and fractals, in practice. Since classificatory grids/taxonomies are a-perspectival scales, they too collide with fractal models. Recall that a fractal model enables changes in perspective so that for any phenomenon to be judged—speech registers, person-types, events, activities, objects—its position on an axis of differentiation depends on what it is compared to. Speakers can switch perspectives—and thus rescale—while staying within the fractal model, even within a single event. A speaker can take the position of farmer with respect to one interlocutor, but with respect to another claim an artisan position. Such fractal comparisons are undermined by any move that *permanently* allocates people-types, objects, practices, events to one or the other side of what participants construct as a distinction. (An imaginary example would be a regulation stating that those who ate potatoes every day, or spoke farmers' German at home, must always identify as farmers and never adopt an artisan voice.) If enforced by law, this obligates participants to take up (only) the perspective of those who force the allocation. It creates what I call a *blockage* of recursivity. The dilemma of an elderly woman (Terus) from an artisan family in Bóly provides an example. Her narratives show how she positioned herself in relation to ever more encompassing categories of identity.

In 1990, she was interviewed, in German, by a younger woman (Mari), who was also a German-Hungarian bilingual but from another region of Hungary. The elder woman was giving examples of artisan language and farmer language, enacting an artisan persona by displaying her expertise in communication. The transcript starts when she suddenly launches into the story of a time when she lived in a largely Hungarian-speaking village. There, she said, she spoke German with those few farmer women who, like her, were German-Hungarian bilinguals. In that village, she was ignoring the farmer/artisan distinction so important in Bóly. Emphasizing that she "likes the German word," and usually watches German TV (via satellite), she segued to the story of a recent trip to Germany, where her excursion group met a German woman (i.e., not from Hungary) who recited in Hungarian a poem and the Hungarian national anthem for the visitors. Terus, the interviewee, conveyed a strongly ambivalent emotional reaction to this performance: "I said then, I don't know what, what this is in me, I am still, after all, Hungarian, the Hungarian anthem, it so moves me and even so I like German. I don't understand this in myself, what this is." And she began to cry.

Example 2. Transcript, Bóly 1990, interview with artisan woman (boldface section Hungarian, otherwise German; orthography standardized for readability; M90:3A9:50):

> Terus: ... I lived in a village [once] where there were only Hungarians, there were just one or two schwäbische [German-Hungarian] women there. When we met in the street we always spoke German because I like the German word. Now I have a TV and a satellite dish and I mostly watch German. Closer ... I don't know, we were out in Germany two years ago. . . . There we, she, a, she was a real Imperial German, she could speak such beautiful Hungarian, though it's so hard. . . . She knew **"Night has come, night has come, to each in repose"; she recites it so beautifully.** That's a Hungarian—
>
> Mari: Poet.
>
> Terus: Poet, whom we love very much; he has a beautiful poem; she did this so, we were so surprised, that she learned such beautiful Hungarian and such a difficult [language] still. . . . And there they, they all liked our **National Anthem** and **the Pledge**. And we sang it there. And they sang all of it along with us; and I, I said then I don't know what, what this is in me; I am still, after all Hungarian, the Anthem and Pledge, presses [my heart]. . . . And even so, I like German. I don't understand this in myself, what this is.

Terus: ... *Ich war auf solchen Dorf gelebt nur Ungarn warn nur eins-zwei schwäbische Frau warn dort. Wenn wir uns getroffen haben wir haben immer nur deutsch weil ich habe gern das deutsch Wort. Jetzt hab ich die Fernseh die Parabola und ich schaue meistens nur deutsch. Näher ... ich weisst nicht, wir waren vor zwei Jahren in Deutschland d'raus ... dort haben wir die, eine, die war aber eine Reichsdeutsche, die kann so schön ungarisch sprechen. Sie kann* **"Este van este van ki ki nyugalomba"** *gyönyörűen elszavalja. Des is ein ungarische—*

Mari: *Dichter*

Terus: *Dichter, den haben wir lieb, der hat schöne Dichtung, sie hat das ganz so, wir waren so überrascht, dass sie so schön ungarisch gelernt hat und so ein schweres, doch ... und dort haben se, sie haben alle gern den unseren* **Himnusz** *und a* **Szózat**. *Und das haben wir dort gesungen. Und sie hat, kann auch alles mitgesungen und ich, hab ich damals gesagt ich weiss nicht was das ist in mir, ich, doch ein Ungar, der* **Himnusz** *und* **Szozat** *so drückt. . . . Und doch habe ich das deutsche [gern]. Das kann ich in mir nicht so verstehen was das ist.*

In the space of a few moments, the elderly woman presented herself as differently situated in a series of linked comparisons, each from a different perspective, iterating the "same" contrasting clusters of qualities, ones summarizable as farmer versus artisan, qualitatively simple versus elaborate. The linguistic forms that invoked the clusters shifted from one comparative frame to another. In the narrating event, she enacted an artisan persona, implicitly contrasted with the farmer type. She then presented two comparisons, distinguished by setting. In the Hungarian village, she aligned via linguistic practice with the few German-bilingual farmers, enacting the "plain, farmer" in contrast to Hungarians. This stereotype needed no explication for the young interviewer; it was the conventional view in Hungary. The next scene was international. When Terus marveled at the German performer's feat of reciting in Hungarian, and called Hungarian "difficult," she was evaluating it as elaborate, with respect to German. Once again, the same contrasting qualities were invoked. In this final scene, the interviewee inhabited neither the artisan role (versus farmer) as in the first scene, nor German-speaker (versus Hungarians), as in the second. Instead, she was the Hungarian with respect to the Germans. This was signaled by deictics ("our" poet, "our" anthem), by a switch to Hungarian in praising the performer, and by her sobs and her report of being emotionally moved. By juxtaposing the three comparisons, she equated the analogies, yet placed herself differently in each one.

This evidently made sense to her. And indeed, in a fractal world, shifts in perspective on oneself are expected.

Why, then, was she so distressed by her own reaction to the final scene? We can understand this by recalling that fractal shifts are contradicted—blocked—by any system that forces participants to take up fixed, exclusionary categories. European linguistic nationalism of the mid-twentieth century was famous for doing so. The contrast of German versus Hungarian became far more significant than the qualitative contrast between artisan language and farmer language that crosscut nationality. Moreover, language was made a sign of national loyalty: ideally, one to a customer. In terms of this linguistic nationalism, our elderly bilingual speaker could be neither properly Hungarian nor German. In this interaction, she was able to confide her distressed reaction to an interviewer who was similarly placed. She revealed a dismayed emotional response to the institutional and ideological pressure to choose one language, as well as her deep puzzlement that she felt what this ideology disallowed: a strong attachment to both.[10]

The process of blockage is widespread. It is evident in Franz Fanon's (1952) famous, enraged description of the way language operated in the colonial situation he experienced: For him, the French/Creole contrast indexed Frenchmen versus Antilleans. Speaking the Frenchman's version of French was the promised ticket to acceptance as French for a black man from the Antilles. Yet no matter how French his speech, that repositioning was denied. In Paris, Fanon noted bitterly, he would be treated as inferior on the basis of skin color: blockage by racial taxonomy.

Extensions and connections across events. The examples so far have shown how people in a *single event* invoke models that contextualize their experience. Using the same qualitative contrasts, they *imaginatively* and analogically placed themselves into wider (and narrower) relational fields: not only farmer/artisan but also Bóly/Pécs or German/Hungarian. The differences of scale we observed were questions of relative encompassment of the categories used. The invocation of the model of qualitative contrasts can also be tracked *across* encounters, where differences of scale are questions of relative spatial or social "spread," the increased number and dispersion of real-time instantiations of the contrasts. Participants not only project analogies of the artisan/farmer model in narratives, but they also use the model to interpret and organize real-time social scenes that do not involve farmers and artisans. The familiar contrasts and categories are extended—by analogy—to novel circumstances; or new scenes are socially linked to scenes of another place or time as (partial) equivalences. This then looks like a "circulation" of the model of qualitative contrasts. When taken up by people outside of Bóly, the model can create social linkages based on perceived similarity among participants and between scenes that are—by other measures—socially, spatially, and/or institutionally distant from each other. Like encompassment, spread and linkage are questions of relative scale. The handling of perspective remains important.

In models that deny or neglect perspective, the perceived fixity of categories across events is assumed. When observers and participants use a-perspectival models to gauge the distribution of a social practice, they presume the practice itself to be fixed. They ask: Is the practice restricted to one locale? Has "it" spread (circulated) to a larger scale of distribution? With a perspectival model, by contrast, one attends to questions of uptake: from what perspective is the particular practice construed as the same as some other instance of practice and therefore interpretable as a *re*iteration (Irvine 1996; Agha and Wortham 2005)? Fractal distinctions add complexity to this question because the phenomena taken up are not practices but qualitative contrasts: instances that are perceived to display opposed qualitative categories—whether the instances are practices, person-types, or objects. Co-constitutive contrasts of qualities enacted by speakers in one scene are reframed—quoted, narrated, cited, voiced—and projected onto other speakers and practices in other events. The clusters of opposed qualities that define a fractal distinction are somewhat transformed through such recontextualizations. Nevertheless, if the uptake perceives the "same difference" in people-types, objects, or practices, then a linkage is established among scenes that are otherwise socially, spatially, or temporally distant, even unrelated.

A glimpse of one moment in this process is evident in example no. 1: The husband and wife were telling stories about the farmer/artisan distinction. Whether or not their friend actually exchanged bread with farmer children (or ever said he did), the husband and wife narrated *about* bread exchanges. Yet the husband as narrator also took up the farmer role by enacting the farmer-*origo* in the storytelling event. The farmer/artisan contrast thus became relevant to characterizing others in the storytelling event around the kitchen table. Participants would be compared to each other with respect to the farmer/artisan axis. It seemed to me that I was cast as the farmer-narrator's opposite: the artisan role. Of course, I was no artisan. But the couple commented on my travels and life in distant places, my speech, and on my elaborate sartorial practices (compared to theirs). These stereotypically artisan qualities could be "found" in my actions and demeanor. And, conveniently, my appreciative consumption of their homemade bread during that storytelling event could be seen, from their perspective (and no doubt with wry amusement), as an enactment of the very transaction that, in the stories, typified the farmer/artisan relationship. If this is an accurate assessment, then a familiar distinction was extended by analogy to make sense of a relatively unusual event, the presence of an American visitor.

The projection of the same contrasts can be tracked across more events, to see how it produces further scalar effects, as connections, as linkages. Stories comparing Pécs and Bóly were told not only to me but also to a Hungarian ethnographer in the late 1980s. Publishing her oral histories of Bóly in a Hungarian social science journal, the ethnographer characterized Bóly in the interwar years as a highly successful example of rural capitalism. She noted that a "raw communist dictatorship" had tried to destroy what remained of rural capitalism after the Second World War. In the ethnographer's view the farmer/artisan distinction itself had been key to the town's pre-war economic success, especially the town's "bourgeois values of hard-work and austerity[,] . . . [its] self-reliance," and ideals of "community autonomy" (Kovács 1990, 76, 34). The farmers, she wrote, were typified as frugal, restrained, and industrious, and she added that all of Bóly shared those qualities, when compared to Hungarian towns of the time.

The article entered Hungarian academic discussions amid heated debates about capitalism and state socialism in the late 1980s. These discussions criticized postwar policies. The arguments were driven in part by a market-oriented, liberal movement of intellectuals in Budapest who were organizing to challenge the agricultural policies of the state socialist government. In her article, the ethnographer described the farmer/artisan distinction in the same terms used by the elderly couple I interviewed. The ethnographer did not take up either the farmer or artisan persona. But she did align herself with Bóly by representing the town in admiring terms, ones widely accepted by her readers in Bóly. However, when read in Budapest scholarly circles, the qualities the ethnographer named and valorized were dramatically recontextualized: Rather than contrasts of plain/elaborate that distinguished farmers/artisans or German towns/Hungarian ones, the article was read as a defense of *community autonomy,* as opposed to centralized planning; *self-reliance,* as opposed to collectivization; *hard work* as opposed to the famously lax labor ethic of "really existing socialism." For readers in Bóly, the italicized terms were their favored forms of self-characterization and fit well with their farmer stereotype. For Budapest intellectuals, the italicized qualities were characteristic liberal values, and these intellectuals invoked, as contrasts, the qualities they attributed to communism. As a result, the qualitative contrasts of Bóly were extended and linked to Budapest's liberal political distinctions.

Were they the same contrasts? Those in Bóly and those in Budapest all found the contrasts recognizable and interpretable, each from their own perspective. Perhaps we can say the contrasts were the "same-enough." Whether she intended it or not, the ethnographer's descriptions were interpreted in Budapest as *evidence* that capitalism had worked, and could work again, in Hungary. At the same time, the article's contrasts allowed politically engaged readers in Bóly to recognize themselves in the rhetoric of pro-market reformers in Budapest. As the Cold War ended, leaders in Bóly and liberal activists in Budapest sought each other out, inspired in part by the article. These uptakes had scalar effects of increased interconnection: The liberal group of Budapest intellectuals gained adherents, extending itself from Budapest to a southern town. People in Bóly gained connections in the capital that they had not had before. One might call this "alliance by mutual appropriation." Increases in connectivity—yielding differences in the scale of their projects—were achieved by two groups of actors as each used the other to advance their own purposes.[11]

INSTITUTIONALIZATIONS

The alliance between leaders in Bóly and liberals in Budapest did not last long. This was not a strongly institutionalized connection. The models that organize qualitative contrasts are often much more firmly established. Indeed, the farmer/artisan contrast in interwar Bóly was maintained for many decades by the separate voluntary associations for artisans and farmers that I have already mentioned. These voluntary societies policed the qualities considered typical of farmers and artisans. They provided venues for displaying, explaining, and reproducing the differences. But fractal models need not be constructed only in small towns; they can be made and projected from many kinds of sites. The invention and imposition of a fractal model by powerful social actors can introduce organizational change that shifts scales. Leaving Bóly behind, I look at Hungarian economic policy in the 1970s, which provides a striking example.

Recall that in the Cold War of that period, two opposed power blocs faced off against each other, operating on what were declared to be antagonistic political economic principles: capitalist and communist, West and East, the so-called First and Second Worlds. No country could be in both camps at the same time, and each side claimed superiority. Each had its own taxonomy of members: the Soviet Union and the United States were the opposed superpowers each in alliance with other states of ranked sizes and influence.[12] Recent revisionist research rightly argues that this is a vastly oversimplified picture. Nevertheless it is largely the way most scholars and politicians saw the situation at the time. It was a rigid classificatory scheme, reinforced by armed force, bloc-internal discipline, mutual propagandistic derogation ("evil empire," "capitalist lackey"), and claims that the ways of life and economies of the two blocs were opposed and incompatible.

As managers, Hungarian economists in the 1970s were faced with repeated crises of their Soviet-style, centrally planned economy. A major problem was that, to compensate for the perennial shortages produced by this system, fully three-quarters of the population participated in a network of illegal, black market activities considered incompatible with the logic of the official, centrally planned and redistributive economy, while they also held jobs in that official economy. Indeed, the two jobs often depended on each other: clerks and professionals in government offices and hospitals profited from tips and gifts from petitioners and patients; workers in state factories and agricultural collectives used factory machinery and materials to produce, during the workday, commodities that they sold independently after hours. Economists tracked this illegal, do-it-yourself economy. Its activities supplied the population with otherwise scarce consumer

108　SUSAN GAL

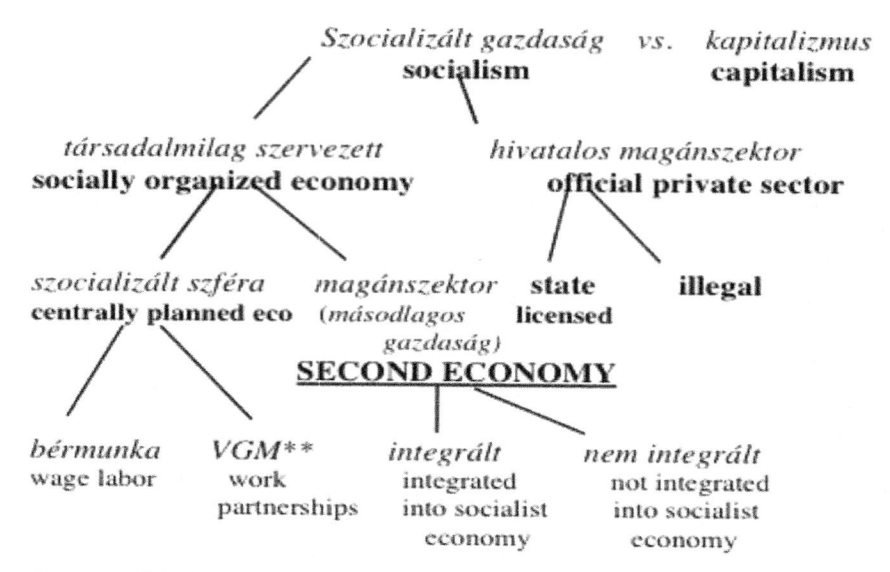

```
                    Szocializált gazdaság    vs.    kapitalizmus
                         socialism                  capitalism
                        /          \

   társadalmilag szervezett          hivatalos magánszektor
   socially organized economy        official private sector
           /        \                    /          \

  szocializált szféra   magánszektor    state         illegal
  centrally planned eco (másodlagos     licensed
      /      \           gazdaság)
                       SECOND ECONOMY

  bérmunka    VGM**      integrált        nem integrált
  wage labor  work       integrated       not integrated
              partnerships into socialist  into socialist
                         economy          economy
```

* note this is **not** a taxonomy but a recursive application of the same distinction, from different perspectives

***Vállalati gazdasági munkaközösség*
enterprise work partnership

FIGURE 4.1. Fractal recursions in Gábor and Galasi's argument (based on Gábor and Galasi 1978).

goods and services, contributing to political stability. But the population also evaded state control in this way, so this underground economy was seen by officialdom as a political danger and embarrassment.

As a solution, two young economists (Gábor and Galasi 1978) reconceptualized their economy to subtly transform the bipolar commonsense of the Cold War. They proposed an alternative way of comparing economic activities. They recast the either/or of capitalism/socialism by formulating contrasting, co-constitutive qualities for the two systems and applied the distinction iteratively. I have analyzed it as a fractal scheme (see figure 4.1). Their writings reveal the logic of this reclassification when they justify it in detail. Starting with the Cold War's classificatory grid—capitalism versus socialism ("communism" was for an ideal future)—they argued that Hungary had reduced capitalism to insignificance through collectivization, so no further consideration of capitalism itself was necessary. Socialism in Hungary still retained a minuscule and stigmatized "official private sector" of small, independent craftsmen and their shops (shoemakers, locksmiths) who operated by state license but were insignificant. All other economic activity comprised the enormous "socially organized economy."

Yet, Gábor and Galasi argued, the activities within this socially organized economy were already subdivided by the same criteria, since some were "centrally planned" and thus controlled by the state, but others happened outside of planning and were simply tolerated by the state. Urging that these tolerated activities be acknowledged, legalized, and thus perhaps better controlled, they baptized it as the "second economy." Admitting that activities in the second economy had many of the qualities that distinguish capitalism from socialism—market principles, profit for individuals, lack of central planning—they nevertheless argued that these activities were not *really* capitalist because they were embedded in a socialized economy. Having applied the socialist/capitalist distinction to the whole economy, and then subdivided the socially organized economy by the same principles, they applied the distinction yet again, this time to the activities in the centrally planned economy of state-owned factories and other large state enterprises. For workers in the centrally planned economy, they proposed a new category of work, distinct from ordinary wage work. This would be called wage partnerships and would occur in the same state factories that operated by wage labor, and would be done by the same individuals. Inside such factories, workers would legally form independent firms. As part of these firms, they would do the factory's work for their own profit, in addition to their regular wages and hours. In effect, the economists proposed creating a second economy for factory workers: an outsourcing to insiders. With some irony, we can call it a whole new kind of "socialist" labor.

From an American perspective, this rescaling justified the legalization of market principles in some parts of the socialist economy. But in their exegesis, the economists never proposed a continuum that would label some jobs or activities as "capitalist," or "more/less capitalist." That was ideologically taboo and, by their logic, also simply inaccurate. The fractally recursive argument enabled Gábor and Galasi to show that all jobs remained socialist and should be embraced and controlled by the state, while admitting that—from some perspectives—many had (relatively) unusual qualities. With these arguments, a single factory activity would display socialist qualities when viewed/compared from one perspective, and capitalist ones when judged from another point of view. Summaries of the young economists' scholarly article were published in popular magazines and later widely discussed in newspapers. Ultimately much of the plan was adopted. People discovered, to their surprise, that they had been participating in the second economy all along! Novels and ethnographies of the time make it plain that different practices—ethics, values, business transactions, even ways of speaking—distinguished the second economy from the rest. And people used the opposed values to position themselves, in everyday interactions, with respect to the qualitative contrasts.

As economists close to the central planning office, Gábor and Galasi were well placed to argue for the acceptance of these changes. Nevertheless, by all accounts, the decision-making process was a tough bureaucratic struggle (Seleny 1994). Recommendations had to persuade many political factions. As it turned out, hard-liners took up the perspective that compared Hungary with the capitalist world. This retained the communist/capitalist distinction as a bedrock classificatory principle, showing continued orthodoxy. It was presentable and acceptable to the Soviets. Those positioning themselves as reformers, by contrast, interpreted the iterations as a legalization of markets in labor and commodities. This was an innovation they proudly displayed to Western scholars. Perspectival rescalings enabled the acceptance of a substantial economic reorganization.

CONCLUSION

Scaling is a relational procedure that starts with comparison. Models for comparison that differ in the handling of perspective create conflicting scalar effects. Fractal recursivity is analogical; it allows perspectival comparisons. There are certainly other techniques that are based on analogy, or that otherwise incorporate perspective. It is important to explore how they work. With analogical practices, people equate phenomena that, by other measures, are of different "size" or extent, or distinguish those that are otherwise deemed the same scale; they connect as similar (or allied) phenomena that, by a-perspectival measures, are distant and distinct; or they distinguish what would otherwise be equated. Perspectival models can contest models that—positing a single point of view—purport to measure the world simply as it is. Conversely, single-perspective scalings can undermine fractal recursivity.

Ideological frameworks define the significant qualities and dimensions of any social scene and the default model(s) for scaling. They shape how scales are justified and authorized: what agendas they serve. When socially embedded and institutionalized, models are enforceable. Taking up or imposing them is a powerful move, as illustrated by the dilemmas of the elderly German-Hungarian woman and Fanon, who were both dismayed by constraints on the identities they could convey. But it is equally illustrated by the success of the Hungarian economists.

The instantiation of models is an indispensable step in scaling. What are the units, categories, and/or qualities to be considered in specific circumstances? By what means are the models invoked? These questions point up the multiple roles of linguistic practices in constructing and construing scale. On the one hand, linguistic materials are among the objects compared by models. For instance, linguistic practices are used as evidence of contrasting qualities. On the other hand, communicative practices—by invoking semiotic models of measurement and comparison—also constitute the pragmatics of scale. They are the means by which scaling-as-practice is situated and accomplished. Communicative, and specifically linguistic, practices are the means by which models are put to work organizationally, institutionally, and interactionally in projects of scale-making.

NOTES

My thanks to Judith T. Irvine for her comments on this paper and for our continuing productive collaboration on matters of language ideology and scale.

1. Moore (2008), Latour (2005, 220), and Tsing (2005), among others, urge us to take up these questions, noting that "micro/macro, local/global" are not neutral frames. *Scale* is a term used in many ways; untangling them is part of the point of this chapter.

2. Qualities and dimensions for scaling are as various as "length," "cost," "consequentiality," or "beauty"; *models* for comparison are the focus of this chapter. This is an analytical distinction we should make before adopting the conventional vertical topography of scales or Latour's flat imaginary.

3. Morgan and Morrison (1999) point out the indispensability of situated narratives for understanding and justifying models in all scholarly disciplines. This is further developed as a Peircean insight in recent understandings of ritual (Silverstein 2004).

4. I thank the editors for asking me to clarify this example. Semiotic infrastructures include lists, forms, scenarios, and charts (Anderson 2008, 167–191; Bowker and Star 1999, 135–163; Lampland and Star 2009), all of which have creative/performative effects.

5. In addition, some ideologies assign dialects to languages in a presumed part/whole relation that is seen as scalar, dialects defined or thought to be somehow "smaller" than and included in languages.

6. Other examples could be equally revealing. Ethnographic and linguistic materials from Europe, Africa, Southeast Asia, and North America have illustrated this process as making differentiation. The point here is to exemplify its relevance for scaling.

7. The best instantiations of these categories were people from the richest farmer and artisan families. A large proportion of the town's population was poor agricultural laborers; they were erased from this ideological regime but aligned themselves with it nevertheless (see Gal 2013).

8. Beauty can serve as an example of how *contrasts, gradients,* and *units* are different ways of conceptualizing values and qualities: if beauty is in the eye of the beholder, then it is a matter of perspective, in opposition to what is not beauty for the beholder. A contrast set is created. Treated as something to be judged in a contest, however, beauty is made into a gradient or ordering that allows first-, second-, and third-place winners. Finally, metrologists have joked about creating a standard unit of beauty, to be called "the helen." The millihelen would then be fixed (perhaps with claims to a-perspectivalness) as the amount that launches one ship (Crease 2011, 180). It is important to note that all languages have resources for creating comparisons and ordinal gradients—for example, in English by inflection as in *pretty, prettier, prettiest,* or adverbially with *more* and *most*. We could posit beauty as a single underlying dimension, as is often done. But making it a dimension (rather than a simple contrast) is itself an ideological move, its motivations and effects worth noticing and analyzing. As the examples here show, beauty is conceptualized and thus ideologized in different ways when viewed through what are conventionally called nominal, ordinal, or ratio measures. In the process, beauty is submitted to different models of scaling, made ready to serve diverse social projects.

9. A census had asked about German mother tongue. Those who claimed it, as well as members of a certain German ethnomilitary organization, were charged with Nazism and expelled. This is deeply ironic, since Hungary was a German ally in the war.

10. Only in the mid-2000s was the idea of "dual identity" for minority-language speakers formulated in Hungary (Bindorffer 2007). Note the parallel to segmentary lineages, though the process is analyzed here as ideological (Evans-Pritchard 1940).

11. Tambiah (1996, 185–193), Latour (2005), and Bockman and Eyal (2002) describe somewhat similar ethnographic situations.

12. The so-called Third World was the venue of proxy wars between the other two. The Non-Aligned Movement, through its name, revealed the structure it was trying to oppose.

5

BALANCING THE SCALES OF JUSTICE IN TONGA

Susan U. Philips

A social phenomenon that is said to operate on a larger or higher scale of social organization typically encompasses a greater spatial area and a greater number of people, among other things, compared with smaller or lower-scale social phenomena. However, space is only one dimension or aspect of scaling. Human cultural construction of scale is multidimensional in general. Furthermore, dimensions of scale can be rendered interdependent—or interscaled—in ways that contribute to their cultural impact, durability, and power. In this chapter, I show how Tongan legal activity is *interscaled* in higher and lower trial courts. This process not only bolsters the institutions themselves but also naturalizes the legal ideologies they espouse. This is made clear by examining the "seriousness" of legal infractions as an effect of the way Tongan courts are (inter)scaled. The scaling processes I describe ultimately allow parties involved in legal proceedings to take the courtroom's legal constitution of seriousness for granted, as if there were no alternative interpretive reality through which to address social conflicts. In this sense, this chapter highlights the role that (inter)scaling plays in the naturalization of institutional practices and products.

. . .

All kinds of dimensions of social life can be scaled, and they are often scaled in relation to each other. To scale something is not only to quantify it but to qualify it as well. Scaling is, after all, a cultural and a semiotic phenomenon. Consider, for example, the interscaling of weddings. A "bigger" wedding is usually associated with more people, but it also is associated with more space taken up, a grander space, more food, fancier food, more and higher-alcoholic-content liquor for free, a fancier wedding dress, a longer train, more formal dress for all, more flowers and more expensive flowers, a more elaborate/longer ritual, and of course greater cost. A number of dimensions of the wedding are scalable. We tend to think that these dimensions somehow go together, so that the fact of more people invited to a wedding can lead to the expectation that there will also be more of everything else. In other words, we take for granted the interdependence of these dimensions of scale, so that a "big wedding" seems to mean all of these things at once.

The hierarchical scaling of Tongan trial courts is similarly multidimensional. For example, a comparison of audio-recorded cases shows that when the Supreme Court handles a case of theft, the trial takes place in a courtroom that is bigger and is located in the country's central city, as opposed to the small rooms out in villages used by the lower-level Magistrate's Courts. Moreover, the higher court judge has more legal education than the lower court magistrate. In the higher court, the procedural and evidence law is more strictly enforced than in the lower court. The higher court's procedures are bilingual, in Tongan and English, rather than just in Tongan, as in the lower court. More people—lawyers, witnesses, jury members, and interpreters—are involved in a higher court trial of theft, which takes days rather than minutes to complete. All of these dimensions of scale come together to reinforce the stature, and authority, of the court as "high."

Just as our commonsense orientations to weddings and court trials are implicitly scaled, so are our ideas about the relationships within geopolitical entities like the nation-state. More specifically, activities associated with a nation-state are seen as operating on a greater scale than activities associated with a region within a state. These activities in turn are seen as operating on a greater scale than activities associated with a tribe or a village. Similarly a phenomenon that is citywide is said to operate on a greater scale than the same phenomenon that is villagewide. Such observations easily move to claims of greater power and cultural pervasiveness for phenomena of greater scale in part, no doubt, because of the same kind of interscaling dynamics we see in Tongan trials or American weddings.

Like geopolitical entities, institutions are scaled, both internally and in the way they are conceived to "fit" within other scaled entities.[1] After all, hierarchy is often, if not always, a built-in feature of institutions—whether governmental branches, churches, health care systems, nongovernmental organizations, mass media, or private workplaces. Hierarchy includes the idea that interactions within an institution are organized into levels, which are respectively supervised by bosses, who are conceived to be under or over the supervision of bosses at other levels.

The distinction between equal and unequal relationships within organizations is readily recognized, enacted, and (often) taken for granted.

Tongan governmental and legal systems are normatively considered to be nationwide, though they may just as easily be scaled as global, or certainly transnational, institutions. As Max Weber made social scientists aware in his conceptualizations of bureaucracies (Bendix 1962; Weber 1951), hierarchically conceptualized and enacted institutions existed in many parts of the world before they were (re)exported by European colonizers over the last several hundred years. European colonial imposition of complex institutions, particularly those of government, law, education, and religion, has often been with the explicit intention of constituting new (albeit dependent) nation-states in the only ways European colonizers knew how to do this. In other words, these institutions are not so much encompassed by, as constitutive of, the state and its relations to other political entities. Thus, the scaled dimensions of activity that distinguish the higher and lower courts in Tonga also distinguish higher from lower courts in other, particularly British-derived, legal systems, even as local Tongan circumstances play a role in determining the relative seriousness of cases.

THE TONGAN TRIAL COURTS: A BRIEF OVERVIEW

Tonga is a Polynesian microstate in the South Pacific, and its designation as a microstate already signals the concept of scale. Tonga is a microstate in that it is, both geographically and demographically speaking, a very small nation recognized by the rest of the world as a sovereign state. The total landmass for the island group is 289 square miles, and the population of the country hovers around one hundred thousand.

In Tonga the lower and higher trial courts are part of a larger legal system that includes police, jails, an appellate process, and articulation with the executive and legislative branches of the government. This system took on its present basic form during the nineteenth century with the ratification of the 1875 Tongan Constitution (Lātūkefu 1974). The Magistrate's Courts, however, were established by written law twenty-five years before the constitution was formed (Lātūkefu 1974). Historically, many hierarchically conceptualized court systems have been created in such a piecemeal fashion, as a strategy of conquest, with the conquerors imposing their own courts as higher-level courts relative to existing conflict management fora (Borah 1983; Tigar and Levy 1977). In the Tongan case, the creation of Magistrate's Courts happened at a time when the chief, Tāufa'āhau, was extending his control over all of Tonga, and it has been interpreted as an act to take authority away from other chiefs. We can see this as the beginning of a functional differentiation between the courts beyond their scaling of seriousness.

Throughout the nineteenth century, British Wesleyan missionaries and high-ranking Tongans collaborated in forming this Tongan national government, which was conceptualized as combining Western and Tongan concepts of rule (Philips 2007). Collaboration between Tongans and non-Tongans in the production of the Tongan legal system continues up to the present day. This is especially true for the higher court. The court is influenced by the Tongan Minister of Justice, the British judges who preside over the Supreme Court, and the mix of British, New Zealander, and Tongan lawyers, and the Tongan and non-Tongan litigants and witnesses who come before the court. Great Britain funds this Tongan Supreme Court judgeship, and New Zealand also provides financial support for the maintenance of the higher court.

As in many other British-derived legal systems, including the legal system in the United States, the primary basis for distinguishing the two courts, conceptualized as higher and lower court levels, is the "seriousness" of the case. In Tongan law, the Magistrate's Courts deal with criminal cases that have possible sentences of up to two years if the defendant is convicted, and civil cases involving claims up to one thousand dollars. The Supreme Court deals with criminal cases that have a possible sentence of more than two years in prison and civil cases where the claim is for more than one thousand dollars (*Tonga Magistrates Bench Book* 2004). The seriousness of crimes is in this way overtly connected with the seriousness of the *consequences* for defendants if they are found guilty. The sentence ranges in criminal cases, and monetary-compensation ranges in civil cases, are encoded in written law. The actual sentences given to people (within the possible ranges) also reflect how seriously the magistrates and judges view the violations to be.

The higher court is higher not only because more serious sentences can be given for crimes but also because it is a court of appeal for the lower court. This means Supreme Court judges ultimately have potential authority over all cases in a way Magistrate's Courts magistrates do not.

The two court levels are kept interactionally separate, which also contributes to the scalar antinomy of "higher" and "lower." For instance, the hearings of each court are held in distinctly separate spaces, even in the capital city of Nuku'alofa, where both levels of court may meet on the same day. They have separate personnel for the purpose of carrying out the public events of court hearings. There are separate sets of people who fulfill the expected roles of judge, clerk, government criminal prosecutor (i.e., police prosecutor in the Magistrate's Court, and Crown prosecutor in the Supreme Court), and there is an additional role of interpreter for the Supreme Court.

While the scaling of "seriousness" is commonly taken to be the basis for tiered trial courts in a number of legal systems influenced by a British colonial presence, these courts still vary in the kinds of cases that end up being constituted as ranging in seriousness, depending on their local histories and present functions. In the collaboration between Tongans and non-Tongans, for example, Tongans are more predominant in the lower court, and here one can see greater Tongan cultural influence, whereas greater British influence is apparent in the higher court.

In addition, from among possible forbidden acts laid out in written law, litigants choose to prosecute only some such acts. There are also alternate conflict resolution venues in Tonga for kinds of problems one doesn't see in court. Prospective litigants are also aware of what others have taken to court and often follow the lead of those others. Not every case a citizen wants heard will be heard, of course. What various sources and interests within the government of Tonga want heard in these courts, which are open to the general public, also shapes what actually appears in court. For instance, conflicts over the inheritance of noble titles and noble lands were at one time handled by the Supreme Court; but control over them was reclaimed by the monarchy, and such cases no longer appear in the trial courts (Marcus 1980).

As a result of such factors interacting, different recognizably British colonial legal traditions in the present-day British Commonwealth and the United States can present very different kinds of cases in the courts. As we will see, the smallness (scale) of Tonga itself is a factor in the frequency with which the higher court plays a role in constituting what is inside and what is outside of Tonga as a nation-state. In spite of sources of cross-national diversity in the cases that appear in lower versus higher courts, the scaled dimensions of court activity that distinguish the higher court from the lower court create coherence through shared, interdependent, scaled dimensions that hold the courts together conceptually.

SCALED DIMENSIONS OF THE TONGAN COURT HIERARCHY

Although the scaling of sentences appears to be the legal basis for the separation of criminal and civil charges into higher and lower courts, in actuality the intersection of dimensions of scale works to constitute cases as more or less serious, both in terms of the perceived qualities of the infraction and the degree of the sentence. In the discussion to follow, I will consider five scaled dimensions of courtroom procedure that differentiate the cases handled by higher versus lower court. These dimensions are interdependent, both reinforcing the institutional distinction between higher and lower courts and determining what sorts of cases are arbitrated there.

1. The legal background of those who preside over the court is scaled. Judges of the Supreme Court in Tonga are British. They have law degrees from British institutions and have been licensed to practice law by the British national government and legal community. This licensing entitles them to wear a wig and a black gown, which lawyers without such an education are not allowed to wear, so that legal education and the semiotic expression of formality in dress are interscaled.

The main reason that Tongans repeatedly offered for their use of British judges in the Supreme Court was that a Tongan in the position of judge would favor his relatives, whereas British judges would not have any relatives in Tonga and would remain in the country for only a few years. Tongans didn't want the favoring of relatives in the lower court either, and magistrates took pains to make sure they were not hearing cases involving relatives. The point remains that Britishness and impartiality or objectivity are interscaled in higher courts.

The magistrates, in contrast, were all Tongan men, who were paid less than the Supreme Court judges. They did not have law degrees, but had less-formal training in legal seminars or workshops held in Tonga, New Zealand, and Fiji. They gained legal experience as court clerks and as police prosecutors in the Magistrate's Courts. Tongans speaking English referred to the magistrates as former "bush lawyers." This meant that they had in the past been hired, without a law degree, by Tongans to represent them in both court levels.

The scaling of education also applied to the lawyers who appeared in the courts. Many bewigged lawyers appeared in the Supreme Court, though most had been licensed in New Zealand rather than Great Britain. When "bush lawyers" in their everyday suits went up against these licensed lawyers in trials, the wigs and gowns—and the knowledge of the law that these markers connoted—often intimidated them. No bewigged lawyers, only bush lawyers, appeared in the Magistrate's Courts, and then only rarely.

2. *The enforcement of law in the courtroom is scaled.* It is assumed that those with more legal training are able to follow the law more effectively than those with less legal training. So one key legal rationale for British-licensed judges in the Supreme Court is the expectation that they will enforce procedural law and evidence law more rigorously in the higher court than will magistrates in the lower courts. For example, in one lengthy criminal jury trial I recorded in full, the jury was told no fewer than five times that procedural law required them to find the defendant guilty only if they were sure beyond a reasonable doubt.

The need to scale evidence law so that it is more strictly enforced in the Supreme Court is based on the idea that in this court it matters more that unacceptably prejudicial information *not* be presented, in part because the crimes and their sentences are expected to be more serious. And enforcement is stricter in jury trials than in trials presided over by the judge.[2] Evidentially irrelevant information is also constrained more often in the higher court. For example, the Tonga-specific speech genres of apology and forgiveness used in noncourt conflict resolution were regularly tolerated and even encouraged in the Magistrate's Court, but did not occur in any case I observed in the Supreme Court and were not raised as relevant to the disposition of a case as they were in the Magistrate's Court. Religious testimonies were also offered by victims and witnesses in the lower courts, to explain persecution and to mitigate illegal behavior. These were not in evidence in the higher court in any way whatsoever. Similarly, written forms of evidence were common in the higher court and rare in the lower court. These differences show how the scaling of whole speech genres is part of the implementation of evidence law, a concept introduced in Meek's discussion of preferred forms of talk in language revitalization efforts (Meek this volume).

3. *Language use is scaled.* The distinction of higher and lower courts is bolstered not only by the scaling of genre but also by choices in the very language(s) spoken in each setting. The Supreme Court is bilingual. The norm reported to me repeatedly was that everything said in English is translated into Tongan by an interpreter, and that everything said in Tongan is translated into English by an interpreter. In practice, there is much more complexity to the allocation of English and Tongan in the Supreme Court. The Tongan rationale for this bilingualism is that the judge is British and won't know Tongan. The Magistrate's Court, in contrast, is conducted entirely in Tongan, except for the rare appearance of non-Tongans in court, in which case the magistrates, all fluent in English, conduct the procedure in English.

The translation between Tongan and English in the Supreme Court had multiple interscalar effects.[3] First, and most obviously, it required more time. When Tongan witnesses were questioned in Tongan by Tongan lawyers, the interpreter would interpret first the question and then the answer in English. When the British Crown prosecutor questioned Tongan witnesses in English, the interpreter interpreted the question into Tongan and the answer into English. When the judge asked questions of witnesses in English, they were usually interpreted into Tongan and the answers from Tongan speakers were interpreted into English.[4]

Although this was not volunteered to me by Tongans, it is clear that there are other factors besides the judges' linguistic competencies that make the use of English in the Supreme Court desirable. Specifically, language choice is interscaled in a number of ways. First, there is the general prestige of English. Even though some Tongans blame the use of English for what they see as the disappearance of some specialized speech registers in Tongan, they still want to give their children the best economic opportunities possible; and to Tongans, this means sending the children to schools where they will learn English.[5] When Tongans encountered a noble and found themselves unable to speak to the noble using chiefly language, a specialized register, they would switch to English if they could, as a way of showing more respect than they felt everyday Tongan could provide (Philips 2011). Thus, it is not just in court that English is scaled as better than everyday Tongan, though not as good as honorific Tongan, for showing respect.

In addition, language choice is interscaled with the geopolitical scaling of each court's reach. Court participants are cast as more or less "local" or "global" in their dealings. The majority of the cases in the Supreme Court that I observed and recorded involved organizational entities that existed both inside Tonga and outside of it, in the United States, New Zealand, and elsewhere, including banks, airlines, lumber companies, and churches. Many of the people representing these organizations in court cases were themselves non-Tongans or Tongans who had lived overseas for long periods and were fluent in English, reflecting the high degree of out-migration among Tongans. The more a case involved institutions, personnel, and written materials from outside Tonga, and litigants who had financial dealings outside Tonga in the English-speaking Tongan diaspora, the more English was used.

The interscaling of English and economic interests in the Tongan court system must also be noted. English makes the court proceedings accessible to those from outside Tonga who have business dealings with Tongans who live in Tonga, and it allows them to judge whether Tongan businesses are supported by legal policies needed to make doing business predictable. The government of Tonga has an interest in encouraging transnational business relationships and in rendering Tongan business practices credible in order to sustain the economic well-being of the country. For all these reasons, English is associated with the production of legal activity that is more serious than legal activity conducted only in Tongan.

4. *The length of time given to cases is scaled.* Lower-level cases brought to completion during a single hearing rarely take more than a few minutes. This is in part because defendants usually plead guilty in the Magistrate's Courts. The longer cases usually involve more extensive moralizing by magistrates in what they define as the more serious cases. Even when defendants plead not guilty, which is rare, their hearings rarely last as long as ten minutes, and the longest trial in my database took only an hour and a half. Higher court trials can last from days to weeks.

This scaling of the time given to each case in turn involves several other scaled dimensions of the organization of courtroom interaction. First, the more people involved in a court hearing, the longer the case takes. Lawyers were always involved in Supreme Court cases, whereas they rarely appeared in Magistrate's Courts. In Supreme Court jury trials, the selection of prospective jurors required additional time, because they had to be interviewed before they could be selected. There was always an interpreter present when the Supreme Court was in session, and interpretation, as noted above, required additional time. And when evidence was presented in the Supreme Court, there was always an additional court employee (usually an assistant registrar) whose job it was to swear in each witness. By contrast, the majority of interactions in the lower court took place between the magistrate and the defendant.[6] Occasionally a witness would testify. Sometimes the witness was a policeman reporting what other witnesses had told him, which meant the evidence was hearsay, a type of evidence that did not get presented in the higher court.

Because of the scaling of evidentiality, lawyers in higher courts are responsible for bringing in more witnesses to interview than appear in cases in the lower court, for asking each witness more questions than would be asked of a witness in the lower court, and for encouraging longer answers from witnesses. In this way interactional units that are similar in their organization of participation can be repeated and/or expanded so as to lengthen the time given to a higher court case. The lengthening of time given to each case in the higher court, then, depends on not only the number of people interactionally involved but also the greater care given to adherence to rules of evidence. More time given to a case allows for greater complexity in the circumstances of a crime to be aired, including accounts of its temporal unfolding. These aspects of variation in how much time is devoted to individual cases are interdependent. So, for example, the presence of fewer lawyers makes the appearance of fewer witnesses more likely, reducing the likelihood of evidence-expanding question-and-answer sequences.

In addition, lawyers introduce whole genres or forms of talk in the higher court that do not occur in the lower court, specifically opening statements, closing statements, and, in jury trials, the voir dire, or questioning of prospective jurors. Supreme Court judges add instructions to juries and judgments in civil cases. Interpreters add translation from Tongan to English and English to Tongan in the higher court. The amount of talk produced is in these ways scaled in this court system, and more talk requires more time.

5. *The spatial jurisdiction of the courts is scaled.* There are three ways in which the courts are spatially scaled. First, there is a scaling of the geographical sizes of their legal jurisdictions. Taking the main island of Tongatapu as the point of reference, the island is divided into three jurisdictional areas for the level of Magistrate's Court: the east side, the west side, and the middle, which contains the capital of the nation-state, Nuku'alofa. A magistrate is assigned to each end, east and west; and two magistrates are assigned to the middle of this main island. These people are then rotated regularly to other jurisdictions to prevent the accumulation of power in a given jurisdiction. The Supreme Court, in contrast, has jurisdiction over the entire island group.

The judge thus has greater jurisdictional authority than the individual magistrates, not only because cases tried by the latter could be appealed to him, but also because his decisions could affect anyone, anywhere in the country. He can also decide when to send some of the procedures under his jurisdiction down to lower courts. Arguably, the lower courts have a different kind of power. They are more numerous, they hear many more cases (of shorter length), far more people appear before them, and far more people in their packed audiences hear their moral messages repeated over and over. They generate activities where Tongan culture is replicated or reiterated time and time again.

A second form of spatial scaling concerns the political economic types of communities in which courts are physically located (Philips 1995). The Supreme Court, as mentioned earlier, is in Nuku'alofa, which has approximately thirty-five thousand people, or half the population of the main island. Magistrate's Courts are located in the capital. too, but they are also located in large villages throughout the rest of the island of Tongatapu and in regional centers of outer islands. The east and west sides of Tongatapu each have three such courts in large, and reportedly troublesome, villages with populations of approximately fifteen hundred people. The magistrate for the west side, along with his clerk, was driven out from the capital one day a week to each of the three villages that had courthouses. The two Nuku'alofa Magistrate's Courts, in contrast, were convened every weekday.

The capital is the primary regional center of the country. It has the only public market on the island, the national government offices, the banks and most of the other commercial enterprises, the main tertiary-educational institutions, and the main offices of all of the churches. This regional center and other, much smaller regional centers in the outer islands are also centers of most of the Tongan-English bilingualism (as opposed to just Tongan) found on a day-to-day basis and functionally associated with government, education, and commerce. The large villages where courts were located had churches, schools, large multipurpose communal sheds, and small roadside grocery stands, but they had none of the institutions found in the capital.

A third kind of spatial scaling is semiotic, and while it is clearly influenced by the geopolitical scaling just discussed, it has distinct elements. In the capital, the Supreme Court is convened in a very large building at the center of town. The opening and closing of Tonga's Parliament are national holidays and occur in the same building, so the building is strongly associated with the national government. The Magistrate's Courts in Nuku'alofa meet in smaller multipurpose buildings either adjacent to the central higher court or in areas peripheral to the center. The Magistrate's Court on the west side of the island in the village where I lived was close to the middle of the village. It was part of a complex that also included a police department and a holding cell.

The actual courtroom of the Supreme Court is far larger than, and has much higher ceilings than those of, the Magistrate's Courts. And the Supreme Court judge's bench is elevated far more than the benches of the Magistrate's Courts. The courtroom of the village Magistrate's Court is the smallest of all. So size of courtrooms, height of courtrooms, and the elevation of judicial personnel are also scaled.

There is a close interdependence between the scaled sizes of the communities where courts are located and the scaled court language choices discussed earlier. The bilingual Supreme Court is held in the most bilingual community in the country, while most of the monolingual Magistrate's Courts are located in the predominantly Tongan-speaking villages. Arguably, too, as will become clearer, most of the crimes that involve bilingual speakers and bilingual written materials take place, at least in part, in the bilingual capital's institutions and are heard in the bilingual Supreme Court.

Together the scaled dimensions of court activity that both differentiate the Tongan court levels and bring them together in a common framework do the work of producing some cases as more serious than other. In other words, these overlapping dimensions work together to scale seriousness. Actual court cases that I observed and recorded in the Tongan courts shed further light on how some issues come to be legally constituted as more serious than others.

THE SCALING OF SERIOUSNESS: MORE AND LESS SERIOUS CRIMES IN THE COURTS

The multiple kinds of scaling involved in constructing higher and lower Tongan courts are interdependent in ways that contribute to their differential authority and power. In the constitution of the two courts, which ideologically are conceptualized as dealing with more and less serious crimes, the lower courts have jurisdictions that are geographically and demographically smaller, and they are presided over by magistrates who have less education, adhere less closely to the country's evidence law, speak primarily Tongan in court, and give less time to each case they hear. The higher court is presided over by judges who have jurisdiction over the entire country's crimes, have more legal education, adhere more closely to the country's evidence law, speak only English in bilingual proceedings, and give much more time to each case they hear.

Clearly some of these scaled dimensions are interdependent, including or even particularly to Tongans. The judges' English legal education is thought to both necessitate bilingual proceedings and enable the judges to know how to more strictly impose evidence law. The greater amount of time given to the cases in the higher court and the adherence to evidence law are related: both are thought to improve the factual basis upon which cases are supposed to be decided. Even the location of the higher court in the bilingual capital, and the bilingualism of proceedings in that court, are interrelated: the capital is the place where bilingual people live, or where they go in order to engage in transnational activities that call for both English and Tongan. As the cases I present here illustrate, the interdependence of these multiple dimensions semiotically thickens (Wirtz 2014, 37) the concept of seriousness that differentiates the two court levels.

The interscaling of seriousness in magistrate's court cases. In the Magistrate's Court in the west-end village where I lived, defendants almost always pled guilty. When a defendant pled not guilty, this meant the magistrate was obliged to conduct a minitrial. Thus, not-guilty pleas regularly led to longer hearings and the elicitation of more evidence about the case. In other words, the cases were scaled in length of time and standard of evidence based on whether the defendant pled guilty or not guilty. But this would usually mean only that a case lasted ten minutes instead of two to five minutes, and these defendants were always ultimately found guilty.

Two kinds of cases were regularly completed, as opposed to those that were postponed or canceled. First were violations of specific government regulations concerning vehicles. These included the lack of an auto license or driver's license, missing taillights, or nonvisible auto licenses. Second were crimes against persons and property, primarily drunkenness on the public road, assault, bad language, theft, and property trespass (Philips 2003). There was a relationship between the category of crime and the social identities of the people who committed them. The defendants charged with auto violations were typically middle-aged men. Many had jobs as drivers for government officials or businessmen, so they were employed. They dressed up for court in relatively expensive clothing: heavy *tupenu*, 'cloth skirts,' in dark colors—blue, gray, and black—covered by the *ta'ovala*, 'waist mat.' The waist mats are worn to show respect and are reportedly required of all in public settings. They wore watches, as well as shoes that fully covered their feet. In contrast, the crimes against persons and property were usually brought against men in their teens and twenties, who wore thin tropical-print *tupenu* (sometimes without the *ta'ovala*) and flip-flops instead of shoes, and who had no watches. The crimes thus appeared to be scaled by age and social class or financial well-being.[7]

Because Magistrate's Courts meet frequently and hear many cases that last only a few minutes each, and because there are many such courts, it is possible to argue that, in court proceedings, the magistrates mobilize commonsensical moral scalings in cases of infractions. This is particularly true in the cases of crimes against persons and property, which, unlike most auto violation cases, can have moral framings. All four of the magistrates that I observed and recorded—two in the capital and two in the large rural village—displayed a similar scaling according to the nature of the infraction. For instance, magistrates gave much less time to the cases of those charged with drunkenness on the public road than to cases of assault, theft, trespass, and bad language; and the fines were lower in the drunkenness cases—a reflection of local norms.

Yet scales of seriousness were not only reflected in lower-court proceedings but produced there as well. Greater time was given to the assault cases than to the drunkenness cases, for instance, in that defendants were asked more questions and lectured more about the ways in which their crimes were morally wrong. Speech genres of apology by defendants and forgiveness by victims also lengthened procedures in cases of assaults. The defendants given more time in court were also sentenced to higher fines and sometimes to prison. In these ways, seriousness was not only scaled before the defendants appeared in court, as spelled out in written law, but also scaled in court through the magistrates' interactions with the defendants.

In addition, magistrates explicitly invoked various aspects of defendants' and victims' identities to assert the greater seriousness of crimes, which were then given more serious sentences.[8] For a variety of group crimes committed by male youth—such as stealing and cooking pigs, throwing rocks at a bus, and making home brew—the older boys in a group were assigned greater responsibility than the younger boys, lectured more, and sometimes given harsher sentences. Once a thirteen-year-old boy was given no punishment at all for being drunk, although he was found guilty. The magistrate had determined that he was the youngest child among many children, born close together, in his family, and that no one from his family was there to support him. The magistrate explained to me that the boy had clearly not been raised with enough attention to his needs in such a family situation. Scaling of seriousness based on relative age, then, was common.

Other invocations of aspects of social identity appeared to be more idiosyncratic, but they followed the broader pattern of scaling of seriousness relative to social identity. For example, in one case, a man in a group who had made alcoholic home brew was singled out because he was a teacher—his being a teacher made what he had done worse. In another case the caretaker of a church building who assaulted a boy from the congregation was singled out both because he was a caretaker and because the assault had been committed inside the chapel, a sacred place. Both these men were also older than most of the defendants charged with crimes other than auto violations. In another case the usual fine of two dollars for being drunk in public was upped to seven dollars because the person had been drunk in a nightclub; the magistrate's rationale focused on the number of people who had been disturbed. In this case, the scaling up of the number of people affected by the infraction meant a scaling up of punishment.

The interscaling of Supreme Court cases. In the Tongan Supreme Court, there were two kinds of "serious" cases at play.[9] First were cases that could be conventionally understood as morally worse versions of lower court cases—that is, as the same kind of infraction, but "more so" in some sense. Second were cases that had no clear analogues in the lower court in that they were conducted through discourses that were transnational in several ways.

The cases I observed that could be understood as intensified versions of lower court cases included thefts of greater financial value than those in the lower courts; murder, which could be seen as a scaling up of assault cases; conflicts over land that had features related to property crimes tried in the lower courts; and "found by night." The latter was the local popular English phrase for a situation in which a defendant sneaked into the bedroom of a young unmarried woman and tried to have sexual contact with her. As I would learn in observing one such court case, the charge in this type of crime asserted a scaling up of harm to women. "Found by night" was locally seen as morally worse than directing bad language at a woman, and worse than physically assaulting a woman, but not as bad as rape.

In a murder trial in the Supreme Court, in which the Crown lawyer for the prosecution was British and the defense team included an overseas-trained Tongan lawyer, nine young men were tried together over a period of three weeks. The case arose out of a situation where boys from a neighboring village came to a dance in the victim's adjacent village. The victim got separated from his friends and was attacked with fists, rocks, and sticks by these nine; the charge specified that he had suffered many injuries to the head. The nine individuals were charged with having collaboratively killed the young man; but to allow for them to be given different kinds of responsibility for this act, each was charged with five different crimes, specified in court as descending in order of seriousness in this exact sequence: murder, manslaughter, grievous bodily harm, bodily harm, and assault. Not surprisingly, the possible sentence for each also descended, in this case from death to time in jail to a fine.

The murder trial took far longer than a lower-court guilty plea for assault—three weeks rather than ten minutes. The murder trial involved more lawyers for the defense and prosecution—three rather than none. This trial also involved formally trained lawyers—one for the defense, one for the prosecution, and one as judge, whereas none appear in the lower court.[10] Although this was never mentioned in the court sessions I attended, my research assistant learned from villagers in the audience that the two villages had together carried out a fairly elaborate ritual of apology and forgiveness, a familiar traditional activity for healing conflicts, as a way to bring the two villages back together. This suggests that that Tongans were engaged in their own culturally specific form of scaling up seriousness, apart from the law-driven scaling that occurs in court. Of course, such community rituals take much more time and preparation than the brief apologies in the Magistrate's Court. Nevertheless, there was a place in court for an abbreviated version of such healing in more serious cases through apologizing and forgiving, which was seen by Tongans, as well as non-Tongan legal practitioners, as having no place in the Supreme Court.

During my fieldwork, I also observed and recorded cases in the higher court that had no obvious analogy or relatedness to lower court cases. These cases were scaled by "transnational" discourses of several kinds. First, they typically involved some kind of financial malfeasance, a concept that itself was widely shared with the Anglo-American legal communities outside Tonga. This concept was lacking in lower court cases, particularly since there were almost no civil cases of the small-claims-court variety. Second, these cases were imagined in court as involving people in Tonga with people in other nation-states, and through this the nation-states themselves were constituted. Relevant events were characterized as taking place inside Tonga, outside Tonga, and between people in Tonga and people in other countries. People, goods, and money were envisioned as moving from one country to another. Third, relevant people were imagined as acting, and relevant events were imagined as taking place, within and through transnational institutions such as banks, lumber companies, airlines, commodities boards, and churches. In larger countries, such transnational elements are likely to be less salient in a court of general jurisdiction such as the Tongan Supreme Court. The very small geographical scale of Tonga contributed to the imagining of crime as taking place on a much larger geographic and geopolitical scale in the higher court than in the lower court. The scaling up, in the Supreme Court, of the British legal education of the judge and some lawyers, the imposition of Anglo-American evidence law, and the use of English were particularly relevant for cases with these transnational elements.

These qualities can be illustrated through a comparative discussion of my audio recordings of two complete trials that took place in the Supreme Court. Each took place over several days, during which seven to nine hours of actual courtroom interaction took place. The first was a civil trial heard before a judge who acted as fact finder, rather than before a jury. The plaintiff was suing a distant relative, who had been in charge of a construction project, for taking money he had agreed to invest in the project and essentially putting it in his own account. The plaintiff wanted that money back. He was also claiming that he had worked on the construction project and never been paid. The Church of Latter-Day Saints was also identified as a defendant because the construction project was for one of their chapels, and the church was the ultimate source of payments for the project. The judge found that the first defendant had violated his contract with the plaintiff, who should have been paid twenty thousand dollars for the work he did. The issue of invested money was left unresolved, and the church was found to have no responsibility for the money owed.

During this civil trial, it emerged that the plaintiff had lived in the United States for twenty-four years and had become a citizen of the United States, although he was living in Tonga at the time of the trial. His citizenship meant that the judge could use U.S. contract law as well as Tongan contract law and find that an oral contract that had no written equivalent was still valid and binding, making the case transnational in law and in this way scaling it up geopolitically.

This plaintiff told me that he wanted to reach the judge in English because the interpreter did not quite say what the man meant when interpreting him. Had this been a jury trial rather than a trial by judge, the plaintiff would have been in a different position. To a Tongan jury, he would have wanted to testify in Tongan. The plaintiff's initial choice to testify in English appeared to have a destabilizing effect on the overall patterning of the situational bilingualism in the other legal procedures I witnessed. Other later witnesses similarly switched into all English, with no translation into Tongan. The scaling up of English was related to the scaling up of the amount of time the plaintiff and other parties to this case had spent in an English-speaking country. Because all the key figures in the case were Mormon and were known to be, to Tongans this upscaling of English was also related to the greater Mormon sponsorship of English in church educational institutions, compared to other Christian religious denominations in Tonga.

The interscaling of the geopolitical locales of the institutions and individuals involved in this case, the amount of money at stake, and the upscaling effect of English, along with all the other dimensions of scale that render the court "high," are also what rendered this crime "serious."

The second complete, multiday trial I recorded was a criminal case heard by a jury. In this case, a female bank employee of the Bank of Tonga was accused of two crimes: taking money under false pretenses and theft from the bank. The person from whom the money was taken under false pretenses I will call Sione, and the defendant I will call Mele. Sione's brother and wife, who were living and working in Hawaii, sent him and his family two thousand dollars, a common way for those overseas to help those at home. They sent the money by telex from the Bank of Hawaii to the Bank of Tonga. Mele, a relative of Sione's wife, was a clerk at the bank. Sione asked Mele to help him transfer the funds from the bank's overseas account into his savings account. Later Mele came to see Sione and told him there had been a mistake at the bank. He actually had been sent, not two thousand dollars, but only two hundred dollars. She told him that if he would return one thousand dollars of the money now, then he could use the rest of the money until the matter was resolved. Later she brought him a withdrawal slip, which he signed. She used his signed withdrawal slip to take one thousand dollars out of his account and put it into an account she shared with her brother. She then used the money in her joint account with her brother as collateral to get a loan from the bank for two thousand dollars to finish a house she was building with her brother on another island.

During the month that Mele was carrying out these activities, Sione contacted his brother in Hawaii. His brother's wife contacted the Bank of Hawaii, which contacted the Bank of Tonga, asking why Sione did not get all of his money. The Bank of Tonga wired back that Sione had gotten all of his money, and implied he was trying to trick someone into giving him more. Sione also repeatedly went to Mele for help in getting his money back. Her story apparently changed to one where the bank had made a mistake and was rectifying it, and she would let him know when that had been done. Eventually Mele put one thousand dollars back in Sione's account, repaying him with half of the building loan she had obtained with his money as collateral. Only then, apparently, did Sione go to a higher level bank official to complain that he still had a loss of two hundred dollars for the phone calls made between Hawaii and Tonga during the past month. At this point the bank looked into the matter and, soon after that, had Mele arrested on the charges of theft and taking money under false pretenses.

When the jury returned from its deliberations, the jurors had found the defendant guilty of taking money under false pretenses, but not theft. When the judge sentenced the defendant to a year in prison, with nine months of that sentence suspended, so that she would spend three months in prison for a first-time offense, he said, "You and other bank employees must be shown that this sort of behavior will not be tolerated and will be punished."

As in the murder case previously discussed, the number of lawyers, and their educational backgrounds, were scaled up in comparison to those of the lawyers present in the Magistrate's Court. The Crown prosecutor was a formally trained British lawyer, and a Tongan bush lawyer appeared for the defense. In this case, as in the previously discussed civil case, the number of witnesses was extensive. Six witnesses were called in this criminal theft case: four Bank of Tonga employees, the victim, and a policeman, all of whom were interpreted and, therefore, testifying bilingually. All of this increased the amount of talk in each case and, as a result, the amount of time given to each case.

Because the higher court cases take more time, they are constituted as more serious than those in the lower court. Great human energy and other precious resources are expended in prosecuting these cases. All these interlocked dimensions of higher court cases are intended to send to the broader Tongan public the message that the parties to court interactions, participating in a nation-state-making activity as they do, do not take lightly the fates of those charged with crimes. Citizens of Tonga learn they should not take these cases lightly either, or they too could be dragged into court in a way that Tongans talk about as embarrassing and harmful to the parties' socially perceived respectability.

The scaling of trans-seriousness. As I noted earlier, both of the multiday cases recorded in full involved financial malfeasance—stealing money from the bank in one case and failing to pay a subcontractor in the other case. This is not an issue or a concept that appeared in lower court proceedings; but elsewhere in the Tongan political public sphere, similar concerns were addressed at the time these cases were recorded. In the Fale Alea, the national legislature (sometimes referred to as "Parliament" by English-speaking Tongans), commoner representatives were trying to impeach the Minister of Finance. And they were publicly accusing their fellow representatives of padding expenses for travel and time spent in Parliament. Candidates in the most recent Fale Alea election were also accused of having bribed voters. If a candidate comes to a charity fund-raising kava party and makes a donation, is that a bribe? Much of this was reported on the radio and in local bilingual publications, the national *Kalonikala/Chronicle* weekly newspaper and the *Matangi Tonga* magazine. Tongan villagers between 1987 and 1990 were highly engaged in following the controversies in the Fale Alea. On Friday evenings, men gathered around kava bowls to listen to recorded excerpts from Fale Alea sessions, riveted by the radio. On the main island, in the areas where I lived, the widely politically engaged citizens generally approved of what the commoner representatives were doing.

This Tongan discourse of financial malfeasance is an old transnational discourse that has evolved over the past one hundred years and more. In the late nineteenth and early twentieth centuries, British colonial administrators complained about financial malfeasance in the Tongan government; and partly as a result, Tonga lost some of its autonomy to Great Britain for a period (Thomson 1894; Scarr 1968). Then, as now, instances of financial malfeasance were imagined as embedded in transnational contexts.

Both of the present-day financial cases that I described also involved transnational organizations or organizations that were conceptualized as engaging in exchanges between people in different nation-states. These cases had an actual material presence in physical locations in different nations. In the civil contract-violation case, the main transnational institution was the Mormon Church, more formally known as the Church of the Latter-Day Saints. This U.S.-based church originally hired a Tongan Mormon building contractor in Hawaii to build its chapel, and that organization subcontracted work to other supposedly similar entities, even though the original contract forbade such subcontracting. In the criminal theft case, banks were the main institutional entities, and a great deal of testimony was devoted to how the Bank of Tonga communicated with the bank in Hawaii that the victim's brother had used to send him money.

In several ways, then, both of these higher court trials represented the events at issue as operating on a geographical and geopolitical scale beyond Tonga: in the imagining of events that were constituted as taking place both inside and outside of Tonga; in framing the discourses in the trials as part of a broader transnational discourse on financial malfeasance that was current in other areas of Tongan public political life at the time, and which had a history in colonial relations between Great Britain and Tonga; and in constructing the events in which the crimes were embedded as being carried out through transnational institutions.

What come to be scaled as more serious in the higher court, then, are crimes that themselves are conceptualized as having involved activities that took place on a larger geographic and geopolitical scale than those addressed in the lower court. The Supreme Court hears cases that implicate not just Tongans in Tonga but also people in other countries connected through institutions that, in turn, also operate on a transnational scale and link Tonga to the rest of the world.

CONCLUSION

In this chapter, I have shown how dimensions of scales are rendered interdependent. Through this process of interscalation, different dimensions of social life are tightly bound up with each other. This interdependence projects wholeness, boundedness, authority, and durability of a kind commonly attributed to institutional complexes like law, education, medicine, and religion. Such is the case with "higher" and "lower" courts in Tonga and the notions of seriousness that derive from this distinction.

The interdependencies contribute to the authority and power of the court system in several ways. First, the legal ideology regarding the courts is that one scaled dimension of court activity cannot be altered without altering other scaled dimensions. Second, there is a tendency to conflate one dimension with another. For instance, in Tonga as in many other legal jurisdictions, there is a basic assumption that when more time is given to a case, the evidence will be better or more reliable, when in fact additional evidence sometimes generates more confusion and contradictions. Furthermore, it is assumed that because a judge has more legal education than a magistrate, he will demand closer adherence to evidence law, when in fact this may not be true. Moreover, English is viewed as evidentially more reliable than Tongan because it is associated with a court that gives more time to each case, and certainly the data indicates that English is seen as preferable for negotiating matters of law, as opposed to matters of fact.

Third, the higher court activities are constituted as having greater authority than the lower court activities, and this is not just because a Supreme Court judge has appellate powers over lower court cases and is literally the boss of everyone below him. This court also derives greater authority from its supposed legal superiority in the scaling of the dimensions discussed here. The Supreme Court has jurisdiction over a larger area; it spends more time on cases; it carries out procedures in English, which has global prestige; it imposes the law more strictly; and the judges have more education.

Fourth, in financial malfeasance cases, the higher court activates aspects of law that operate on a transnational and even global scale in ways that the lower court does not. Its language, law, and lawyers all participate in relations between nation-states, culturally constructing Tonga as a nation-state whose citizens have legal relationships with people in other nation-states. Litigants in the Supreme Court are constructed as participants in transnational institutions and as engaged in transnational relationships through those institutions.

Finally, these same scaled dimensions also differentiate court levels in many former British colonies, and it is the higher courts that have the most in common and are interconnected. This resemblance contributes to the prestige of this multiscalar hierarchy. As noted earlier, the actual kinds of cases brought to such court systems can vary considerably, so that the tiny size of the Tongan nation-state increases the likelihood that legal cases will involve other nations, which is not true of cases in larger countries. The resemblances among British-derived court systems send a message of predictability and familiarity to Western and westernized outsiders who wish to do business with Tonga.

An examination of scaling in the Tongan courts indicates that there is, in addition to a spatial concept of scale, a stunning range of cultural phenomena that can be scaled along continua. In the Tongan court system, the degree of seriousness of a crime can be thought of as the product of the multiscalar distinction between lower and higher courts as much as the functional foundation for the distinction. Furthermore, the semiotic thickening that accompanies interscalation also strengthens institutions: their processes and products are naturalized, as is the moral authority they wield. And examination of the Tongan court system ultimately demonstrates that the scale of institutions and their authority must not be taken for granted. Rather, we must tease out the many scalable dimensions of cultural semiotic phenomena and identify their interdependencies in order to understand how institutions wield their power and to appreciate the production of scale.

NOTES

I particularly acknowledge the Michicagoan Faculty Seminar for our workshop readings and discussion that led to this volume and my paper in particular. Participants include the contributors to this volume and Bruce Mannheim, Kristina Wirtz, Hilary Dick, John Lucy, Justin Richland, Matt Hull, Webb Keane, and Robin Queen. Earlier efforts on my part to characterize the Tongan Supreme Court and how it differs from the Magistrate's Courts include papers for past sessions at meetings of the Association of Social Anthropologists of Oceania and the American Anthropological Association. These sessions were organized by Karen Watson-Gegeo; Barbra Meek and Diane Riskedahl; Beverly Stoeltje and myself; and Summerson Carr and Michael Lempert. I am grateful to the government of Tonga for allowing me to carry out the research on which this paper is based.

1. Institutions are systems of interaction, which are held together by a common interpretive framework shared by those involved, including ideas about the nature of activities within the institution and the nature of the social identities that will carry out the activities. The activities that make up an institution are commonly recognized as, and thought of as, reoccurring, reiterated, or routinized. This enduringness means that institutions persist even as the people who constitute them move in and out of them.

2. In legal ideology it is argued that a judge can eliminate from his thinking any evidence that should not have been admitted in the first place, when the time comes to decide guilt or innocence. It is assumed that jury members cannot do this, even when told to.

3. When court personnel characterized how this worked, they told me the proceedings were fully bilingual, meaning everything said in one language was "interpreted" rather than "translated"—the interpreter's very deliberate distinction—into the other language.

4. The most systematic exception to this basic pattern of bilingualism was when the lawyers engaged in direct exchanges with the judge, whether these exchanges were initiated by the judge or the lawyers. When this happened, the entire exchange was in English with no translation into Tongan. All of the bush lawyers thus had to be fluent in English as well as Tongan. If parties to a conflict, jurors, or audience members did not know English, they did not know what was being discussed. Often the discussions concerned legal rather than factual matters, and at least one legal practitioner offered this as the reason why these exchanges were not translated.

5. The school on the main island that taught English from the first grade on was, for that reason, the most sought-after school by parents, in spite of the fact that the government recommended that English not be taught until the fourth grade.

6. Rarely, a bush lawyer appeared on behalf of a defendant, but overseas trained lawyers did not appear in any cases observed and recorded in the rural court. Interestingly, bush lawyers often requested that cases from the rural area be moved to the town court so they would not have the inconvenience of driving to the rural area. This meant the number of people involved in a case, and the time they took, scaled up as one moved from the geopolitical periphery to the center of the country, even in just the Magistrate's Courts.

7. What was not common were small-claims civil cases of the sort shown on reality television shows in the United States—for example, cases brought by landlords and renters, or property damage cases. There is no small-claims culture in the Tongan Magistrate's Courts, unlike in the higher court.

8. Elsewhere I have discussed how magistrates regularly invoked the possible or actual presence of brothers and sisters as a reason why the defendant's bad language was so very bad (Philips 2000).

9. The cases heard in the Supreme Court during the period I was doing research are more difficult to characterize. Because far fewer cases are heard on a day-to-day basis, it is difficult to see patterns in the handling of interactions. I observed and recorded two complete trials, as well as a number of segments of other contested cases. I also draw on my collection of court calendars and annual reports to the government from the court system.

10. The number of defendants tried together may sound unusual, but in a lower court I saw as many as seven young men tried together for throwing rocks at a bus.

6

INTERSCALING AWE, DE-ESCALATING DISASTER

E. Summerson Carr and Brooke Fisher

The mass of concrete was bigger than anything anyone dared imagine, a harbinger, it seemed, of our worst fears.

—LORI TOBIAS, THE OREGONIAN

On June 5, 2012, a dock from Misawa—a northern Japanese town devastated by the Great East Japan Earthquake and Tsunami of March 2011—floated ashore on Agate Beach, in Oregon.[1] By the time the soon-to-be-famous "mass of concrete" docked on Oregon's shores, American oceanographers and computer programmers had spent over a year tracking debris from the disaster in order to render wave patterns visible and predict what residents might expect in the way of future visitors. Nevertheless, the dock's landing awed a range of American audiences—from seismologists and marine biologists to park officials and beachgoers—confronting them with the limits of what can be known, daringly imagined, or otherwise anticipated. As spokesperson for the Oregon Department of Parks and Recreation, Chris Havel, put it to local reporter Lori Tobias:

> The dock is sort of this big turning point.... It was like a 200-ton alarm clock. All eyes turned to the coast. Everyone was like, "I guess it is really here." ... In the couple of months before the dock showed up, everyone was noticing there was more debris, Styrofoam and plastic.... This is exactly what we were told to expect—light stuff drifting across the waves. We were getting ready for that.... The fear was that if we were wrong about that, what else were we wrong about? ... Are there 20 of these things waiting offshore? Nobody knew. As hard as they'd been looking ... they missed this. In spite of the size to us, it is very small compared to the ocean. So there was that fear and that scramble to try and prepare for the unknown.[2]

Of course, a two-hundred-ton slab of concrete, in and of itself, hardly exceeds the imagination. And certainly, it is fathomable that something that size floated roughly five thousand miles across the ocean, another metric that the prolific commentary on the dock is keen to point out. As Havel concedes, the dock is very small compared to the ocean, and debris from Japan was expected to make the overseas journey all along. If the dock was "bigger than anything anyone dared imagine,"[3] it is not because it was a ready-made sign of the awesome events that had unfolded in Japan, nor because it immediately indexed American futures. Rather, the dock was so alarming because of how it was (inter)scaled by the various commentators who engaged it.

Interscaling involves drawing connections between disparate scalable qualities so that they come to reinforce each other (See Carr and Lempert this volume; Philips this volume). As we document here, the American media on the "200-ton alarm clock" is characterized by an almost compulsive interscaling that moves briskly between the dock's heaviness, its height, the distance it traveled, and the enormity of the natural disaster that sent it on its way, as well as the quantity and diversity of "nonnative" marine species attached to it. Significantly, while a variety of experts detected and defined particular scalable qualities of the dock, they commonly betrayed the conclusion that no single way of seeing and scaling the dock was sufficient on its own, potentially rattling the very basis of their expertise.

In fact, when speaking with journalists, experts were curiously up-front that the dock defied the scales most closely associated with their respective domains of knowledge. Among those who took responsibility for comprehending the visiting dock, many joined Havel in confessing that "there was that fear and that scramble to try and prepare for the unknown." For instance, one marine scientist commented on the species-encrusted dock's arrival: "That was the first time that anyone ever considered that marine organisms could drift across the ocean.... We're still finding species we haven't seen before. It doesn't make sense to us."[4] Ecologists soon joined marine biologists in projecting uncertainty, taking the dock's arrival as "the largest experiment in invasion ecology ever run" and warning that the "invaders ... have the potential to extinguish native species, destroy fisheries and permanently alter ecosystems."[5] Whether the dock was cast as a giant "alarm clock" or the "largest experiment ... ever," these comparisons scaled the dock as something that could not be descriptively captured by way of standard measurements alone (see also Gal this volume). So if the dock became big by means of interscalar accretion, it grew awesome and even threatening as its expert interlocutors projected it as exceeding their established ways of seeing, scaling, and knowing.

The dock was also scaled by way of synecdoche—discursively rendered and materialized as part of otherwise inchoate wholes. More specifically, and as we will see, scalers figured the dock as a fragment of ecologies, histories, and futures too disastrous and overwhelming to otherwise imagine. Scaling by way of synecdoche was a literal as well as figurative project at the Oregon State University's Hatfield Marine Science Center, which now displays part of the dock as "an educational exhibit" designed to serve as "a vivid reminder that a similar earthquake and tsunami could just as easily happen here in the Pacific Northwest."[6] This foreboded catastrophe is what *New Yorker* writer Kathryn Schulz calls "the big one," or, worse, the "really big one": a disastrous amalgam of earthquake and tsunami expected to occur along the Cascadia subduction zone, which runs seven hundred miles along the Pacific Northwest. According to Schulz, seismologists anticipate that the magnitude of "the big one" will be somewhere between 8.0 and 8.6, with the "really big one" reaching between 8.7 and 9.2.[7]

Yet for Oregon officials charged with disaster preparedness, seismic scales capture only the most rudimentary feature of the future calamity. From their perspective, what makes the portended event so "big" is that the average Oregonian is still unaware of and unprepared for that which is inevitable.[8] The arrival of the dock provided an opportunity to publicly establish that Japan's disaster could one day become Oregon's own, all the while pinning responsibility for weathering that future on more-or-less properly alarmed individual citizens, who reasonably accept the limits of state preparation and intervention. In order to do this, the dock was officially scaled as a sign of a threat too big to prevent, too big to centrally manage, and too big to individually ignore.

As we will see, scalers of all stripes and with very different agendas worked to multiply the symbolic magnitude of the dock for the Oregonians who beheld it. And if the dock was rendered *big* by way of interscaling, and *awesome* through the recurring suggestion that it exceeded even the most sophisticated scalers' sense-making abilities, yet another pragmatics of scale emerges in the mediation of the Misawa dock. Namely, the scientists, public officials, museum curators, and laypeople who came to know the dock—whether as experimental fodder, educational exhibit, or memorial—engaged in a process of *de-escalation,* forging intimacy out of fear, threat, and awe.

In popular parlance, to de-escalate a crisis is to de-intensify it by bringing its disoriented participants to their senses.[9] In other words, de-escalation changes the qualities of a crisis only to the extent that it changes participants' perceptions of it. In the case of the dock, Oregonians came to understand what was far by touching what was now near, to feel the pain of Japanese victims by imagining their own future pain, to appreciate the "sea creatures that had survived hundreds of blistering days and nights crossing the thrashing Pacific,"[10] if eventually annihilating them. Accordingly, de-escalation—as we illustrate below—is not a matter of erasing or reducing the scalar qualities of phenomena. Rather, de-escalation involves forging explicit connections between the human senses and that which has been scaled as awesome and alien.

Along these lines, the media coverage of the dock suggests that its interlocutors, whether expert or lay, not only came to better know the dock from a number of angles but also began to *feel connected* to all that the dock had come to represent. As Havel commented, "One year later [the dock] has become the epitome of tsunami debris—an object that brought with it lessons, surprises and helped shape our response to every piece that's floated ashore in its wake."[11] Those lessons and responses, we argue below, would be impossible without the intensive scalar labor of the dock's many interactants as they (inter)scaled awe and de-escalated disaster.

In studying the media descriptions of the dock's landing,[12] we demonstrate that scaling is a practice that can—among other things—spawn a sense of intimacy and an ethic of interrelatedness at the same time it serves projects that discriminate, individuate, and alienate (cf. Tsing 2012, 2015). This is so because there is more than one pragmatics of scale: different sorts of sign activities amount to distinctive modes of scaling, each enjoying its own productive potentials.

BEHOLDING THE MONOLITH: EXERCISES IN INTERSCALATION

U.S. media coverage of the dock's landing often includes striking photographs: some feature a bare, straightforward aesthetic, while others, like those included in a *National Geographic* photo essay by journalist Brian Handwerk from June 2012, are more atmospheric. These photographs depict the dock marooned upon a crescent of beach, haloed in fog, and tucked into a curve of evergreen-dotted hills. The photograph in figure 6.1, titled *Monolith*, portrays the concrete slab as almost unworldly: cloaked in slime, bearded with sea life, and host to a variety of not readily identifiable creatures. In the foreground are two human bodies, gendered in blue and pink raincoats and holding hands as they tentatively approach the once floating object now resting in a shallow tide pool. Subject of the couple's transfixed gaze, and surrounded by other landsmen's buckets and tools, the "monolith" has been transported, apparently, from the umbra of the vast Pacific to the penumbra of Agate Beach–goers' field of sensation. Indeed, the photograph highlights the relationship of the life on the dock to its new human neighbors.

Such visual representations alone do little to tell us just what is "monolithic" about the Misawa dock. After all, it appears only slightly taller than the couple who stand before it, and a modest, five-step ladder has evidently lifted another person to its top. If the dock was to be beheld as alarmingly big, scaling was in order. Media descriptions almost always begin by emphasizing the dock's physical dimensions. Repeatedly, readers are told how much the dock weighs (132–165 tons, depending on the surveyor) and what its height (seven feet), width (sixty-six feet), and depth (nineteen feet) measure. And while *National Geographic* deemed the

FIGURE 6.1. *Monolith*. Photography by Robin Loznak/ZUMA Press/Corbis. From Brian Handwerk, "Pictures: Tsunami Dock Is 'Alien Mother Ship' of Species," *National Geographic* (June 13, 2012).

dock a "monolith," other journalists less poetically describe it as "massive," "enormous," or a "hulking monstrosity."[13]

The dock only continued to grow as its physical dimensions were interscaled with the distance it traveled and the time it took to arrive on Oregon's shores. Consider, for instance, this characteristic titling in a *Time* magazine article: "Massive Fishing Dock Washes Ashore in Oregon, 15 Months after Japanese Tsunami."[14] In a *USA Today* piece, the journalist not only recites the thousands of miles the dock traveled—a standard metric in the media descriptions of the dock—but also assigns the dock an agency usually reserved for animate entities. The journalist writes, "For a dock that was ripped from its pilings in the Japanese port city of Misawa during the March 2011 tsunami and then floated 5,000 miles across the Pacific Ocean—thanks to its Styrofoam filling—it seemed fitting it would put up a fight."[15]

The dock is also frequently interscaled relative to the size of the seaside town in Oregon where it landed, Newport—described in one article as a "small port city" and a "quiet, friendly town."[16] "Not for long!" the dock seemed to say through those who described it. "This past summer, residents of Newport were abuzz and tour buses shuttled people to the shoreline to check out the big slimy excitement that had washed ashore—a 20 meter long, 6 meter wide chunk of concrete," one journalist remarked.[17] The dock, when interscaled with the "thousands of visitors from the US and Canada" who came to visit it, does more than simply place the small town on the proverbial map.[18] It also arguably makes the dock even bigger in light of its popularity, prompting one journalist to title the dock a "tourism sensation" and others to deem it a "slimy celebrity."[19]

As the Oregon Parks and Recreation Department (OPRD) was counting seventy-three thousand cars in the Agate Beach parking lot between the dock's landing and dismantling—indicating a momentous "spike in tourism"[20]—others were counting the revenue generated by its now famous Japanese visitor. Once subjected to economic scaling, the dock became sign of potential boom, with locals lobbying the state not to bust it. Indeed, in several articles, the dock is interscaled with dollars, from the amount of money a tourist would spend to behold it (about $3,000) to the bids that the OPRD received to wreck it, dismantle it, and remove it from Oregon's jurisdiction ($79,922 to $128,702).[21]

While readers expect the *Wall Street Journal* to engage in economic scaling, the newspaper's explicit temporal scaling of the dock betrays its understanding that the monetary values of the dock dramatically intensify when interscaled. Consider that the *WSJ* article "Tsunami Relic Puts Beach on Map" begins this way: "Some use the word 'historic' to describe the big thing that washed ashore here. Others call it 'important.' For most, though, it elicits a simple phrase: 'The tsunami brought it in.'"[22] In article after article, the dock is scaled not simply as *big*, but as a *big event* with even bigger implications about the past and for the future. To call the dock a "relic," after all, is to imply a quasi-sacral connection to a history that promises to endure in perpetuity. Accordingly, journalists sometimes refer to the tourists who "flock to the site" as "pilgrims," reinforcing the idea that the dock confers transcendental knowledge and experience. Said one such pilgrim: "We had to bring the kids, the whole family, and at least touch it. . . . It's a piece of history."[23] Furthermore the "lasting impression" that the dock[24] was said to leave upon pilgrims—such as the hooded, hand-holding couple—was not just in relation to a disastrous past but also a portended future.

The dock's historic significance was thematized at Hatfield Marine Science Center (HMSC), which salvaged a corner of the dock for a permanent exhibit. The interim director's note in the newsletter begins, "It came ashore at night. Rather than the beginning of a bad novel, it is the middle of an interesting saga."[25] And while seismologists affiliated with the science center read this "saga" as an epochs-old tale of subduction and eruption, for the marine scientists at HMSC the big story was that, as the dock made its journey, "along for the ride were hundreds of millions of individual organisms, including a tiny species of crab, a species of algae, and a little starfish all native to Japan that have scientists worried if they get a chance to spread out on the U.S. West Coast."[26]

From the start, these sea creatures were central to the semiotic projection of the dock as monolithic and monstrous. Consider this description with attention to its interscaling virtuosity: "The 66-foot dock originated from the Japanese fishing port of Misawa and during its year-long, 5,000 mile journey has picked up a host of sea creatures including Asian crabs, sea stars, algae, urchins, barnacles, snails, and other life-forms. In fact, there are so many creatures on it that the Oregon Department of Fish and Wildlife estimate that they weigh over 100 tons."[27] Clearly, it is not just the aggregate weight of the tiny sea creatures attached to the dock that helps to interscale it as big here. It is also the ecosystemic threat that those creatures were feared to pose, given the alien agencies assigned to them. Indeed, the marine biologists who flocked to Agate Beach to study the dock and speak to journalists made clear that, aside from the dock-clinging sea organisms' physical size, there was nothing diminutive about them.

These marine organisms grew even bigger as they acquired anthropomorphic qualities in the descriptions by journalists and the scientists they quoted. The sea creatures are alternately described as "troublemakers," "invaders," "refugees," and "hitchhikers,"[28] given their "unprecedented" ability to withstand vast distances and time and survive extreme conditions. Although a few journalists use the quintessentially American monikers of "pilgrims" and "pioneers," the sea creatures are most commonly anthropomorphized as threatening Others. So while ecosystemic threat was marine biologists' and ecologists' most present concern, there are nevertheless echoes of xenophobic rhetoric deployed in discussions of human migration over the course of U.S. history (see also Cardozo and Subramaniam 2013; Helmreich 2009). For instance, in one case a quoted invasive-species biologist raises concerns about the organisms' reproductive capacities, noting that "they can disrupt entire ecosystems by outcompeting native creatures, . . . [and that by] compromising commercially valuable species—oysters or crabs, for example—invaders can damage economies."[29] A reader of the *Wall Street Journal* apparently inferred the analogy. In the online comments section on January 12, 2015, the reader recites a line from the article's interview with Oregon's aquatic invasive species coordinator—"You just don't know which ones are going to explode and become harmful"—to set up his own disturbing commentary: "Much like human migration, it seems."[30]

Before assuming this comment is an idiosyncratic one, we would be wise to consider that at the time of the Japanese sea species' arrival, the migration of the human species to the United States was at the very center of post-9/11 public debate. Perhaps in an effort to raise public awareness, and likely with little to no reflexive intent, interscalers nevertheless tethered a political-sociological discourse to a scientific one.[31] As a result, the dock grew even bigger, a sign of a looming social, economic, political, and ecological threat. Given this implied linkage of human and nonhuman migration, there is something profoundly discomfiting when one marine biologist—in reference to alien species and with a presumed cache of expert knowledge at hand—declares, "Kill them. Kill them all."[32]

SCALING THE ALIEN AND THE PRODUCTION OF AWE

John Chapman, of Oregon State University's Department of Fisheries and Wildlife and its affiliated Hatfield Marine Science Center, was the one who issued that warlike cry. A marine biologist with over forty years of experience and a scholarly focus on aquatic biological invasions, he was among the most vocal in his accounts of the dock's "unprecedented" journey and, therefore, one of the most accomplished interscalers when it came to the Misawa dock. For instance, in the caption accompanying the *National Geographic* photo pictured above (see figure 6.1), Chapman is quoted as saying, "While invasives sometimes find their way across oceans, the journey of this 'floating island' was unprecedented. So was the idea that hundreds of millions of organisms could survive in relatively food-poor, open-ocean waters without being picked clean by predators."[33] Scaling up the dock, from human-made structure to self-sustaining ecosystem and landmass, Chapman's description suggests that swift, expert intervention was required to deal with the two hundred species, including 1.5 tons of barnacles, mussels, urchins, crabs, sea stars, snails, algae, and marine microbes of all kinds, that he and his colleagues had identified.

Indeed, Chapman and others indexed expertise by way of their intensively scalar descriptions of the dock.[34] In doing so, they helped make the dock an object of public attention, and themselves the knowing purveyors of the lessons necessary to comprehensively see and understand it (see also Carr 2010; Silverstein this volume). At the same time, the dock's expert interlocutors commonly confessed that they had failed to predict what they so often referred to as "unprecedented." They further conceded that the dock defied their own established standards, thereby suggesting that it was conceptually unwieldy, even alien. Accordingly, the dock was commonly presented by the journalists—who relied heavily upon experts to tell them just what the dock really was—as a symbol of the very limits of what can be predicted, seen, and known, standing for what awes and can only be imagined.

When metrics fail, scalers can always turn to metaphors. In the case of the dock, metaphoric scaling abounds. In addition to the likening of the dock to "freight train boxcars" or colossal "alarm clocks,"[35] extraterrestrial comparisons further grew the dock. When the dock was scaled in reference to the "invasive" species attached to it, it was not simply in terms of their aggregate weight but also through reference to other, resonant kinds of invasions. And while Chapman, as a marine biologist, was obviously most concerned with "alien" sea creatures, his and others' descriptions of the dock elide the word's shades of meaning, evoking notions of the alien as extraterrestrial, foreign, exotic, disturbing, unassimilated, and (almost) unassimilable. Said Chapman himself, "It was like a spaceship landed on the beach. It was impossible except for one thing: it wasn't."[36] Whatever they claimed to definitively know about the dock, Chapman and his colleagues were also quick

INTERSCALING AWE, DE-ESCALATING DISASTER   141

FIGURE 6.2. Scaling the monolith. Still from *2001: A Space Odyssey* © MGM/Photofest.

to confess that when the dock first arrived, "we were caught flat-footed. . . . This was a close-encounter-of-the-fourth-kind type of event, where an alien mother ship from outer space lands on our shores."[37]

To be flat-footed, by popular definition, is to be either unprepared or uncompromising; and in Chapman's use of the term, both meanings seem to be in play.[38] He reflects that the scientific community was wholly unprepared to understand the "alien" invasion based on their already established cache of expertise. However, this lack of knowledge hardly halted efforts to prove how big the dock—as object, event, and possibility—really was. Rather, experts began to metaphorically scale what was already known with what could only be imagined, thereby growing the merely massive into the definitively awesome. We see this as Chapman digresses from knowing talk of alien sea creatures to reference another sort of invasion: one alien because it is outside of the bounds of scientific knowledge.

The *National Geographic* image pictured earlier—in both its composition and Chapman's captioning of it—invites comparison to another "monolith" in popular representation: the alien object of Stanley Kubrick's *2001: A Space Odyssey* (1968). Much like Agate Beach–goers are figured wonderingly assembling around the dock's cuboid form, the opening movement of Kubrick's film portrays awestruck hominids gathering around an extraterrestrial object. When Kubrick's "monolith" appears in the middle of a bare, prehistoric landscape, the tribe of hominids begin to interrogate it with their senses—its size, materials, temperature, texture, behaviors. Their habitual curiosity brings them increasingly closer, and they cry out at the monolith, tentatively approaching, and then touching it with fingertips and palms (figure 6.2).

The parallels between the hominids of Kubrick's film and of Oregon's coast extend beyond the fact that both tribes assemble around a mysterious object, called a monolith, which has arrived without seeming precedent. In both cases, initially, there is mutual wonder at the alien strangeness, followed by efforts to manage the awe by establishing patterns of relation. But before this can happen, what has come from afar needs to be brought near, through what Chapman refers to as a "close encounter." Beginning with Hynek's scaling,[39] famous among those who study unidentified flying objects (UFOs), as well as among fans of science fiction, ufologists have used the concept of the close encounter to establish a quasi-scientific classificatory system for humans' sightings of UFOs. In a seeming paradox, the UFO must be close enough for the viewer to be reasonably sure that it is not actually a mistaken plane or satellite. In other words, the UFO by definition is that which is scaled as unscalable with terrestrial tools. Awe is produced in the close encounter when the witness realizes that the UFO defies or exceeds its existing ways of seeing, scaling, and knowing.

Yet a close encounter of *the fourth kind*—the kind invoked by Chapman's description of the dock's arrival—complicates the agencies involved in the process of seeing, scaling, and knowing the unidentified object. After all, a close encounter of the fourth kind refers to human abduction by aliens. It was ultimately by way of abduction, in the sense of the term as used by American pragmatist Charles Sanders Peirce, that Chapman and others regained their footing in relation to the alien. They took the alien as the starting ground of their inquiry. For before one can abduct, in a Peircean sense, one must be abducted, in a Hynekian sense—by acknowledging the limits of existing ways of knowing (cf. Helmreich 2007). If induction is inference from a sample to a whole, abduction is inference from an observed body of data to an explanatory midlevel hypothesis, which need not be true, or even verifiable, but merely provide promising guidelines for further action and investigation (Peirce 1997; see also Carr 2015). In this sense, abduction motors knowledge production precisely to the extent that it radically troubles what is knowable in advance—a leitmotif of the scientific discourse about the dock.

To be sure, Chapman and his colleagues did not remain flat-footed for long. He continued to be a key protagonist in the process of knowledge production about the dock—a process heavily reliant on scaling techniques. As an affiliate of the science center where part of the dock would eventually be displayed as an educational exhibit, Chapman also understood that his profession would be served if the dock's accumulated awesomeness could be preserved through ongoing discursive management.

LOGGING THE DOCK, AND THE OFFICIAL MANAGEMENT OF AWE

While experts worked to demonstrate that they were acquiring ways to know and scale the dock in all its awesomeness—awesomeness they had helped discursively generate—state officials set about showing how the threat of the monolith would and should be managed. That the pragmatics of scaling the dock advanced particular state, as well as scientific, agendas is suggested by the Oregon Parks and Recreation Department (OPRD), whose spokesperson is quoted as saying, "The tsunami debris brought marine debris up to this high level of awareness. . . . I almost feel like knocking on wood when I say this but we're stronger than we were a year ago."[40]

When the dock washed ashore on Agate Beach, one of Oregon's public recreation sites, it entered OPRD's jurisdiction. Almost immediately, park officials initiated their own process of documenting the dock though an online "logbook."[41] The logbook is most obviously a textual exercise in identifying the dock, delegating responsibility, allocating resources for its management, and handling the uncertainty expressed by scientists and laypeople alike. That the logbook's entries are explicitly scalar invites us to think about the role of scaling in state bureaucracy (see also Meek this volume), and the scaling of risk more particularly.

According to the logbook, when OPRD staff first "responded to the site," the origin of the dock was still unknown. Loggers resorted to more proximate calculations: the dock was documented as "very large and heavy: 7' tall, 19' wide and 66' long," and as fashioned "primarily of concrete and metal," though "clearly designed to float." These rudimentary calculations promptly compelled a risk managerial response from the OPRD officials, who announced that the "large and heavy," yet buoyant, structure—nudged ever the more insistently by incoming tides—might pose a threat to curious or intrepid humans. Interscaling the dock with Newton's first law of motion and the tide table, park officials recorded their first of many warnings in the log: "Because of its size and the chance it could continue to settle or be moved by wave action, state park staff are posting warning tape and signs instructing the public to stay off the structure." Significantly, loggers nevertheless informed tourists that the beach would remain open, with one caveat: "Just stay off the dock."[42]

In subsequent log entries, scales and scalers proliferate, and a specific approach to risk management comes into view. On "Day Two" of the log, during the short time it took Japanese consulate officials to confirm that the metal placard inscribed in Japanese was evidence of the dock's origins, loggers note both that the dock had been tested for radiation, with negative findings, and that local scientists had discovered that some of the marine life attached to the structure were "specific to Japan." Having determined that the dock posed a potential ecological, if not radiological, threat, the loggers announced that they had elicited the help of fellow officials at the Oregon Department of Fish and Wildlife "to contain this threat."

The ODFW's engagement with the dock-as-threat is chronicled in the June 7 entry of the OPRD logbook. Bright and early, as marked by an 8:15 AM entry, a hybrid team of about a dozen ODFW staff and volunteers, with John Chapman among them, assembled alongside the marine biota that encrusted the dock's steel and concrete bearings. Their task was to make good on Chapman's call to "kill them all," in reference to what he had identified as nonnative species. Once the dock dwellers had been exterminated, loggers turned their attention to the disassembly of the dock itself. The June 13 entry lists the privately owned companies that placed bids to remove the "derelict dock at Agate Beach." Through that entry, the OPRD also advertises that it is "checking references" of the bidders, thereby indexing its own fiscal responsibility as a state agency.

In the meantime, park officials were counting tourists who had come to see what loggers had deemed a threatening and derelict site, making note of a sixfold increase of cars in its parking lot between June 2011 and June 2012. Scaling the dock in terms of tourists, logging officials, like the scientists they had enlisted, apparently gathered that it was best to preserve the awesomeness that the dock had acquired even as it was being physically disassembled. Significantly, the state's response was never to cordon off the dock from human visitors but, rather, to continue to engage them while issuing reminders that any risks those visitors took were their own. Accordingly, OPRD promised to post pictures of the dock's dismantling on its log and made note of the footbridge it had built for tourists so that they could watch the demolition live. Some of the tourists who did so reported boredom to journalists, as if their awe had been deflated as the dock was dismantled. However, the loggers continue to make note of the "surprises" and "difficulties" the demolition crew encountered, including the discovery that the dock was "heavier than expected," and that inspection of its underside revealed pink Japanese acorn barnacles.

Interestingly, the log ends not when the very last chunk of dock is carried off, but rather with a promise that the barnacles that adorned it are dead and the "stiff foam" has been "contained." That the logbook textually begins at these alien entities' end can be read as a projection of the OPRD's increasing managerial "strength," to recall their spokesperson's self-description. One might therefore conclude that if the professionals who interacted with the dock were emboldened, it was precisely because they portrayed themselves as responsibly managing the monolith: soliciting private corporations to remove it from state property and volunteers to help eliminate ecological threats to Oregon's shore. At the same time, loggers clearly delegated responsibility for human injury to those individuals who crossed state-erected footbridges. As we will see, this approach to risk management—one in which disaster risk is perceived as external to technological or social risks within modern life, and solutions hinge upon the public heeding technocratic knowledge (see also Hewitt 1995)—carried over to the project of disaster preparedness, once a chunk of the dock was relocated to the Hatfield Center.

If the OPRD's scaling furthered risk management strategies that individuated the dock's interlocutors, they were simultaneously participants in *de-escalating* the dock, rendering the awesome and alien features it had acquired intimate and relatable. For at the same time that they politically individuated the Oregonians they invited to the dock, loggers also made "the monolith" conceptually and affectively, as well as physically, approachable. Indeed, if park officials removed the dock from its shores and scientists exterminated the life that it once hosted, both groups were central in heightening the dock's affective dimensions.

DE-ESCALATING DISASTER, AND DOCKING (POST) HUMANISM

According to Kubrick, the Dawn of Man comes precisely when hominids begin to interrogate their relationships to objects and their ability to manipulate those objects to achieve certain ends. This first occurs when a bone is taken up in the hand of the hominid protagonist, who studiously weighs it and turns it over, considering its dimensions. He then hefts it overhead, letting it fall to splinter and scatter ribs and scapulae. Through experimentation he learns that interrelationships—among the forces of gravity, his arm muscle's contraction, the weight of the bone, the brittleness of the skeleton, and countless other inputs—can break, threaten, cudgel, and kill. For Kubrick, this knowledge-production process, and the relationality it spawns between hominid and bone, rock, tapir, and other hominids, is precisely what makes the human.[43] Similarly, media accounts of the Misawa dock suggest that Pacific Coasters who heeded loggers and visited the dock came to new understandings of themselves and their worlds by appreciating the extent of their interrelationships with others.

Scholarly advocates of the ontological turn in anthropology, sociology, and neighboring disciplines work to document precisely this kind of relationality, seeing it as the evidential fodder of posthumanism. This strain of thought is united by the shift of methodical attention away from individuated subjectivity and toward the patterns of relations that connect and constitute human and nonhuman things (see, for instance, Kohn 2013; Raffles 2002). Consider, for example, Donna Haraway's premise that "relationships are the smallest possible patterns for analysis; the partners and actors are their still-ongoing products. It is all extremely prosaic, relentlessly mundane, and exactly how worlds come into being" (2008, 25–26). Haraway (2003; 2008) and others are interested in the ethical implications of this relational ontology, suggesting that the ethics and politics of subjectivity may be overtaken by the ethics and politics of relations, but only if we begin to seriously consider nonhuman actors—whether dogs or docks—and accept our posthuman condition.

Accordingly, anthropologist Eduardo Kohn suggests that "what we learn about the world and the human through the ways in which humans engage with the world . . . undoes any bounded notion of what the human is" (2015, 313). While this may be the case, we are wise to keep in mind that taking relationships to be "the smallest possible patterns," as Haraway advises, is a matter of rescaling our analytical lens. After all, it is not that some underlying or essential interrelatedness is simply revealed by way of attentive scholarship. Relations, too, are a product of scaling, which is a profoundly perspectival and therefore humanistic endeavor, even when posthuman entities are constitutive participants (see Carr 2015).

One cannot help but recognize and appreciate the posthumanist overtones in the public discourse on the Misawa dock, focused as much of it is on the intimate relations forged with once-alien entities. And while much of the scalar discourse is concertedly scientific, the mediation of the dock-as-monolith nevertheless exalts the sensorial and imaginative capacities of those who behold it. This resonates with Stefan Helmreich's 2009 account of the sensitized scientists aboard the research vessel *Lobos* who explore the "alien ocean." Taking exception to Chandra Mukerji's account of deep sea research as "the expression of signatory techniques . . . [that] gives scientists a way to assert their culture, and not be overwhelmed by the scale of the ocean" (153), Helmreich proffers this observation: "To imagine scientists on *Lobos* hungering after some exterior, transcendent position would be to miss the more intimate relations they develop to their subjects of study. . . . On *Lobos*, the sensation is not of detachment from nature but of a pleasurable, technological immersion *in* it—an experience of being 'in the field' at once immediate and hypermediated" (44).

If such sensorial experiences are at once immediate and hypermediated, as Helmreich suggests, we should examine the pragmatics of scale in which those charged with knowing the ocean participate. Along the same lines, consider the way the OPRD logbook de-escalates the dock in the eyes of its interlocutors, thereby reorienting their senses. For although, at first blush, the logbook may simply appear to be a textual exercise of enacting expertise, more than risk management seems to be at play when the loggers warn: "Stay off the dock. Look, touch, reflect on the original tragedy that brought this visitor to Oregon's shores, but do not compound the sadness of that day by suffering an injury."[44] The dock is portrayed as a special "visitor" that other visitors might thoughtfully (if carefully!) engage. Furthermore, the at-risk Oregonians the loggers address are explicitly connected to those who fell victim to the "original tragedy," a tragedy that is putatively approachable and apprehensible through human touch.

Indeed, touch played an especially potent role in the dock's de-escalation. Even the *Wall Street Journal* found that *homo economicus* had ulterior motives for "flocking" to the "132-ton slab of reinforced concrete" when a quoted father explains that he wanted his family to "at least touch" what he called "a piece of history." Yet another father in the same article is quoted as saying, "'It's the tsunami![,]' . . . hoisting his son onto his shoulders so the boy could touch the concrete."[45] To the extent that the dock had been scaled as synecdoche—as in "it's the tsunami!" or "a piece of history"—these visitors apparently feel that they are accessing what is otherwise inchoate and barely imaginable when they touch the dock.

As little boys on their fathers' shoulders touched the dock, as synecdoche, in an effort to feel the awesomeness firsthand, other visitors described a profound experience of *continuity* with the dock and—by extension—all that it had come to represent; they too attributed their experience to the power of touch. Oregonians' physical encounters with the Misawa dock made the large, awesome, even alien feel proximate and intimate, at least in their sensorial self-portraiture. Consider this prototypical account:

> Kate Brown, 55, a resident of Newport, was one of those who rushed to see the dock after hearing about it. Touching it, she thought back to what happened in Japan, recalling horrific images of entire communities being swallowed by the ocean. Since the same ocean brought the 20-meter-long concrete and metal slab weighing over 100 tons from Misawa, Aomori Prefecture, all the way to her doorstep, thoughts of tsunami tearing apart the Oregon coast also flashed through her mind. "I was at a loss for words. I became a part of the tsunami. The tsunami and earthquake became a part of Oregon. People around me were shocked," she said.[46]

To extend Helmreich's (2009) terminology, an "immediate" reading of Brown's narrative goes something like this: Touching the dock instigates a series of thoughts, which we might conventionally assume to be in her own head. First she "[thinks] back to what happened in Japan"—that is, to "entire communities being swallowed by the ocean." Brown then realizes that it is the very "same ocean" that has brought the object she touches—described here again in concertedly interscalar terms—to her relatively diminutive doorstep. With that, she is thrust forward in time, almost as if riding a huge wave, confronted with the idea that the Oregon coastline could be similarly destroyed. The narrative is graced with a strikingly posthumanist climax as Brown feels herself to be part of the tsunami, which in turn became part of Oregon.

The sublime experience is typically figured as an experience *beyond language*. Note how Brown eloquently claims that she was at a loss for words in encountering the dock, though it seems that she is anything but. While Brown attributes the approximation of her own here and now, a shocking Oregon future, and "what happened in Japan" to the power of touch, let us underscore the semiotics of scale that allowed for this culminating experience. Recall that the dock had been synecdochically scaled in the media as *part of* all the entities Brown names as her experience: tsunami, history, and past and future devastation. The pragmatics of scale has also linked the dock, metaphorically and indexically, to a web of other relations within which Ms. Brown now includes herself. This is not to take away from the profound experience of being part of and in relation to, but rather to point to the scaling processes that allow for that experience. Of particular note here is the way that Kate Brown, like so many others, de-escalates what has been thought alien and Other by her claims of intimacy and relationality.

Significantly, the dock's de-escalation occurred across what is understood to be distinctive temporal planes, extending webs of relation across time. For as the "100 tons from Misawa, Aomori Prefecture" lands on Kate Brown's proverbial doorstep, it seems that future as well as past devastation is at the forefront of her mind. As we will see below, experts and officials alike worked hard to make the dock a sign of a portended American future. As an effect of these scalers' labors, Oregon residents absorbed the dock into their imaginaries of crisis (Povinelli 2011), leading them to ponder the ways that their fate was bound inextricably to (inter)actions among other people, places, and things. De-escalation reveals to interlocutors that the processes that threaten and secure their lives, such as "natural" disasters and preparedness efforts, are diachronic in ways that can be visualized, imagined, predicted, and forestalled.

Children hoisted upon parental shoulders learn that the relations that constitute them are highly contingent upon the mercurial weather patterns and tides. Tourists, like Kate Brown, travel way farther than they had planned as they recognize, through a complexly scaled dock, that their lives are the product of unfolding interactions that seem to outpace current horizons of knowledge and management. These sensibilities and socialities challenge the common scholarly implication that scaling degrades or defies human experience rather than, conversely, making it possible and apprehensible. The phenomenal experience of being "part of" and "related to" described by Brown and celebrated by posthumanists is not generated despite the pragmatics of scale but is, rather, their very product. To be sure, scaling is necessarily perspectival (Gal, this volume; Irvine, this volume), which directs the human eye/I to an object of interest. Yet the story of the Misawa dock also poignantly shows us how people can *feel,* as well as see, themselves as part of something larger through their scalar practices. So contrary to the concern that scale obviates "transformative relations" between species (Tsing 2015, 40), we suggest that scaling practices can illuminate the world and orient the human senses to others, even when there are competing pragmatics at play. After all, if we are to take Brown and her fellow Oregonians seriously, we must recognize that de-escalating the dock radically challenged notions of human beings as atomized or unique, unaware of their surrounds, and made them see and feel themselves to be "awash in relationships" (Whitington 2010, 166), whether with sea creatures, unpredictable waters, or Japanese victims.

SCALING SOCIALITIES AND EXHIBITING DISASTER

While overseeing the dock's demolition, amid the crowd of tourists, OPRD spokesperson Chris Havel predicted, "Once that last piece is off and gone . . . all this interest will probably evaporate like the morning clouds."[47] In this prognostication, Havel clearly underestimated the dock's enduring impact, for even after it was physically dismantled, its symbolic capacities endured. Proving that scaling work is never done, the dock continued to acquire new meanings as its ever-growing number of interlocutors made use of previous scalings in the service of a diverse range of projects.

For instance, the idea that the dock phenomenally connected Oregonians to a Japanese disaster and its victims was clearly fodder for the dock's exhibition at the Hatfield Marine Science Center (see figure 6.3a). And while the HMSC's institutional mission is to "improve scientific understanding of marine systems, coastal processes and resources, and appl[y] this knowledge to social, economic, and environmental issues,"[48] public officials focused on risk management recognized that this concertedly scientific endeavor could serve state interests.

Consider that among the many speakers at the exhibit's dedication—including representatives from the HMSC, Oregon Sea Grant, the City of Newport municipal government, and Oregon Emergency Management—all organizations that, according to an HMSC newsletter, "have been instrumental in developing the exhibit and increasing preparedness on the coast"—stood Japan's consul general, Hirofumi Murabayashi, and former Newport mayor Mark McConnell.[49] Their job was to read aloud in English and in Japanese, respectively, the posthumanist tract that had been inscribed on the dock exhibit's dedication plaque (figure 6.3b). The paired public officials initiated a moment of silence to honor the tsunami's Japanese victims as their audience contemplated the plaque's instructions to appreciate "the great power of the ocean to shape our lives, binding us to the natural world, and to each other"—a relationality that the dock had come to represent through the pragmatics of scale we detail above.

Though ritually reinforcing the human connection forged between those gathered at the dedication and those who lost their lives and livelihoods in Japan, it turns out that the dock's exhibit was not simply, nor primarily, a matter of memorialization. Rather, the exhibit was instrumentally geared toward educating Oregonians to prepare for, if not avoid, a similar fate. George Boehlert, biologist and former director of the HMSC, explained: "We're not putting it up as a shrine per se; it's really more for educational purposes. The real meaning here is really related to the disaster, and to give visitors a sense of the power and how serious the potential impact can be. Because people will be attracted to this piece of dock, I think the signage accompanying it will really serve a very valuable educational tool to educate folks about what the threats are and what could happen here."[50]

FIGURE 6.3A. Docking relations. Photograph by Rio Romero-Jurado.

This monument is dedicated to those who lost their lives
in Japan's Tohoku Earthquake and Tsunami
on March 11, 2011.

It honors the multitude of lives saved
by the preparedness efforts of the
Japanese government and its people.

May this dock's transoceanic journey remind us
of the great power of the ocean to shape our lives,
binding us to our natural world, and to each other.

Dedicated by the Community of Newport, Oregon
March, 2013

───────────────

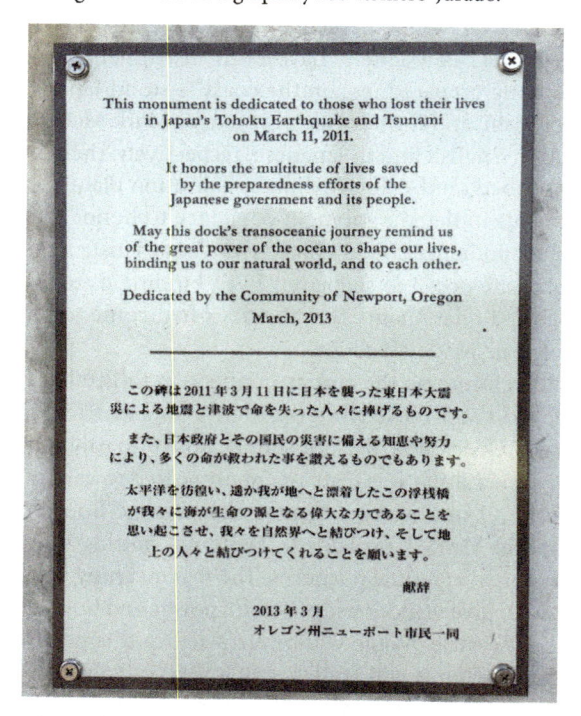

この碑は2011年3月11日に日本を襲った東日本大震
災による地震と津波で命を失った人々に捧げるものです。

また、日本政府とその国民の災害に備える知恵や努力
により、多くの命が救われた事を讃えるものでもあります。

太平洋を彷徨い、遥か我が地へと漂着したこの浮桟橋
が我々に海が生命の源となる偉大な力であることを
思い起こさせ、我々を自然界へと結びつけ、そして地
上の人々と結びつけてくれることを願います。

献辞

2013年3月
オレゴン州ニューポート市民一同

FIGURE 6.3B. Docking relations. Photograph by Rio Romero-Jurado.

FIGURE 6.4. Scaling disaster: head of the Tsunami Evacuation Interpretive Trail. Photograph by Rio Romero-Jurado.

Now adorned with signage that points not to a Japanese past (see figure 6.4) but rather to an Oregonian future, the dock is reendowed with the threat it had acquired through previous scalings. The director imagines that those American individuals "attracted to the piece of dock" can be empowered to assert individual agency in the face of what they now understand to be a serious threat, thanks to the museum's educational efforts. Significantly, the dock's indexical capacities were not just carefully aimed at an American future but also literalized: the dock exhibit now stands at the entrance of an evacuation route, or as the HMSC puts it, the "starting point for the new Tsunami Evacuation Interpretive Trail leading visitors to high ground."[51]

Explicitly coupling interpretation and evacuation, the posthumanist values the dock had acquired through its scaling were repurposed to support utilitarian science and state projects. It was therefore not surprising that, when asked about the exhibit at the dedication, McConnell recalled his visit to Sendai, Japan, to view the wreckage from the disaster this way: "You realize when you see it first-hand that you can't plan or build for an event of that magnitude, but you can prepare for it by educating yourself about the risks and creating strategies for safe evacuation. The exhibit will be a reminder that the tragedy in Japan could just as easily happen here."[52] With that, a familiar political narrative, one that absolves the state of responsibility to "plan and build" for natural disasters while urging citizens to nevertheless "prepare" through self-education, was mobilized by means of the representational apparatus the dock had acquired through its scaling.

If the primary purpose of the dock's permanent exhibition was science education, then the agenda of disaster preparedness and, by extension, the political program of neoliberal individuation, was clearly serviced by the dock's de-escalation. Consider, for instance, how the power of touch perdured in the remediation of the dock at the dedication. Speaking of the exhibit, the former mayor further remarked, "I wanted people to see it. To educate the people who visit Newport and the local residents about tsunamis and the debris washing up. It connected us to the people on the other side of the Pacific. It made the tsunami something they could touch."[53] Once erected at the museum as literal and figurative synecdoche, the dock served as a way to render science, as well as politics, as personal and sensorial.

The scientists affiliated with Hatfield also saw how the sensory experience produced by the scaled dock could focus their own efforts to predict and prevent natural and ecological disaster in Oregon. According to Mark Farley, the manager of the HMSC visitor center, one of the most popular features of the exhibit is the tsunami simulator, a "hands-on educational tool" that "offers a firsthand look at how destructive a tsunami can be."[54] As Farley sees it, the sensorial responses cultivated by the dock's scaling are crucial to getting Oregon residents to take seriously the impending disaster threat and educate themselves about the risks and preventive measures—that is, to appreciate and feel what is scientifically predictable if not known.

CONCLUSION: BEAUTIFUL, BOUNTIFUL SCALING

Contra Havel's prediction that the symbolic potency of the dock would fade, others rightly insisted that the "saga" of the dock would not end anytime soon. One spokesperson for another tsunami-debris exhibit, at the Columbia River Maritime Museum in Washington, implied that the dock's symbolic tenacity was closely linked to its scalability. He stated, "Almost exactly two years and 5,000 miles later and here is a piece of wreckage from a natural disaster almost beyond comprehension, 10 miles from the museum on the shores of Washington. It has connected us in this almost unimaginable way. Fifty, 100 years from now, I think it will continue to be an interesting story."[55]

Scaling never ceases, and its products can never be fully determined in advance nor forever stabilized. The saga of the dock illustrates that scalings can be used for various projects, and that scalers—whether ecologists, marine biologists, public officials, humanists, or posthumanists—borrow each other's metrics and metaphors, putting those terms to work toward different ends. And while we may bemoan the way the dock was ultimately used in a political project of individuation, if not alienation, we must recall the lability that things acquire precisely because they are subject to our sign practices, including scaling. As we have seen, scaling means that all forms of life can be brought close as well as cast afar. Scaling can create collectivities, bringing nonhuman entities within them, as easily as it can individuate them.

To be sure, scaling fixes our perspective and, accordingly, propels some projects at the expense of others. But there is nothing inherently dehumanizing nor atomizing about scaling. The story of the Misawa dock demonstrates that while certain governance strategies are served by scaling projects, so too are sensory experience, relationality, and our very understanding of who, where, and what we are. People may use scalar discourse to anchor themselves in profoundly moral, deeply felt relationships forged across established geographical, national, temporal, and experiential borders. So while we must be ever alert to the ways institutions impose constraining scalar logics that limit our imagination, we must also remember that scaling can transport us across space and time, introduce us to countless other actors, and dock us to any number of shores.

NOTES

We acknowledge the following people for their helpful comments on and contributions to this paper: Richard Bauman, Susan Gal, Michael Lempert, and Rio Romero-Jurado.

1. Misawa was one of the towns devastated by the magnitude 9.0 undersea earthquake that occurred off the coast of Japan. The earthquake unleashed a massive tsunami that wrought widespread death and destruction, particularly along Japan's northeastern coastline. This compound disaster resulted in the deaths of tens of thousands, widespread injury, over twenty-five hundred people missing, and more than two hundred thousand people internally displaced—many of whom are still living in temporary housing as the nation confronts bureaucratic obstacles and construction delays. Japan also sustained unprecedented damage to homes, property, land, and infrastructure, leading the World Bank to deem the natural disaster the costliest in world history (Victoria Kim, "Japan Damages Could Reach $235 Billion, World Bank Estimates," *Los Angeles Times*, March 21, 2011, http://articles.latimes.com/2011/mar/21/world/la-fgw-japan-quake-world-bank-20110322).

2. Lori Tobias, "Japanese Tsunami Dock Came Bearing Lessons for Oregon Officials, Coastal Residents," *The Oregonian/Oregon Live*, June 4, 2013.

3. Ibid.

4. Jes Burns, "More Japanese Tsunami Debris Will Wash Up This Winter on Northwest Shores, Scientists Predict," *Northwest Public Radio*, December 9, 2014.

5. Eric Wagner, "The Tiniest Tsunami Refugees," *Slate*, August 15, 2013, www.slate.com/articles/health_and_science/science/2013/08/tsunami_and_earthquake_debris_from_japan_washes_ashore_in_the_united_states.html; Katy Muldoon, "After Long, Cold Trip across Pacific on Tsunami Debris, Sea Creatures Find Little Warmth," *Wall Street Journal*, January 12, 2015, www.wsj.com/articles/after-long-cold-trip-across-pacific-sea-creatures-find-little-warmth-1421108242.

6. "OSU's Hatfield Marine Science Center to Unveil Japanese Dock Exhibit on March 10," Oregon State University News and Research Communications, February 27, 2013, http://oregonstate.

edu/ua/ncs/archives/2013/feb/osu%E2%80%99s-hatfield-marine-science-center-unveil-japanese-dock-exhibit-march-10.

7. Schulz writes, "In the Pacific Northwest, the area of impact will cover some hundred and forty thousand square miles, including Seattle, Tacoma, Portland, Eugene, Salem (the capital city of Oregon), Olympia (the capital of Washington), and some seven million people. When the next full-margin rupture happens, that region will suffer the worst natural disaster in the history of North America." What's more, "the science is robust . . . [and] the odds of the big Cascadia earthquake happening in the next fifty years are roughly one in three. The odds of the very big one are roughly one in ten." "The Really Big One," *New Yorker*, July 20, 2015, www.newyorker.com/magazine/2015/07/20/the-really-big-one.

8. Ibid.

9. The American English term *de-escalate*, which appears to be of Cold War origin, means: "to reduce the intensity of a war or international conflict." The term is now widely used in American policing, where it means: "to defuse conflict and potential violence through communicative techniques." And most recently, in relation to the widespread public concern about overzealous policing, it means: "to reduce the chance of using force against a citizen during a suddenly antagonistic encounter" (Timothy Williams, "Long Taught to Use Force, Police Warily Learn to De-escalate," *New York Times*, June 27, 2015). It has a similar meaning in American parenting discourse, where to de-escalate is to calm a potential outburst or tantrum through verbal and other communicative techniques.

10. Muldoon, "After Long, Cold Trip."

11. Tobias, "Japanese Tsunami Dock Came Bearing Lessons."

12. We conducted a comprehensive literature review and document analysis of North American media sources covering the dock, beginning with its arrival in June 2012 and continuing through early 2015. These sources included local and national newspapers, magazine articles, blog posts, official documents released by Oregon state department officials, presentations by local scientists, newsletters for the Hatfield Marine Science Center and other local organizations made available online, and written materials from tourism websites, among others. Alongside these media sources, we considered English-language Japanese publications, such as the *Japan Times* and the *Asahi Shimbun*, English edition.

13. Its descriptions as "massive" and a "hulking monstrosity" come from Nick Carbone, "Massive Fishing Dock Washes Ashore in Oregon, 15 Months after Japanese Tsunami," *Time*, June 7, 2012, http://newsfeed.time.com/2012/06/07/massive-fishing-dock-washes-ashore-in-oregon-15-months-after-japanese-tsunami/print/; and its description as "enormous" is from Max Eddy, "Japanese Dock Torn Loose in Tsunami Washes Ashore in Oregon Bringing Unwelcome Guests," *The Mary Sue*, June 8, 2012, www.themarysue.com/japanese-ghost-dock/.

14. Carbone, "Massive Fishing Dock Washes Ashore."

15. Cara Pallone, "Dock from Japan Leaves a Lasting Impression," *USA Today*, August 2, 2012.

16. Tomoji Watanabe and Yu Miyaji, "Misawa Pier Becomes Slimy Celebrity on Oregon Beach," *Asahi Shimbun*, January 13, 2013.

17. Ibid.

18. Tobias, "Japanese Tsunami Dock Came Bearing Lessons"; Joel Millman, "Tsunami Relic Puts Beach on Map," *Wall Street Journal*, June 20, 2012.

19. Lori Tobias, "Tsunami Dock Memorial Unveiling Planned on March Anniversary Date," *The Oregonian/Oregon Live*, September 15, 2012; Watanabe and Miyaji, "Misawa Pier Becomes Slimy Celebrity."

20. Pallone, "Dock from Japan Leaves a Lasting Impression."

21. Millman, "Tsunami Relic Puts Beach on Map."

22. Ibid.

23. Ibid.

24. Pallone, "Dock from Japan Leaves a Lasting Impression."

25. Janet Webster, "Notes from the Interim Director," *Upwelling* (Hatfield Marine Science Center newsletter) 10 (August 2013), http://hmsc.oregonstate.edu/files/main/upwelling_v10_1_2013.pdf.

26. RT.com, "Boxcar-Size Dock from Japan Tsunami Washes Up on US Beach," June 7, 2012, www.rt.com/news/japan-tsunami-beach-us-280/.

27. Timon Singh, "Japanese Tsunami Dock Hits Oregon Beach with Army of Alien Species Attached!" *Inhabit*, June 19, 2012, http://inhabitat.com/japanese-tsunami-dock-hits-oregon-beach-with-army-of-alien-species-attached/.

28. The quotations "troublemakers" and "hitchhikers" are from Brian Handwerk, "Pictures: Tsunami Dock Is 'Alien Mother Ship' of Species," *National Geographic*, June 13, 2012, http://news.nationalgeographic.com/news/2012/06/pictures/120613-tsunami-dock-japan-oregon-aliens-invasive-species-science/; "invaders" is found in both Rebecca Jacobson and Jenny Marder, *PBS NewsHour*, June 27, 2012, and Muldoon, "After Long, Cold Trip"; and "refugees" comes from Wagner, "Tiniest Tsunami Refugees."

29. Handwerk, "Pictures: Tsunami Dock Is 'Alien Mother Ship.'"

30. Graham Sanders, comment on Muldoon, "After Long, Cold Trip," www.wsj.com/articles/after-long-cold-trip-across-pacific-sea-creatures-find-little-warmth-1421108242.

31. Consider also Stefan Helmreich's (2009) book, *Alien Oceans*, which addresses how taxonomic and political questions get entangled in the classification of marine organisms. He argues that in Hawaii, where the term for native marine species is also the term that indigenous Hawaiians use to describe themselves, feelings of nationalism and xenophobia get baked into marine science, which in turn compounds a sense of alienation and threat.

32. Muldoon, "After Long, Cold Trip."

33. Handwerk, "Pictures: Tsunami Dock Is 'Alien Mother Ship.'"

34. Alongside marine biologists and ecologists, ocean seismologists seized upon the dock as a way to project the predictive potential if not the established knowledge of their vocation. For instance, a computer programmer in the University of Hawaii's International Pacific Research Center—which, according to an article in the *Christian Science Monitor*, reportedly tracked "the 1.5 million tons of tsunami debris estimated to still be floating across the Pacific"—told reporters, "Just how the dock float happened to turn up in Oregon was probably determined within sight of land in Japan. . . . That's where the winds, currents and tides are most variable, due to changes in the coastline and the features of the land, even for two objects a few yards apart" (Jeff Barnard, "Tsunami Debris: Dock from Japan Floats 5,000 Miles to Oregon [+ Video]," *Christian Science Monitor*, June 7, 2012, www.csmonitor.com/USA/Latest-News-Wires/2012/0607/Tsunami-debris-Dock-from-Japan-floats-5-000-miles-to-Oregon-video).

35. Ibid.; Tobias, "Japanese Tsunami Dock Came Bearing Lessons."

36. Muldoon, "After Long, Cold Trip."

37. Handwerk, "Pictures: Tsunami Dock Is 'Alien Mother Ship.'"

38. According to the 2015 *Oxford English Dictionary* online, *flat-footed*, meaning "unready, not 'on one's toes,'" is from U.S. baseball slang of the early twentieth century. In its prior use, beginning in the early nineteenth century, it had meant "downright, plain and positive," in the sense of planting one's feet firmly.

39. J. Allen Hynek, PhD, an American astrophysicist who served as chair of the Astronomy Department at Northwestern University and as scientific adviser to the United States Air Force on studies of UFOs following the Second World War, developed his eponymous scale in an effort to classify UFOs in a way that he claimed was compatible with science. For Hynek, this relation between fact and (mis)representation presents a fundamental "UFO problem," outlined in his book *The UFO Experience: A Scientific Inquiry*: "Either UFO observations represent genuinely new empirical observations—that is, new in the sense that they do not fall immediately into place in the present scientific framework—or they simply are misperceptions and misidentifications" (1972) 1998, 10). Hynek asserts that UFOs fall

into the former category, but that an inherent conservatism in science resists any explanation of phenomena that exceeds current scales. Referencing the ideas of philosopher of science Thomas Goudge, Hynek writes, "Throughout history any successful explanation scheme, including twentieth-century physics, acts somewhat like an establishment and tends to resist admitting new empirical observations (unless they have been generated directly within the framework of that explanation scheme).... 'For,' Goudge continues, 'if the establishment assimilates the new observations into the present explanation scheme, it implies that the empirical observations are not genuinely new.'"

40. Tobias, "Japanese Tsunami Dock Came Bearing Lessons."

41. "Dock Ashore at Agate Beach," Oregon.gov, www.oregon.gov/OPRD/PARKS/pages/agatebeach_dock.aspx. According to historian Margaret Schotte, the nautical logbook emerged in fifteenth- and sixteenth-century Europe. Its purpose was anticipatory as well as documentary: it helped the captain record important information, such as the ship's speed and location, so as to assist in future voyages. Shortly thereafter, the practice of keeping logbooks expanded, and the information contained within them became "standardized, pooled, and exchanged deliberately with 'virtual communities of observers dispersed over time and space'" (2013, 286). Then, in the early- to mid-seventeenth century, the logbook's function expanded further to include a "daily record about distant geography, climate patterns, and geopolitics, to say nothing of the events—economic, social, even legal—that occurred on board ship" (284). The eighteenth century saw a decline in logging amid concerns about its efficiency; though it remained standard to keep logbooks, their records tended to be less comprehensive and were thought to be less reliable.

42. "Dock Ashore at Agate Beach," Oregon.gov, entry for June 5, 2012.

43. Arguably, the humanness that emerges in the film might be thought of as an assembling of living (e.g., the tapir) and nonliving (e.g., rock, bone) things, as well as a practice of (inter)scaling that is not limited to humans but rather is performed, in varying ways and to varying degrees, by other intelligent alien and machine (re)actors in the film, including the alien monolith and the sentient computer HAL 9000. To become human is more than a genetic legacy: it is also the embodiment of practices of scaling.

44. "Dock Ashore at Agate Beach," Oregon.gov, entry for June 8, 2012.

45. Millman, "Tsunami Relic Puts Beach on Map."

46. Rene Chen, "Washed-Up Dock Stirs Awareness in Oregon," *Japan Times,* March 20, 2013.

47. Pallone, "Dock from Japan Leaves a Lasting Impression."

48. Oregon State University Hatfield Marine Science Center, *Oregon State University Hatfield Marine Science Center Strategic Plan* (Corvallis: Oregon State University, December 2006), https://ir.library.oregonstate.edu/xmlui/bitstream/handle/1957/5036/HMSCStratPln1206.pdf?sequence=1.

49. "The Story of the Tsunami Dock," *Upwelling* (Hatfield Marine Science Center newsletter) 10 (August 2013), http://hmsc.oregonstate.edu/files/main/upwelling_v10_1_2013.pdf.

50. Tobias, "Japanese Tsunami Dock Came Bearing Lessons."

51. "OSU, City of Newport Plan for Exhibit Featuring Piece of Tsunami Dock," *Oregon State University News and Research Communications,* September 12, 2012, http://oregonstate.edu/ua/ncs/archives/2012/sep/osu-city-newport-plan-exhibit-featuring-piece-tsunami-dock.

52. Ibid.

53. Chen, "Washed-Up Dock Stirs Awareness."

54. Ibid.

55. Tobias, "Japanese Tsunami Dock Came Bearing Lessons."

PART THREE

PREDATORY SCALES

Encompassment and Evaluation

7

SCALING RED AND THE HORROR OF TRADEMARK

Constantine V. Nakassis

OWNING THE SOLE OF ANOTHER

... I see a red shoe with my red sole. I can't see anything else.
—CHRISTIAN LOUBOUTIN DEPOSITION, JUNE 13, 2011, CHRISTIAN LOUBOUTIN V. YVES SAINT LAURENT (2011)

In 1992, Christian Louboutin was a well-known, if still up-and-coming, women's shoe designer. The now famous, and much repeated, story of his success was one of the material contingencies of quality. Inspecting one day a factory prototype made from a design sketch of his, he was disappointed. The color was different on leather than it was on paper. It had a "black thickness" to it that wasn't in his original drawing. Attempting to make the color on the shoe match the color on the paper, he commandeered the bright red nail polish of his nearby assistant (who was busily doing her nails) and began to paint the outsole of the shoe (Christian Louboutin v. Yves Saint Laurent 2011, doc 32–1, p. 9).[1] This lacquered red sole immediately became, so the story goes, Louboutin's signature design element. Indeed, since 1992, Louboutin has made almost none of his popular and expensive shoes without it. As Lauren Collins (2011, 83) wrote in the *New Yorker*, the red sole "render[ed] an otherwise indistinguishable product instantly recognizable." The "lacquered red sole" on "women's high fashion designer footwear" was finally trademarked in the United States in 2008, recognized by the government as a source-indexing sign of Louboutin's authorial production, of his brand, his identity (see figure 7.1).

Two years later, in the fall of 2010, legendary French fashion house Yves Saint Laurent (YSL) released its 2011 Cruise collection (see figure 7.2). Among many other clothing items and accessories, the Cruise collection featured YSL's signature

Int. Cl.: 25

Prior U.S. Cls.: 22 and 39

United States Patent and Trademark Office

Reg. No. 3,361,597
Registered Jan. 1, 2008

TRADEMARK
PRINCIPAL REGISTER

CHRISTIAN LOUBOUTIN (FRANCE INDIVIDUAL)
24 RUE VICTOR MASSÉ
PARIS, FRANCE 75009

FOR: WOMEN'S HIGH FASHION DESIGNER FOOTWEAR, IN CLASS 25 (U.S. CLS. 22 AND 39).

FIRST USE 0-0-1992; IN COMMERCE 0-0-1992.

THE COLOR(S) RED IS/ARE CLAIMED AS A FEATURE OF THE MARK.

THE MARK CONSISTS OF A LACQUERED RED SOLE ON FOOTWEAR. THE DOTTED LINES ARE NOT PART OF THE MARK BUT ARE INTENDED ONLY TO SHOW PLACEMENT OF THE MARK.

SEC. 2(F).

SER. NO. 77-141,789, FILED 3-27-2007.

NORA BUCHANAN WILL, EXAMINING ATTORNEY

FIGURE 7.1. Christian Louboutin's U.S. Patent and Trademark Office–registered trademark for "a lacquered red sole on footwear."

monochromatic Tribute, Tribtoo, Palais, and Woodstock women's shoe designs. One of the colors used was red (in fact, four different reds). The overall color palette (the so-called DNA of the brand) of the Cruise collection, and the use of reds in particular, was a citational *renvoi* to the 1960s signature wear of the house founder, Yves Saint Laurent, including to his first advertising campaign in color, which featured a bright red dress (CL v. YSL 2011, doc 34, p. 3).

In January 2011, Louboutin became aware of YSL's all-red shoes, shoes whose sole was, he claimed, "virtually identical" to his own (CL v. YSL 2011, doc 1, p. 15). On April 7, 2011, after a series of communiqués that failed to resolve what Louboutin saw as YSL's attempt "to take unfair advantage" of his brand's "goodwill," Louboutin filed for a preliminary (and, if successful, thereafter permanent) injunction in the southern district of New York against YSL's production of its all-red shoes, arguing that it was likely that the case, if it went to trial, would prove trademark infringement and dilution (under state law and the federal Lanham

DNA OF THE BRAND – YSL COLORS

" A chaque coin de rue, à Marrakech, on croise des groupes impressionnants d'intensité, de relief, des hommes et des femmes où se mêlent des caftans roses, bleus, verts, violets....c'est étonnant de se dire qu'ils ne sont en fait que l'improvisation de la vie"

" On each corner of the street, in Marrakech, you find impressive group with intensity, with relief, men and women where rose, blue, green and violet caftans are mixed together...It is incredible you might think there are actually the improvisation of life"

Yves Saint Laurent

1967

In 1967, Mr. Saint Laurent discovered Marrakech. He bought his first house located in the medina. Dazed by the bright colored garments in the street of the city, he has been strongly inspired by this combination of vivid tints.

Throughout his collection, he has explored audacious mix creating the YSL color palette. Fuchsia/orange Rive Gauche logo and opium/purple Opium fragrance, are the emblematic association the designer has created

1984   1996   1996

Cruise 2011

Quintessential YSL color palette creates a tonic and feminine look

For internal use only   Women's Cruise 2011 – Shoes training

FIGURE 7.2. Yves Saint Laurent's "DNA of the Brand—YSL Colors" (from CL v. YSL 2011, doc 34–1, p. 6).

Act), and unfair competition and false designation of origin (under the federal Lanham Act). YSL, Louboutin's lawyers argued to the district court, had to be stopped. Otherwise, the very basis of Louboutin's identity—his red sole—would be crushed under the weight of so many others' soles.

Central to this case was a confounding question: can the color red be trademarked? Can it be owned, enclosed from the commons and tied to a brand identity, transformed into a distinguishing mark on commodities circulating in the market under the name of their source, Christian Louboutin? Or would claiming the red of the outsole constitute an unfair monopoly? Would it stifle "the market" and impoverish "the commons" by allowing Louboutin's brand name to encompass both, contracting the space for competition by disallowing others to use "his" color on their shoes?

The district court of southern New York was called on to draw the line between the commons and intellectual property, between what should be available to all and what can be owned by some, between the market (and the commodity designs that compete within it) and the mark, between Yves Saint Laurent and Christian Louboutin. Not only did Christian Louboutin's and Yves Saint Laurent's brand identities, and thus businesses, depend on where that line was drawn, so did the very contours of the fashion market itself, a domain that turns both on the free play, and availability, of particular qualities (e.g., color as design element) and on the intelligibility of brand identity (e.g., Louboutin, YSL). As this case demonstrates, deciding on a trademark is a decision on what a market is, just as it is a decision on what the extent of the commons is.

In this chapter I show how these questions and decisions are fundamentally scalar in nature, as are the entangled terms upon which they turn: *market, commons, monopoly,* and *trademark.* I demonstrate how central to trademark law, to the adjudication of the red of a high-heeled shoe, are the pragmatics, and metapragmatics, of scale.

METAPRAGMATICS OF SCALE

Scales, as geographers and anthropologists have argued, are *made* through social practices (Carr and Lempert this volume; Latour 2005; Moore 2008; Agha 2011; Lempert 2012). There is always a social project, and thus a pragmatics, of scale. As linguistic anthropologists have suggested, the pragmatics of any social activity are mediated through their *metapragmatics,* the particular ideologies and reflexive practices that construe and regiment, mediate and materialize, that very activity (Silverstein 1993; Agha 2007). Studying scale-making practices requires us to attend to those ethnographic sites where scale itself is reflexively attended to, where the pragmatics of scale are themselves the object of concern and action. As I show in this chapter, trademark law is both a site of scale-making and is characterized by reflexive worry about itself as a site of scale-making, a (metapragmatic) worry that is part and parcel of how the law (pragmatically) makes scale. The play of this dialectic, I further suggest, is how the law makes claims to speak authoritatively. That is, the reflexivity of the law to its scalar practices and their effects is central to the law's attempts to constitute its jurisdiction (Richland 2013) *as* a site for scale-making.

QUALITY OF SCALE, SCALING OF QUALITY

To speak of practices of (meta)scaling is to speak of the categories and relations between categories that constitute the scale in question (Moore 2008, 215). Such categories and relations are always fleshed out by particular *qualities,* whether these are the qualities of "verticality," "hierarchy," or "spatiality" that (early) geographers used in scaling their objects of inquiry (Moore 2008, 206 and references therein); the "star-shaped" "flatness" described by Latour (2005, 171–2); the "empty, homogenous time" of the scaling of the nation-state (Anderson 2008) or the durative, continual unfolding of other modes of sovereignty and (national) belonging (Eisenlohr 2006); or even the "real-time" quality of discursive interaction (Silverstein 1997; Wortham 2006).

There is a *quality of scale* and a *scaling of quality,* the way in which, say, U.S. case law constitutes the scale of trademarks and the market (according to what the law calls "functionality," as I discuss below) and the way in which such a quality of scale is imbricated in scaling a quality—say, the red of a shoe's outsole.[2] In the pages below, I explore the ways in which trademark case law attunes itself to the qualities of the scales that it draws on in the process of adjudication, and how such attunement is caught up with the project of scaling qualities and the anticipated effects therein. In doing so, I focus on two types of (meta)scaling: first, that of determining the *extent* of particular categories like trademark vis-à-vis the commodities and markets with respect to which they operate, and how the constitution of those categories may engender certain desired or undesired scalar effects. In particular, I show how courts are concerned with how their adjudication of categories like trademark may alternatively create a healthy market wherein competition is encouraged, or an unhealthy one where pernicious monopolies reign and competition is hindered. Second, I focus on legal practices that reflect on scalar relations internal to the law—that is, on the relationship *between* particular qualities of trademarks and commodities (e.g., as representational, functional, source-indexing) and types of intellectual property (copyright, patent, and trademark). The law attempts to keep such relations distinct and, thus, such categories pure and coherent. However, as I show, the qualities that characterize different kinds of intellectual property continually threaten to migrate *across* these categories, creating paradoxes that play into courts' reflexive worries about their scalar performativity (e.g., to allow unfair monopolies and thus hamper markets). Such problematical interscalarities, as I suggest later in the chapter, threaten to undermine the very justification of trademark law and, thus, are horrific to it. And yet, they follow from a contradiction that resides at the very heart of intellectual property: namely, that intellectual property law demands that trademarks simply index their source and do no more even as every trademark, as a material, aesthetic (de)sign, is necessarily more than a source-designating index. This contradiction follows, as I argue in the conclusion, from the very distinction of trademark and commodity.

FUNCTIONALITY AND TRADEMARK

These boots are made for walkin', and that's just what they'll do. One of these days these boots are gonna walk all over you.
—LEE HAZLEWOOD, "THESE BOOTS ARE MADE FOR WALKIN'," 1966, AS SUNG BY NANCY SINATRA

Trademark law is a scalar project, one that attempts to determine simultaneously the extent of "the market" (and to increase its size through limited monopolies) and the extent of "the commons" (and to maintain, and even increase, it through protections against unfair monopolies). This is based on a particular scalar logic that is equal parts pragmatic and ideological.

In the U.S. legal context, the default assumption is that free competition in the market is founded on a "right to copy" (McKenna 2011). Such a right is, in some sense, what constitutes a market, that domain of comparable goods that, by virtue of their differentiable sameness vis-à-vis some aspect or use value, compete. Against this right to copy, intellectual properties like copyright and patent are partial exceptions, granted precisely because the unhindered play of the market distorts the public good that accrues through such "free" organization of economic activity. Intellectual property, so goes its justification, provides limited monopoly rights precisely so as to *encourage* market activity. Without such exceptions, the market would suffer. The incentive for producers to invest in product creation and innovation would be undermined by the ability of other producers to cheaply copy such goods. Such copying would stifle economic growth and efficiency, disincentivize innovation and creativity, and thus dampen the ability of the market to serve the larger public. The "market" here is construed by the law as both the effect and limit of intellectual property protection.

The ideological stakes of American intellectual property law, then, turn on a tension between market and monopoly, a tension that materializes in the category of intellectual property, that which can be justifiably withdrawn from the "commons" and yet does not also constitute an unfair, and hence illegal, monopoly. This tension is a result of the law as much as it is the law's object of jurisdiction. The quality that mediates this tension, and thus this scalar project, is what is called, in legal discourse, "functionality."[3]

Intellectual property categories of copyright and patent are determined on the (impossible) distinction between the aesthetics or representational "content" of some commodity (or aspect thereof)—which may be protected by copyright—or by its utility or "function," which may be protected by patent.[4] "Function" here has a double valence. On the one hand, it appeals to commonsense notions of utility, the good as something that is bought or sold so as to perform some function (e.g., a shoe that protects the foot), as opposed to representing an idea or a concept (e.g., a book that expresses a method for accounting). On the other hand, function is also routed through the detour of the market, which is to say that function denotes that which is inherent to a good qua commodity, that which defines a good such that it competes with other (similar) goods in a market.

In contrast to copyright and patent rights, which protect (aspects of) the commodity itself, trademark rights protect the semiotic relation that the mark mediates. Trademarks protect, or rather instate, the indexical relation—more specifically, the rigid-designating relation (Kripke 1981; Nakassis 2012)[5]—between a commodity and its nominal production source for some relevant social domain of consumers (Coombe 1998); or, in a more modern idiom where "source" is often anonymous and perhaps irrelevant to consumer activity (Klein [1999] 2000), trademarks protect the iconic indexical relationship between commodity and brand image (Nakassis 2013a). The trademark distinguishes goods not by their commodity type or "market" (the functional category within which competitors compete—say, "shoes") but by the entity that stands as their putative origin (say, Louboutin). The trademark, then, is defined by the law as a transparent medium that allows consumers to rationally navigate otherwise opaque markets where origin and source are unclear, thereby protecting them against fraud and "confusion."[6] The trademark thus is not functional (in the sense of patent), nor does it represent (in the sense of copyright). Rather, it is a supplement to the commodity, a sign independent from it that merely acts as a relay of the good's origin and, as far as the law is concerned, no more.[7]

And indeed, the trademark, *as* a trademark, should *not* be representational or functional. Hence, if one can show that some putative mark is representational with respect to the market within which it circulates, as in the case of "generic" trademarks that denotationally describe the commodity type to which they are appended (e.g., "Shoe" brand shoes; see Coombe 1998; Nakassis 2012), then such a mark may be canceled. And if a putative mark can be shown to be functional—that is, if some quality of it is essential to the purpose or use of a good (if it is critical to the commodity genus within which firms compete, which is also to say if it constitutes the relevant market) and thus disadvantages other firms and "unfairly" distorts competition (e.g., by raising their costs to compete or by forcing them to lower the quality of their goods)—then it should not be protected as a trademark. Function, in trademark law, then, draws the line where the commodity begins and the trademark ends, and this, again, not simply to define the extent of the category of trademark but also to prevent the limited monopoly afforded by the mark from distorting the market within which commodities compete.

Of course, the lines between representationality and functionality,[8] and thus copyright, patent, and trademark, are far less clear than the law would seem to require. This lack opens up the potential for "mutant" forms that operate across categories (Ginsburg 2008), as well as for forms that fall "between the seams" (Cox and Jenkins 2008). The design of fashion items like designer shoes, to take an example of the latter, have historically been excluded from both copyright and patent (Schmidt 1983, 864; Raustiala and Sprigman 2006; 2012).[9] On the one hand, this is because the design of shoes presumably has an "intrinsic utilitarian function that is not merely to portray the appearance of the article or to convey information" (17 USC §101). On the other hand, it is because, even as "useful articles," fashion designs rarely fit the criteria for patenting—that is, that the innovation be nontrivial and nonobvious (Hagin 1991, 354–356; Tsai 2005, 455–458; Scafidi 2006, 122–123).

Whatever we think of the ideological work that goes into making such distinctions—for example, the assumption that high-heeled shoes are bought and worn because they are functional for walking, that the work of fashion designers isn't truly innovative, or even that the world is parsable into things and signs[10]—what is of interest to me here is that in such situations where commodity design falls "between the seams," trademark rights are often invoked precisely because, as noted above, trademarks are legally defined as distinct from the (functional) commodities with which they comingle. And indeed, without easy appeal to copyright and patent, fashion brands have increasingly depended on trademark to protect their designs. This creates a conundrum since trademark law is not intended to protect design (in fact, quite the opposite, as noted above), a conundrum strategically materialized in goods whose trademarks *are* their designs and whose designs *are* their trademarks, in trademarks whose qualities are difficult, if not impossible, to distinguish from the commodity designs to which they are appended.[11] Think, for example, of Louboutin's red outsole (cf. Louis Vuitton v. Dooney & Bourke 2008).

SCALING A MARK

Never has a red sole meant so much.
—FASHION CONSULTANT ROBERT BURKE, COMMENTING ON LOUBOUTIN'S SHOES (QUOTED IN FOOTWEARNEWS.COM 2010, CITED IN CL V. YSL 2011, DOC 22-37, P. 2)

Single colors have historically been considered untrademarkable. For nearly a century, the law held that colors could never function as trademarks, except as part of some otherwise trademarkable symbol. To trademark color alone would give rise to unfair monopoly because, it was variously argued, the number of distinguishable colors is limited, and for any one competitor to "own" a color would "deplete" the colors available to other competitors, thereby disadvantaging them in commodity design, production, and sale. It would also discourage new entrants to the market and thus adversely affect market vitality (e.g., see Campbell Soup Co. v. Armour & Co. 1949 and references therein; Life Savers Corp. v. Curtiss Candy Co. 1950; Summerfield 1993).

In 1995, however, the Supreme Court, in *Qualitex v. Jacobson*, definitively argued that single colors could be trademarks under two conditions. First, single colors could be trademarked if they were shown to have "secondary meaning" (that is, that an *appreciable* number of consumers associated the color in question exclusively with a particular brand [as we will see below, the scale of the mark's recognizability is one important basis upon which courts adjudicate trademark cases—see, e.g., EMI Catalogue P'ship v. Hill et al. 2000]).[12] Second, a single-color mark could be trademarked if protection wouldn't significantly put other competitors at a "non-reputation-related" (i.e., non-brand-related) disadvantage (e.g., by increasing the cost of the good or by decreasing its quality)—that is, if the colors in question weren't "functional" with respect to the market, or commodity type, in question.[13]

Turning to *Christian Louboutin v. Yves Saint Laurent*, where it was a single color qua trademark that was at issue, critical to Louboutin's claim was the scale of the semiotic relation between the red outsole and his brand (the first condition noted above). Indeed, Louboutin's initial 2001 application to the U.S. Patent and Trademark Office (USPTO) for trademark registration was rejected precisely because the red outsole was decided to be "merely an ornamental feature of the good"—that is, part of the shoe's design. And this, further, was because Louboutin failed to show that his putative mark had "secondary meaning," which is also to say that he failed to show that enough people associated red outsoles with his brand. Louboutin's 2008 application (CL v. YSL 2011 doc 22–7, 22–8, 28), which provided a preponderance of evidence (from advertising, sales, and press coverage) of the wide scale of the red outsole *as* an exclusive sign of Louboutin, by contrast, succeeded. No longer commodity design, given the demonstrated scale of association of the red outsole as an index of his production, the red outsole was now officially a trademark (see figure 7.1).

In attempting to protect the Louboutin mark from YSL, Louboutin's lawyers rehashed much of the same ground covered in his USPTO application. Louboutin's lawyers submitted copious affidavits, reports, and declarations from lawyers (CL v. YSL 2011, doc 1, 18), survey experts (doc 21), fashion industry insiders (doc 46), and corporate honchos (doc 22–24) to demonstrate the popularity of his shoes, as evinced by sales (240,000 shoes sold in the United States in 2011, worth upward of $135 million), fan websites, and numerous public awards honoring his success. Multitudes of press clippings were submitted by the lawyers describing the red outsole as an exclusive and distinctive sign of Louboutin (doc 22-2, 22-9 to 22-25). Lengthy corporate documents (doc 22-30, 22-33) detailed the enormous media coverage of Louboutin's red shoes (e.g., in celebrity events where celebrities wore his red-soled shoes, in films and television shows that featured them, and even pop songs about them). All of this was to demonstrate the sheer scale of Louboutin's mediatized presence, the sheer size of the social domain that took the red sole *as* a rigid designator for Louboutin. All of this was, like Melville's description of the whale's carcass discussed by Carr and Lempert in this volume's introduction, to invoke, and create, the leviathan of his brand. Louboutin's lawyers wrote to the court:

> Each article and product placement results in attention from <u>tens of thousands,</u> and often <u>millions</u> of individuals for the Louboutin Footwear and especially its Red Sole Mark. By reason of the <u>remarkable</u> unsolicited media coverage of Louboutin Footwear, product placements, celebrity appreciation and Plaintiffs' marketing strategy, the Red Sole trademark is known to relevant consumers <u>throughout the United States and the world.</u> . . . The Red Sole has become synonymous with Christian Louboutin and high fashion. (CL v. YSL 2011, doc 1, p. 9; my underlining)

Or, as they wrote in a later document: "<u>Massive</u> and *undisputed* evidence of <u>broad</u> media coverage and <u>public</u> recognition demonstrate that the Red Sole Mark is distinctive, protectible [*sic*], and even <u>famous</u>. From Oprah to Barbie's special Louboutin shoes and Louboutin's <u>half-million</u> fans on Facebook, luxury goods consumers and the <u>general public</u> have <u>overwhelming</u> exposure to the Red Sole Mark" (ibid., doc 40, p. 6; original italics, my underlining). Everyone (who mattered) knew about the "flash of red," which is why it was critical that competitors like Yves Saint Laurent not imitate and steal that which allowed consumers to identify a shoe as a Louboutin.

In their defense, YSL's lawyers took a number of tacks. For example, they argued that consumers did not exclusively associate a red outsole with Louboutin; indeed many other designers had used red outsoles on shoes before Louboutin, including YSL. They also argued that Louboutin's surveys, which purported to show that consumers were likely to be confused by YSL's shoes (that is, take them to be Louboutin shoes), were flawed. Their own survey data showed little likelihood of consumer confusion (CL v. YSL 2011, doc 36). Moreover, the absence of any evidence reported by Louboutin of any actual consumer being confused, especially given that YSL had sold thousands of its monochromatic red shoes over the years, indicated that Louboutin's move for preliminary injunction would likely fail. The scale of the infringement wasn't enough, YSL's lawyers argued, to carry Louboutin's case forward.

But the most fundamental question YSL's lawyers raised was whether the very use of red in a shoe obviated protection as such: that is, was Louboutin's red a "functional" element of the shoe's design and thereby untrademarkable? Was red part of the commodity per se? Was red part of the commons, something public that anyone should be able to use in a design, something that was part of the market and not anyone's exclusive property? Asking these questions, YSL hit back against Louboutin with a counterclaim that Louboutin's mark didn't even qualify for protection at all (CL v. YSL 2011, doc 8). They wrote, "Louboutin claims to have the <u>exclusive</u> right to use red outsoles on women's footwear—even on shoes, like all the YSL models challenged in this lawsuit, that are entirely red. Louboutin's attempt to <u>monopolize</u> the use of red outsoles—even to the extent of claiming that <u>no other</u> designer can make an all-red shoe—is unsupported by law, defies common sense and would <u>unduly restrict</u> the design options available to competitors in <u>this market</u>" (CL v. YSL 2011, doc 8, p. 2; my underlining). At the heart of YSL's counterclaim was that the red outsole was, to return to the USPTO's rejection of Louboutin's original trademark application, merely an "ornamental design feature" of the shoe—that is, that the trademark was "aesthetically functional" and thus shouldn't be able to serve as a source-designator.

Here we see how functionality, definitionally excluding of trademark, reappears through the trope of the "aesthetically functional." That which excludes fashion from copyright (functionality) is merged with that which is irrelevant to patent (aesthetics), manifesting in a chimerical noun phrase that specifies the functional quality of fashion commodities *as being their aesthetics*. Red—as an aesthetic design feature of the shoes—is a tool in the color palette of all designers aiming to compete in the fashion market for women's designer shoes. Hence, to concede a monopoly in a context where the "aesthetic use of color is literally the function of the productions" would "[impoverish] other designer's palettes" (CL v. YSL 2011, doc 33, p. 8, citing Jay Franco and Sons v. Clemens Franek 2010, p. 11) and thus unfairly disadvantage them in the market. Louboutin's lawsuit, then, YSL's lawyers argued, was "part of an anti-competitive campaign to <u>monopolize</u> use of a <u>common</u> design feature and thereby inappropriately <u>limit</u> the design options available to competitors" (CL v. YSL 2011, doc 8, p. 4; my underlining).[14] It was an attempt to rescale, unjustly, YSL's lawyers argued, the market by appropriating those qualities that should be part of the commons (the color red) to a brand identity (Louboutin).

YSL also argued that their own use of red on the outsole was not as a trademark at all but as part of a more general design concept: monochromaticity (CL v. YSL 2011, doc 33, p. 29). Their design, in that sense, was a "fair use."[15] It "expressed" and "described" a concept rather than designated a source (CL v. YSL 2011, doc 33, p. 29, also see doc 8, p. 4) and, thus, was of a different ontology than Louboutin's use of red as a mark. It was an expression of an idea and hence was not an infringement.

Rather than address the scale of Louboutin's mark (which they implicitly conceded), YSL's arguments addressed the courts' concerns regarding the law's performative power to make scale, contending that protecting a single color as a mark would in effect constitute a monopoly on a commodity type, contracting the market (in this case, women's designer shoes) and the commons (in this case, colors available for fashion design). Moreover, YSL's lawyers argued, affording Louboutin's red sole trademark protection would not simply unfairly and deleteriously rescale the market and commons, it would also contradict the very legal conditions of possibility for trademarkability. YSL's lawyers articulated and anticipated, and thus provoked, the court's reflexive attunement to its own scale-making powers by appealing to the very logics that organize the law itself—that is, by invoking the quality of functionality.

Scaling a quality turned on the law's quality of scale. YSL attempted to shift the scale in question, away from the scale of the mark and toward the question of "aesthetic function." This was a gambit to change the legal category of the semiotic form in question (the color red), to shift from the idiom of recognition and confusion to monopoly and function—that is, from mark to market, property to commons.

The threat and danger to Louboutin was real, for these arguments had recently held traction in a similar type of case in the French courts (Christian Louboutin v. Zara 2012; see CL v. YSL 2011, doc 32–2, pp. 5ff.).[16] Indeed, without a trademark, Louboutin would lose the main legal instrument he had to police his brand, to stay the qualities that made it intelligible in the marketplace, that made it unique and desirable to consumers. As Louboutin's lawyers anxiously noted, designers like Christian Dior, and legions of unnamed counterfeiters and midgrade copy brands, were awaiting the outcome of this case so as to unleash their own red-soled shoes (CL v. YSL 2011, doc 40, p. 14, and fn. 11, p. 10). The court stood as the sole dam holding back a flood of goods that would drown Louboutin. Palpably worried, Louboutin's lawyers wrote, "But when YSL ignores <u>countless</u> color choices, including other reds, and apes the <u>famous</u> signature of the LOUBOUTIN brand, it infringes and exposes Louboutin to irreparable harm via a loss of control over its own brand identity and ravaging of the goodwill painstakingly built in the Red Sole Mark. Other competitors will likely join YSL with their own red soles. Unless this court enjoins YSL, the <u>floodgates</u> will open, and the Louboutin business will be devastated" (CL v. YSL 2011, doc 40, p. 6; my underlining).[17] A single color controlled the fates of market and brand.

Two sides, two scalar arguments: on the one hand, not protecting Louboutin would wipe them off the fashion map by unleashing unbridled copying, by the proliferation of the qualities they claimed as their brand dominion; on the other hand, protecting Louboutin would create an unfair monopoly, allowing Louboutin to unfairly expand their control of the commons, thereby contracting the space for legitimate competition.

A WHITMANESQUE QUESTION

On August 10, 2011, Judge Victor Marrero issued his decision and order. Recognizing that Louboutin's use of red was indeed indexical of his brand, Marrero framed the main issue as such: "The issue now before the Court is whether, despite Christian Louboutin's acknowledged innovation and the <u>broad</u> <u>association</u> of the high fashion red outsole with him as its source, trademark protection should not have been granted to that registration" (CL v. YSL 2011, doc 53, p. 5; my underlining). Having dryly reviewed the facts of the case, Marrero continued:

> Hence, this case poses a Whitmanesque question. Paraphrased for adaptation to the heuristics of the law, it could be framed like this. A lawyer said *What is the red on the outsole of a woman's shoe?* And fetching it to court with full hands asks the judge to rule it is
> [A] gift and remembrancer designedly dropt,
> Bearing the owner's name someway in the corners, that we may
> see and remark, and say *Whose?* (CL v. YSL 2011, doc 53, pp. 7–8, citing Whitman's *Leaves of Grass*, "Songs of Myself," poem 6; italics in my source)

Taking poetic license with both Whitman's poetry and YSL's arguments, Marrero posed Louboutin's request to rule its red outsole exclusively distinctive of its brand as an impossible task. Indeed, the opening of Whitman's poem—the second line of which is neither paraphrased nor quoted by Marrero—is filled with doubt:

> A child said *What is the grass?* fetching it to me with full hands;
> How could I answer the child [here, the lawyers]? I do not know what it [here, the red of a shoe] is any more than he.

Notwithstanding his initial skepticism and hesitation, Marrero went on in his decision, like Whitman in his poem, to offer some decisive judgments on the matter.

For Marrero, the fundamental question was whether a color could be a trademark in fashion *at all*. Or put otherwise, could color in fashion ever *not* be functional—that is, not be a quality of the good as such? Comparing fashion to painting, Marrero reasoned that color furthers the aim of the object itself, "to attract, to reference, to stand out, to blend in, to beautify, to endow with sex appeal—all comprise nontrademark functions of color in fashion" (CL v. YSL 2011, doc 53, p. 20). Citing *Qualitex v. Jacobson* (1995), citing G. K. Chesterton's *Simplicity and Tolstoy,* Marrero noted that "color serves an additional significant nontrademark function: 'to satisfy the "noble instinct for giving the right touch of beauty to common and necessary things""' (CL v. YSL 2011, doc 53, p. 20). Red, Marrero suggested, was irreducibly aesthetic and, thus, in fashion at least, irreducibly functional. Marrero found that a red outsole was simply part of the shoe's design itself—part of its function as an aesthetic good—and, thus, part of the market within which such goods competed: women's designer footwear. Note that

Marrero's reasoning turned, not simply on rescaling Louboutin's mark vis-à-vis the market for women's shoes, but more fundamentally on rescaling the market and the commons vis-à-vis the question of color in fashion per se.

But perhaps a more troubling scalar conundrum to Marrero was the question of what exactly was the quality of Louboutin's particular red.[18] Could it be determined with sufficient specificity such that it wouldn't threaten to spill out of itself, bleeding into surrounding colors, shades, and hues, cannibalizing the fashion market by denying whole color swatches to other designers (cf. NutraSweet v. Stadt 1990; Summerfield 1993 on "shade confusion")? Voicing a concern about the potential effects of protecting Louboutin's red as a single-color mark (not simply in this case but in every future scenario where this case could be cited as precedent), Marrero apocalyptically warned of "fashion wars" (CL v. YSL 2011, doc 53, p. 457) and other dystopic futures where the color spectrum would be divvied up and owned by different brands. In short, Marrero asked whether the fuzzy quale of a single color could be disciplined enough to serve as a sign of identity. Or is color always blurry as to where its boundaries lie, a blurring that is also an expansive, monopolistic projection into the market, a menacing halo rendering contiguous shades and hues always potentially infringing?

And even if the red line of identity could be drawn, how would it be *registered* as a public fact?[19] As emphasized during oral arguments by YSL's lawyers (CL v. YSL 2011, doc 54, p. 10, 32) and taken up by Marrero in his decision (CL v. YSL 2011, doc 53, p. 455), the materiality of the quality of Louboutin's red—even if specified by Pantone color—rendered its referent problematic: the "same" Pantone color on a computer screen is noticeably distinct from its materialization of a piece of paper, and both are distinct from the "same" color materialized on a piece of leather (also see CL v. YSL 2012, doc 89, p. 21). (Remember here the founding myth of Louboutin's lacquered red shoes discussed at the outset of the chapter.) That is, Louboutin's particular red couldn't be a rigid-designating trademark precisely because, it was suggested, its referent couldn't be stably "fixed" (Kripke 1981); or to put it otherwise, it couldn't be reliably scaled in relation to other shades, hues, colors.[20]

In the end, Marrero decided that Louboutin was unlikely to succeed in his attempt to prove his claims, because his mark wasn't, well, actually a mark. This wasn't because it didn't have wide-scale recognition. It did. But to concede it protection would result in monopoly rights that contracted the space for competition. Marrero's decision, then, was as much about the (meta)pragmatics of scale as it was anything else: what scalar entailments would follow if protection was provided? On this basis Marrero denied Louboutin's motion for injunction. He further noted, regarding YSL's counterclaims, that Louboutin might not even have a valid mark, throwing the sign of their brand identity into question and threatening its cancelation.[21]

Here I would like to dwell on Marrero's invocation of Whitman, for it strikes upon the scandal and horror of the case (indeed, Marrero's decision scandalized and horrified many in the fashion world—including Tiffany and Company, with its trademarked blue box, and the International Trademark Association, both of whom wrote amicus curiae on behalf of Christian Louboutin), and trademark mark law more generally, as I discuss in the next section. In the original poem, the line that Marrero quotes is preceded by the line "Or I guess it is the handkerchief of the Lord"—that is, this gift and remembrancer, the grass, is the sign of God himself (*The* Source known to all true believers). Whitman next suggests, voicing the grass, that—like the bounty of God—the grass belongs to all: "Growing among black folks as among white, Kanuch, Tuchahoe, Congressman, Cutt, I give them the same, I receive them the same." We all know the grass's source, and yet it exists for all. Whitman's next line is beautifully ominous, forming the crux of the rest of the poem and retroactively framing its opening. Whitman writes, "And now it seems to me the beautiful uncut hair of graves." This is the horror and scandal of Marrero's decision for Louboutin: the death of his (brand) identity, the return of his mark to the commons. Marrero answers this "Whitmanesque question," then, like Whitman: a single color in fashion, like the green grass, cannot be owned. This ruling threatened all color marks (and implicitly all trademarks), making them no more than the beautiful adornments of their owners' now unmarked mass graves.

AVOIDING AESTHETIC FUNCTION

The Court of Appeals for the Second Circuit, on September 5, 2012, resoundingly rejected Marrero's decision (CL v. YSL 2012, doc 121). Underwriting their rejection was a sense of Marrero's impropriety in scale shifting. Marrero's decision operated at the wrong legal scales, covering whole types of marks ("single color marks") and entire economic-productive domains ("fashion"). His issuance of a blanket "per se rule" was, they argued, inappropriate and outside of the mandate of the district court (cf. Philips this volume). Rather, as they implied, a piecemeal, ad hoc approach must be followed, each case taken on its own merits and particularities (Summerfield 1993). The scale of any judgment within the citational entailments of future cases should be small, contained, particular (cf. Marrero's precedential concern with future "fashion wars").[22]

In its legal reasoning, the Second Circuit court's decision, written by Judge José A. Cabranes, followed a rather conservative path. Following the precedent of the Second Circuit's discussions about "aesthetic functionality," the court defined the test for aesthetic functionality as whether the putative trademark significantly limits the range of competitive designs available to other market actors. Would protection bar the use of features necessary to compete in the relevant market? Having laid out what counts as functionality, however, the court did *not* decide on the question of whether a red outsole was functional per se, or whether a functional *use* of a trademark (like YSL's) should be protected in general. Rather, following the ad hoc method necessitated by their rejection of Marrero's "per se rule," they concluded that the Louboutin trademark—as defined in the USPTO's trademark registry—was overbroad. It didn't accurately describe Louboutin's *actual* trademark as understood by the public (which is to say, how the court's methodological individualism construed how "consumers" evaluated the trademark). They noted that Louboutin's trademark was *not,* in fact, "a lacquered red sole on footwear" but a "red outsole contrasting with the remainder of the shoe" (CL v. YSL 2012, doc 121, p. 11).

The court, in effect, canceled and rewrote Louboutin's trademark at once. Note the result: for with the trademark modified, YSL's monochromatic red shoe—now defined by fiat as an exception to Louboutin's trademark ("The use of a red lacquer on the outsole of a red shoe of the same color is not a use of the Red Sole Mark," the court intoned [CL v. YSL 2012, doc 121, p. 11])—ceased to infringe. The court complexified the mark so that it was no longer a single color, but a *contrast* of colors (red/nonred) between parts of the shoe (outsole versus "upper").[23] This judgment, in effect, found for both parties. Christian Louboutin got to keep his trademark (now modified), and YSL got to keep its monochromatic shoe (now noninfringing).

Like Marrero in the district court, the Second Circuit engaged in its own scale-making, this time, though, to rather different effect. By redefining the qualities that constituted the trademark, the Second Circuit redefined the market for designer women's shoes itself, redrawing the line between the space of exception (red outsoles + nonred uppers = Louboutin monopoly) and the space of free competition, "functionality," and the "right to copy" (i.e., everything else—namely, women's designer shoes that do not have a red outsole contrasting with the rest of the shoe). This was accomplished by the court nimbly navigating the interscalar entanglement between, on the one hand, the constitutive *quality* of the law's internal scalar organization (functionality) and, on the other hand, the scalar *effects* of the law vis-à-vis that very quality (e.g., to create monopolies and contract the commons, or to demolish corporate futures). Through deft definitional footwork, the Second Circuit managed to sidestep this entanglement, "dodg[ing] the functionality issue"—as Rebecca Tushnet (2012) put it[24]—by avoiding a decision that framed Louboutin's mark as functional while also avoiding the implication that Louboutin's mark constituted an unfair monopoly on the market. The court's redefinition obviated the very arguments and tests for aesthetic functionality that it so meticulously reviewed, in fact, reviewing them precisely so that their redefinition would make them nonissues.

With a repressing silence, the Second Circuit met the scandal that Marrero had raised. By dodging the issue of aesthetic functionality, the court dodged the conundrums of scale that constitute the very intelligibility of its practices (viz., the question of functionality) and thus the internally contradictory pragmatics of its scale-making. Such conundrums, I suggest below, threaten to unearth the difficult, and perhaps impossible, to resolve legal relation between the trademark's source-indexicality and its aesthetics. This insolubility, I argue, puts trademark law's very coherence and authority into question.

UNAVOIDABLE AESTHETIC FUNCTION

As noted earlier, the trademark as an ideal legal type is supposed to be, relative to the commodity it marks, a pure index, a transparent medium that simply points to, and invokes, the commodity's source. And yet, every trademark in order to do so must be materially embodied and thus must itself have its own qualities and aesthetics (cf. Keane 2003; Nakassis 2013b).[25] This was, of course, Marrero's point: in domains like fashion—where aesthetics *is* consumer desire, *is* the market, *is* competition, and thus *is* function, insofar as the trademark is part of the aesthetics of the good (or, put in reverse, insofar as design can be[come] source-indexing)—the distinction of source-designation and aesthetics/function is rendered permanently problematic. The challenge that lurks under the surface of this case, then, is precisely this: what do we make of the fact that a trademark can and perhaps must also be, unto itself, a site of aesthetics and desire, and that this—the law notwithstanding—might simply be its function (cf. Nakassis 2012; 2016, 33–86)? The challenge of "aesthetic functionality" points to an internal contradiction within trademark law: that the unavoidable aesthetics of a mark are necessarily possibly functional, that a trademark always is itself a design and, by being contiguous with the so-marked commodity, part of *its* design. The quality that negatively defines the mark (functionality), curiously undermines the mark's very identity through its return in the mark's necessary aesthetics, in its inhering qualities.

The law attempts to work around and manage this internal contradiction in various ways. In this case, and others like it (e.g., Louis Vuitton v. Dooney & Bourke 2008; Fleischer Studios, v. A.V.E.L.A. 2011), this self-contradictory quality of scale appears as silence, elision, avoidance, and ad hoc-istry, as noted above. This is because to face up to the self-contradiction of this founding quality would constitute trademark law's very negation. Such a scene of self-reckoning, as I suggest below, is horrific to the law.[26] It is avoided when possible (as in CL v. YSL 2012) and, when impossible, met with explicit disavowal.

Consider the Ninth Circuit case *Au-Tomotive Gold v. Volkswagen et al. (2006)*.[27] Au-Tomotive Gold (also referred to as Auto Gold) produced key chains and license plate holders featuring the names and logos of well-known car companies. One of the facts of the case was that consumers bought such goods because they wanted their license plate holders and key chains to match the logos of their cars.

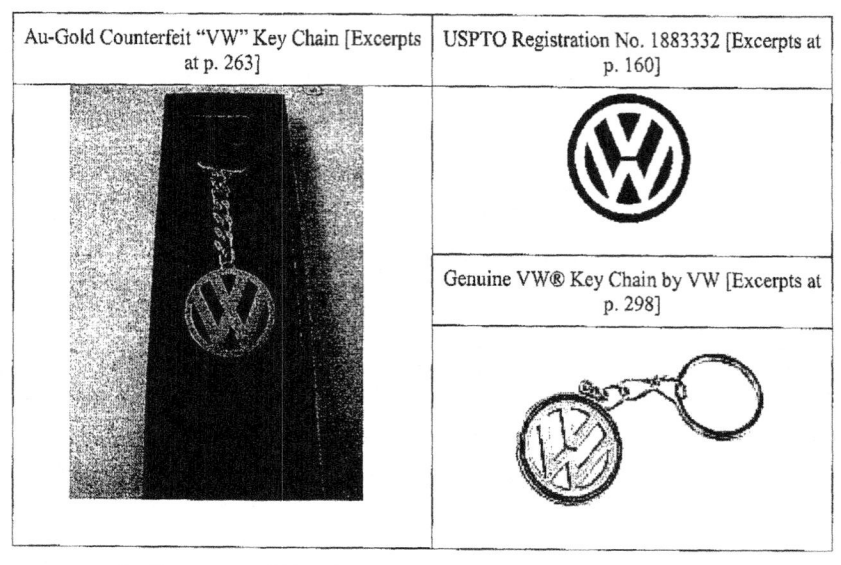

Au-Gold Counterfeit "VW" Key Chain [Excerpts at p. 263]	USPTO Registration No. 1883332 [Excerpts at p. 160]
	Genuine VW® Key Chain by VW [Excerpts at p. 298]

FIGURE 7.3. Au-Tomotive Gold keychain compared with the VW registered trademark and a VW key chain (from Au-Tomotive v. Volkswagen et al. 2007, doc 165, p. 3).

While the trademarks on such goods invoked brands like Volkswagen or Audi, they explicitly did not function as indexicals of the source of the key chain or license plate holder itself (i.e., Au-Tomotive Gold) and, thus, did not impute the production source of the goods to Volkswagen or Audi.

While Au-Tomotive Gold had gotten licensing rights from many of the car companies whose logos they reproduced on their accessories, they hadn't gotten permission from Volkswagen and Audi. Arguing against the idea that their products were infringing, Au-Tomotive Gold noted that the marks were being used not *as* trademarks but as functional elements in an aesthetics of trademarkedness (cf. Nakassis 2013c; 2016, 33–86). In order to cater to this market and to consumers' desires ("the actual benefit that the consumer wishes to purchase," Au-Tomotive v. Volkswagen et al. 2006, p. 9515, citing Auto-Tomotive's arguments)—that is, in order to operate as matching elements within a total car gestalt—trademarks had to be used in the design of these goods. Otherwise, how could Au-Tomotive Gold compete in the market for car accessories, a market defined by consumers' demand for logo bejeweled accessories (see figure 7.3)?

The district court found in favor of Au-Tomotive Gold. The court noted that the "VW and Audi logos are used not because they signify that the license plate or key ring was manufactured or sold (i.e., as a destination of origin) by Volkswagen or Audi, but because there is a[n] aesthetic quality to the marks that purchasers are interested in having" (as cited in Au-Tomotive v. Volkswagen et al. 2006, p. 9519)—namely, the marks themselves. Here we see most clearly, and threateningly, the trademark as both trademark *and* aesthetic bundle of qualities. The qualities that the trademark comprises overwhelm it, allowing it to be refunctioned to new purpose by new economic actors, allowing Au-Tomotive Gold to appropriate Volkswagen's mark as a design element in its car accessories.

The case was appealed to the Ninth Circuit; and like the Second Circuit, the appellate court of the Ninth Circuit decisively reversed the district court's finding, remanding the rest of the case back to the district court for infringement and dilution charges. In its judgment, the Ninth Circuit stared into the abyss and saw only death and destruction. In its decision, the court wrote, "Accepting Auto Gold's position would be the death knell for trademark protection. It would mean that simply because a consumer likes a trademark, or finds it aesthetically pleasing, a competitor could adopt and use the mark on its own products. Thus, a competitor could adopt the distinctive Mercedes circle and tri-point star or the well-known golden arches of McDonald's, all under the rubric of aesthetic functionality" (Au-Tomotive v. Volkswagen et al. 2006, p. 9515). In the next paragraph, the court noted, "Taken to its limits, as Auto Gold advocates, this doctrine would permit a competitor to trade on any mark simply because there is some 'aesthetic' value to the mark that consumers desire. This approach distorts both basic principles of trademark law and the doctrine of functionality in particular" (Au-Tomotive v. Volkswagen et al. 2006, p. 9515). That is, the qualities of the trademark—its aesthetics unto itself—always threaten to suspend the trademark's identity as a proxy of the brand. The shifty promiscuity of the trademark as a (de)sign that may change function across contexts,[28] its duality as a sign of elsewhere *and* as an aesthetic object unto itself, potentially subordinates its status as a trademark to its aesthetics and thus augurs its negation. This passing bell, this desire for the mark as such, threatens to kill the trademark and have it resurrected as an undead object, possessable and revivifiable by anyone, a body with no mind. And indeed, this "aesthetic functionality defense" has been termed by certain legal commentators as a "zombie apocalypse" (Heavner 2012; also Fletcher 1985, 2011), an exanimate threat that continually rises to cannibalize trademark law, a horror that can never quite be, but must be, buried.[29]

The Ninth Circuit court, of course, recognized that "consumers sometimes buy products bearing marks . . . for the appeal of the mark itself, without regard to whether it signifies the origin or sponsorship of the product" (Au-Tomotive v. Volkswagen et al. 2006, p. 9521). And yet, the registering of this fact in trademark law could *not* come to pass. Indeed, in the face of this horror, this death knell, the court responded by disavowal: We know, and yet we act as if we don't. It continued: "As a general matter courts have been loathe to declare unique, identifying logos and names as functional" (Au-Tomotive v. Volkswagen et al. 2006, p. 9522).[30] And indeed, like the Second Circuit, the Ninth Circuit could only respond by normative fiat, writing (note the shifts in modality, which I have underlined): "While that <u>may</u> be so, the fact that a trademark <u>is</u> desirable <u>does not</u>, and <u>should not</u>, render it unprotectable" (Au-Tomotive v. Volkswagen et al. 2006, p. 9530). Later in its decision, the court reissued the following abnegation: "We [the Ninth Circuit] have squarely rejected the notion that 'any feature of a product which contributes to the consumer appeal and saleability [*sic*] of the product is, as a matter of law, a functional element of that product' [citing Vuitton, 644 F.2d at 773]. Such a rule would eviscerate the very competitive policies that functionality seeks to protect" (Au-Tomotive v. Volkswagen et al. 2006, p. 9531).[31]

Why would it "eviscerate" trademark law, gutting it and leaving it permanently incontinent? Because it implies a performative contradiction and paradox immanent in the heart of the quality of scale through which trademark is defined: being a trademark entails the necessary possibility of others desiring the trademark and thus "aesthetically" consuming it, thereby rendering the trademark "functional" and obviating its protection. Being a trademark, then, would negate the mark's very ontology as a trademark. This result is, not surprisingly, anathema to the court, for this would discourage the investment in and use of trademarks and, thus—as the Ninth Circuit put it—negate the "competitive policies" that functionality serves. It would negate trademark law as such.

The contradiction immanent to the mark, then, is the performativity of its aesthetics. Trademarks performatively open up aesthetic spaces, functional spaces, markets. Consider again the "flash of red" of Louboutin's shoes. As reported in the case's files, Louboutin's red-soled shoe *created* an aesthetic space in the market for women's shoes where there was none before. Louboutin's mark established a space of citational possibility for other designers, the very space for competition, for copying, for aesthetic function:

> Louboutin took a part of the shoe that had previously been ignored and made it not only visually interesting but commercially useful. (Elizabeth Semmelhack, curator at Bata Shoe Museum in Toronto, quoted in Collins 2011, p. 83, reproduced in CL v. YSL 2011, doc 22-2, p. 4)

> Louboutin made a colored outsole into <u>a trend</u> with his red lacquer mark and built the Red Outsole Mark over twenty years into an iconic identifier. (Lewin et al. [Louboutin's lawyers], CL v. YSL 2012, doc 99, p. 16; my underlining)

The fashionable use of the outsole for aesthetic purposes was, on these accounts, *brought into being* by Louboutin's mark. This performativity is precisely the contradiction faced by the Ninth Circuit in *Au-Tomotive v. Volkswagen et al.* (2006) and "dodged," by the Second Circuit in *Christian Louboutin v. Yves Saint Laurent* (2012; cf. Flagg Mfg. v. Holway 1901, cited by McKenna 2011, 837).[32] Function and aesthetics are not distinct from source-indexicality (or commodity/market from mark, or quality from identity) but, in a very real sense, performatively follow from it.

THE TRANSMIGRATION OF SOLES

In this chapter I have explored the interscalar relationship that mediates, and is mediated by, trademark law: on the one hand, the law's reflexivity to its own scale-making effects within and beyond the law; on the other hand, the law's self-contradictory scalar infrastructure, that undead quality of scale, "functionality." In concluding, I suggest that this interscalarity, its conundrums, and its horrors follow from the rather banal and uncontroversial opposition of trademark and commodity. The death knell of trademark follows from the cut into the market that *is* the trademark, the impossible foundation of a finite identity amid a world of infinite qualities, an impossibility created by the paradoxes that result from the untenable division between sign and metasign, and from the ideological fantasy that semiotic function (e.g., source-indexicality) and the sign-vehicle's materiality can be kept distinct.[33] Indeed, as I have suggested, trademarks are not merely indexes of the source of commodities in the market but are elements of/in the market itself. They are not simply meta-commodities, or rather, if they are, then they too partake in the commodity worlds that they are meant simply to hover above. The line between trademark and commodity is far from clear. In short, the (meta)pragmatics of scale in these cases is linked to foundational, if internally contradictory, semiotic ideologies inherent to the law: oppositions of word and thing, representation and function, trademark and good.

This cut, which is also a purification, makes possible trademarks and brand identities. It also makes them impossible. This purification abstracts identity out of quality. It elicits the authoritative force of necessity out of the impishness of possibility. But how can quality be stayed, stabilized, and held steady, and can it? How can a shifty aesthetic form be made into a rigid designator of brand identity? And for how long? The court (re-)creates the very line between identity and quality, and thus between mark and market/good, by arbitrating it. And yet every such arbitration is tinged with danger and possibility.

Identity is a tenuous achievement, where the proliferation of difference and indifference is attempted to be stayed and kept at bay. And yet qualities of sameness and difference always slip away, undermining those identity projects even as they constitute them as sites of desire and semiotic potency. No trademark can be without its qualities and aesthetics, even as a trademark's legal definition turns on the very denial of the significance of that very fact. This fantasy of the pure designator and its rigid reference constantly gives way to copies and citations, flaccid commodities like an all-red shoe or a "VW" keychain, commodities that elicit and detach those qualities that constitute the identity of that which they (are taken to) cite, materializing them in a novel, if uncannily familiar, form. Such forms continually threaten to extinguish that identity by promising to open the floodgates of quality, by breeching the bounds that keep legal categories like trademark coherent and continent. The law's scalar logics and practices found, and find themselves in, this leaky space.

But if this is so, perhaps the death knell heard by the Ninth Circuit and avoided by the Second is no death at all, but simply another occasion for life. Beyond the question of identity and essence, of ownership and origin, is another world of possibility, a world beyond the trademark. Whitman finished the poem, which Judge Marrero elliptically cited in his ruling on the *Christian Louboutin v. Yves Saint Laurent* case, thusly:

> The smallest sprouts show there is really no death,
> And if ever there was it led forward life, and does not wait at the end to arrest it,
> And ceased the moment life appeared.
> All goes onward and outward . . . and nothing collapses,
> And to die is different from what any one supposed, and luckier.

NOTES

This chapter is based on a presentation given at the 2013 American Anthropological Association meetings for the panel "The Pragmatics of Scale" and on an earlier essay written for the Michicagoan faculty seminar in January 2013. It has benefited from discussion in both forums, as well as from readings by and discussions with E. Summerson Carr, Michael Lempert, Justin Richland, Julie Chu, Jennifer Cole, Rebecca Tushnet, Nancy Munn, and Julie Cousin. John Acevado provided able research assistance.

1. In this chapter I abbreviate this case as CL v. YSL, for both the 2011 district hearing (SDNY) and the 2012 appeal (Second Circuit). Documents from the courts' case files, downloaded from www.pacer.gov, are referred to by the document (doc) number listed in the docket and the page number of the file. Unless otherwise specified, all other citations to other court cases are to published opinions.

2. I thank Justin Richland for the stimulating conversation from which this relationship was made clear to me.

3. This isn't to say that functionality is the only such quality, of course. Another important quality of this scale-making is the temporality of such protections, which are historically limited precisely so that protected innovations and creative products may be "returned" to the (now-enlarged) commons after allowing sufficient time to encourage investment in their production in the first place. Trademarks, in an important contrast to copyright and patent, have no such time limit.

4. For discussion of utility and functionality in intellectual property law, see Knitwaves v. Lollytags 1995, 1002; Hagin 1991, 349; Bharati 1996, 1693; Firth 2008, 517.

5. Indexical relations, following Peirce (1998), are semiotic relations where the sign-vehicle and its object are articulated causally, by copresence, or by contiguity. Indexical signs "point to" their objects, not simply or only by convention or similarity, but also by a relation of contextual association (where that context may be of larger or smaller extent). Rigid designators (e.g., proper names, cf. personal pronouns) are particular kinds of indexical signs whose indexical relation is "fixed" so that it inheres across contexts of use by always indexically returning to a particular imputed event, or source, of "baptism" (Kripke 1981).

6. More recently and secondarily, trademark law has been expanded to explicitly protect producers' brand image (and their marketing investment in it) as such, regimenting and guarding the semiotic capacity of marks to distinguish goods and producers, in addition to, or rather than, protecting against consumer "confusion." Such an expansion of the law protects marks from being "diluted" or "tarnished"

by marks whose similarity erodes the distinctiveness and uniqueness of the to-be-protected mark (Coombe 1998, 41–87; Arvidsson 2005; Bently 2008). In the cases I discuss, while dilution was alleged, because the question of the mark itself was problematized dilution never emerged as a significant issue. For this reason I don't discuss this important expansion, and partial reorientation, of trademark law away from its putatively original mandate to protect against consumer confusion.

7. Notice how, in this way, what distinguishes a trademark from a commodity mirrors, and reapplies, the differentiation of commodities into utilitarian or representational forms. See note 10.

8. Such a distinction has long raised for courts the sticky issue of what it means for an object to be defined by *either* its "intrinsic" utility or its representationality (or its aesthetics). In legal discussions of copyright, this comes under the legal doctrine of "separability" (Mazer v. Stein 1954), wherein qualities inextricable from the utility-conferring form of the article are excluded from copyright (see Raustiala and Sprigman 2006, 1699–1700; Marshall 2007, 315ff.; Cox and Jenkins 2008, 7ff.; H. R. Rep. No. 94-1476, p. 9, cited in Tu 2010, 426). Courts, however, have been reluctant to recognize the conceptually separable aspects of fashion design, except in certain cases: notably, fabric/print design that can be replicated in other media while maintaining its conceptual/aesthetic identity. (On separability and fabric design, see Peter Pan Fabrics v. Brenda Fabrics 1959; Knitwaves v. Lollytags 1995; Scafidi 2006, 120; Cox and Jenkins 2008, 9.) While extractability of quality from form is one way that copyright can be used to police copying, it practically applies only in a limited number of cases and, when it does apply, often so does the more powerful, and temporally unlimited, trademark law.

9. U.S. law has generally not been supportive of increased intellectual property rights over fashion design. There have been numerous attempts to pass legislation to protect fashion design in the United States. Over seventy different bills have been proposed since 1914 (see Weikart 1944; Schmidt 1983; Tu 2010; and Raustiala and Sprigman 2012, for discussion). No such proposed bill has, to date, succeeded, though some hold out hope for the 2012 Innovative Design Protection Act, which, as of the time of writing, is stuck in congressional limbo.

10. The distinction of utility and representation instates an Enlightenment language ideology of "words" and "things." Hence, the law distinguishes useful objects (functions for patent) versus expressive signs (ideas for copyright), and further between that which is functional or representational (and hence untrademarkable but potentially patentable or copyrightable) and that which is properly source designating (and thus trademarkable). Note the fractal recursion: things versus signs, and within the latter category of signs, denoting texts versus referential marks, where this latter opposition replays the former. Also see note 7.

11. This has been enabled by the historical expansion of what counts as trademarkable (e.g., the extension of rights to colors [Qualitex v. Jacobson 1995], not to mention sounds and smells [Ginsburg 2008] and even whole commodified experiential envelopes [Two Pesos v. Taco Cabana 1992; see also Wal-Mart v. Samara Brothers 2000; Abercrombie & Fitch v. American Eagle 2002; Adidas-Salomon AG v. Target 2002; for discussion see Bharathi 1996; Wong 1998; Cox and Jenkins 2008, 14) and the increasingly blurry boundaries between the domains of intellectual properties (see Moffat 2004; McKenna 2011, 2012).

12. The term *secondary meaning* diagrams the disavowed tension at the heart of trademark law's semiotic, for while it recognizes that every trademark is also something else (i.e., its "primary" meaning—e.g., Nike is the name of a Greek goddess, red is a color), as far as the law is concerned it is the arbitrary or fanciful secondary meaning (the association with the commodity's source) that is primary. It is, however, the perpetual primacy of the nontrademark status of trademarks that enables the tensions and contradictions that I discuss in this chapter.

13. This decision came after a number of lower courts argued that color alone could be protected, a broadening that followed from the Lanham Act of 1946 (Summerfield 1993). Before the Lanham Act, colors alone were generally refused trademark protection by definition (see Owens-Corning Fiberglas Corp. 1985 for discussion). Following the Lanham Act, where colors were not subject to a blanket

disbarring, courts that allowed the trademarking of colors have advocated judicious avoidance of "per se" rulings, an issue that comes up, as we see, in the Second Circuit's response to the district court's ruling in CL v. YSL 2011.

14. Part of YSL's allegation that Louboutin waged an "anti-competitive" campaign also included the claim that Louboutin unfairly forced retailers of YSL (who also did business with Louboutin) to pull YSL's shoes off their racks (CL v. YSL 2011, doc 8, p. 4).

15. Following from the First Amendment, fair use doctrine in trademark law covers, to varying extents, so-called parodic uses, nominative uses (i.e., mere mention), and descriptive uses (i.e., uses of the "primary" meaning of the trademark rather than its rigid-designating "secondary meaning").

16. As with the U.S. case, the French case involved the lack of clarity of Louboutin's trademark. The French court of appeals canceled the mark, though Louboutin quickly reregistered—an action allegedly approved by an European Union appellate court (appellate because YSL contested this reregistration) on June 16, 2011—using a new description of the mark that added a level of clarity (e.g., rendering the model in 3-D, specifying its use only with high-heeled shoes, and designating the particular shade of red, Pantone 18-1663 TP, or "Chinese red"; see CL v. YSL 2011, doc 40, p. 6, fn. 1; also doc 48-1).

17. Compare the scalar rhetoric here of "countless" color choices to that of "limited" color choices, as typically voiced by proponents who argue against trademarking single colors (Summerfield 1993; see discussion in the main text below).

18. Note, incidentally, that the issue isn't simply with the color red, for what do we make of the adjective "lacquered" used to describe the mark? Does it describe the quality of glossiness of the red or the type of red? And where would we draw the lines of either? (See CL v. YSL 2011, doc 54, doc 61, p. 28, where Marrero addresses these questions.)

19. Marrero's concern here turned on the ability of a mark to be registered such that its registration could communicate to other market actors what is, and is not, already protected.

20. Louboutin's lawyers pointed out, however, that the fixation of color is no different than that of any other kind of sign. It is accomplished by whatever token-exemplar of red is registered with the USPTO (CL v. YSL 2011, doc 54; cf. Summerfield 1993). *That* red is the trademark. And whatever that red is, the measure for infringing similarity is consumer confusion, obviating the problem of designating (e.g., by Pantone reference) *what* the red is as such. Of course, whether this solves the issue that USPTO marks are registered so as to warn off competitors (see note 19), or whether it addresses the fundamental epistemological question of the gap between a quality and its materialization, is unclear.

21. Marrero refused to cancel Louboutin's mark then and there, however, since procedurally Louboutin should have the right not simply to appeal—which they did—but also to argue why the mark should not be canceled.

22. Here we see another kind of metapragmatics of scale—in fact, a second-order, or meta-metapragmatics of scale—that is oriented to the scalar performativity of the law through the detour of the citational futures of precedence. And, of course, the Second Circuit's decision is oriented to the district courts' own meta-metapragmatic worry, making it a third-order metapragmatics.

23. This finding was prefigured from the first letter sent by YSL to Louboutin's lawyers, before the complaint was even registered (CL v. YSL 2011, doc 22–63; doc 89, fn. 4, p. 41), and was repeated throughout the trial. Indeed, YSL early on noted that its monochromatic shoes didn't infringe, because Louboutin's signature shoes involve the contrast of red bottoms with nonred uppers. This complexification, following a long line of legal reasoning about color (Summerfield 1993), made Louboutin's mark more distinctive and less generic and, thus, less likely to be seen, in the law's eyes, as functional or constraining of the market.

24. In its efforts to avoid the issue, the court, as Tushnet (2012) points out, also sidestepped the fact that the change in definition didn't address the possibility that the monochromatic shoe, even if excluded by the definition of the trademark, could still be similar enough to "confuse" consumers (thereby raising the issue of color and functionality again). The court passed over this in silence. The

court also avoided the question of whether a feature (such as a color) could be functional in one context but a trademark in another (see note 28 for more discussion).

25. The point isn't that the law is unable to recognize this fact, for it certainly does (see McKenna 2011). Rather, it is that it cannot resolve this tension between source-designation and aesthetics except in an ad hoc, and often contradictory, way. While some courts emphasize that the functionality of an alleged mark bars it from serving as a mark despite its secondary meaning (e.g., Au-Tomotive v. Volkswagen et al. 2006; see McKenna 2011, 856), others recognize that marks will, of necessity, have aesthetic properties (that make them desirable), though such aesthetics do not, or should not, interfere with their status *as* marks (see CL v. YSL 2011, doc 61, p. 17, 19; doc 45, p. 36ff.; Fabrication Enter v. Hygenis 1995).

26. This horror is why the Second Circuit, in *Christian Louboutin v. Yves Saint Laurent* (2012), advocates a piecemeal method and finds Judge Marrero's "per se rule" anathema. It is also, perhaps, why it makes no mention of the amicus curiae written by Rebecca Tushnet, which pressed the court to confront precisely this issue. In the face of foundational challenge, ad hoc–istry is a necessity for life, for without it trademark law is rendered incoherent. The irony, of course, is that this putative inherence of value, aesthetics, and "function" in the body of the trademark is the very reason that trademarks are so valuable on the market (Klein [1999] 2000; Lury 2004; Arvidsson 2005)—and thus, a reason that corporate interests have pushed the law to protect the trademark and brand as such (e.g., through dilution laws; see note 6). The ontological complexity and tension of the trademark as both a sign of origin and a (non-source-designating) aesthetic object presents the frightening and exciting possibility that the trademark may simply be desired because it *is* a trademark, not because of what it stands in for. In such situations, should the trademark be protected? Or does such desire permanently decenter the trademark by rendering it aesthetically functional?

27. Au-Tomotive was the plaintiff in this case, because in 1996 they were sued by BMW for trademark infringement. Afraid that they would get sued by Volkswagen, they acted first so as to make the case that their activities didn't constitute infringement or counterfeiting.

28. McKenna (2011) and Tushnet (CL v. YSL 2012, doc 92 [amicus curiae]) argue that marks, and their aesthetic functionality, are inherently contextual. While the law often recognizes different "markets" as different contexts for marks (so that Delta Airlines is not infringed by Delta Dental)—so that these are, in effect, different semiotic types (*Delta* being homonymic here)—McKenna and Tushnet are interested in the multiplicity and unbecoming of the trademark as an ontological form across contexts (e.g., *Delta* as a proper name, common noun, and graphic form). Note that the idea that trademarks may be contextually shifty doesn't square with trademark law, which, as an institution tasked with keeping source-designation rigid, protects the mark across *all* contexts (or "possible worlds," we might say, analogizing Kripke 1981 on proper names). The mark, if protected, is *necessarily*, rather than contingently, protected. This ideological and normative commitment to a particular semiotics of the mark, however, flies in the face of the empirical realities of how marks are construed, used, and consumed, as McKenna and Tushnet powerfully show (also see Nakassis 2012; 2013c; 2016, 33–86, and references therein). Tushnet, moreover, argues that while the Second Circuit avoided the issue of contextuality by redefining the Louboutin mark, it also implicitly endorsed just such a contextualist view, creating an internal contradiction in its decision. As Tushnet (2012) asks, what indeed was the basis for the cancelation of the original Louboutin mark if not that a *use* of a red outsole was aesthetically functional (e.g., on a monochromatic shoe), even if it was nonfunctional in other contexts (e.g., on a nonmonochromatic shoe)? Compare this with *Louis Vuitton Malletier, S.A., v. Hyundai Motor America* (2012), where a reference to the Louis Vuitton mark—even if not used *as* a mark—was found to be infringing.

29. For a review of the history of the aesthetic functionality defense, see Fletcher 1985, 2011; and CL v. YSL 2012, section 3 and references therein.

30. Note the metapragmatic verb phrase "loathe to declare," which implicitly admits the potential aesthetic function of a mark (a fact that courts "loathe") while performatively disavowing that very possibility (in this case, by refusing to "declare").

31. Also see the Fifth Circuit's decision in *Pebble Beach Company v. Tour 18 I, Limited* (1998, 539).

32. The Second Circuit went out of its way to avoid this death knell in the *Christian Louboutin v. Yves Saint Laurent* case (even if YSL lawyers attempted to resurrect the zombie threat of aesthetic functionality in their defense; see CL v. YSL 2011, doc 28). The Second Circuit wrote, "Therefore, in determining whether a mark has an aesthetic function so as to preclude trademark protection, we take care to ensure that the mark's very success in denoting (and promoting) its source does not itself defeat the markholder's right to protect that mark" (CL v. YSL 2012, doc 120, p. 8).

33. A parallel problematic, of course, is the expression–idea distinction in copyright law.

REFERENCES CITED

Legal Cases

Abercrombie & Fitch Stores, Inc., v. American Eagle Outfitters, Inc., U.S. Court of Appeals for the 6th Circuit, 2002.

Adidas-Salomon AG v. Target Corp., U.S. District Court, Oregon, 2002.

Au-Tomotive Gold, Inc., v. Volkswagen of America et al., U.S. Court of Appeals for the 9th Circuit, 2006; U.S. District Court of Arizona, 2007.

Campbell Soup Co. v. Armour & Co., U.S. Court of Appeals for the 3rd Circuit, 1949.

Christian Louboutin v. Yves Saint Laurent, U.S. District Court, SDNY, 2011; U.S. Court of Appeals for the 2d Circuit, 2012.

Christian Louboutin v. Zara, Court of Appeal of Paris, 2012.

EMI Catalogue P'ship v. Hill et al., U.S. Court of Appeals for the 2d Circuit, 2000.

Fabrication Enter., Inc., v. Hygenis Corp., U.S. Court of Appeals for the 2d Circuit, 1995.

Flagg Mfg. Co. v. Holway, U.S. District Court of Massachusetts, 1901.

Fleischer Studios, Inc., v. A.V.E.L.A.. Inc., U.S. Court of Appeals for the 9th Circuit, 2011.

Jay Franco and Sons, Inc., v. Clemens Franek, U.S. Court of Appeals for the 7th Circuit, 2010.

Knitwaves, Inc., v. Lollytags, Ltd. (Inc.), U.S. Court of Appeals for the 2d Circuit, 1995.

Life Savers Corp. v. Curtiss Candy Co., U.S. Court of Appeals for the 7th Circuit, 1950.

Louis Vuitton Malletier v. Dooney & Bourke, Inc., U.S. District Court SDNY, 2004; 2d Circuit U.S. Court of Appeals, 2006; U.S. District Court SDNY, 2008.

Louis Vuitton Malletier, S.A., v. Hyundai Motor America, U.S. District Court SDNY, 2012.

Mazer et al. v. Stein et al., U.S. Supreme Court, 1954.

NutraSweet Co. v. Stadt Corp., U.S. Court of Appeals for the 7th Circuit, 1990.

Owens-Corning Fiberglas Corp., U.S. Court of Appeals, Federal Circuit, 1985.

Pebble Beach Company v. Tour 18 I, Limited, U.S. Court of Appeals for the 5th Circuit, 1998.

Peter Pan Fabrics, Inc. v. Brenda Fabrics, Inc., U.S. District Court SDNY, 1959.

Qualitex Co. v. Jacobson Products Co., U.S. Supreme Court, 1995.

Two Pesos, Inc. v. Taco Cabana, Inc., U.S. Supreme Court, 1992.

Vuitton et Fils S.A. v. J. Young Enters., Inc., U.S. Court of Appeals for the 9th Circuit, 1981.

Wal-Mart Stores, Inc. v. Samara Brothers, Inc., U.S. Supreme Court, 2000.

8

SEMIOTIC VINIFICATION AND THE SCALING OF TASTE

Michael Silverstein

In contemporary life in the First World, people orient to commodities such as edibles and potables through normative cultural schemes that inform and shape their perception of the qualities thus rendered salient. In such terms they classify, categorize, and come to judge the good from the bad—not only the things they ingest but as well those they wear, drive, or make use of in other ways in their daily lives, and even, I suggest, those personae they vote for or vote against.

Wine in particular, among potables, has long ranged across many modes of judgment that differentiate categories of consumers. At one position in a space of use-value, it is a consumable commodity, whether accompanying food or not, a beverage providing the enjoyment of shared sociality, of (generally) mild inebriation, of sophistication, and sometimes of occasion. It is poised, along with wine-derived spirits, as an alcoholic beverage between beer and so-called hard liquor, which contrast along one or more of these dimensions of use-value. At another, more rarefied position of use-value, wine is less a beverage commodity and more an object of aesthetic valuation, of connoisseurship even. But even at the other extreme, something of the fact of the aesthetics of wine has long given it its contrastive position with respect to other potables—a position from which, and in the image of which, those involved with each of these other commodities have increasingly sought to duplicate a space of comparably distributed use-values.

Thus, the emergence of microbreweries of connoisseur-worthy artisanal beers and ales, and the emergence of microdistilleries of connoisseur-worthy gins, vodkas, (scotch) whiskies, bourbons, rye whiskies, and so on—all have come to be framed by an efflorescence of winelike semiotic activities. The process of creating these parallel spaces *in the image of wine*—a metaphorical or citational (cf. Nakassis this volume) vinification, to be sure—resituates these other commodities and transforms the overall envelope of institutionalized, connoisseurship-anchored taste, bringing new, intersemiotically structured nodes of consumer experience into this network. It also, I maintain, reanchors new prestigious and prestige-conferring commodities in the enveloping political economy of stratified consumption—that is, consumption bespeaking one's position in a stratified political economy.

Key to how this dynamic of reimaginative assimilation operates is the spread of the semiotic means provided to the consumer for engaging with things brought close to and especially into the human body, the very senses and naturalized aesthetic sensibility of which are mobilized to and in acts of judgment. In such judgment, language is central, in the form of what I term an aggressively cultivated *register effect*. Spreading like vines to encompass multiple foci of connoisseurship, it creates a scaled-up envelope of interdiscursivity (Silverstein 2005, 2013) in and by the process of semiotic vinification.

SEMIOTIC EVENTS AND INTERSEMIOTIC NETWORKS IN JUDGMENTS OF TASTE

In contemporary mass social formations, any semiotic event—for example, an event of verbal communication or any other social transaction—occurs within a phenomenal context defining its particular mode of social locatability. For example, we can recognize the primordial, spoken, face-to-face conversational dyad of interlocutors in bodily copresence; or the group-defining, web-mediated broadcast distribution (simultaneous or over an interval of availability) of pixelated text to multiple receivers' terminals; and as well the generalized circulation of commodities to a mass category of users through distribution sites like stores. Yet socioculturally considered, each such "local" event occurs and has effect only because it is linked by form and significance to other semiotic events as one site or node in which or at which intersect multiple networks—tendrils or vines—of connection to other semiotic events. Many such networks intersect in any particular event, of course. Each inscribes its own implied, if perhaps not locally experienced, order of chronotopic framing,[1] suggesting the dimensions of an immanent sociological envelope of its own making. In this way, analytically, we can see how particular sign-mediated events, multiply connected one to another in an encompassing socio-space-time, are rendered meaningful as instantiations of systems of values. Social institutionality in particular—such as the practices in the world of wine—exists in this duplex chronotopic order: semiotic forms emergent at particular sites of social interaction (with their own local chronotopic character as events) are endowed with significance for social actors insofar they orient to and/or contest immanent normative defaults established in the implied chronotope of multiply interdiscursive socio-space-time.[2]

Every encompassing social formation of which social scientists (and laypersons) speak—think of "the state," "capitalism," "kinship"—is such a socio-spatiotemporal envelope manifest through events connected intersemiotically and thus implying chronotopic networks of social practice. Thus, to make visible this more abstract scalar order of institutionalized social life—here I concentrate on the contemporary, particularly North American (and Anglophone), cultural order of prestige comestibles—we must start within some genre of event-bound semiotic practice and attempt to trace its connections to other semiotic practices, both those that seem to have intersected in it so as to license it and give value to its semiotic forms, and those that it has come mutually to license and to valorize at a growth-edge of emergently grafted chronotopy. This brings me to the matter of wine itself.

Working on the semiotics of linguistic registers thirty years ago led me to discover that, indeed, *in vino veritas*; there is at least semiotic "truthiness" in wine—or at least a certain important culturally revelatory quality in the register of language in which American English speakers have learned to talk about it.[3] I dubbed the register *oinoglossia*, or "wine talk." Understanding this phenomenon will help us recognize a general semiotic process that is all around us: how the generally verbally conveyed assertive projection of *qualia*—value-laden qualities or properties of things/people/experiences (see Chumley and Harkness 2013; Harkness 2015)—as discerned and communicated through verbalized assessment, further entails, via verbal enregisterment, a reciprocal positioning in social space of the one who discerns and communicates such qualia. This is true whether within a chronotopic envelope already established or one being created in and by this very enregisterment of judgment.

Our descriptions of things/people/experiences in the first instance index—they presume upon—the existence of shared conceptual schemes of qualia, differentiable values in quality-spaces (some even scaled) made relevant to the context of judgment in and by the act of evaluation or assessment. One's description places the referent in a field of other entities all belonging to a relevant universe of differentiated, sometimes explicitly dimensionalized—even graded or scaled—value: "large, extra-fancy" versus [uncharacterized other] apples, or "plum" versus "beefsteak" tomatoes at the greengrocers;[4] "well-marbled" ("prime") versus "lean" ("choice") beefsteak at the butcher shop. The description-as-thought/communicated presumes upon (indexes) the existence of that which it evaluates in its relevant quality-space(s). But in and by this act of evaluating-by-describing, there is a counterdirectional (as I term it) "second order" indexical process (Silverstein 2003) that indicates—that "performs" or constructively entails—one's very identity as an evaluator so as to affirm or call into question one's license or claim to authority to construe what one is perceiving and about which communicating a judgment.[5]

Aesthetic response to, and in particular developed connoisseurship of, everything from plastic and graphic art to viniferous art has long been recognized in Euro-American ideologies of human "faculties" and their perfectibility; thus, not surprisingly, they are deeply anchored in institutions of our political economy of social stratification and prestige. The late Pierre Bourdieu, taking a cue from decades of nondisinterested market researchers, developed this point in *Distinction* (1984). It is important to see, however, that such a relationship is a dynamic emergent of a semiotics of enregisterment, of much, much wider and more fundamental nature in our contemporary sociocultural condition. It has been spreading or circulating in an ever more encompassing chronotope of its own making, seemingly emanating from oinoglossia and its descriptive object, spreading to an analogously "vinified" semiotics of register fashioned for describing other realms of comestible consumption. In turn, these come to presume upon quality spaces in wine's image as affordances of identity-conferring connoisseurship that can as well be communicatively performed.

One should note as well that this luxuriant growth of "vinification" frequently seems, to those inside the phenomenon, to depend directly on the human sensorium, rather than on multiple institutional orders that stabilize the semiotics of evaluational judgments and their reciprocal effects of positioning the judges. Here we claim the centrality of institutional processes of enregisterment to the upscaling of scaled-up regimes of commodity value, the tendrils of oinoglossia having crept into talk about such consumables as coffee, chocolate, beer, spirits, and so on. This growth means not only that winelike quality spaces have been extended and elaborated for an increasing number of comestibles but also that those who consume such comestibles have ever more opportunity to, as it were, climb multiple vines to higher elevations. Endowed with their own "wine"-talk, once lowly, humble consumables are felt to undergo an elevation in cultural taxonomies of relative prestige. This allows for the parallel elevation of consumers in the distinct but parallel domain of consumptive class stratification so widely naturalized as refinement of the sensorium. Recalling the reciprocal indexical effects of enregisterment, we will come to appreciate how such homologies develop as ideological cultural concepts of how the scaling of consumables into emergently more and less prestigious categories relates to scaling of humans into higher and lower class strata.

THE AESTHETIC TALK OF THE TOWN

The verbal phenomenon of oinoglossia itself is widely recognized. For people with a certain wide experience of English prose, it is the register of an unmistakable textual genre.

TABLE 8.1 A Wine-Tasting Note by Sir Michael Broadbent, Formerly of Christie's

First tasted in 1963. Surprisingly soft and lovely on the palate even in the mid-1960s but the nose curiously waxy and dumb, developing its characteristic hot, earthy/pebbly bouquet only latterly. Ripe, soft, lovely texture, but not as demonstrably or obtrusively a '61 as the other first growths. Fine, gentlemanly, understated.

SOURCE: Broadbent 1980.

Table 8.1 displays what we recognize as demonstrably and obtrusively a wine-tasting note—in fact, one of the thousands published in 1980 by Sir Michael Broadbent, whose evaluations had for many years set price for Christie's auction house. English speakers outside of the social fields where such discourse is the norm can recognize the special quality, the "fine, gentlemanly, understated" quality, we might term it, of this kind of language, but only a much smaller number can actually produce equivalent prose in the register that would make sense to professional and serious avocational insiders of wine connoisseurship.

As a kind of text, a genred organization of language, the well-formed wine-tasting note is highly structured. Its narrative line follows what connoisseurs understand to be the event-dimensions of aesthetic experience and evaluation that serially or temporally give structure to one's perceptual encounter with the obscure object of oenological desire.

As seen in figure 8.1, the aesthetic encounter with wine is itself conceptualized as a phased space-time of dimensionalities to be focused on in serial order. Along each dimension of perception, the qualities—the qualia—that characterize the current object of evaluation can be denoted by using one or more from among a taxonomy of contrasting descriptors for that perceptual field, whether ready-to-mind simple words from the expert's lexicon or more complex phraseological expressions built around them. As is the case for so many areas of connoisseurship, such descriptions, as well, comparatively locate the current particulars in each of the phases of wine-as-experienced in relation to other occasions of comparable experience; one may have experienced this particular named wine in a different vintage or phase of its bottle life, or with other named wines one has encountered. Through such accumulated familiarity one can conceptualize a whole sensorial universe of possibilities aggregated across evaluational dimensions within which the characteristics of any one wine or any category of wines can be differentially imagined and, through language, communicated. A structured hierarchy of qualia emerges for each phase of evaluation in multiple intersecting qualia-spaces with their own possibly conventionalized descriptors. As well, this wine—say, a red one now being tasted—can be comparatively described in relation to others of its point of origin (vineyard, producer, region, etc.) in different years of production; it can be compared to other named wines of its locale; compared to other red wines with

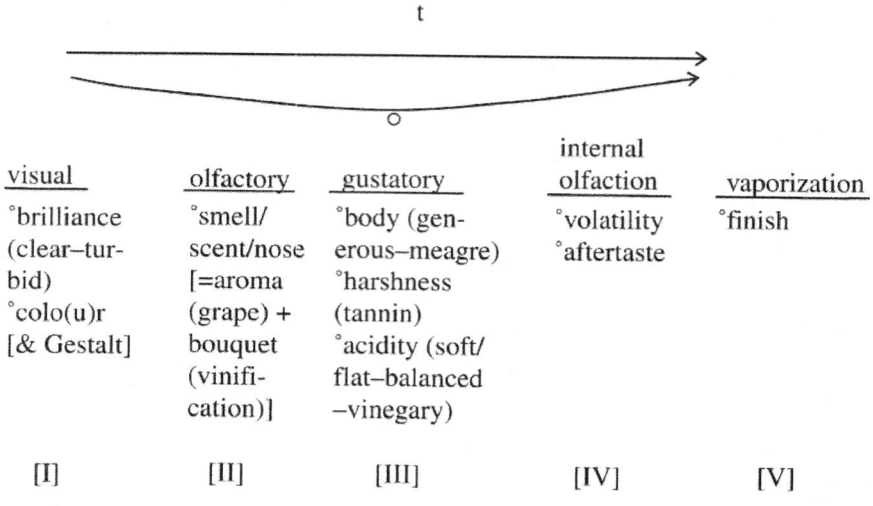

			internal	
visual	olfactory	gustatory	olfaction	vaporization
°brilliance	°smell/	°body (gen-	°volatility	°finish
(clear–tur-	scent/nose	erous–meagre)	°aftertaste	
bid)	[=aroma	°harshness		
°colo(u)r	(grape) +	(tannin)		
[& Gestalt]	bouquet	°acidity (soft/		
	(vinifi-	flat–balanced		
	cation)]	–vinegary)		
[I]	[II]	[III]	[IV]	[V]

FIGURE 8.1. Evaluative dimensions of the serial phases of the aesthetic encounter with wine.

its predominant (or exclusive) grape type, no matter the locale of origin; compared to other red wines of other grape types; and so on.

A common mode of description is the use of multiple comparisons to other olfactory and gustatory sensations identified with substances other than wine—flowers that smell a certain way, fruits that taste a certain way, objects that give off pleasant or, as the case may be, unpleasant smells. (There is both a metaphorical or, as Peirce would note, an iconic predication involved in such comparisons, with wine the tenor, and the standard of comparison the metaphorical vehicle.) Another is a kind of ontogenetic identification of percepts with their presumptive origins in the production history of wine from vine to glass, such origins and developmental trajectories through time themselves contributing descriptive dimensions, such as one's ability to discern in the beverage experience the pebbly soil in which the grapes had grown before harvesting and vinification as such began. (Imagine being able to discern what kind of chicken under what conditions produced the eggs in the omelet or soufflé you've recently eaten, just from its characteristics as a prepared foodstuff.)[6]

In fact, analysis of hundreds of such tasting notes allows us to organize in diagrammatic form what Sir Michael had to say about Château Haut-Brion, 1961, claret of the Graves district of Bordeaux, on tasting in November 1979. We can diagram the way the very orderliness of this "spontaneous" bit of English prose in fact follows its rigid structural pattern.

The diagram in table 8.2 separates on the right the phrases composed of the technical terms professionals use for each of the dimensions along which they evaluate the substance. For example, under stage II, *nose*, Broadbent was surprised

TABLE 8.2 Genre Structure of the Wine-Tasting Note of Table 8.1, Exemplifying Register Usage

Château Haut-Brion, 1961

(A. Placement in history of
acquaintance/connoisseurship)   First tasted
                                in 1963.

(B. Perduring characteristics
of such occasions—summary
note [stage III])   Surprisingly *soft* and
                                              lovely   on the **palate** even
                                                                      in the mid-1960s

(C. Tasting note per se)
    (II:)   but the **nose** curiously
                                                                      waxy and *dumb*,
                                                                      developing
                                                                      its characteristic
                                                                      hot, earthy/pebbly
                                                                      bouquet
                                                                      only latterly.
                                                                      Ripe, soft
    (III:)   **texture**,
                                              lovely
                                              but not as demonstrably
                                              or obtrusively a '61   as the other first
                                                                      growths.
                                                                      Fine [cf. **finesse**],
                                    Gentlemanly, understated.

to find the smell *waxy* and initially difficult to discern (<u>dumb</u>),[7] but later was reassured to experience the <u>hot</u>, <u>earthy</u>/<u>pebbly</u>-ness of the *bouquet* component of scent, the conditions of growth on hot, calcareous slopes presumably enhanced by the techniques of vinification of its particular grapes (merlot and cabernet sauvignon). As should be clear, there are what we term *taxonomies* of possibly discerned characteristics for each dimension through which the taster moves in cognizing the experience, among the members of which contrast-set at each phase or stage a taster distinguishes. A maximal note records values along all five phased dimensions, in their proper order; a more telescoped or minimal one generally concentrates on stage III, for which there are the most taxonomic differentiators, and perhaps as well stage II, since olfaction is so much a part of what is considered to be "taste" in the mouth.

Now, in addition to such highly organized technical terminologies of evaluative wine connoisseurship, there are other bits of prose, shown on the left of the textual diagram. These tend to be characterological, almost anthropomorphic, and bespeak, by their use, a kind of assumed social position on the part of the user we nowadays associate with the rarefied precincts of a now receding male preppy and clubby culture in the city and, on weekends, with great estates and country clubs of toney suburbia and exurbia. My research reveals, however, that it is this vocabulary and these phrases that those who live socially distant from oenological pursuits actually identify as the shibboleths, the salient contributory elements, of the verbal register of wine talk, and about which there is the usual kind of class-associated anxiety peaking in the lower-to-mid-bourgeoisie—as is the case for many realms of connoisseurship. James Thurber catches this in his famous 1944 *New Yorker* drawing that pictures and quotes a dinner party host as he tastes the wine he has just served, noting for his guests, "It's a naive domestic Burgundy without any breeding, but I think you'll be amused by its presumption." All of this talk is, as can be seen, characterological phraseology, all verbal material from the left-side of a would-be tasting-note diagram, to be sure. But it is richly communicative of the predicament of the anxious readership of would-be wine aficionados for whom Thurber's joke still resonates. (There are still takeoffs of Thurber's joke—interdiscursive *renvoi*, technically speaking—used in television sitcoms and other pop culture these days; recall the similar fate of Magritte's "non-pipe" in his 1928–29 painting *La trahison des images*, parodied in visual text, even by its author, ever after. Both have become—to use the term—memes.)

And yet, this oinoglossic register continues to be the very medium of this particular area of connoisseurship, particularly at its professional peak top-and-center. Table 8.3 reproduces a couple of examples that came onto my desktop screen not long ago for a white wine from France's Côte de Beaune region of Burgundy, Girardin's 2007 Puligny Montrachet, Folatières.

The text genre and especially the register are unmistakable. We can render these two recent exemplars in precisely the same analytic framework as we were able to do with Sir Michael's canonical prose.

Notice in the diagram[8] of the *Wine Advocate*'s tasting note in table 8.4 how remarkably active and agentive the aesthetic essence of the chemical substance seems to be, how almost like an encountered subject-alter in character to whom the taster develops an appreciative reaction! The aesthetic object presenting here "mingles" (active nomic); it is "vivacious" and "bright" in its brimming-ness; it "finishes with almost startling grip and tenacity"; and it "compensates for" what it seems to lack in the way of complexity. But it presents itself to us, as it were, phase by phase as a temporally organized aesthetic encounter through qualia-as-experienced: first in the *aroma* dimension "malt and toasted brioche" giving way to "sea breeze, fresh citrus, ripe white peach, floral perfumes." Next, in the mouth it *tastes* of "primary fruit" and feels—its *texture*—"silken" on the tongue. And as it vaporizes as it is swallowed or expectorated, it still seems to be there, its *finish* in other words "tenacious," in fact "startlingly" so. It's an in-your-face wine, not a subtle one: full of "sheer energy and excitement" that makes up for lack—can you imagine, after all this verbiage!—of "complexity." (Naive domestic burgundy, anyone?)

TABLE 8.3 Tasting Notes on 2007 Puligny Montrachet, Folatières

"93 out of 100.... Girardin's 2007 Puligny-Montrachet Les Folatières mingles aromas of malt and toasted brioche with sea breeze, fresh citrus, ripe white peach, and myriad floral perfumes. Vivaciously and brightly brimming with primary fruit, yet silken in texture and suffused with salinity and notes of toasted grain, this finishes with almost startling grip and tenacity. Anything it might lack in complexity today vis a vis the very best of the vintage it compensates for in sheer energy and in promise. Expect more excitement over the next 7–10 years." —*Wine Advocate*

"93 out of 100.... Perfumed nose offers lovely lift to the aromas of flowers, violet and saline minerality. Juicy, stony and high-pitched, combining a strong impression of saline minerality with obvious chewy extract. Seriously sexy, precise wine, finishing vibrant and long." —Stephen Tanzer

2007 **Puligny Montrachet, Folatières** (Girardin, Vincent) (750 ml)—$49.50 per bottle

TABLE 8.4 Genre Structure of the *Wine Advocate* Wine-Tasting Note of Table 8.3, Exemplifying Register Usage

Overall Point Evaluation		93 out of 100.... Girardin's 2007 Puligny-Montrachet Les Folatières
II. Olfaction	mingles ... with ... and myriad ...	*aromas* of malt and toasted brioche ... sea breeze, fresh citrus, ripe white peach, ... floral perfumes
III. Taste and Tongue-Feel	Vivaciously and brightly brimming with ... and suffused with ...	... primary fruit, yet silken in *texture* ... salinity and *notes* of toasted grain
IV. Finish	... almost startling grip and tenacity	this *finishes* with ...
Overall Comparison and Futurity	in sheer energy ... more excitement ...	Anything it might lack in *complexity* today vis a vis the very best of the vintage it compensates for ... and in *promise*. Expect ... over the next 7–10 years.

Wine Advocate on 2007 **Puligny Montrachet, Folatières** (Girardin, Vincent) (750 ml)

TABLE 8.5 Genre Structure of the Stephen Tanzer Wine-Tasting Note of Table 8.3, Exemplifying Register Usage

Overall Point Evaluation		93 out of 100
II. Olfaction	... offers lovely lift to ...	Perfumed *nose* ... the *aromas* of flowers, violet and saline minerality
III. Taste and Tongue-Feel	... high-pitched, ... combining a strong impression of ... obvious	Juicy, stony and ... saline minerality with ... chewy *extract*
(2) IV. Finish	... vibrant and ...	*finish*ing ... long
(1) Overall Impression	Seriously sexy, precise ...	... wine, ...

Stephen Tanzer on 2007 **Puligny Montrachet, Folatières** (Girardin, Vincent) (750 ml)

The shorter note by Stephen Tanzer, too, as diagrammed in table 8.5, constructs an aesthetic object in waves of pleasurable sensation-inducing qualia as described in the rightmost column of my chart; it is so pleasurable an aesthetic object, apparently, as to render itself "lovely . . . high-pitched . . . vibrant . . . [and] seriously sexy!" One blushes to think of the even metaphorical tingling bodily reaction of the taster, and yet here we see illustrated the important notion that the event of tasting is an encounter with a virtually living structure of qualia—rendered into a verbal report—to which the sensitive, indeed, the hypersensitive aesthete responds with unmistakable affect, even emotion, all the while able to cognize, to verbalize, the experience.

If such tasting notes are truly authoritative—think of those of Sir Michael Broadbent or of the American Robert Parker of the *Wine Advocate,* eagerly sought out by aficionados—they become normative standards for other tasters to share the experience, indeed to *have* the experience *or at least to aspire to have it* in the same way and with the same degree of subtlety and multidimensional elaboration of a structure of qualia as the wine authorities manage to convey in their tasting notes published as beacons of aesthetic orientation for the wine-consuming public. The tasting note becomes a verbal component of a normative cultural schema for experiencing and enjoying the object of aesthetic contemplation. It authoritatively constructs that aesthetic object as one that will, in phases, reveal its dimensionalized qualia to the experienced sensorium of someone who purports to construe it, to interpret it with appropriate descriptive verbalization (whether thought to oneself or uttered or written).

Taken all together, the aggregated dimensions of evaluation, particularly considered against certain reference benchmarks for the qualia generally associated with type, terroir, vintage, and so on, give way to a summary judgment of aesthetic value in the instance, as in any field of connoisseurship. ("It's definitely a Monet, but not a particularly good example of his production at the height of his imaginative and technical powers.") The French government already in 1855 established an outline rubric of grades of distinction—first growths, second growths, and so on, they are termed—for the then notable château wines of the Bordeaux region (since expanded and revised). The concept of comparative ranking on various encompassing scales has widened and scaled up in all sorts of ways: scales of five degrees of distinction, scales of twenty degrees of distinction (though rarely does one see a number below twelve), scales of one hundred degrees, as in the *Wine Spectator* (where ratings below 80 are rare indeed, for why even note such products!). Speaking of scales, such evaluative numbers—"92 points"; "***"—are prominently displayed in signage in a wide variety of retail outlets, perhaps along with some minimal tasting note, so that the would-be consumer encountering a new wine from afar need pay attention to nothing but the ratio of price to numerical rating to calculate against desired optimal value in advance of purchase of a bottle. Such a consumer wishes to trust the experts quoted by retailers, who have thus made it easy to drink by number.

OUR REGISTERS, OUR SELVES

As a linguist, I am of course concerned with the forms and meanings of words and expressions by which people communicate with one another, in the instance about their experiences as users and judges of commodities. In such communication, even the same word form can be associated with many different conceptual schemes depending on degrees of socially recognized shared expertise; think of what we term the technical meanings of otherwise ordinary words, like lattice (algebra), or bouquet (wine tasting), and contrastively think of words even the forms of which are known only among those with certain technical knowledge, such as muon (particle physics) or climat (viticulture).

In effect, then, using a word or expression in a certain way in an event of evaluative communication frequently does double classificatory work. A word used in a certain descriptive way categorizes or classifies both things-in-the-denotable-world (whether "real" or fictive/imagined/theorized), to be sure; it indexes—makes immanently relevant in the communicative here and now—one or more schemata of qualia, as I have noted, of which the distinctive value is differentially signaled by that particular word or expression. But additionally, the particular differential application of the word at the same time reveals—it points to, or indexes—the social identity, the category of person, who would stereotypically invoke such a use of the word, aligning or figuring the user with respect to that category. This is an example of what, as adumbrated above, is *a dialectically duplex indexical register effect* built into the use of such linguistic material (an effect that is, by the way, universal in all known language communities).

Verbal registers, let us recall, constitute a particular kind of sociolinguistic fact.[9] For language, the idea is that there is a mode of folk consciousness (an ethno-metapragmatics) of "superposed" (Gumperz 1968, 383–84) indexical variability that posits the existence of distinct, indexically contrastive ways for a speaker to convey what counts as "the same thing"—that is, to communicate the same denotational content over intervals of text-precipitating discourse that differ as to their appropriateness to and effectiveness in conceptualized contexts of use. These contexts may be defined along any of the usual sociolinguistic or social anthropological dimensions describing who normatively communicates with what forms to whom about whom/what, where, and under what institutional conditions.

So registers emerge from the interaction of the inherent indexicality of linguistic form—how forms of language signal their contexts of use—and the very particular folk understanding of that indexicality as grasped by native speakers, who conceptualize indexicality as alternate ways of being able to communicate "the same thing" in more than one way. That is, for the nonsemiotician native speaker, using the proper register means representing or describing—referring to and modally predicating about—something in the usual sense, only with a sensitivity to the message's appropriateness to and effectiveness in context, for which one chooses the "just right" linguistic form. For a semiotic like language *enregisterment*—the quality of being differentiated into registers—is organized around certain key *register shibboleths,* such that the overall compatibility of the other linguistic material in a text containing the shibboleth seems to guide native sensitivities to understanding what register the text is in. It is very much like the way the eye alights on certain parts or features of a painting before moving on to others that it tries to encompass in a single coherent whole, comprehended variously in generic, thematic, and stylistic modes. Here, in verbal communication, we seem to operate conceptually in terms of the indexical salience of the shibboleths that in the first instance enregister a text in which, then, the other forms of the message are evaluated for compatibility.

Language users thus evaluate discourse with intuitive metrics of coherence of enregistered features of form that co-occur across relevantly cohesive stretches, generally focusing on highly salient register shibboleths that reveal a basic register setting around which cluster other aspects of usage whether compatible or lacking compatibility.[10] "Standard" registers, too, within fuzzier margins of performance, set up a gradience of expectation for adherence and thus for indexical self-identification. One's usage is recognized as standard when marked by the coherent co-occurrence of a sufficient number of prescriptive standard shibboleths (English: use *he and I* in Subject position) and the nonoccurrence of the preponderance of proscribed nonstandard ones (English: don't use *him and me* in Subject position; never use *ain't*) under the cultural order of institutionalized standardization. Enregisterment of standards of this kind produces both a conscious and an unconscious anxiety in speakers about conforming to them. As William Labov's work of fifty years ago (1966, 1972) classically demonstrated, the acuteness of such anxieties also has a profile of social differentiation within the population comprising the language community. Linked to such demographic characteristics of speakers as socioeconomic class, ethnicity, age, and sex, speakers' orientation to—and hence anxiety about—use of standard register is a metasemiotic framework that gives indexical potency to the very prescribed and proscribed forms. They become guides for interpretation of who (sociologically speaking, what category or kind of person) is speaking and under what conditions of social context (sociologically speaking, at what site of using language where normative demands for inhabiting a role challenge the speaker to succeed in navigating these demands). A speaker successfully or not so successfully doing so places himself or herself within relevant orders of stratification.[11] Both registers as such and manifest orientations to/from such enregisterment thus socially position the people who use them in relation to those who take note of them.

Now, what is interesting about wine talk is certainly not its being a register phenomenon as such but the curious bidirectional and tiered, dialectical indexical

The "Eucharistic" Quality of Qualia-fication

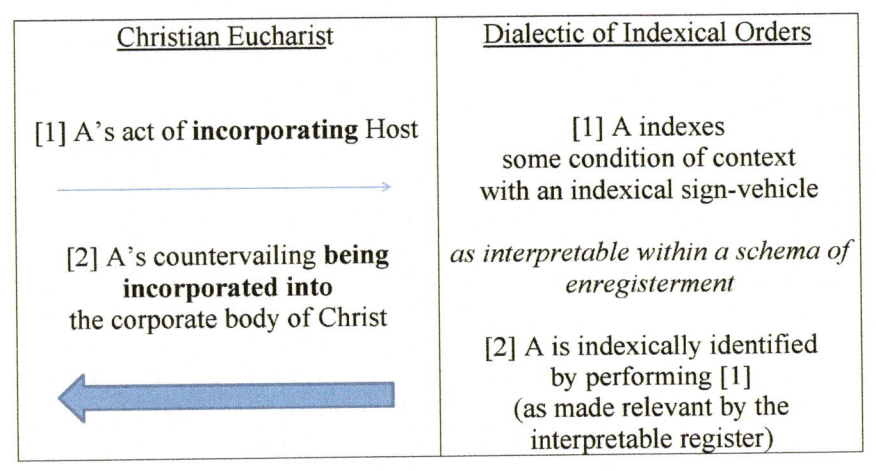

Christian Eucharist	Dialectic of Indexical Orders
[1] A's act of **incorporating** Host	[1] A indexes some condition of context with an indexical sign-vehicle
[2] A's countervailing **being incorporated into** the corporate body of Christ	*as interpretable within a schema of enregisterment* [2] A is indexically identified by performing [1] (as made relevant by the interpretable register)

FIGURE 8.2. The "eucharistic" semiotics of aesthetic evaluative discourse.

character—I like to call it, appropriately enough for wine, eucharistic—of this kind of aesthetic and evaluational discourse, as shown in figure 8.2. For if, as we've seen, it is the case that, in using oinoglossic register in the well-formed, genred tasting note, one is engaged in an activity of *construal* of the aesthetic object, interpreting and ultimately evaluating it in terms of certain dimensions or qualities manifest to the discerning taster, one is, in and by this act of construal, at the same time performatively *constructing oneself,* making one's social identity salient within the macro-order of prestige consumption. One is then not only characterizing the aesthetic object but also, in effect, placing or locating oneself socially with respect to a "community of practice," those "in the know"—or not—about matters oenological within the complex intersection of institutionalized practices that bring the aesthetic object and the judging aesthete together.

To be sure, all discursive manifestations of so-called expert knowledge inevitably suggest both directions of such tiered indexicality (Cf. Carr 2010). In the aesthetic realms its deployment grounds the authority of professional or avocational connoisseurship. Expert discourse is denotationally *terminologized*: its lexical forms—its set words and expressions—as we've already seen, index specific points of conceptual distinction in the normative ontologies of such expertise; their use perspectivally reveals how the world is structured so as to produce the referent one is differentially describing and thereby evaluating along its presenting dimensions.[12] Expert discourse is, furthermore, *genred*: one must use the words and expressions just so, in a highly policed cotextual organization of discourse, coherently to communicate all the relevantly conceptualized dimensionalities of the object one is describing and how they interrelate in the expert ontological perspective. Thus, thinking and talking like—or, in varying modes and degrees of fault, unlike—an expert positions an individual, associating him or her with the societal places where experts ply their trade. Moreover, convincingly expertlike talk endows such an individual's views with a certain degree of authority in the particular realms of expertise, even by those who can do no more than identify that an expert register is in use.

This should remind us of Thurber's wine-serving and -evaluating host, who, no doubt socially situated far from the precincts of Sir Michael or Robert Parker or Stephen Tanzer, knows there is an oinoglossic register and perhaps genred discourse in it. He constructs his own "tasting note" to alert his guests to what they are about to imbibe, entirely out of the characterological fluff of the genre. It's an attempt at oinoglossic enregisterment at an anxious, if therefore somewhat bombastically snobbish, distance from the authorizing center of semiosis.

OINOGLOSSIA'S INSTITUTIONAL MATRIX—INTERSECTING CHRONOTOPES

Every encounter of a wine drinker and wine, and in particular every aesthetic-evaluative encounter of a wine taster and wine, exists within an abstract envelope projected by the fact that wine is an agricultural product rendered into a marketable cultural commodity at the retail level. There are multiple versions of wine's course from grape to enjoyed beverage that depend on, and result in locating it in, distinct segments and sectors of its ultimate retail market. Such alternative chronotopes are shaped by processes and operations that run along a cline from industrial agribusiness through degrees of artisanal and ultimately exquisitely artistic technique. Given these, as it were, multiple "biographical" trajectories of wine, institutional factors associated with one or more of the phases of its life apply to it according to, and determinative of, its various gradations, all intersecting to affect the way wine—and its drinkers—are classified and scaled.

One such institutional factor is that of applied science, in particular oenological and viticultural sciences such as geomorphology, soil and climate science, and botany, on the one hand, and on the other the organic chemistry of esters, aldehydes, and alcohols, and human psycho-physiology, sciences of olfactory and gustatory perception. A second shaping factor emerges from the institutions of aesthetic connoisseurship in the organized world of collecting, auctions, and "capital appreciation" of heirlooms and the like, central or peripheral in the cline ranging from the professional through the serious avocational to the rank amateur or even happenstance wine drinker. Yet a third arises in the institutional world of retail marketing of commodity circulation, in particular of so-called lifestyle commodities—that is, personal-value-conferring commodities of domestic consumption, in some of which, for example, brand has become very important as an index of distinction. Each of these institutions, organized via networks of nodes of social practice, endows the experience of engaging wine and, in particular, of verbally engaging with it with a distinctive effect on enregisterment that has been spreading from wine to other comestibles.

First, from the applied science institution, anchored in organizational sites in schools of oenology and viticulture and industrial research laboratories, emerge guidelines on everything from horticultural interventions suitable to vines of particular ecologies to methods of maceration, vinification, blending, barreling, and bottling with specific biochemical (and ultimately aesthetic) goals and ends uppermost. At the receptive end of these processes, tasting can be seen as a kind of psychophysical response to the raw, biochemical data of empirical reality in ways that can be isolated and terminologically standardized by laboratory methods.

A particularly interesting and influential example is the "standard system of wine aroma terminology," from the University of California, Davis, Department of Viticulture and Enology, as shown in figure 8.3. The circular visual array notwithstanding, it depicts the conceptual classification of aroma in the form of a taxonomy with three degrees of inclusive specificity, locating each ultimately terminologized aroma lexeme in a pie-shaped area at the circumference of the circle. Each of these specific lexical forms was operationalized in the laboratory with reference standards of olfactory percepts, based on putting certain precise amounts of some substance into a precise amount of a reference white wine in a covered test tube, waiting a precise amount of time, and then uncorking and smelling. The idea is to establish a reference standard for use of each of the descriptive terms. The center point of the circle represents undifferentiated aroma and the intermediate inner circle's circumference labels clusters of aromas into affinity groups of what the researchers presume are substantively similar kinds.[13]

Particularly in the consumer environment of a trained and credentialed bourgeoisie (physicians, lawyers, business executives, academics, etc.), a class fraction in which serious wine tasting or at least interested consumption is notable, the suggestion is appealing that our olfactory sensoria respond psychophysically to aroma in much the same way as our visual sensoria respond to dimensions of hue, saturation, and brightness organized into a psychophysical perceptual space of what is commonly termed "color." The human perceptual acuity for color is such that every non-color-blind human organism can differentiate somewhere in the range of 7.5 to 10 × 10^6 j.n.d.s measured in the three-dimensional psychophysical color space of stimuli in the visible spectrum. Looking at the verbalizations of aroma in wine-tasting notes (such as the ones quoted above), it appears that people at the professional end of the wine-tasting cline experience waves of precise simultaneous and serial reactive olfactory percepts of the substance they are encountering.

Research Note
Modification of a Standardized System of Wine Aroma Terminology

A. C. NOBLE[1*], R. A. ARNOLD[2], J. BUECHSENSTEIN[3], E. J. LEACH[4], J. O. SCHMIDT[5], and P. M. STERN[6]

A modified version of the wine aroma wheel has been constructed to clarify and improve the proposed list of standardized wine aroma terminology. The order of terms has been reorganized to facilitate its use. Terms describing the "nutty" aromas in wine have been added. In addition, reference standards are suggested to define

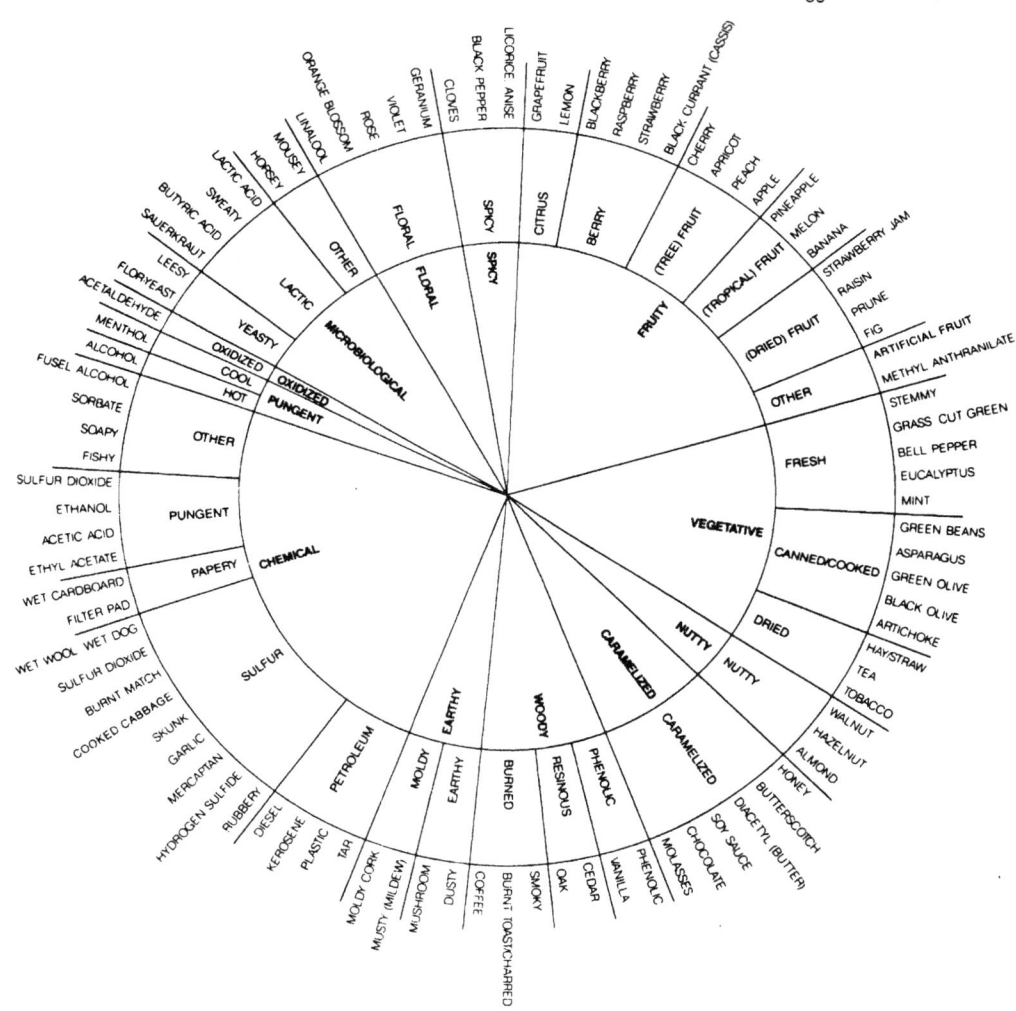

Fig. 1. Modified ASEV Wine Aroma Wheel showing first-, second-, and third-tier terms.

FIGURE 8.3. The "aroma wheel" of Noble et al. (1987).

So to the interested layperson in the target category of advanced-degreed consumers, the idea is inherently appealing that such degrees and admixtures of precise, verbally realized connoisseurship can in fact be substantiated by laboratory calibration. This was, in fact, the presentation of the aroma wheel in upscale print media, as scientific backing to the enregistered genre being inculcated by professionals through wine-tasting educational outreach. And, perhaps like colorimetric psychophysical training, one can, through guided practice, become a more acute and accurate perceiver of aroma as of other characteristics of wine. Such acuity or refinement of palate, in other words, could as well be confidently acquired as a kind of aesthetics backed by applied science—like acquiring an additional quasi-professional degree or certificate of aesthetic competence (compare art- or music-appreciation courses in secondary schools and colleges as opposed to studio art and music performance).[14]

The second institutional realm we should consider is aesthetic connoisseurship as such. The analogue is, of course, connoisseurship in plastic, graphic, and performance arts, and in matters of "collectibles" of all kinds with pasts and futures in chronotopes of fluctuations in value. There are professional connoisseurs whose expertise and judgment set price in the art and collectibles markets, and these people are valued for the subtlety of their judgment in discerning inherent aesthetics, historicity, and so on, and in projecting stable or volatile futurities, as the case may be, amid all the risks to collectors and other avocational enthusiasts. In such matters not only is professional status and authority associated with fineness of aesthetic sense (and sensoria!), but it is also dependent on a wide, cumulative familiarity with histories of production, circulation, and consumption/possession of objects, genres of objects, styles and registers of material aesthetics, and so on. Art critics need to have examined the pen-and-ink drawings related to paintings and sculptures, the chalk cartoons related to grand frescoes, and so on, to know the history of how and to whom they circulated as instruments of process, then as objects of possession, and the values, pecuniary and otherwise, attached thereto. The authoritativeness with which such aesthetic acuity is combined with fingertip knowledge of a work's historical minutiae, and mobilized in evaluative discourse, undergirds the authority with which a connoisseur commands respect for—and confidence in—his or her informed judgment.

Among comestibles, wine seems to have been the first, and remains the *primus inter pares*, of those where such connoisseurship is now highly developed. It is surely the case that wine as an aesthetic experience is associated first and foremost with people in those sectors and segments of the population where aesthetic connoisseurship in realms of "[high] culture" and collecting have long been highly developed. And as the very notion of oenological connoisseurship has become linked to class mobility, anxiety has developed about the register with which one verbalizes the rationale of a perhaps ultimately scalar judgment—and, of course, through which one is, conversely, judged as to position in a political economic and cultural scale. And from wine, the process continues to other comestibles made to be worthy of association in its image. There have long been published print runs of the *Wine Spectator* and the *Wine Advocate;* and, according to Google (queried on June 1, 2014), no fewer than 18,600,000 sites on "wine appreciation" and 819,000,000 on "wine terms" are accessible to search, all part of a thriving industry-supporting oenological avocationalism and oinoglossic enregisterment. But so also do we now have the *Beer Advocate,* the *Malt* [i.e., whiskey] *Advocate,* the *Cheese Advocate,* and so on, both in print and online. The imitative parallelism—how these forms of avocational fandom mimic that of wine—is quite extraordinary.

The third institution is mass lifestyle retailing, which relies on the existence of the first two and brings them together. What you are in consumption class is what you eat, drink, wear, and so on—and what you discover you have to say about the experience or reveal in other cultural modalities makes others aware of your consumptive patterns. In such retailing, a product that can be a performative emblem of distinction always hovers between total individuation (one-of-a-kind artisanal and artistic achievement) and brand dependability (label, logo, insignia on the display/packaging of the very object), of course. Total individuation in wine gets down to the level of the individual bottle tasted on some particular occasion; the best oenological connoisseurs facing the most rarefied of wines, operate at this level. (Note how this cultural concept of distinctiveness informs the practice, at serving, of never filling a glass with fluid from bottle number $n+1$ if there is still present in the glass some of wine of bottle number n, for example. Even where it is ridiculous not to do so, it is a gesture of interdiscursive reference, a little performative nod to, an imitative figuration of, the top and center of viticultural distinction.) At the other extreme, it is brand, brand, brand that is the principle of marketing, like the mass-produced couturier-authorized lines that self-advertise on the products themselves. At the middle ranges of the wine market in the United Sates, brandedness is the key to marketing; the consumer must be made to feel the equivalent—for wine, certainly anchored in France and things French—of prominently showing off a Prada article of clothing on the body, or a Miele dishwasher in the fabulously up-to-date kitchen.

It is in this institutional framework that we can see how the above-named publications and websites are not simply providing connoisseurs' tasting notes and other such evaluations to consumers that would guide them in wisely using the financial resources they devote to consumable comestibles. They are providing, through a rhetoric not unlike that of fashion (Barthes 1983), images of a life built around focal interest in the comestible and all that goes congruently along with it. These have become vehicles of total personal self-fashioning, as it were, no different in genred appeal from the gendered appeal of the obsessively bodily focused magazines and websites like *Cosmopolitan, Marie Claire,* and so on for (young) women and *Details, Men's Health,* and so on for (young) men, mirror images across the gender line. Garments, gadgets, gizmos, things with which to surround oneself corporeally and in life and leisure activities, training regimes and tips for everything from abdominal musculature to sexual experiences, and so forth, are the repetitive content of each issue of the latter. In like form, the connoisseurship-focal publications also market through imaging as well as verbiage how to devote oneself, to whatever degree, to wine, to beer, to whiskey, or to whatever as a lifestyle totalization. Vacation in a wine-producing region; see how the stuff is made and purchase it. Remodel your kitchen not with any old ordinary appliances but with a special wine refrigerator. Here is the perfect wine glassware for each of your favorite kinds of wines. Wear our *Wine Enthusiast* T-shirt to inform others of your life's passion. Why drinking wine is ultimately superhealthy and compatible with your exercise regimen to keep fit.

All of this cyclically produced as a guide to the good—no, a better, more accomplished—life that becomes, in each of these aspects, more of life's "work" even in one's so-called leisure.

At the culminating moment of consumption, the tasting and evaluation of the experience, the wine consumer is poised in a place where all these institutions have intersected with distinctive shaping influences.

"VINIFYING" PRESTIGE IN COMESTIBLES AND BEYOND

But now we can move beyond wine to think about parallels to the oinoglossic phenomenon that seem to emanate from it and project an expanding chronotopic space of iterative parallels in the wider universe of consumption. The mechanism of such iteration has been the strength and institutional entrenchment of the doubly indexical—the "eucharistic"—oinoglossic register and associated nonverbal semiotics that continue their spread or emanation to other realms of would-be prestige in the universe of potables and comestibles. Indeed, each of these areas of lifestyle has come to prestige fruition as a branch of the growing semiotic vine of oinoglossia.

Wine's prestige as a comestible manifests its well-developed register effect, not only in language, but also in a large number of penumbral sign systems that frame the production, circulation, consumption, and memorialization of this substance and people's relation to it. And, this register effect is spreading, or has been spreading, from the domain (the *domaine*, if you will!) of the oenological to draw in any comestible that aspires to distinction—that is, any comestible that as well aspires to confer distinction upon its consumer. In terms of the framing of myriad other comestibles undergoing stimulated stratification by prestige, a kind of semiotic vinification, turning them into metaphorical wine, has been taking place both in

TABLE 8.6 Wine-Note-Like Coffee-Tasting Notes from a 1991 Starbucks Customer Flyer

Mocha Sanani: "Properly brewed [as espresso, it] . . . combines unrivalled intensity of aroma with thick, creamy body and bittersweet chocolate finish."

Ethiopia Sidamo: ". . . a delicate yet sprightly new crop coffee. . . . Flowery bouquet (with a hint of eucalyptus), light and elegant body, and a honeyed natural sweetness. . . . [O]ne of the most seductive of all African varietals."

Kenya "AA": "At the very top of the mountain (literally and figuratively) [t]his coffee, like a fine Bordeaux, balances heft and heartiness with bell-like clarity of flavor and blackcurrant fruitiness."

Ethiopia Harrar: ". . . a carefully cultivated coffee with a flavor that's usually anything **but** cultivated! The Chianti-esque, slightly gamy aroma gives Harrar a certain rustic charm that has family ties to Mocha Sanani (though it usually lacks that coffee's complexity, balance and breed). It is . . . 'a coffee for people who like excitement at the cost of subtlety.'"

Tanzania, Zimbabwe, Malawi: ". . . better used in blends than as varietals, since their flavors, while pleasant, are much less clearly delineated."

the language surrounding them and in the other sign systems by which we make their virtues known—for example, in the visual codes of advertising.

In other words, the institutional world of wine as a node has itself become a center point of "emanation" of ways of constructing prestige throughout a whole world of construable comestibles, edible and potable commodities that are brought into the stratified precincts in which wine has long had a social life. So today, just as one can be admired/reviled and imitated/shunned for being a "wine snob" (a folk term of opprobriousness from outside the fold, note), so also can one find a parallel place in the social world of those seeking to experience coffee, beer, cheese, ice cream, olive oil, vodka, and so on—examples in my data of all those things that through artisanal labor represent nature turned into culture. Let me illustrate this process of value-emanation, which transfers the register effect of bidirectional, thing-human cocategorization to any such commodity for which interested parties now wish to claim the possibility of stratified prestige. We will see that we are—sociologically speaking—what we communicate about what we eat or drink.

An early 1990s corporate flyer from Starbucks, for example, displays the distinctive oinoglossic register in discussing its beverages. Observe the way the tasting note genre in table 8.6 is used first off as a way to make the implicit argument that at least Starbucks coffee and wine are consumable commodities of comparably complex dimensionality in qualia space. We may observe in particular the dimensionality of coffee qualia here revealed and even the characterological anthropomorphism we have come to expect in the tasting note: "Seductive" Ethiopia Sidamo has "flowery bouquet (with a hint of eucalyptus), light and elegant body, and a honeyed natural sweetness"; Harrar's "Chianti-esque, slightly gamy

SEMIOTIC VINIFICATION 205

Appellation Colombie Contrôlée.

FIGURE 8.4. Advertisement for Colombian coffee growers.

aroma" gives it "a certain rustic charm" as "a coffee for people who like excitement at the cost of subtlety." The explicit comparisons to (high-value) Bordeaux and (lesser-value) Chianti should be noted. But more importantly, these tasting notes put the consumer on notice that, in learning to experience coffee-as-drunk in this

TABLE 8.7 Starbucks' Explanation of "Barista Talk" for Its Retail Customers

If you're nervous about ordering, don't be.
There's no "right" way to order at Starbucks. Just tell us what you want and we'll give it to you.
But if we call your drink in a way that's different from what you told us, we're not correcting you.
We're just translating your order into "barista-speak"—a standard way our baristas call out orders.
This language gives the baristas the info they need in the order they need it, so they can make your drink as quickly and efficiently as possible.
"Barista speak" is easy to learn. It's all about the order of information. There are five steps to the process. (Starbucks 2003, n.p.)

(1) cup (a cup for hot, cold, or "for here" drinks), (2) shots and size, (3) syrup, (4) milk and other modifiers, to (5) the (kind of) drink itself.

"I'd like to have an

ICED,	DECAF, TRIPLE, GRANDE,	CINNAMON,	NONFAT, NO WHIP	MOCHA."
CUP	SHOTS AND SIZE	SYRUP	MILK AND OTHER MODIFIERS	THE DRINK ITSELF
1	2	3	4	5

fashion, he or she will become defined by refined tastes that learn to discern and thus to favor this or that among the offered possibilities. Note how the Bordeaux comparison goes with the highest-end coffee varietal, and that of Chianti with the "coffee for people who like excitement at the cost of subtlety." Speaking of the "vinification," as it were, of coffee, figure 8.4 displays one of the most extraordinary visuals in this tenor—could it be less subtle in analogical form as a full-page glossy advertisement?—on behalf of the producers of Colombian coffee.

In its corporate heyday in shaping a prestige coffeehouse-like image, and concerned about the total contextualization of their products in relation to those who drink them, the Starbucks firm licensed a certain persnickety attitude on the part of its retail vendors, the baristas and other faces of the corporation in sales, who insist on having would-be customers use the corporate-specific formulaic genres in ordering their drinks when they belly up to the coffee bar. Paul Manning (2008) has written brilliantly about Starbucks barista register and its realization in the stylized genre of the drink order. Material excerpted from the corporation's own guide to ordering (see table 8.7) avers that of course there is no "right" and "wrong" way to order; it is just that "barista talk"—that is, the actually preferred and normative register and constructional genre—seems to impose itself as the rationalized, precise, and efficient verbal currency in such establishments.

And this verbal currency is again one that constructs the commodities for purchase at a Starbucks location as cells within a whole multidimensional matrix of complex objects defined by substances primary and secondary, shapes, sizes, and

TABLE 8.8 Barista "Rant" about an Encounter with a Noncompliant Customer

Me:	Hi, what can I get for you today, sir?
Man:	A small.
Me:	You would like a tall what sir?
Man:	I said I want a small.
Me:	Would that be a tall coffee sir?
Man:	No I want a small regular, I don't want to supersize my drink.
Me:	No sir, tall is small. Here at Starbucks small is tall, medium is grande and large is venti.
Man:	Well what I want is a small.
Me:	Okay, tall traditional it is. *grinding teeth* *get him the drink and give it to him*
Man:	*Takes off the lid* I thought I told you I wanted a small regular. This is just black.
Me:	Sir, you can find milk and sugar for your coffee over at the condiment bar. We have various types of dairy for your coffee and also many different types of sweeteners.
Man:	What I want is a regular small coffee. Why can't you do this for me? Is that too hard for you? At what I am paying for a cup of coffee you should be able to put the milk and two spoonfuls of sugar in for me.
Me:	Well sir, here at Starbucks we feel that you are better served by arranging your coffee however you like. That will be $1.52.
Man:	Are you sure? I can't get this for free being that it has taken over 5 minutes just to get me a small coffee and ring me up?
Me:	I am sorry that took so long. That will be a dollar and 52 cents for your TALL TRADITIONAL cup of coffee.

Why oh why do we have to go through this EVERY FREAKING DAY!!! Why!!!!

SOURCE: Manning 2008.

so on as it purports to be the most accurate description (i.e., construal) of them. Thus customers' violations of bellying up to the coffee bar with the proper formula trippingly articulated stimulate barista rants on the employees' website. Table 8.8 reproduces one of my favorites—and demonstrates the venomous condescension toward those who apparently pretend to the value of the Starbucks experience but who are thought by the service personnel to be distinctly unfit to consume Starbucks liquids, since they have not yet learned or—can you imagine?—they actually resist learning the rarefied uniqueness of genre and register for ordering them.[15]

There is revealed here a socio-spatiotemporal distance-from-the-authorizing-center involved for those failing the test as consumers no different from the distance indexed by inability to experience and properly notate oinoglossic aesthetics in the act of drinking wine. The totalizing corporate enregisterment of verbal style, both as a way to present and construe/construct that which is proffered for sale and as a way to present oneself in the saying as a consumer desirous of purchasing the comestible, constitutes in essence the imposition of a conical structure of the familiar kind in regimes of enregisterment. At the top and center are those "of" the lifestyle; at the down-and-out circumferential edges are those against whom baristas rant. Such a sociology—and sociolinguistics—distinctly reinforces the semiotics of what we term consumptive class, the key kind of class distinction in late capitalism, the one that drives people's anxieties of identity manifest by the second-order indexicals of verbal enregisterment insofar as this indexes the very conceptual framing of their approach to consumption.

But the mechanism of self-definition by virtue of projective construal of objects is certainly not limited to wine and prestige- (or at least class-) conferring coffee. It has come to encompass much in the contemporary world. Not long ago I was reading the automotive supplement to one of my city's newspapers, the *Chicago Sun-Times,* and noted this automobile connoisseur's excuse in a review of a 2014 Infiniti: "From my point of view, exterior looks are not the M56's strong suit. *There are really no distinguishing characteristics that immediately conjure up a specific feeling or thought or an attitude of excitement.* With the competition in this class incredibly strong when it comes to looks, approaching the exterior from a different direction is a great strategy to try to get noticed. However, if you miss the mark, you will limit your appeal" (John Stein, automotive editor, *Chicago Sun-Times,* October 15, 2012, emphasis added). If we think a bit about this, the point is that the qualia-as-apprehended of the Infiniti vehicle are supposed to resonate with a feeling—an affective or emotional interpretant, Peirce would say—in the reviewer, who confesses not to feel much of anything (except perhaps disappointment) as a response to the styling of this new vehicle. (One can, of course, find views of the very vehicle online, so as to gauge for oneself if one resonates with it in properly enregistered evaluative commentary.)

In conclusion, I suggest that there is an institutionalized social semiotic at work here, one that is perhaps clearest for commodities, since culturally these exist at the intersection of our ideas about the sensorium, our anxieties about the political economy of class, and our responsiveness to how marketing is integrated into every organized form of modern life. To be sure, Marx, one of the nineteenth century's great semioticians, already wrote illuminatingly of commodity fetishism, in which what he saw to be macro-socioeconomic structures of production, circulation, and consumption get projectively misrecognized as essential qualia of the very commodities that come to people in a market and are used by them. In some sense, a transformational skewing of the commodity form can be seen even in regimes of aesthetic connoisseurship, where value rests on the commodity's scarcity, historical uniqueness, and so on, as well as on "inherent" objectual properties. Wine as a fetishized commodity is thus closer to the extreme of fine art along such a scaled continuum of relevant gradations that runs from the absolutely unique all the way to forms of Benjaminian "mechanical reproduction" (of "brand," for example) in a variety of areas of circulation and consumption. The other potables I have mentioned above in their own ways imitate wine, particularly by making their own claims to bestow second-order indexical distinction on those who know how properly to fetishize them, how properly to project construable qualia discernable in them. For each, one does so by constructing appropriately enregistered language as legitimated by an authorizing center, whether corporate or—as for wine itself—in a more abstract intersection in socio-space-time.

But the emergence of such qualia driven by the duplex indexical processes discussed here has scaled up; it has become a ubiquitous phenomenon in our world of consumption. Why? Clearly, since even before the Lockean Enlightenment in western Europe, people have had ethno-psychological ideas of the sensorium, the faculty underlying the ability to discern and to judge properties or qualities of the individual persons, things, and so on of experience. With the institutionalization of Enlightenment ideas, sensory data—especially as extended by epistemic prostheses, especially those, like gauges, that render and calibrate qualia as numerical or scalable in type—have been moved to the very center of both professional and lay cultural ideas of rational response to the universe. So all of our evaluative projections of qualia deep down suggest to us the potential for an applied science, for an objective, even numerically gradated equivalent of the "aroma wheel." We train our sensoria and use epistemic prostheses emerging from the laboratory to extend our sensoria, calming ourselves in relation to the significant properties of things "out there" and thus "objectively" anchoring our ontologies within our worlds of experience.

The very capacity for ever finer human discernment of qualia as, itself, a capacity or a quality of one's sensorium intersects precisely with notions of personal "distinction," as, noted earlier, the late Pierre Bourdieu elaborately wrote about some years ago (1984). It is swept up into the political economy of class insofar the sensorium can be educated and trained as a mechanism of class mobility—as certainly can be one's facility with the registers and genres of reportage that we've seen exemplified in wine, coffee, and so on (and of course any technical registers—even those of semiotics!). There thus develops a kind of anxiety in those most aspiring to class mobility, as though the finer the discernment—reported in such registers as oinoglossia—the more distinguished one's consumptive class affiliation. Thus the phenomenon of wine-tasting seminars and practicums for the aspiring bourgeoisie, such as the noncredit course at my university's Graduate School of Business keen to provide its MBAs with the cultural wherewithal (cultural "capital," indeed!) to have an interview dinner that reveals their fitness for career placement in middle management. Think also of the idiot-savant sensorial monster, who, without explicit training of the sensorium in such modes, manages to have a refined taste articulated in proper genre and register (Robert Parker of the *Wine Advocate*, by reputation).

Such anxieties of self-identification are, of course, the very semiotic grist of advertising as a communicative institutional form. After all, the very essence of advertising semiosis consists of conveying the second-order indexical connection between the addressee's identity and his or her discerning—or at least assenting—projection of particular qualia of things and services and corporate identities for sale. As Richard Parmentier (1994, 151–153) has pointed out, in the United States, since circa 1976, because of Supreme Court rulings advertising has significantly shifted from explicitly rendered statements about products—predicating propositions about them—many of which were understood to be "puffery," exaggerated claims about the benefits of soap A or cigarette B. Advertising semiosis has shifted to nonpropositional "qualia-fication" of the product, service, corporation, and so on relative to which the hearer or viewer of the ad is positioned in, in the best of cases, the receptive would-be second-order indexical position. How one feels about imagining the qualia of the object-as-obtainable (the "obscure object of desire") gets projected onto the hearer or viewer, so that the latter's personal biography—one already lived or merely imagined—can be aligned with whatever is being marketed. Even American political campaigns, the central method of which is marketing a politician's "message" (see Lempert and Silverstein [2012]), are strategically organized around the second-order indexicality of identity politics. For this, a constantly updated quasi-biography of the candidate is the semiotic medium, a composite of certain qualia of personal biography and alignment or association with issues, so as to stimulate imaginative affiliation or disaffiliation—of the voters/consumers and ultimately result in their votes.

So the semiotics of qualia-fication are all around us, I would claim, and we experience "selves" that reflect at second-order indexical remove the sum total of the various institutionally relevant qualia projectively construed—that is to say, constructed under authority—by us and for us in our daily lives. And that is why oinoglossia thrives as a generative semiotic cultigen in its chronotope of identity-making.

NOTES

1. A *chronotope*, a conceptualization of M. M. Bakhtin (1981), is a space-time-like envelope in which characters and presumed others who populate narrated worlds are understood to interact according to emplotted trajectories of their unfolding interests as social beings in that fictive world. It can be seen that insofar as events of experienced social life, too, are understandable and narratable in the plotlike cause-and-effect terms of "realism," they, too, lend an inherently chronotopic character to each individual's real-life semiotic experience—sometimes one revealed only through careful tracing of multiple trajectories of connection that may not have been clearly conceptualized by the very protagonists themselves (ourselves).

2. Institutional defaults for how social relations are to be engaged in are, of course, not so much binding norms as value-conferring *affordances;* they can just as well be creatively violated and/or transformed in local practice as straightforwardly instantiated—as they regularly are!

3. A *register* of a language is, for its users, a contextually distinctive and formally contrastive style of communicating a message (denotational content) that could be more or less equivalently com-

municated in another, at least partially contrasting, way. A register setting thus provides a distinctive coherence to verbal communication over a stretch of discourse—a verbal *text*—as being appropriate to and indicative of (that is, it functions as an *index* of) the particular interactional *context* in which it occurs or, normatively, should occur. Contrast two possible forms of report in English of the same event: He went to see the eye doctor, in everyday lexical and syntactic vernacular, and He consulted his ophthalmologist, which includes at least two medical-technical terms, consult (cf. the billing term consultation) and ophthalmologist, a professionally dubbed medical specialist. Any and all planes of linguistic form may be "enregistered" in this way, and registers tend, as well, to be associated with particular communicational genres, socially deployable textual forms, and thus stereotypically with types of social beings who are thought characteristically to engage in using such communicational genres in particular loci of social life. Nonlinguistic culture, too, comes to be enregistered through the mediation of the discourse associated with it.

4. Decades back, the *New Yorker* had a "drawing" showing two carts stacked high with this vegetable, the one labeled "tomatoes 39¢" the other "tomahtoes 89¢," the joke turning on the two register variants (for most American English speakers) of the word, one with stressed vowel [ɛ·ʸ], the other with stressed vowel [ɑ·]. These two pronunciations of the word tomato—enregistered respectively as vernacular versus snooty; cf. the Gershwin song of 1937—would also be simultaneously seen as appropriate to small, irregularly shaped tomatoes versus large, beautifully rounded ones, I should think.

5. Linguists would as well observe that this reciprocally stacked or tiered indexicality in the social act of evaluation is independent of systems of so-called grammatical evidentiality and inferentiality, themselves deictic (indexical-denotational) markers that indicate, in the act of someone's communicating a proposition, his or her presumed license or authority so to do by virtue of (a) having been the addressee of the information in a prior communicative event ("hearsay evidentiality"); or (b) having been an observer via the senses of the factuality of what is currently being communicated-as-true ("eyewitness evidentiality"); or, contrastively, (c) communicating a proposition indexing that one has merely inferred its truth, or even just the possibility of its truth ("inferential" and "potential" epistemic grounds) on the basis of a cognitive operation.

6. Summerson Carr (personal communication) calls my attention to a scene in the American television spoof *Portlandia* in which the would-be diners in a restaurant are riven with just such anxieties about a menu item involving chicken, available for viewing at www.youtube.com/watch?v=ErRHJlE4PGI. We see here anxieties of a more generalized "vinification" still!

7. Forms denoted as forms (not sense-bearing signs) are underlined.

8. Here and in table 8.5 the text is still to be read, as in table 8.2, from left to right and top to bottom. But in these two representations I have used three dots to indicate that the next phrase is the next-occurring in the other column. Thus "mingles . . ." in the left text-column indicates that the phrase "aromas of malt and toasted brioche," the first in the right column, occurs next in the *Wine Advocate* text. A phrase in the left column preceded by three dots occurs after one without them in the right column.

9. See now Agha 2004 for an extended discussion. The term, building on the Reid (1956)—McIntosh—Halliday et al. (1964) precedent in the use of the term, alludes to the pipe organ, where different registers manipulated by stops provide distinct timbral envelopes for what is otherwise precisely the same melodic sequence of pitch-over-time.

10. For users of European languages, consciousness of "honorification," how one pays deference to Alter's relative status, for example, has long focused on saliently enregistered second-person personal deictic usage (think of saying German *du* as opposed to *Sie* as the Subject of a statement about—as well as to—an addressee); on form of terms of address (think of addressing someone in English as "Liz" rather than "Your Majesty," or as "Pops" rather than "Sir"); and on certain formulae for mands (in French, asking someone to sit down by using *Veuillez, s'il vous plaît, vous asseoir* versus *Assois tu!*). But co-occurring with these salient shibboleths, many other indexically loaded variants within their own

paradigms of contrast concurrently operate at many different planes so as to differentiate such deferential uses so long they compatibly co-occur with the more salient shibboleths noted here.

11. Registers, it should be noted, have all the properties of languages as structures immanent in denotational discourse; since registers are, however, indexically particular to context, whether by positive or negative stipulation, the set-theoretic union of the elements of all registers in a community, sociolinguistically viewed, thus constitutes the inclusive envelope of what can be termed the community's "language." Note also that most languages of the world do not have standard registers in the way the modern languages of nation-states do, even if they have valued registers of one or another sort—for example, for ritual use.

12. It is useful to compare medical diagnosis, which, as a procedure, begins from a cluster of "presenting symptoms" and a medical history that might be compatible with a number of possibilities regarding a patient's medical condition. In diagnostic intervention the goal is to produce a "differential diagnosis" that can be precisely described and thus indicate a course of therapy, perhaps even what is termed in the vernacular a "cure." In frustrating instances, the differential diagnosis emerges only after the fact, when a specific course of therapy has "worked" or when multiple ones have failed, eliminating all but one possibility.

13. See Noble et al. 1987. Of course, one would want a hierarchical cluster analysis or an analysis of common "errors" of labeling of a sufficiently large number of trials with each of the olfaction stimuli to extract inductively based groupings at this intermediate level, which would probably not lend themselves to representation around the circumference of a circular array.

14. See Silverstein (2013, 351–55) for a discussion of the influence of the Noble et al. aroma wheel as it has "emanated" from wine to other beverages and beyond.

15. I use here the "ethnographic present," though it is arguably the case that, since the expansionist corporate heyday of Starbucks represented in these ethnographic and text-artifactual materials, there have been reactions, especially among the fashionable urban young, of two sorts that have moved this brand into a different market image and space. One is the realignment of customer loyalty to down-market coffee, as for example that available at Dunkin' Donuts—earnest and genuinely "of the people." The other is to shun Starbucks as tantamount to the McDonald's of café experiences and to seek out, particularly in gentrifying urban enclaves, truly local, truly artisanal, truly unique and noncorporate "un-brands" of coffee at small internet cafés, and so on. The widespread emergence of the latter, ironically enough, no doubt depends on the prior brand history of Starbucks' success.

9

GOING UPSCALE

Scales and Scale-Climbing as Ideological Projects

Judith T. Irvine

In *Argonauts of the Western Pacific,* Bronislaw Malinowski famously wrote about the difference between two perspectives, the native's and the ethnographer's:

> The Kula is thus an extremely big and complex institution, both in its geographical extent, and in the manifoldness of its component pursuits. It welds together a considerable number of tribes, and it embraces a vast complex of activities, interconnected, and playing into one another, so as to form one organic whole.
>
> Yet it must be remembered that what appears to us an extensive, complicated, and yet well ordered institution is the outcome of ever so many doings and pursuits, carried on by savages, who have no laws or aims or charters definitely laid down. They have no knowledge of the total outline of any of their social structure. They know their own motives, know the purpose of individual actions and the rules which apply to them, but how, out of these, the whole collective institution shapes, this is beyond their mental range. Not even the most intelligent native has any clear idea of the Kula as a big, organized social construction. . . .
>
> The integration of all the details observed . . . is the task of the Ethnographer. ([1922] 1961, 83–84)

Today, many readers of this text would contest Malinowski's assertion that Trobrianders or other "natives" are unable to analyze the workings of their own social relations—that they are unable to take a "system" perspective. Clearly, Malinowski presumed that there was a major difference between himself and the Trobrianders in positioning and point of view, and he took this difference to be scalar: it was an epistemological metric, contrasting an ability (his) with a lack of ability (theirs) to see the "big picture." For him, moreover, Trobrianders could collectively be seen as tokens of a type, "savages," or "primitive man" as opposed to Europeans or "civilized humanity" (as he labeled these two types on p. 96 and elsewhere). Whether Trobrianders themselves see—or, in 1922, saw—human societies exactly this way, divided into primitive and civilized according to Malinowski's criteria, is doubtful. *Argonauts* does not tell us how they compared themselves to Europeans; perhaps other social distinctions, such as a contrast between Trobrianders and Dobuans, were more salient to them. And while Malinowski took it for granted that they were entirely immersed in the local, perhaps their cosmology offered a different view of the extralocal and the systemic. At any rate, since it is now rare for ethnographers to draw on "primitive man" as a social type, Malinowski's assertion looks to us today like a bit of ideology, in the most negative sense of that term. It is also an example of scale-making, in several respects: the relationship between a particular ethnographic case (Trobrianders) and a social type; the particulars of social relations and an encompassing social system; and the degrees of ability to discern what that social system might be.

If these kinds of scalar assumptions can no longer be taken for granted, then they must be examined more closely. What are the logics and interpretive practices—in a word, the ideologies—that guide people in the making and use of social and linguistic scales? Why do they so often favor whatever is construed as the big over the small? These logics can be called ideologies, for several reasons: because they are totalizing visions that shape construal, linguistically and socially; because these visions contextualize experience, imaginatively placing the phenomena of experience in wider (or narrower) relational fields; and because ideologizing and scale-making are semiotic processes that presuppose point of view. Construal, being a human activity, is socially situated, and there's always more than one position from which construal might take place. In scale-making, too, there must be a point of view, a perspective—a line of sight, as it were—along which a scale is constructed and its values measured. So the concepts of scale and ideology are linked, both of them requiring us to consider point of view (see also Gal this volume). In short, scale-making practices are ideological, hence semiotic, activities reliant on perspective and social positioning.

The Malinowski passage emphasizes a scale-implicating contrast in perspective between himself, as "civilized" European ethnographer, and the "natives" he observed. But while there is an obvious and familiar difference in point of view between ethnographer and ethnographee (so to speak), is that difference inevitably *scalar*, as Malinowski took it to be? Moreover, this is not the only perspectival difference that matters. There are multiple points of view among the people ethnographers study, not just one. And there is also a difference in point of view between Malinowski and ourselves, since we now see his work in the light of almost a century of subsequent ethnographies and later political contexts. To elevate the one difference—between ethnographer and those the ethnographer studies—as if it were the only difference that mattered, and to downplay the society-internal differences and the historical differences, would itself be an example of ideologized scaling.

Notice now that this passage from *Argonauts* has shown Malinowski invoking scaling along several different lines. There are metrics of personnel: the number of persons included in a social scene (the individual Trobriander and the many tribes); also the scope of the social categories these persons are deemed to represent. There are metrics of institutional complexity: the range of kinds of practices that are deemed to form an integrated system. There are metrics of geographical space: the text refers to the Kula as "big" in its geographical extent. And there are metrics of time: Malinowski wrote in the ethnographic present, except when describing events in which he himself took part; yet we now see Malinowski's work as situated in a particular historical moment, and we cannot now suppose that social conditions on the Trobriand Islands or the ideas of their inhabitants remain the same as in Malinowski's day. To these metrics one could add others, more language-focused: for example, the amount of talk that occurs on a particular social occasion, such as meeting one's Kula trade partner; or the range of linguistic varieties participants employ (although Malinowski's text doesn't tell us much about them).[1]

As this ethnographic description of the Trobriands illustrates, in any scene or site of analysis of social life there are many scalable dimensions or variables. In Malinowski's eyes, all these dimensions coincided. And even though he was sufficiently invested in the workings of scale to appreciate how the Kula as a "system" could be built up in practice, he claimed a sovereign voice. It was he, not the Trobrianders, who saw the big picture; and to him, the big picture was what counts. For scholars today, however, that privileged vision warrants interrogating, along with its role in scalar analytics and the idea that the big picture must be best.

Like the editors of this volume, I argue against off-the-shelf versions of "scale" (such as "micro-macro") that assume social life takes place on a single dimension of bigness (or smallness).[2] Instead, the many dimensions of social life, each of which might be scalable, must be considered independently in an ethnographic analysis. What dimensions are seen as scalable (and by whom); whether the scalar ladders are seen as lining up together; and whether there is a particular step that is especially salient—these are empirical questions about the construction of scales in particular ethnographic cases (see, for example, Philips this volume). The assumption inherent in so many "big picture" analytics, however, is that we know a priori how these dimensions cluster—that they form a single metric, "scale" *tout court*—and that the value of an analysis is similarly scaled, so that the bigger the picture, the more worthwhile the analysis. Often, however, those analyses can be achieved only by dismissing such troublesome things as facts that don't fit, aspects of social life that point in a different direction, and perspectives that don't agree. To assume, as is so often done in invoking a micro-macro binary, that scalable dimensions must coincide—or that there's only one kind of scale at all—is an ideological construction, perhaps emerging from the institutions that regiment people's lives (including our own) and align scales according to some social project.

So let us not suppose that scalable metrics just sit out in abstract space, with predictable relations among them. Along with the other contributors to this volume, let us ask, instead: what can ideological projects of scale-making do? In what follows, I offer some examples illustrating how scale-making emerges in ideological projects, and how those projects are perspectival, stemming from particular points of view. The examples also show that more than one kind of scale might have been relevant to the particular case, and these scales cannot simply be supposed to coincide or to be encompassed within the "big picture." They show, too, how frequently scale-making links bigness to privilege, institutions, and inertia. Most of all, the examples reveal some of the troubles that follow when the big picture is assumed to be the best picture or the only picture that matters. To show the pervasiveness of these projects and some of the variety of the topics in which they appear, my examples range among many ethnographic cases (thus illustrating a scale-making endeavor of my own, though I hope not a troubling one).

As Bruno Latour has remarked, "The problem is that social scientists use scale as one of the many variables they need to set up before doing the study, whereas scale is what actors achieve by scaling, spacing, and contextualizing each other.... It is of little use to respect the actors' achievements if in the end we deny them one of their most important privileges, namely that they are the ones defining relative scale. It's not the analyst's job to impose an absolute one" (2005, 183–184). Yet there is more to be said. Beyond the task of deconstructing absolute and a priori scales lies the task of exploring how and why scales are made—by analysts or by actors or by analysts-as-actors; how the logic of scale-making works; and how some scale-making and scale-climbing efforts are privileged.

CENSUS-TAKING: SCALES OF POPULATION, LANGUAGE, TERRITORY

Every ten years the United States conducts a census of its population. One of the major purposes of the census is to determine how many congressional representatives each state will have in the coming decade, since representation is proportional to population. More detailed versions of the census provide population figures for counties, cities, and towns—smaller administrative units. The number of people, then, is the scalar metric by which those administrative units are compared. Census tables line up the states and the subunits within them. With a closer look one might ask—as is increasingly done when the next census-taking looms, but may be forgotten or overlooked by many people in between—how the population figures are to be derived. Who counts as a resident of a town or a county, or any other administrative unit, and why? Obviously, the answers to these questions have consequences (in politics, education, and more). The practices for constructing the answers—for conducting and compiling the census—can be institutionalized, and indeed it is necessary that they should be stabilized before a decennial census can actually take place. Yet because of all the political and economic consequences of the results, there is disagreement about how a census is to be conducted.

That the scale of population (of a social unit) should determine the scale of resources—political representation, among other things—to which that unit gets access is itself a matter of ideology and political contestation. In the early republic, the Constitutional Convention of 1787 saw rancorous debate over whether representation in the national legislature should be based on a population scale (proportional representation), or unscaled, representing each state equally. With the less populous states deeply discontented and threatening to withdraw, weeks of discord elapsed before a compromise could be found. In what was later called the "Great Compromise" of 1787, a bicameral legislature was created in which each state would be equally represented by two seats in the upper house (Senate), while seats in the lower house (House of Representatives) would be scaled by population.[3]

What we see in this familiar example is a project of linear scale-making—lining up units according to population—whose political entailments transparently advantaged some units over others. At the time, it was not obvious to everyone that any scale-making to rank states with respect to each other was necessary at all, hence the discord. Moreover, the example also shows how *projects of scale-making can select a particular metric as the relevant one,* more important for some project than any other measure that might have been adduced. A state's territorial size, for instance, might have been selected as the relevant metric, rather than its population.

A linguistic census works in a similar way. Just as one can ask questions about residence in a state, similar questions can be asked about figures for speakers of a language. Who counts as a speaker—and what counts as a language? What kinds of projects select numbers of speakers of a language as the most relevant metric? Projects seeking to document languages deemed endangered, and to develop educational materials and language-learning activities for them, could be a contemporary illustration. Language endangerment is measured in large part by numbers of speakers.

As a historical illustration of a census in which numbers of speakers of a language were key to the project, consider census-taking in British African colonies in the days of empire. It was a principle of colonial governance—elevated to a policy of "indirect rule" or "native administration"—that the governed should be grouped along ethnic lines for uniform and enlightened administration, especially for the jurisdiction of native courts and participation in native councils. Although this principle was not put into practice everywhere, where it was applied a census was to determine the population figures for ethnic groups (then usually called "tribes") in each province and town. The colonizers assumed, however, that ethnicity normally depended on language. In fact, one of the rationales for organizing courts and councils by tribe was the idea that, on the whole, an ethnic group would share one "mother tongue" language, have homogeneous customs, and (except for nomads) inhabit a more or less contiguous territory. Supposedly, the resulting jurisdictions would be homogeneous, and their proceedings comprehensible to all the people subject to them. Moreover, in tracking ethnic groups it was thought to be most convenient to count people by language, rather than to delve into the complexities of their customs. Thus the census of "tribes" was actually a linguistic census.[4]

Since from the early 1920s onward there was an effort in southeastern Nigeria to put the policy of indirect rule into practice, the census of 1921 tracked the numbers of tribal populations in rural communities in order to redraw the boundaries of administrative units. But the task of matching administrative districts to ethnicity (via language) proved to be difficult. Populations seemed to be intermingled and multilingual, and they had their own notions as to which court and which district officer they preferred. Although the census results were published (Talbot [1926] 1969), together with maps, for the benefit of a metropolitan audience, the maps' visual effect of tidiness—with neatly delimited territories supposedly corresponding to tribes and subtribes whose population figures were provided in systematic tables—was achieved only at the expense of detail. The maps' geographical scale is too gross to reveal whether the figures match the bounded territorial units. Moreover, since the census questions did not distinguish "tribe" from "language," just assuming they were the same thing, the report offers no information about multilingualism or about the basis on which individuals were assigned to named groupings. Unless an especially astute policy-maker in London were to look beyond the maps, any discrepancy between tribe, language, and territory must have seemed to be an entirely local problem, a difficulty to be managed by local district officers. Discussing the maps and census in the 1926 survey volume, anthropologist P. Amaury Talbot seems to have thought these problems could be easily resolved: "As detailed information is here given for each sub-division of the population, it will be a simple matter to separate out any people which may be found to be incorrectly classified" ([1926] 1969, 17).

It is curious that Talbot, who had some firsthand experience in southern Nigeria, should have considered this matter "simple." As it turned out, any such optimism was short-lived. The very next year (1927), Talbot and C. M. Meek, an administrator with some anthropological training, were sent by the colonial government to southern Nigeria to investigate the "breakdown of local administration there" (Kuper 1973, 128). There were no quick solutions. For decades to come, local colonial officers were faced with endless troubles in which local inhabitants contested their assignment to this or that jurisdiction.

For example, a village cluster called Ika-na-Anang seems to have been a sore spot for British administrators for decades. The colonial archives reveal a record of disputes from the 1920s to the 1950s (a record traced and documented by A. E. Afigbo; see Afigbo 1987). At issue was whether the cluster should be assigned to a Ndoki Igbo administrative unit or an Ibibio unit. To which "tribe" did the cluster belong? The residents of these villages were almost all bilingual or multilingual. Their genealogies linked them to Ibibio clans, but they had also intermarried with people from nearby villages identified as Ndoki Igbo, with whom they had trade and property relations. They seldom met with their "parent" Ibibio clans for traditional rituals or anything else.

British officers acknowledged the problems attending this case from the 1920s on but, nevertheless, assigned the villages to a Ndoki Igbo administrative district, retaining an assignment that had been made somewhat more arbitrarily earlier in the twentieth century. Disputes over the assignment emerged regularly, accelerating after the early 1930s, when the colonial government tried to reactivate more of what it saw as its subjects' precolonial political institutions—and in so doing, increased the powers of the Ndoki Native Court. Moreover, court proceedings were to be conducted and, if possible, recorded "in the local tongue"—that is, in some variety of Igbo rather than in English (Afigbo 1987, 100). Some of the Ika-na-Anang villagers objected to the greater power the Ndoki court would now have over them.

Several years of discussion between village representatives and colonial officers ensued, culminating in formal petitions in 1939. In these petitions, a group of elders claimed that as Ibibios, they could not speak the Igbo language of the Ndoki Igbo council; so they petitioned to be removed from the Igbo district and placed in an Ibibio jurisdiction in a neighboring province.[5] The issues prompting the petitions seem to have been complex and were certainly not limited to language, although language differences were highlighted in the petition text. Other factors the elders emphasized included the villagers' minority status in the Igbo council that was managing some of their taxes and decisions affecting them. (Not emphasized in the petitions but relevant to the case were land rights and rents and the fact that taxes in the Ibibio district were a little lower.) Unpersuaded, the district officer at the time found against the petitioners—partly because one of the elders discussed the case with him in Igbo.[6] But the trouble did not go away. A new set of petitions in 1953–54 made the same argument: that the villages should be reassigned on linguistic grounds. By now the voices clamoring for reassignment were more numerous and insistent, and they now included newly educated people who were making common political cause with colleagues in the Ibibio Welfare Union. African political activity was becoming more organized, with new institutional forms that took on the colonizers' discourses of ethnicity.

This time the colonial administrators were more willing to ignore the villagers' (multilingual) competence in Igbo and focus, instead, on their command of the Ibibios' language.[7] They were also willing to consider subdividing the region by ethnicity. Accordingly, in April 1953 the British authorities transferred some eleven villages in the cluster to an Ibibio jurisdiction. As for the remaining villages, however, the district officer decided against a transfer. A visit to the area convinced him that he would have to subdivide them into Igbo and Ibibio groupings that were tiny and geographically complicated—unlike his vision of "tribal" territories. He seems to have concluded, therefore, that the issues could not really be about ethnicity at all. They could only be about personal conflicts (as if these have nothing to do with ethnicity). In short, he threw out the case, rather than revising the model it failed to match—a model of language-ethnicity-territory, with language indexing the other two factors, as long as contiguous swaths of territory met a certain minimum geographical magnitude.

In sum, bureaucratic scale-making in this Nigerian case identified populations according to language and ranked "tribes" on the scale according to numbers of speakers of the linguistic variety supposedly identified with the tribe. Language was selected as the relevant metric, indexing the values of other metrics. Yet because these metrics were assumed to coincide, if the value of one of them looked "wrong"—as the territorial one did, for Ika-na-Anang—the others seemed to be invalidated.

This particular ideological project, universally identifying ethnicity with language—a project summed up perhaps in the concept of "ethnolinguistic groups"—is stunningly persistent. The concept is even institutionalized in such catalogues as *Ethnologue*, a listing of such groups. This catalogue, produced by the Bible-translation organization Summer Institute of Linguistics, provides each group on the list with (asserted) information about its geographical location and speaker population. *Ethnologue* has even been taken up by the Linguistic Society of America in its administrative arrangements: the catalogue appears online as a list of options by which the society's members are to register their particular linguistic expertise.

STANDARDS AND DIALECTS

Identifying the linguistic varieties in use in southeastern Nigeria was difficult in itself, since linguistic documentation was sketchy and the analyses available in the colonial period for languages of the region tended to lump together quite different varieties under a single label. What if there had been an accepted standardized version of one or more of these languages? The difficulty and the contestations would not have disappeared. Taking language as the most important measure—the sign and determinant of a person's primary ethnic (or national) identity—is an ideological practice that can still lead to trouble when it fails to match the world it purports to represent. Actual speech does not conform to the standard; many people are multilingual; an ethnic identity recorded by outsiders is not necessarily the way people see themselves, or not necessarily an identification they take to be important. The affiliations of multilingual people can shift, depending on context and activity.[8]

Closer to home than the 1921 Nigerian census is the case of an Italian-American student I once had who wrote a term paper titled "Why I Can't Speak My Language." His grandmother had come from Calabria, but his father had rejected the Italian community, including its language; so the student grew up speaking only English, although he heard his grandmother speaking what he called "Italian." At college he enrolled in Italian classes as a "heritage student." But he was unhappy in class and found it difficult. What was taught there did not match the Calabrian variety his grandmother spoke. There was a scalar misalignment that (he argued in his paper) created his distress: thinking of himself as "Italian," not "Calabrian," he identified a national language as "his," rather than a regional one. (In the end he acquired neither one.) In cases like his, the ideological practice of taking language as principal ethnic identifier involves scale-making in two ways: first, because it selects the standardized variety, whether or not the relevant persons speak anything like that; and second, because it selects one scalable measure rather than another. This process entails either suppressing attention to other scalables—other aspects of a person's life—or presuming covariation.

What is the logic of the scale-making, or scale-invoking, practices involved in identifying a particular way of speaking as a dialect of language X (say, "English," or "Italian")? In these practices an entity—a "language"—is posited as a whole, a type, of which any particular dialect is an instantiation that has emerged in local social circumstances. Dialect differences are disattended to, for purposes of imagining some overarching "thing" that encompasses all of the dialects as instantiations. It is part of the ideology of standard language that the standard exemplifies that imagined whole, even though the standard does not itself include the dialects, except perhaps lexically. (Consider, for example, the Abbé Grégoire's survey of French patois, undertaken in 1790–92, just after the revolution. In surveying all the local dialects of France, the project aimed to collect any words for local referents not yet included in metropolitan French. After those words were collected, the patois were to be eradicated.) Instead, the standard is to be considered the best and most elaborated exemplar of the (imagined) type, which does encompass the dialects. Clearly, there are differences among the dialects. But except when the boundaries of the whole language (say, French) are debated—is Haitian Creole (or Kreyòl) a kind of French, or something else? What about Béarnais? Or Picard, officially recognized as a distinct language in Belgium but not in France?—the differences are often erased in discussions referring to French as type or as whole.[9]

By similar reasoning, the posited linguistic "type" might include among its tokens a historical form of that language, as when a language attested in ninth-century texts is termed "Old English"—not "Late West Germanic," or even "Anglo-Saxon," but "Old English"—thus positing a national/linguistic persistence over twelve hundred years and in spite of the incursions of Norman French.[10] The choice among these labels is not politically innocent.

These examples illustrate, in the realm of standard language and its corresponding dialects, how *type-token relationships are relations of scale. This is scale-making as encompassment.* It pertains as much to these ideologized linguistic relationships as to the passage from *Argonauts* quoted earlier in this chapter. There, Malinowski made a rapid move from Trobrianders to "primitive man," and from Kula transactions to "primitive exchange." In making this move Malinowski was not interested in, or at least not calling attention to, the differences in particulars between Trobrianders and other "primitives," much as he surely knew that there were some. Instead, the Trobrianders are taken as instantiating a more general type. And when attention is called to type rather than to tokens, the differences between tokens are taken as irrelevant. With coins—often the prime example of token/type relations—it is perfectly possible to notice a difference between this particular dime and that one, as well as the systematic differences that result from changes in dime designs over time, like the change from the liberty head to Roosevelt's portrait; but when we use the dimes as money we ignore those things. What Malinowski's analysis shows is how *ideological projects can construct type-token relationships,* and this is a form of scale-making. That is, within an ideological project, people can imagine a type, of which some concrete phenomenon or instance is taken to be a token. Insofar as the type is envisioned as related to and summarizing all its tokens, the type is more encompassing—a scalar relation. Attending to it and not to the differences among its putative tokens is to climb the (putative) scale and look toward the bigger picture.

Dialects, registers, and styles of speaking are not identical, of course, nor do they each exist in isolation. They come in sets. A linguistic variety is identifiable not just in what it (linguistically) *is*—what its linguistic characteristics are—but also in what it is *not:* how it contrasts with some other style(s). The same is true, if not always appreciated, of sociolinguistic variants. A particular way of speaking can only index some particular social category if it differs from other varieties that index other categories. These relationships of contrast—that is, contrast sets—are scalable. The linguistic differentiation, mapped into an ideological system, can follow a pattern Susan Gal and I have called fractal recursivity (Irvine and

Gal 2000; see also Gal this volume). In such cases—in those complex linguistic ideologies—*measures of encompassment are organized recursively,* through iterations of the contrastive features.

Consider, in this light, some aspects of linguistic differentiation in the United States, taking into account the linguistic varieties' historical origins. The ancestors of Euro-Americans spoke various languages when they first came to the New World; not all of them spoke English. Speaking, say, Yiddish as opposed to some other European language marked a difference between European Jewry and European gentiles, who, even if multilingual, were unlikely to include Yiddish among the languages at their command. So, in a narrower categorization that applies to those Europeans' descendants in America, a Yiddish-infused American English (as opposed to other ways of speaking American English) marks a difference between Jewish and gentile Americans. The recursion here takes a contrast between categories—a language indexing Jewishness and languages indexing other social identifications—and uses it to create distinctions within one. Individuals contrast with one another, too, as to how much Yiddishkeit they choose to display, and in what circumstances. But a system of fractal recursions also includes the possibility of moving to broader categorizations—that is, ignoring differences that were relevant in one situation but are deemed, in some other situation, to be trivial (like the differences among tokens of a type). Proponents of the English-only movement do not worry about the differences between Yiddish-inflected and Italian-inflected American English. Both of these are just "English," grouped together as opposed to Spanish or some other language the English-only folks consider foreign and threatening to American nationhood.

Several aspects of scale-making are at work in this American example. There is the nesting of categories—relations of encompassment. There is the comparison between the ethnic identities and their populations, as well as comparisons between the linguistic varieties that index them. Moreover, the linguistic relationships are scalable linearly, in terms of the number of linguistic features that distinguish the varieties: many (distinguishing Yiddish from, say, Italian) and fewer (distinguishing Yiddish-inflected English from Italian-inflected English).[11] So the example illustrates a semiotic system in which linear scale-making combines with relations of encompassment to form a complex ideological configuration.

As with other kinds of scale-making projects, these complex systems are subject to regimes of value. Ideological projects of scale-making can *establish a particular magnitude, or a particular degree of encompassment on a scale, as "real" or "authentic" or legitimate,* relegating other magnitudes—whether more encompassing or less encompassing—to the status of metaphors, or projections, or even ignorable things. That the courses my Italian-American student was taking were in standard Italian, not in the Calabrian variety his grandmother spoke, is not just due to the administrative convenience of grouping many students into one classroom. Nor is standard Italian simply a leveled variety in comparison with which Italy's regional dialects just add some differentiating features. (If it is seen that way, there's an ideologized vision for you.) Instead, the standard is taken to be socially more encompassing—at least in terms of a range of social groups for whom it is a reference point—and, especially, more legitimate. As the language of the Italian state and of contemporary mainstream Italian literature, it is the variety deemed legitimate for classroom teaching in American universities.

SCALAR ISSUES IN LEXICAL DENOTATION

Let us consider a more extended example of how *scale-making ideology can establish a particular degree of encompassment, within a recursively nested system, as "real" compared to other scalar degrees.* This example comes from my early fieldwork in Senegal and concerns the Wolof lexeme *jaam,* commonly translated as "slave," and its social reference. "Slaves," as opposed to free persons, are a major social category among Wolof people, and the category remains meaningful as a social condition even though "slave" is no longer a legal status.[12] But the term *jaam* can also refer to the patrilateral cross-cousin (father's sister's child, abbreviated as FZch in anthropological shorthand; or the classificatory cross-cousin, FFZSch). There are other possible referents, too, applying to clan relations and even to the relations between ethnic groups: for some Wolof-speakers, at least, the ethnic group Serer may be called *jaam* in relation to Wolof. In the discussion that follows, I use the English gloss "slave" for the social category and "cross-cousin" for the kin relation (thus applying a terminological distinction Wolof lexicon does not make, a fact that will deserve comment).

The term *jaam* can be understood as recursively denoting persons in a state of dependency, owing menial forms of service to their "masters." Both the slaves and the cross-cousins stand in that relation. Thus the patrilateral cross-cousin, FZch (*jaam*) owes services to his or her matrilateral cross-cousin (the mother's brother's child, MBch); that is, if you are my FZch, I am your MBch and you must serve me. This matrilateral cross-cousin is termed *sàngg,* which also translates as "master" or "lord." There are no other Wolof lexemes for these kin. Meanwhile, certain pairs of patriclans claim one another as *jaam;* and as for the Serer, in the days of the slave trade Serer were prime targets for slave raiding by Wolof kings and aristocrats. The Serer areas, even their polities, were outliers in a Wolof-dominated regional political system.

The various referents of the lexeme *jaam* and their contrast with non-*jaam*—"free"—can be scaled along several dimensions.[13] One such dimension would concern the number of people, or at least the genealogical range, these terms encompass. Thus an individual EGO (propositus) in a kinship framework has only a few persons who stand toward him or her in a cross-cousin relationship, while patriclans number far more people. Pairs of patriclans as wholes stand in cross-cousin relation with each other, a relationship that supposedly pertained between their ancestors.[14] Even larger in numbers and in social range are the statuses of "slave" and "free," categorizations that apply throughout the Wolof population and within neighboring ethnicities as well. (Regarding numbers, consider that the total population self-identifying as Wolof ethnics numbers several million.) Given that the status of "slave" is not legally recognized today, it is not clear how many Wolof people are considered to belong to this category, and the numbers would vary depending on who is doing the considering. Meanwhile, the ethnic classification that contrasts all Serer with all Wolof encompasses yet a larger social range, in the sense that the referents on the Wolof side would include "free" Wolof together with Wolof *jaam*. Notice that an individual might have *jaam* status in many senses: a person might be of Serer background, be classified as a "slave" within a Wolof community, and be somebody's patrilateral cross-cousin.

Other dimensions along which the referents of *jaam* can be scaled include the nature and extent of the services to be performed. The cross-cousin *jaam* owes the "master" fewer services, often in ritual contexts and, in any case, only a few days a year, compared with the extensive agricultural labor and more unpleasant menial duties of the "slave" *jaam*. The time horizon of the relationship with the "master" is scalable as well. It is permanent for the patrilateral cross-cousin; supposedly finite and alterable for the "slave," whose freedom could be purchased, at least theoretically; and unrealized for the Serer, who do not accept that they owe service to Wolof on ethnic grounds.

However, the referents of the term and the relationships the term implies are not, in Wolof consultants' eyes, all equally "real" or "literally true." As a Wolof villager put it to me: "Do you know the difference between a *jaam* and a *jaam*? The real *jaam* are the people whose grandfathers were bought or were captured in war. The *jaam* who is the child of one's paternal aunt, that's somebody we just call *jaam*." In other words, the term as applied to the cross-cousin—or to the Serer ethnic group, for that matter—is a metaphor, an extension. It is not the "real thing." The ideology attaching to the recursive system establishes one of its category sets—one degree of encompassment—as the "real" reference for the terminology. *Jaam* is a polysemous word, but only one of its referents counts as literally real and true.

The fact that some of these usages are understood as metaphors is relevant to the pragmatics of their actual use. Members of the paired patriclans call one another *jaam* in the context of conventionalized joking relationships; the joke is conventional and consists in the very fact that the joking partners do not actually differ in status in this way. The joking is a mock contest of status, each partner claiming the other as his or her dependent. In contrast, for a free person to call someone a *jaam* literally—that is, outside the framework of joking relationship partners or the genealogical framework of cross-cousin relations—is deeply serious. It is either an insult (if someone is not actually of slave status) or an act of exclusion: you (*jaam*) may not sit upon my mat; you may not eat from the same bowl as I; you are not eligible for such-and-such political office; you may not consort with my daughter; and so on.

The pragmatics of the term's use in an interethnic context (in regard to Serer) is more ambiguous and is complex in ways that reflect the role of Wolof people and language in the postcolonial nation. Recent literature on Serer indicates that in relation to Tukulor or Joola—other Senegalese ethnic groups—an interethnic pair can be assimilated to the joking relationship, so that two people of different ethnicity, say one Serer and one Tukulor, can draw on the same kinds of conventional joking, accusing one another of being the dependent "slave," as occurs with paired clans. Along with Smith (2006) and De Jong (2005), I take this pattern—or at least the conspicuousness of it—to be fairly recent, an extension of the joking relationship "up" in scale from patriclan to ethnic category. The pragmatics seem to be largely political, activated when, for example, a Tukulor official is posted to a Serer region, or, in the 1990s, when Joola communities in the far south of Senegal were showing sympathy for a separatist movement. The claim, asserted by agents of the state and by some intellectuals, was that an interethnic joking relationship was a deeply traditional way of defusing hostility, turning it away from violence and toward convivial coexistence. Although historical sources from the colonial period do attest to these interethnic joking partnerships, their recent celebration looks very much like a reconstituted tradition, if not quite an invented one.[15]

I mention these interethnic extensions of the joking relationship because the joking talk often takes place in Wolof—and therefore refers to *jaam*—even though Wolof as an ethnicity does not seem to be involved. Wolof language is a lingua franca in much of Senegal, and people whose first language is something else (Joola, for example) are far more likely to acquire Wolof than to become multilingual in other African languages, such as Pulaar (spoken by Tukulor) or Serer. The interethnic pairs who engage in this joking are the peripheral ones, who, Smith (2006) argues, in thus affirming their solidarity and equal status, support one another in opposition to the nationally dominant Wolof.[16] Although I sometimes heard Wolof refer to Serer as categorically *jaam* and make ethnic jokes about them—somewhat analogous to the old (and offensive) category of "Polish jokes" in the United States—I did not witness any such joking directed toward a Serer person face to face or even in their presence. To call a Serer person *jaam* to his or her face would be rude, just as it would be to a Wolof addressee. I was cautioned by a village consultant not to discuss *jaam* status in the presence of a locally resident family of Serer background, "because it would embarrass them." Wolof domination of Serer, past and present, is no joking matter.

In short, although particular Serer individuals and families may actually have slave status, Serer do not (as I've mentioned previously) accept that the term *jaam* could denote them as a whole in relation to Wolof. That notion of the term's reference is evidently a Wolof point of view, not a Serer one. Not only do Serer not accept *jaam* as literally denoting them, but they do not accept it as metaphorically applying, except perhaps when used by Tukulor or Joola in the joking relationship's mock contestation. As we have seen, scalar ideologies are subject to differences in point of view—and to different contexts of deployment.

Notice, however, that there is a scalar ambiguity about the interethnic usage, as well. Compared to the other usages, does an interethnic reference go upscale—to be more encompassing than the social status of slave—or not? On the one hand, the traditional categories of Wolof society include both slave and free.[17] In that sense the ethnic group, as referent, encompasses the slave social category. On the other hand, slave statuses are found (historically, and in some respects still today) in most of the social systems of West and North Africa. Across the Sahel, certain statuses, including slave status, are recognizable across ethnicities and polities. In that sense, slave status—the "true" referent of the term *jaam*, according to my Wolof consultants—is "bigger" than ethnicity, because it includes slaves of many ethnicities. So it is not clear that these social categorizations, ethnicity and slave status, can be incorporated into any single linear scale of population or social range.

To summarize, this lexical example—like the previous section's examples (dialect and standard, and ethnic varieties of American English)—shows how a scalar ideology can pick out one degree of encompassment as counting the most, in talk and in social life. But there is a little more to be said concerning the difference between the Wolof lexicon and the English expressions I have had to mobilize to describe it. The pertinent difference between these languages emerges especially when we consider the relationship between *jaam* as social status category and *jaam* as patrilateral cross-cousin. Notice now that in this Wolof lexical system it is the social category term for "slave" that has been imported into the genealogical kinship terminology, not the other way around.

Some decades ago, there was much debate in anthropological circles about the semantics of kinship terms, with many scholars asserting that genealogical kinship was always the primary meaning of a term, even if the term had other referents. But this Wolof system shows us, if we needed showing (since that debate has been left behind for other reasons), that those scholars' "family-first" assumption about kinship semantics was itself a piece of (linguistic) ideology. For those scholars, the semantic priority of genealogical kinship was assumed to be universal and to offer an all-encompassing framework—the big picture—for comparison of terminological systems around the world. The Wolof-speaker's point of view is different. So are the Wolof scale-making ideologies. My Wolof consultants had their own ideas about what is universal, the "big picture," and what is merely local or particular. These interlocutors did not hesitate to expatiate upon slavery, former slaves, and what they deemed to be appropriate understandings of social statuses in America.

For good or ill, however, their views have little institutional support on this side of the Atlantic.

A REFLECTION: PARODY AND POINT OF VIEW

Big-picture visions have their critics, to be sure, ranging from those who celebrate the particular and the local (think *locavore*) to those who argue against the "view from nowhere." The critiques are too many and too various to review here. What I want to point out, however, are the scale-making issues that are involved in both the visions and their critiques. The issues are three: whether bigger is always better; whether the big picture encompasses the smaller, including whatever the smaller picture can see and then some; and whether one grand scale fits all, incorporating all aspects of social life within the zoom function of one's analytical camera. The examples discussed in this essay, like those in other essays in this volume, offer materials with which one might try to pick at these scalar tangles.

For a last moment of reflection on the ways in which scale-making entails point of view, let us briefly consider an example of parody, a parody directed in this case at those who would equate size with value. As in all parody, clashing points of view—here, about bigness—are embedded. As Bakhtin argued in his writings on the "double-voiced utterance," in parody the speaker or writer represents two points of view at the same time. It is, in Bakhtin's words, an "intentional hybrid" (1981, 75): "What we are calling a hybrid construction is an utterance that belongs, by its grammatical [syntactic] and compositional markers, to a single speaker, but that actually contains mixed within it two utterances, two speech manners, two styles, two 'languages,' two semantic and axiological belief systems" (304). The authorial point of view comments upon the utterance or speech manner being commented upon.

The text from which I offer the following excerpt parodically comments upon—and critiques—the value placed in the state of Texas on bigness as best and boastable, no matter what quality the bigness measures. The excerpt comes from *Stupid Texas Song,* recorded by the Austin Lounge Lizards (1998):

> Texas is a big state, North to South and East to West
> Alaska doesn't really count, we're bigger than the rest
> You can waltz across it, though, so grab your yellow rose
> And sing another song of Texas—this is how it goes:
> One more stupid song about Texas, for miles and miles it rambles on
> Biggest egos, biggest hair, biggest liars anywhere, let's sing another
>   stupid Texas song
> . . .
> Our accents are the drawliest, our howdies are the y'alliest,
> Our Lone Star flag's the waviest, our fried steak's the cream-graviest

Our rattlesnakes the coiliest, our beaches are the oiliest
Our politicians most corrupt, our stop signs most abrupt
Our guitars are the twangiest, our guns are the kerblangiest.
Our cows are the Long-horniest, our yodels the forlorniest,
Our cook-offs are the chiliest, our Waylon is the Williest,
Our sausage is the smokiest, our neighbors are the Okiest
. . .
One more stupid song about Texas, just cause we're braggin', that don't mean it's wrong
Biggest heads and biggest hearts, biggest various body parts,
Let's sing another stupid Texas song.

Even if the text had not included the line "we're bigger than the rest," it would be clear that any claim of the "biggest" whatever—or the (adjective)-est—is a scale-making project, whether or not "the rest" (the places, things, and beings that are asserted to be lower in scale) are specified. Starting from Texas's geographical size, the text moves on to claims that bigger is the boastable best, in any quality that could be measured—many of which, such as the coiliness of rattlesnakes, are not commonly measured at all. The boast of bigness, a staple of Texas's state tourism industry, is shown up as empty of value.

Performances of this song receive big laughs in places like Ann Arbor, Michigan, and even in Austin, Texas (which is said by some Texans not really to belong to the state at all, because its politics and outlook differ from those of the rest of the state). Yet this pattern of bigness evaluation is not limited to Texans. It is not unusual for non-Texan Americans, visiting Europe, to comment that American houses, roads, cars, distances, or whatever are bigger than their European analogues. Their European interlocutors, I'm told, may resent the assertion, hearing in it an ideology, a regime of value that translates "bigger" into "better."

. . .

This chapter's discussion has moved far away from the Kula ring, apparently. But maybe not. Many of my examples touch upon our training and work as academics: close-to-home institutionalizations of some piece of linguistic ideology that involves scalar issues. The Kula ring, Malinowski's emphasis on the divide between ethnographer and "native," kinship studies, "heritage" language courses, "ethnolinguistic groups," and the so-called micro-macro problem (with its tendency to relegate many linguistic topics to the micro—read, "trivial")—all these are regimentations that some of us are, or have been, affected by, sometimes to our sorrow. Scale-making does not have to be evil, I hasten to point out (see also Carr and Fisher this volume). I have indulged in some myself, by enlisting many ethnographic examples in an effort to make a more general point than I thought I could make with just one. (It is a strategy that resembles, within one chapter, the strategy taken by this volume as a whole, you may notice; and if you do, you're noticing yet another kind of scale.) What matters is how the "big picture" is tied up with projects, institutions, and power relations, and what it might erase or make invisible.

Remember, however, that the thing about ideology is that there are always other points of view, other perspectives. Sometimes those differences in point of view lead to distress, sometimes to conflict, sometimes to parody, and sometimes to opportunity—the opportunity to follow some other roadmap, engage in more rewarding projects, construct other scales, and perhaps sometimes to deny that either scale-making or scale-climbing is valuable for a particular project at all.

NOTES

My thanks to Susan Gal for comments on this paper and, especially, for our ongoing conversations about ideology and language, including scales and scale-making. Thanks also to the volume editors for their comments and encouragement. Permission from Hank Card and the Texas Lounge Lizards to reprint excerpts from "Stupid Texas Song" is gratefully acknowledged.

1. In *Coral Gardens and Their Magic* (Malinowski 1935), the discussion of the language of magic provides an early illustration of register differentiation. Malinowski does not, however, offer any focused account of Trobriand dialectology or multilingualism, or the range of linguistic varieties found in the Kula system, except for a brief statement in *Argonauts* ([1922] 1961, 39) about the wider distribution of the Dobuan language, compared to Kiriwinian, the language of the Trobrianders.

2. Notice, by the way, the ambiguity of the term *scale* itself: it can refer either to a *metric* (some dimension or angle that might be measured, made into a ladder, as it were), or to a particular value—that is, a *magnitude* on that metric, a step on the ladder.

3. As is well known, and now infamous, in the early republic the population scale required an additional compromise concerning how slaves were to be counted.

4. P. Amaury Talbot, author of the extensive report discussed here concerning the 1921 census of southern Nigeria, makes it clear that the "tribal" classification in the census depended on language: "It has been necessary in this volume to use language as the sole means of classification" ([1926] 1969, 16–17). In his view, however, language was but a poor substitute for a racial ("somatological") classification system on which a "correct" classification would be based.

5. A compromise ruling earlier that year had accorded Ika-na-Anang its own separate, Ibibio-language native court but still assigned the villages to an Igbo district's clan council for other purposes. See Afigbo (1987) for more detail and documents relating to the Ika-na-Anang case, and Irvine (2015) for additional discussion and background on the linguistic issues at stake.

6. That is, in some linguistic variety the officer took to be Igbo. The ways of speaking that have counted as Igbo have been disparate. See Irvine 2015.

7. In fact, at this point the (new) district officer asserted that the villagers' command of Igbo was actually not good, and that they spoke it "haltingly and with a strong Anang accent" (Afigbo 1987, 113).

8. An interesting recent discussion of this phenomenon among multilingual Africans is provided by Lüpke and Storch (2013).

9. What counts as "French" and who counts as its speakers is important for the politics of *la francophonie*, an international project supported by the French state and promoting cooperation among francophone peoples. In a work accorded a prize by the Académie Française, Xavier Deniau (2001) counts as speakers of "French" all residents of France as well as various other regions, such as parts

of Belgium and Luxembourg, but also the francophone populations of Quebec, "l'Acadie" (New Brunswick and Nova Scotia), and Louisiana. These are counted without regard for linguistic differences. As for Haiti, since the 1987 constitution recognized Kreyòl as distinct, Deniau comments that French has now been joined by "le créole" because of this constitutional move (2001, 37).

10. I owe this point to Dan Segal, from an unpublished manuscript.

11. In phonology, William Labov's sociolinguistic research on New York City's Lower East Side showed that among Jews and Italians, the second generation—children of immigrants—hypercorrected the vowels associated with their parents' language. Yet, while they avoided those particular stigmatized sounds, their speech was still differentiated, since it followed different patterns of hypercorrection (1966, 1972). Other linguistic features mark ethnicity more dramatically; but it is possible that some of these characterize the third generation—who are interested in ethnic distinctiveness, "heritage," and ties to their grandparents—more than the second.

12. Wolof traditions provide two cross-cutting principles of social hierarchy: noble/artisan and free/slave. These principles combine in a complex calculus of rank and status, with various subcategories. The noble/artisan divide is described in the literature in terms of caste, since the various categories concerned are endogamous, engage in occupational specialties, and are understood as morally distinct (sometimes via expressions of "purity" or physiological difference). Though impure, artisans are free. "Slaves" can derive (ancestrally, through capture or purchase) from any caste and can belong to any caste, which then determines their marital options. The calculus of category rank and distinction is complex and, in principle, generative of endless subcategories, limited only by demography and practicality.

13. There is more than one term that contrasts with *jaam*, depending on which aspect of the referent is concerned. *Sàngg*, "lord, master," and *borom*, "owner," emphasize the dependence of the *jaam* on a particular person. Although either of these terms could be used for any of the kinds of *jaam* I have described, in practice *sàngg* seemed most often to be used in the cross-cousin relation. *Jaambur*, which also means "respectable person," refers to "free" in the sense of having no ancestor who was bought or captured into slave status.

14. There is usually room for debate as to which patriclan counts as which cross-cousin—that is, which clan stands in a dependency relation to the other. To establish a consistent dependency relation between patriclans would require consistent marriage arrangements, such that one clan of the pair was always wife-giver, the other always wife-receiver (hence always in a FZch status). Wolof marriage arrangements do not systematically maintain those arrangements over many generations, although particular local clan segments seemed to me to make some effort to do so.

15. See discussion and detail in Smith 2006.

16. As Smith and others have also pointed out, Wolof as a category is somewhat de-ethnicized and de-territorialized, compared with other Senegalese ethnicities. Yet the matter of de-ethnicization is complicated and easily entangled with the spread of multilingualism (acquisition of Wolof as a second language), ethnic assimilation, and Wolof political dominance—factors that may encourage de-ethnicization but are not the same thing. My own rural consultants did not hesitate to discuss Wolof identity in terms comparable to ethnic categorizations elsewhere, while taking their Wolof dominance, social and linguistic, as given.

17. Each of these categories has subdivisions as well. Moreover, as noted previously, the system is best analyzed as the complex interaction of two different forms of status differentiation: slavery and caste. Thus there are free persons of low caste. These are the *nyenyo*, the artisan castes. Nyenyo could own slaves, who would rank lower than the slaves owned by persons of higher caste.

ACKNOWLEDGMENTS

This book arose from a collaborative initiative of the "Michicagoan" group, a group founded over eighteen years ago to serve anthropology faculty and graduate students from both the University of Michigan and the University of Chicago. Early drafts of our chapters were workshopped over the course of several Michicagoan faculty meetings in Ann Arbor and Chicago, with developing papers presented at a double panel at the American Anthropological Association meetings in 2013. We benefited from conversations with many people, not the least with our fellow Michicagoan participants from earlier phases of the project, especially Hillary Parsons Dick, Matthew Hull, Webb Keane, John Lucy, Bruce Mannheim, Justin Richland, and Kristina Wirtz. Daniel Listoe provided the inspiration to turn to Melville to frame our questions of scale, and Patricia Round lent an editorial eye on early drafts of the introduction. Jennifer Cole, Julie Chu, Judith Farquhar, and Joseph Masco offered insights and encouragement along the way.

For their exceptionally generous support of this publication, we owe special thanks to the University of Michigan's Office of the Vice President for Research, College of Literature, Science, and the Arts, and the Department of Anthropology. Additionally, the School of Social Service Administration at the University of Chicago provided funds for an indexer. Thanks are also owed to the University of Chicago Anthropology Department's Lichtenstern Fund, which made possible one of the workshops out of which this volume grew. For the all-too-rare gift of time during the final phase of this project, Michael Lempert is grateful for a 2015–2016 residential fellowship at the Center for Advanced Study in the Behavioral Sciences (CASBS) at Stanford University, supported by a Lenore Annenberg and Wallis Annenberg Fellowship in Communication.

Two external reviewers for the University of California Press offered incisive comments, for which we are grateful, and our editor Reed Malcolm saw this project through with sage advice and characteristic efficiency.

REFERENCES CITED

Aboriginal Language Services (ALS). 1991. *A Profile of the Aboriginal Languages of the Yukon.* Whitehorse, Canada: Yukon Executive Council Office.
———. 2004. *Sharing the Gift of Language: Profile of Yukon First Nations Languages.* Whitehorse, Canada: Yukon Executive Council Office.
Afigbo, Adiele Eberechukwu. 1987. *The Igbo and Their Neighbours: Inter-Group Relations in Southeastern Nigeria to 1953.* Ibadan, Nigeria: University Press Limited.
Agha, Asif. 2004. "Registers of Language." In *A Companion to Linguistic Anthropology,* edited by A. Duranti, 23–45. Malden, MA: Blackwell.
———. 2005. "Introduction: Semiosis across Encounters." *Journal of Linguistic Anthropology* 15 (1): 1–5.
———. 2007. *Language and Social Relations.* Cambridge: Cambridge University Press.
———. 2011. "Small and Large Scale Forms of Personhood." *Language and Communication* 31 (3): 171–180.
Agha, Asif, and Stanton E. F. Wortham. 2005. "Special Issue: Discourse across Speech Events: Intertextuality and Interdiscursivity in Social Life." *Journal of Linguistic Anthropology* 15 (1): 1–150.
Ahlers, Jocelyn. 2006. "Framing Discourse." *Journal of Linguistic Anthropology* 16 (1): 58–75.
Alder, Ken. 1995. "A Revolution to Measure: The Political Economy of the Metric System in France." In *The Values of Precision,* edited by M. Norton Wise, 39–71. Princeton, NJ: Princeton University Press.
Alexander, Jeffrey C., ed. 1987. *The Micro-Macro Link.* Berkeley: University of California Press.
Alexander, Jeffrey C., Bernhard Geisen, Richard Münch, and Neil J. Smelser. 1987. "From Reduction to Linkage: The Long View of the Micro-Macro Debate." In *The Micro-Macro Link,* edited by J. C. Alexander and B. Geisen, 1–42. Berkeley: University of California Press.

Althusser, Louis. 1994. "Ideology and Ideological State Apparatuses (Notes toward an Investigation)." In *Mapping Ideology*, edited by Slavoj Žižek, 100–140. London: Verso. Originally published 1970.
Anderson, Benedict. 2008. *Imagined Communities*. 3rd ed. London: Verso.
Appadurai, Arjun. 2006. *Fear of Small Numbers: An Essay on the Geography of Anger*. Durham, NC: Duke University Press.
Armstrong, Robert Plant. 1971. *The Affecting Presence*. Urbana: University of Illinois Press.
———. 1975. *Wellspring: On the Myth and Source of Culture*. Berkeley: University of California Press.
———. 1981. *The Powers of Presence: Consciousness, Myth, and Affecting Presence*. Philadelphia: University of Pennsylvania Press.
Arvidsson, Adam. 2005. *Brands: Meaning and Value in Media Culture*. London: Routledge.
Austin Lounge Lizards. 1998. "Stupid Texas Song." In *Employee of the Month*. Sugar Hill Records, SHCD-3874, compact disc.
Bakhtin, M. M. 1981. *The Dialogic Imagination*. Austin: University of Texas Press.
———. 1986. *Speech Genres and Other Late Essays*. Austin: University of Texas Press.
Barnes, Barry. 2001. "The Macro/Micro Problem and the Problem of Structure and Agency." In *The Handbook of Social Theory*, edited by George Ritzer and Barry Smart, 339–352. Thousand Oaks, CA: Sage.
Barnes, J. A. 1962. "African in the New Guinea Highlands." *Man* 62 (1): 5–9.
Barthes, Roland. 1983. *The Fashion System*. New York: Hill and Wang. Originally published in French in 1967.
Baskerville, Barnet. 1979. *The People's Voice: The Orator in American Society*. Lexington, KY: University Press of Kentucky.
Bauman, Richard. 1986. *Story, Performance and Event*. New York: Cambridge University Press.
———. 2004. *A World of Others' Words: Cross-Cultural Perspectives on Intertextuality*. Malden, MA: Blackwell.
Bauman, Richard, and Patrick Feaster. 2004. "Oratorical Footing in a New Medium: Recordings of Presidential Campaign Speeches, 1896–1912." In *SALSA 11: Texas Linguistics Forum*, vol. 47, edited by Wai Fong Chiang, Elaine Chun, Laura Mahalingappa, and Siri Mehus. Austin: Texas Linguistics Forum.
Bendix, Reinhard. 1962. "Bureaucracy." In *Max Weber: An Intellectual Portrait*, 423–431. New York: Anchor Books.
Benjamin, Walter. (1936) 1969. *Illuminations*. Edited by Hannah Arendt. New York: Schocken Books.
Bently, Lionel. 2008. "The Making of Modern Trade Mark Law: The Construction of the Legal Concept of Trade Mark (1860–1880)." In *Trade Marks and Brands*, edited by L. Bently, J. Davis, and J. Ginsburg, 3–41. New York: Cambridge University Press.
Berlant, Lauren. 1997. *The Queen of America Goes to Washington City: Essays on Sex and Citizenship*. Durham, NC: Duke University Press.
———. 2008. *The Female Complaint: The Unfinished Business of Sentimentality in American Culture*. Durham, NC: Duke University Press.
Bharathi, S. Priya. 1996. "There Is More Than One Way to Skin a Copycat: The Emergence of Trade Dress to Combat Design Piracy of Fashion Works." *Texas Tech Law Review* 27 (4): 1667–1695.

Bindorffer, Györgyi, ed. 2007. *Változatok a kettős identitásra*. [Variations on dual identity]. Budapest: Gondolat.
Blommaert, Jan. 2007. "Sociolinguistic Scales." *Intercultural Pragmatics* 4 (1): 1–19.
———. 2010. *The Sociolinguistics of Globalization*. Cambridge Approaches to Language Contact. Cambridge: Cambridge University Press.
Blommaert, Jan, and Ben Rampton. 2011. "Language and Superdiversity: A Position Paper." Working Papers in Urban Language and Literacies 70, King's College London.
Blommaert, Jan, Elina Westinen, and Sirpa Leppänen. 2015. "Further Notes on Sociolinguistic Scales." *Intercultural Pragmatics* 12 (1): 119–127.
Bockman, Johanna, and Gil Eyal. 2002. "Eastern Europe as a Laboratory for Economic Knowledge." *American Journal of Sociology* 108 (2): 310–351.
Borah, Woodrow. 1983. *Justice by Insurance: The General Indian Court of Colonial Mexico and the Legal Aides of the Half-Real*. Berkeley: University of California Press.
Bourdieu, Pierre. 1984. *Distinction: A Social Critique of the Judgement of Taste*. Translated by Richard Nice. Cambridge, MA: Harvard University Press.
———. 1991. *Language and Symbolic Power*. Cambridge, MA: Harvard University Press.
———. 1996. *The State Nobility: Elite Schools in the Field of Power*. Stanford, CA: Stanford University Press.
Bourdieu, Pierre, and Jean-Claude Passeron. 1977. *Reproduction in Education, Society, and Culture*. London: Sage.
Bowker, Geoffrey C., and Susan Leigh Star. 1999. *Sorting Things Out*. Cambridge, MA: MIT Press.
Brenner, Neil. 2004. *New State Spaces: Urban Governance and the Rescaling of Statehood*. Oxford: Oxford University Press.
Briggs, Charles L. 2004. "Theorizing Modernity Conspiratorially: Science, Scale, and the Political Economy of Public Discourse in Explanations of a Cholera Epidemic." *American Ethnologist* 31 (2): 164–187.
Briggs, Charles L, with Clara Mantini-Briggs. 2004. *Stories in the Time of Cholera: Racial Profiling during a Medical Nightmare*. Berkeley: University of California Press.
Broadbent, [J.] Michael. 1980. *The Great Vintage Wine Book*. New York: Knopf.
Broffenbrenner, Urie. 1979. *The Ecology of Human Development*. Cambridge, MA: Harvard University Press.
Brooks, Tim. 1999. "High Drama in the Record Industry: Columbia Records, 1901–1934." In *The Columbia Master-Book Discography*. Vol. 1. Westport, CT: Greenwood Press.
Brubaker, Rogers. 2002. "Ethnicity without Groups." *European Journal of Sociology* 18:163–89.
———. 2005. "The 'Diaspora' Diaspora." *Ethnic and Racial Studies* 28:1–19.
Brubaker, Rogers, and F. Cooper. 2000. "Beyond 'Identity.'" *Theory and Society* 29:1–47.
Bryan, William Jennings. 1896. *The First Battle: A Story of the Campaign of 1896*. Chicago: W. B. Conkey.
———. 1911. *Speeches of William Jennings Bryan*. 2 vols. New York: Funk and Wagnalls.
Bryan, William Jennings, and Mary Baird Bryan. 1925. *The Memoirs of William Jennings Bryan*. Chicago: John C. Winston.
Burnaby, B. 2008. "Language Policy and Education in Canada." In *Encyclopedia of Language and Education*, 2nd ed., vol. 1: *Language Policy and Political Issues in Education*, edited by S. May and N. Hornberger, 331–341. New York: Springer Science+Business Media.

Cabezón, José Ignacio. 1994. *Buddhism and Language: A Study of Indo-Tibetan Scholasticism*, edited by Frank E. Reynolds and David Tracy. SUNY Series: Toward a Comparative Philosophy of Religions. New York: State University of New York Press.

Callon, Michel. 1986. "Some Elements of a Sociology of Translation: Domestication of the Scallops and the Fishermen of Saint Brieuc Bay." In *Power, Action and Belief: A New Sociology of Knowledge*, edited by J. Law, 196–233. Sociological Review Monograph. London: Routledge and Kegan Paul.

———. 2013. *Acting in an Uncertain World*. Boston: MIT Press.

Callon, Michel, and Bruno Latour. 1981. "Unscrewing the Big Leviathan: How Actors Macrostructure Reality and How Sociologists Help Them to Do So." In *Advances in Social Theory and Methodology: Toward an Integration of Micro- and Macro-Sociologies*, edited by K. D. Knorr-Cetina and A. V. Cicourel, 277–303. Boston, MA: Routledge and Kegan Paul.

Cameron, Deborah. 2007. "Language Endangerment and Verbal Hygiene: History, Morality and Politics." In *Discourses of Endangerment: Ideology and Interest in the Defense of Language*, edited by Alexandre Duchêne and Monica Heller, 268–285. New York: Continuum.

Canning, Charlotte. 2005. *The Most American Thing in America: Circuit Chautauqua as Performance*. Iowa City: University of Iowa Press.

Canovan, Margaret. 1999. "Trust the People! Populism and the Two Faces of Democracy." *Political Studies* 47:2–16.

Cardozo, Karen, and Banu Subramaniam. 2013. "Assembling Asian/American Naturecultures: Orientalism and Invited Invasions." *Journal of Asian American Studies* 16:1–23.

Carr, E. Summerson. 2009. "Anticipating and Inhabiting Instiutitional Identities." *American Ethnologist* 36 (2): 317–36.

———. 2010. "Enactments of Expertise." *Annual Review of Anthropology* 39:17–32.

———. 2011. *Scripting Addiction: The Politics of Therapuetic Talk and American Sobriety*. Princeton, NJ: Princeton University Press.

———. 2015. "Occupation Bedbug: Or, the Urgency and Agency of Professional Pragmatism." *Cultural Anthropology* 30:257–85.

Choy, Timothy. 2011. *Ecologies of Comparison: An Ethnogrpahy of Endangerment in Hong Kong*. Durham, NC: Duke University Press.

Chu, Julie. 2010. *Cosmologies of Credit: Transnational Mobility and the Politics of Destination in China*. Durham, NC: Duke University Press.

Chumley, Lily H., and Nicholas Harkness, eds. 2013. "Qualia." Special issue, *Anthropological Theory* 13 (1–2): 3–183.

Coletta, Paulo E. 1964. *William Jennings Bryan*. Lincoln: University of Nebraska Press.

Collins, James. 2012. "Migration, Sociolinguistic Scale, and Educational Reproduction." *Anthropology and Education Quarterly* 43 (2): 192–213.

———. 2013. "Voice, Schooling, Inequality and Scale." *Anthropology and Education Quarterly* 44 (2): 205–210.

Collins, James, and Stef Slembrouck. 2005. "Editorial: Multilingualism and Diasporic Populations; Spatializing Practices, Institutional Processes, and Social Hierarchies." *Language and Communication*, 25: 189–195.

Collins, James Phillip, Stefaan Slembrouck, and Mike Baynham. 2009. *Globalization and Language in Contact: Scale, Migration, and Communicative Practices*. London: Continuum.

Collins, Lauren. 2011. "Sole Mate." *New Yorker,* March 28, 2011. www.newyorker.com/reporting/2011/03/28/110328fa_fact_collins.

Coombe, Rosemary. 1998. *The Cultural Life of Intellectual Property.* Durham, NC: Duke University Press.

Cox, Christine, and Jennifer Jenkins. 2008. "Between the Seams, a Fertile Commons: An Overview of the Relationship between Fashion and Intellectual Property," 4–20. Paper presented at Ready to Share: Fashion and the Ownership of Creativity, a Norman Lear Center Conference, USC Annenberg School of Communication, January 28, 2005. http://learcenter.org/pdf/RTSJenkinsCox.pdf.

Crease, Robert P. 2011. *World in the Balance.* New York: Norton.

Daston, Lorraine. 1992. "Objectivity and the Escape from Perspective." *Social Studies of Science* 22:597–618.

De Jong, Ferdinand. 2005. "A Joking Nation: Conflict Resolution in Senegal," *Canadian Journal of African Studies* 39:389–413.

Deniau, Xavier. 2001. *La Francophonie,* 5th ed. Paris: Presses Universitaires de France.

Dinkin, Robert J. 1989. *Campaigning in America: A History of Election Practices.* New York: Greenwood.

Dinwoodie, Graeme B., and Mark Janis, eds. 2008. *Trademark Law and Theory.* Northampton, MA: Edgar Allan.

Doane, Mary Ann. 2003. "The Close Up: Scale and Detail in the Cinema." *differences* 14 (3): 189–11.

Dreyfus, Georges. 1997. "Tibetan Scholastic Education and the Role of Soteriology." *Journal of the International Association of Buddhist Studies* 20 (1): 31–63.

———. 2003. *The Sound of Two Hands Clapping: The Education of a Tibetan Buddhist Monk.* Berkeley: University of California Press.

Duchêne, Alexandre, and Monica Heller, eds. 2007. *Discourses of Endangerment: Ideology and Interest in the Defense of Language.* New York: Continuum.

Durkheim, Émile, and Marcel Mauss. 1963. *Primitive Classification.* Chicago: University of Chicago Press.

Eisenlohr, Patrick. 2006. *Little India.* Berkeley: University of California Press.

Errington, J. Joseph. 2003. "Getting Language Rights: The Rhetorics of Language Endangerment and Loss." *American Anthropologist* 105 (4): 723–732.

Espeland, Wendy N., and Mitchell L. Stevens. 1998. "Commensuration as a Social Process." *Annual Review of Sociology* 24:313–343.

Evans-Pritchard, Edward E. 1940. *The Nuer.* New York: Oxford University Press.

Fanon, Franz. 1967. *Black Skin, White Masks.* New York: Grove Press.

Feliciano-Santos, Sherina, and Barbra A. Meek. 2012. "Interactional Surveillance and Self-Censorship in Encounters of Dominion." *Journal of Anthropological Research* 68:373–397.

Ferguson, James. 2006. "Transnational Topographies of Power" (1998). In *Accelerating Possession: Global Futures of Property and Personhood,* edited by B. Maurer and G. Schwab, 76–98. New York: Columbia University Press.

Field, Margaret. 2009. "Changing Navajo Language Ideologies and Changing Language Use." In *Native American Language Ideologies: Beliefs, Practices and Struggles in Indian Country,* edited by Paul V. Kroskrity and Margaret C. Field, 31–47. Tucson: University of Arizona Press.

Firth, Alison. 2008. "Signs, Surfaces, Shapes and Structures—the Protection of Product Design under Trade Mark Law." In *Trademark Law and Theory*, edited by Graeme B. Dinwoodie and Mark Janis, 498–522. Northampton, MA: Edgar Allan.

Fishman, Joshua A. 1991. *Reversing Language Shift*. Clevedon, England: Multilingual Matters.

———, ed. 2001. *Can Threatened Languages Be Saved? Reversing Language Shift, a 21st Century Perspective*. Clevedon, England: Multilingual Matters.

Fletcher, Anthony. 1985. "The Defense of 'Functional' Trademark Use: If What Is Functional Cannot Be a Trademark, How Can a Trademark Be Functional?" *Trademark Reporter* 75 (3): 249–268.

———. 2011. "Defensive Aesthetic Functionality: Deconstructing the Zombie." *Trademark Reporter* 101 (6): 1687–1709.

Footwear News. 2010. "Footwear News Person of the Year: Christian Louboutin." November 29, 2010. http://footwearnews.com/2010/business/news/footwear-news-person-of-the-year-christian-louboutin-69322/.

Foucault, Michel. 1973. *The Order of Things: An Archaeology of the Human Sciences*. New York: Vintage Books.

Gábor, István R., and Péter Galasi. 1978. "A 'másodlagos gazdaság': A szocializmusbeli magánszféra néhány gazdaságszociológiai kérdése" [The "secondary economy": The private sphere of socialism and some questions it poses for economic sociology]. *Szociológia* 3:329–345.

Gal, Susan. 1991. "Bartók's Funeral: The Rhetoric of Europe in Hungary." *American Ethnologist* 18 (3): 440–458.

———. 1994. "Diversity and Contestation in Linguistic Ideologies: German-Speakers in Hungary." *Language in Society* 22:337–359.

———. 2002. "A Semiotics of the Public/Private Distinction." *differences: A Journal of Feminist Cultural Studies* 13 (1): 77–95.

———. 2013. "Tastes of Talk: Qualia and the Moral Flavor of Signs." *Anthropological Theory* 13 (1–2): 31–48.

Gal, Susan, and Judith T. Irvine. 1995. "Boundaries of Languages and Disciplines." *Social Research* 62 (4): 967–1001.

Gamson, Joshua. 1994. *Claims to Fame: Celebrity in Contemporary America*. Berkeley: University of California Press.

Ganapathy, Sandhya. 2013. "Imagining Alaska: Local and Translocal Engagements with Place." *American Anthropologist* 115 (1): 96–111.

Garfinkel, Harold. 1967. *Studies in Ethnomethodology*. New York: Prentice-Hall.

Geertz, Clifford. 1973. *The Interpretation of Cultures*. New York: Basic Books.

Giles, Howard, and Nancy Niedzielski. 1998. "Italian Is Beautiful, German Is Ugly." In *Language Myths*, edited by Laurie Bauer and Peter Trudgill, 85–93. New York: Penguin Books.

Ginsburg, Jane. 2008. "Of Mutant Copyrights, Mangled Trademarks, and Barbie's Beneficence: The Influence of Copyright on Trademark Law." In *Trademark Law and Theory*, edited by Graeme B. Dinwoodie and Mark Janis, 481–497. Northampton, MA: Edgar Allan Publishing.

Glad, Paul W. 1960. *The Trumpet Soundeth: William Jennings Bryan and His Democracy, 1896–1912*. Lincoln: University of Nebraska Press.

———. 1964. *McKinley, Bryan, and the People*. Philadelphia: J. B. Lippincott.

Glück, Zoltán. 2013. "Between Wall Street and Zuccotti: Occupy and the Scale of Politics." *Fieldsights-Hot Spots, Cultural Anthropology Online*, February 14, www.culanth.org/fieldsights/67-between-wall-street-and-zuccotti-occupy-and-the-scale-of-politics.

Gluckman, Max. 1954. *Rituals of Rebellion*. Manchester, England: Manchester University Press.

———. 1963. *Order and Rebellion in Tribal Africa: Collected Essays, with an Autobiographical Introduction*. London: Cohen and West.

Goffman, Erving. 1957. "Alienation from Interaction." *Human Relations* 10 (1): 47–60. doi: 10.1177/001872675701000103.

———. 1959. *The Presentation of Self in Everyday Life*. New York: Doubleday.

———. 1966. *Behavior in Public Places: Notes on the Social Organization of Gatherings*. New York: Free Press.

———. 1971. *Relations in Public*. New York: Basic Books.

———. 1974. *Frame Analysis*. New York: Harper and Row.

———. 1981. *Forms of Talk*. Philadelphia: University of Pennsylvania Press.

———. 1983. "The Interaction Order." *American Sociological Review* 48:1–17.

Goodfellow, Anne. 2003. "The Development of 'New Languages' in Native American Communities." *American Indian Culture and Research Journal* 27 (2): 41–59.

Goodman, Nelson. 1972. "Seven Strictures on Similarity." In *Problems and Projects*, 437–458. New York: Bobbs-Merrill.

Gumperz, John G. 1968. "Language III. The Speech Community." In *International Encyclopedia of the Social Sciences*, vol. 9, edited by David L. Sills, 381–386. New York: Macmillan; Free Press.

Gupta, Akhil, and James Ferguson. 1992. "Beyond 'Culture': Space, Identity, and the Politics of Difference." *Cultural Anthropology* 7 (1): 6–23.

Guyer, Jane. 2004. *Marginal Gains: Monetary Transactions in Atlantic Africa*. Chicago: University of Chicago Press.

Gyatso, Tenzin. 2000. *Srid zhi'i rnam 'dren gong sa skyabs mgon chen po mchog nas slob grwa khag sogs la shes yon slob sbyong byed sgo'i skor stsal ba'i bka' slob phyogs bsdebs bzhugs so*. Vol. 1. Delhi: Paljor Publications at Creative Advertisers.

Habermas, Jürgen. (1962) 1989. *The Structural Transformation of the Public Sphere: An Inquiry into a Category of Bourgeois Society*. Cambridge, MA: MIT Press.

Hagin, Leslie. 1991. "A Comparative Analysis of Copyright Laws Applied to Fashion Works." *Texas International Law Journal* 26 (2): 341–388.

Halliday, Michael A. K. 1964. "The Users and Uses of Language." In *The Linguistic Sciences and Language Teaching*, edited by Michael Halliday, Angus McIntosh, and Peter Strevens, 75–110. London: Longmans.

Hanks, William F. 2000. *Intertexts: Writings on Language, Utterance, and Context*. Lanham: Rowman and Littlefield.

Haraway, Donna. 2003. *A Companion Species Manifesto: Dogs, People, and Significant Otherness*. Chicago: Prickly Paradigm.

———. 2008. *When Species Meet*. Minneapolis: University of Minnesota Press.

Harkness, Nicholas. 2015. "The Pragmatics of Qualia in Practice." *Annual Review of Anthropology* 44:573–589.

Harpine, William D. 2005. *From the Front Porch to the Front Page: McKinley and Bryan in the 1896 Presidential Campaign.* College Station: Texas A&M University Press.

Heavner, B. Brett. 2012. "Trademark Aesthetic Functionality: A Zombie Apocalypse?" *BNA's Patent, Trademark and Copyright Journal* 85 (December 7). www.finnegan.com/resources/articles/articlesdetail.aspx?news=b1e7f45e-8896-4d51-ae4d-4afc4f9c878e.

Heller, Monica. 2010. "The Commodification of Language." *Annual Review of Anthropology* 39:101–114.

Heller, Monica, and Alexander Duchêne. 2011. *Language in Late Capitalism: Pride and Profit.* New York: Routledge.

Helmreich, Stefan. 2007. "Induction, Deduction, Abduction and the Logics of Race and Kinship." *American Ethnologist* 34:230–232.

———. 2009. *Alien Oceans: Anthropological Voyages in Microbial Seas.* Berkeley: University of California Press.

Henne-Ochoa, Richard, and Richard Bauman. 2015. "Who Is Responsible for Saving the Language? Performing Generation in the Face of Language Shift." *Journal of Linguistic Anthropology* 25 (2): 128–149.

Hewitt, Kenneth. 1995. "Sustainable Disasters? Perspectives and Powers in the Discourse of Calamity." In *Power of Development*, edited by Jonathan Crush, 112–123. London: Routledge.

Hill, Jane H. 2002. "'Expert Rhetorics' in Advocacy for Endangered Languages: Who Is Listening, and What Do They Hear?" *Journal of Linguistic Anthropology* 12 (2): 119–133.

Hull, Matthew. 2012. "Documents and Bureaucracy." *Annual Review of Anthropology* 41:251–267.

Hymes, Dell. 1972. "On Communicative Competence." In *Sociolinguistics: Selected Readings*, edited by J. B. Pride and J. Holmes, 269–293. Harmondsworth, England: Penguin.

Hynek, J. Allen. (1972) 1998. *The UFO Experience: A Scientific Inquiry.* New York: Marlowe.

Irvine, Judith T. 1990. "Registering Affect: Heteroglossia in the Linguistic Expression of Emotion." In *Language and the Politics of Emotion*, edited by Catherine Lutz and Lila Abu-Lughod, 126–161. Cambridge: Cambridge University Press.

———. 1996. "Shadow Conversations: The Indeterminacy of Participant Roles." In *Natural Histories of Discourse*, edited by Michael Silverstein and Greg Urban, 131–159. Chicago: University of Chicago Press.

———. 2001. "Style as Distinctiveness: The Culture and Ideology of Linguistic Differentiation." In *Style and Sociolinguistic Variation*, edited by Penelope Eckert and John Rickford, 21–43. Cambridge: Cambridge University Press.

———. 2015. "Language as Cultural 'Heritage': Visions of Ethnicity in Nineteenth-Century African Linguistics." In *The Politics of Heritage in Africa: Economies, Histories, and Infrastructures*, edited by Derek Peterson, Kodzo Gavua, and Ciraj Rassool, 191–208. Cambridge: Cambridge University Press.

Irvine, Judith T., and Susan Gal. 2000. "Language Ideology and Linguistic Differentiation." In *Regimes of Language*, edited by Paul V. Kroskrity, 35–83. Santa Fe, NM: School of American Research.

Jaffe, Alexandra. 2007. "Discourses of Endangerment: Contexts and Consequences of Essentializing Discourses." In *Discourses of Endangerment: Ideology and Interest in the*

Defense of Language, edited by Alexandre Duchêne and Monica Heller, 575–577. New York: Continuum.
Jameson, Fredric. 1992. *The Geopolitical Aesthetic: Cinema and Space in the World System.* Bloomington: Indiana University Press; London: British Film Institute.
Jensen, Richard. 1969. "Armies, Admen, and Crusaders: Types of Presidential Election Campaigns." *History Teacher* 2 (2): 33–50.
Kazin, Michael. 2006. *A Godly Hero: The Life of William Jennings Bryan.* New York: Alfred A. Knopf.
Keane, Webb. 1997. "Religious Language." *Annual Review of Anthropology* 26:47–71.
———. 2003. "Semiotics and the Study of Material Things." *Language and Communication* 23 (3–4): 409–425.
Kelly, Larry J. 1969. "An Historical and Rhetorical Analysis of the 1896 Indiana Campaign of William Jennings Bryan." Master's thesis, Department of Speech and Theatre, Indiana University.
Klein, Naomi. (1999) 2000. *No Logo.* New York: Picador.
Knorr-Cetina, Karin, and Aaron V. Cicourel, eds. 1981. *Advances in Social Theory and Methodology: Toward an Integration of Micro- and Macro- Sociologies.* New York: Routledge.
Kohn, Eduardo. 2013. *How Forests Think: Toward an Anthropology beyond the Human.* Berkeley: University of California Press.
———. 2015. "Anthropology of Ontologies." *Annual Review of Anthropology* 44:311–27.
Kovács, Katalin. 1990. "Polgárok egy sváb faluban." [Bourgeois/citizens in a Schwäbisch village]. *Tér és Társadalom* 1:33–76.
Krauss, Michael. 1998. "The Condition of Native North American Languages: The Need for Realistic Assessment and Action." *International Journal of the Sociology of Language* 132:9–22.
Kripke, Saul. 1981. *Naming and Necessity.* Cambridge, MA: Harvard University Press.
Kroskrity, Paul V. 2014. "To 'We' or Not to 'We' (+/- Inclusive): Some Artful Uses of *Taitaduhaan* in a Western Mono Construction of Multiple Publics." Paper presented at the American Anthropological Association Meetings, Washington, DC, December 2–6.
Krugman, Paul. 2013. "The Decline of E-Empires." *New York Times,* August 26.
Kubrick, Stanley. 1968. *2001: A Space Odyssey.* Beverly Hills, CA: Metro-Goldwyn-Mayer Studios.
Kuipers, Joel Corneal. 1998. *Language, Identity, and Marginality in Indonesia: The Changing Nature of Ritual Speech on the Island of Sumba.* New York: Cambridge University Press.
Kula, Witold. 1986. *Measures and Men.* Princeton, NJ: Princeton University Press.
Kuper, Adam. 1973. *Anthropologists and Anthropology: The British School, 1922–1972.* New York: Pica Press.
Labov, William. 1966. *The Social Stratification of English in New York City.* Washington, DC: Center for Applied Linguistics.
———. 1972. "On the Mechanism of Linguistic Change." In *Directions in Sociolinguistics,* edited by John J. Gumperz and Dell Hymes, 512–538. New York: Holt, Rinehart and Winston.
Lampland, Martha, and Susan Leigh Star, eds. 2009. *Standards and Their Stories.* Ithaca, NY: Cornell University Press.

Latour, Bruno. 1993. *We Have Never Been Modern*. Translated by Catherine Porter. Cambridge, MA: Harvard University Press.
———. 1999. *Pandora's Hope: Essays on the Reality of Science Studies*. Cambridge, MA: Harvard University Press.
———. 2005. *Reassembling the Social: An Introduction to Actor-Network-Theory*. Oxford: Oxford University Press.
Lātūkefu, Sione. 1974. *Church and State in Tonga*. Canberra: Australian National University Press.
Lefebvre, Henri. 1991. *The Production of Space*. Oxford: Blackwell.
Leinwand, Gerald. 2007. *William Jennings Bryan: An Uncertain Trumpet*. Lanham, MD: Rowman and Littlefield.
Lemke, Jay L. 2000. "Across the Scales of Time: Artifacts, Activities, and Meanings in Ecosocial Systems." *Mind, Culture, and Activity* 7 (4): 273–290.
Lempert, Michael. 2012a. *Discipline and Debate: The Language of Violence in a Tibetan Buddhist Monastery*. Berkeley: University of California Press.
———. 2012b. "Interaction Rescaled: How Monastic Debate Became a Diasporic Pedagogy." *Anthropology and Education Quarterly* 43 (2): 138–156.
Lempert, Michael, and Michael Silverstein. 2012. *Creatures of Politics: Media, Message, and the American Presidency*. Bloomington: Indiana University Press.
Leonard, Wesley. 2011. "Challenging Extinction through Modern Miami Language Practices." *American Indian Culture and Research Journal* 35 (2): 135–160.
Levinson, Bradley A., Douglas E. Foley, and Dorothy C. Holland, eds. 1996. *The Cultural Production of the Educated Person*. New York: State University of New York Press.
Lopez, Donald S. 1998. *Prisoners of Shangri-La: Tibetan Buddhism and the West*. Chicago: University of Chicago Press.
———. 2002. *A Modern Buddhist Bible: Essential Readings from East and West*. 1st Beacon Press ed. Boston: Beacon Press.
———. 2008. *Buddhism and Science: A Guide for the Perplexed*. Chicago: Chicago University Press.
Lüpke, Friederike, and Anne Storch. 2013. *Repertoires and Choices in African Languages*. Berlin: Walter de Gruyter.
Lury, Celia. 2004. *Brands: The Logos of the Global Economy*. London: Routledge.
Lynch, Michael. 1985. "Discipline and the Material Form of Images: An Analysis of Scientific Visibility." *Social Studies of Science* 15 (1): 37–66.
Maliha, Safri, and Julie Graham. 2010. "The Global Household: Toward a Feminist, Postcapitalist International Political Economy." *Signs* 36 (1): 99–125.
Malinowski, Bronislaw (1922) 1961. *Argonauts of the Western Pacific*. New York: E. P. Dutton.
———. 1935. *Coral Gardens and Their Magic*. Vol. 2. New York: American Book Co.
Manning, [H.] Paul. 2008. "Barista Rants about Stupid Customers at Starbucks: What Imaginary Conversations Can Teach Us about Real Ones." *Language and Communication* 28 (2): 101–126.
Manson, Steven M. 2008. "Does Scale Exist? An Epistemolopgical Scale Continuum for Complex Human-Environment Systems." *Geoforum* 39:776–78.
Marcus, George E. 1980. *The Nobility and the Chiefly Tradition in the Modern Kingdom of Tonga*. Wellington, NZ: Polynesian Society.

———. 1998. *Ethnography through Thick and Thin.* Princeton, NJ: Princeton University Press.

———. 1999. *Paranoia within Reason: A Casebook on Conspiracy as Explanation.* Chicago: University of Chicago Press.

Marshall, Laura C. 2007. "Catwalk Copycats: Why Congress Should Adopt a Modified Version of the Design Piracy Prohibition Act." *Journal of Intellectual Property Law* 14 (2): 305–331.

Marston, Sallie A. 2000. "The Social Construction of Scale." *Progress in Human Geography* 24 (2): 219–242.

Marston, Sallie A., John Paul Jones III, and Keith Woodward. 2005. "Human Geography without Scale." *Transactions in the Institute of Bristish Genographers* 30: 416–432.

Matsutake Worlds Research Group. 2009. "A New Form of Collaboration in Cultural Anthropology: Matsutake Worlds." *American Ethnologist* 36 (2): 380–403.

Matthews, Andrew. 2009. "Unlikely Alliances: Encounters between State Science, Nature Spirits, and Indigenous Industrial Forestry in Mexico, 1926–2008." *Current Anthropology* 50 (1): 75–101.

Maurer, Bill. 2005. *Mutual Life, Limited: Islamic Banking, Alternative Currencies, and Lateral Reasoning.* Princeton NJ: Princeton University Press.

McKenna, Mark. 2011. "(Dys)functionality." *Houston Law Review* 48 (4): 823–860.

———. 2012. "Dastar's Next Stand." *Journal of Intellectual Property Law* 19 (2): 357–387.

Meek, Barbra A. 2007. "Respecting the Language of Elders: Ideological Shift and linguistic Discontinuity in a Northern Athabaskan Community." *Journal of Linguistic Anthropology* 17 (1): 23–43.

———. 2009. "Language Ideology and Aboriginal Language Revitalization in Yukon, Canada." In *Native American Language Ideologies: Beliefs, Practices and Struggles in Indian Country,* edited by Paul Kroskrity and Margaret Field, 151–171. Tucson: University of Arizona Press.

———. 2010. *We Are Our Language: An Ethnography of Language Revitalization in a Northern Athabaskan Community.* Tucson: University of Arizona Press.

Melder, Keith. 1965. *Bryan the Campaigner.* United States National Museum Bulletin 241. Washington, DC: Smithsonian Institution.

Moffat, Viva R. 2004. "Mutant Copyrights and Backdoor Patents: The Problem of Overlapping Intellectual Property Protection." *Berkeley Technology Law Journal* 19 (4): 1473–1532.

Moore, Adam. 2008. "Rethinking Scale as a Geographical Category: From Analysis to Practice." *Progress in Human Geography* 32 (2): 203–225.

Moore, Robert. 2006. "Disappearing, Inc.: Glimpsing the Sublime in the Politics of Access to Endangered Languages." *Language and Communication* 26:296–315.

———. 2012. "'Taking Up Speech' in an Endangered Language: Bilingual Discourse in a Heritage Language Classroom." *Working Papers in Educational Linguistics* 27 (2): 57–78.

Morgan, Mary S., and Margaret Morrison, eds. 1999. *Models as Mediators: Perspectives on Natural and Social Science.* New York: Cambridge University Press.

Mountz, Alison, and Jennifer Hyndman. 2006. "Feminist Approachs to the Global Intimate." *Women's Studies Quarterly* 34:446–463.

Muehlmann, Shaylih. 2007. "Defending Diversity: Staking Out a Common Global Interest?" In *Discourses of Endangerment: Ideology and Interest in the Defense of Language*, edited by Alexandre Duchêne and Monica Heller, 14–34. New York: Continuum.

———. 2012a. "Rhizomes and Other Uncountables: The Malaise of Enumeration in Mexico's Colorado River Delta." *American Ethnologist* 39 (2): 339–353.

———. 2012b. "Von Humboldt's Parrot and the Countdown of Last Speakers in the Colorado Delta." *Language and Communication* 32:160–168.

Mufwene, Salikoko. 2003. "Language Endangerment: What Have Pride and Prestige Got to Do with It?" In *When Languages Collide: Perspectives on Language Conflict, Language Competition, and Language Coexistence*, edited by Brian D. Joseph, 324–346. Columbus: Ohio State University Press.

Mukerji, Chandra. 1989. *A Fragile Power: Scientists and the State*. Princeton, NJ: Princeton University Press.

Nakassis, Constantine. 2012. "Brand, Citationality, Performativity." *American Anthropologist* 114 (4): 624–638.

———. 2013a. "Brands and Their Surfeits." *Cultural Anthropology* 28 (1): 111–126.

———. 2013b. "Materiality, Materialization." *Hau* 3 (3): 399–406.

———. 2013c. "The Quality of a Copy." In *Fashion India*, edited by T. Kuldova, 140–163. Oslo: Academia Forlag.

———. 2016. *Doing Style: Youth and Mass Mediation in South India*. Chicago: University of Chicago Press.

Noble, Ann C., et al. 1987. "Modification of a Standardized System of Wine Aroma Terminology." *American Journal of Enology and Viticulture* 38:143–146.

Oppenheim, Robert. 2007. "Actor-Network Theory and Anthropology after Science, Technology, and Society." *Anthropological Theory* 7 (4): 471–493.

Palumbo-Liu, David, Bruce Robbins, and Nirvana Tanoukhi. 2011. *Immanuel Wallerstein and the Problem of the World: System, Scale, Culture*. Durham, NC: Duke University Press.

Parmentier, Richard J. 1994. *Signs and Society*. Bloomington: Indiana University Press.

———. 1997. "The Pragmatic Semiotics of Cultures." *Semiotica* 116 (1): 1–115.

Patrick, Donna. 2007. "Indigenous Language Endangerment and the Unfinished Business of Nation States." In *Discourses of Endangerment: Ideology and Interest in the Defense of Language*, edited by Alexandre Duchêne and Monica Heller, 35–56. New York: Continuum.

Peirce, Charles S. 1932. *Collected Papers of Charles Sanders Peirce: Elements of Logic*. Vol. 2. Cambridge, MA: Cambridge University Press.

———. 1955. "Logic as Semiotic: The Theory of Signs." In *Philosophical Writings of Peirce*, edited by Justus Buchler, 98–119. New York: Dover.

———. 1966. *The Collected Papers of Charles Sanders Peirce*. Edited by Paul Weiss Charles Hartshorne. Cambridge, MA: Belknap Press of Harvard University Press.

———. 1997. *Pragmatism as a Principle and a Method of Right Thinking*. Albany: State University of New York.

———. 1998. *Essential Peirce*. Vol. 1. Bloomington: Indiana University Press.

Philips, Susan U. 1995. "The Political Economy of Language and Law in Tonga: Magistrate's Courts in Town and Village." In *Research Frontiers in Anthropology*, edited by Carol Ember and Melvin Ember, 3–22. Englewood Cliffs, NJ: Prentice Hall.

———. 2000. "Constructing a Tongan Nation-State through Language Ideology in the Courtroom." In *Regimes of Language,* edited by Paul V. Kroskrity, 229–257. Santa Fe, NM: School of American Research.
———. 2003. "The Organization of Ideological Diversity in Discourse: Modern and Neo-traditional Visions of the Tongan State." *American Ethnologist* 31:231–250.
———. 2007. "Changing Scholarly Representations of the Tongan Honorific Lexicon." In *Language Ideologies and Sociocultural Transformations in Pacific Societies,* edited by Miki Makihara and Bambi B. Schieffelin, 189–215. New York: Oxford University Press.
———. 2011. "How Tongans Make Sense of the (Non-)Use of Lexical Honorifics." *Journal of Linguistic Anthropology* 21:247–260.
Porter, Theodore M. 1995. *Trust in Numbers: The Pursuit of Objectivity in Science and Public Life.* Princeton, NJ: Princeton University Press.
——— 2006. "Speaking Precision to Power: The Modern Political Role of Social Science." *Social Research* 73:1273–1294.
Povinelli, Elizabeth. 2011. *Economies of Abandonment: Social Belonging and Endurance in Late Liberalism.* Durham, NC: Duke University Press.
Power, Cormac. 2008. *Presence in Play: A Critique of Theories of Presence in the Theatre.* New York: Rodopi.
Prentice, Michael. 2015. "Managing Intertextuality: Display and Discipline across Documents at a Korean Firm." *Signs and Society* 3 (S1): S70–S94.
Raffles, Hugh. 2002. "Intimate Knowledge." *International Social Science Journal* 54:325–335.
Raustiala, Kal, and Christopher Sprigman. 2006. "The Piracy Paradox: Innovation and Intellectual Property in Fashion Design." *Virginia Law Review* 92 (8): 1687–1777.
———. 2009. "The Piracy Paradox Revisited." *Stanford Law Review* 61 (5): 1201–1225.
———. 2012. *The Knockoff Economy.* Oxford: Oxford University Press.
Reid, T[homas] B[ertram] W[allace]. 1956. "Linguistics, Structuralism and Philology." *Archivum Linguisticum* 8 (1): 28–37.
Richland, Justin. 2013. "Jurisdiction: Grounding Law in Language." *Annual Review of Anthropology* 42:209–226.
Riles, Annelise. 1998. "Infinity without Brackets." *American Ethnologist* 25 (3): 378–398.
Roberts, Susan M. 2004. "Gendered Globalization." In *Mapping Women, Making Politics,* edited by Lynn A. Statheli, Eleonmore Kofman, and Linda J. Peake. London: Routledge.
Rotman, Brian. 1993. *Signifying Nothing: The Semiotics of Zero.* Palo Alto, CA: Stanford University Press.
Safri, Maliha, and Julie Graham. 2010. "The Global Household: Toward a Feminist and Post-capitalist Political Economy." *Signs* 36 (1): 99–126.
Saussure, Ferdinand de. 1983. *Course in General Linguistics.* Translated by Roy Harris. La Salle, IL: Open Court.
Scafidi, Susan. 2006. "Intellectual Property and Fashion Design." In *Intellectual Property and Information Wealth,* volume 1, edited by Peter K. Yu, 115–131. Westport, CT: Praeger.
Scarr, Deryck. 1968. *Fragments of Empire: A History of the Western Pacific High Commission, 1877–1914.* Honolulu: University of Hawai'i Press.
Schelling, Thomas. 1978. *Micromotives and Macrobehavior.* New York: Norton.
Schmidt, Rocky. 1983. "Designer Law: Fashioning a Remedy for Design Piracy." *UCLA Law Review* 30:861–880.

Schotte, Margaret. 2013. "Expert Records: Nautical Logbooks from Columbus to Cook." *Information and Culture: A Journal of History* 48:281–322.
Scott, James. 1998. *Seeing Like a State*. New Haven, CT: Yale University Press.
Segal, Dan. n.d. [2000]. "Translation Effects in Historical Writing." Unpublished manuscript.
Seleny, Anna. 1994. "Constructing the Discourse of Transformation: Hungary, 1979–1982." *East European Politics and Societies* 8 (3):439–466.
Silverstein, Michael. 1981. "Metaforces of Power in Traditional Oratory." Lecture to Department of Anthropology, Yale University, New Haven, CT.
———. 1993. "Metapragmatic Discourse and Metapragmatic Function." In *Reflexive Language*, edited by John Lucy, 33–58. Cambridge: Cambridge University Press.
———. 1997. "The Improvisational Performance of "Culture" in Real-Time Discursive Practice." In *Creativity in Performance*, edited by Robert Keith Sawyer, 265–312. Greenwich, CT: Ablex.
———. 1998. "Contemporary Transformations of Local Linguistic Communities." *Annual Review of Anthropology* 27:401–426.
———. 2003. "Indexical Order and the Dialectics of Sociolinguistic Life." *Language and Communication* no. 23 (3–4): 193–229.
———. 2004. "'Cultural' Concepts and the Language-Culture Nexus." *Current Anthropology* 45 (5): 621–652.
———. 2005. "Axes of Evals: Token vs. Type Interdiscursivity." *Journal of Linguistic Anthropology* 15 (1): 6–22.
———. 2013. "Discourse and the No-thing-ness of Culture." *Signs and Society* 1 (2): 327–366.
Silverstein, Michael, and Greg Urban, eds. 1996. *Natural Histories of Discourse*. Chicago: University of Chicago Press.
Singer, Milton. 1955. "The Cultural Pattern of Indian Civilization: A Preliminary Report of a Methodological Field Study." *Far Eastern Quarterly* 15 (1): 23–36.
———. 1958. "From the Guest Editor." *Journal of American Folklore* 71 (281): 191–204.
———. 1972. *When a Great Tradition Modernizes: An Anthropological Approach to Indian Civilization*. New York: Praeger.
Smith, Etienne P. 2006. "La Nation 'par le côté.'" *Cahiers D'Etudes Africaines* 184:907–965.
Smith, Neil. 1992. "Contours of a Spatialized Politics: Homeless Vehicles and the Production of Geographical Scale." *Social Text* 33:54–81.
———. 1996. "Spaces of Vulnerability: The Space of Flows and the Politics of Scale." *Critique of Anthropology* 16:63–77.
———. 2004. "Scale Bending and the Fate of the National." In *Scale and Geographic Inquiry: Nature, Society, and Method*, edited by E. Sheppard and R. B. McMaster. Malden, MA: Blackwell.
Springen, Donald K. 1991. *William Jennings Bryan: Orator of Small-Town America*. New York: Greenwood Press.
Springer, Simon. 2014. "Human Geography without Hierarchy." *Progress in Human Geography* 38:402–419.
Stasch, Rupert. 2011. "Ritual and Oratory Revisited: The Semiotics of Effective Action." *Annual Review of Anthropology* 40:159–174.
Statistics Canada. 2012. *Statistics Canada Catalogue no. 92–142–XWE*. Ottawa, Ontario: Statistics Canada.

Steedman, Carolyn Kay. 1987. *Landscape for a Good Woman: A Story of Two Lives.* New Brunswick, NJ: Rutgers University Press.
Strathern, Marilyn. 2004. *Partial Connections.* Walnut Creek, CA: AltaMira Press.
Summerfield, Craig. 1993. "Color as a Trademark and the Mere Color Rule: The Circuit Split for Color Alone." *Chicago-Kent Law Review* 68 (2): 973–1003.
Sunder Rajan, Kaushik, and Sabina Leonelli. 2013. "Introduction: Biomedical Trans-actions, Postgenomics, and Knowledge/Value." *Public Culture* 25 (3): 463–476.
Suslak, Dan. 2009. "The Sociolinguistic Problem of Generations." *Language and Communication* 29:199–209.
Swyngedouw, Erik. 1997. "Neither Global nor Local: 'Globalization' and the Politics of Scale." In *Spaces of Globalization: Reasserting the Power of the Local,* edited by Keven Cox, 137–166. New York: Guilford Press.
———. 2004. "Globalisation or 'Glocalization'?: Networks, Territories, and Rescaling." *Cambridge Review of International Affairs* 17 (1): 25–48.
———. 2010. "Place, Nature, and the Question of Scale: Interrogating the Production of Nature." *Diskussionspapier 5.* Berlin: Brandenburgische Akademieder Wissenschaften.
Talbot, P. Amaury. (1926) 1969. *The Peoples of Southern Nigeria: A Sketch of Their History, Ethnology and Languages with an Abstract of the 1921 Census.* Vol. 4, *Linguistics and Statistics.* London: Frank Cass.
Tambar, Kabir. 2009. "Secular Populism and the Semiotics of the Crowd in Turkey." *Public Culture* 21:517–537.
Tambiah, Stanley. 1981. *A Performative Approach to Ritual.* London: British Academy.
———. 1996. *Leveling Crowds.* Berkeley: University of California Press.
Taylor, Peter J. 1982. "A Materialist Framework for Political Geography." *Transactions of the Institute of British Geographers* 7 (1): 15–34.
Thomson, Basil. 1894. *Diversions of a Prime Minister.* London: Blackwell.
Tigar, Michael E., and Madeleine R. Levy. 1977. *Law and the Rise of Capitalism.* New York: Monthly Review Press.
The Tonga Magistrates Bench Book. 2004. Pacific Islands Legal Information Institute. www.paclii.org/to/other/tonga-magistrates-court-bench-book-2004.pdf.
Tsai, Julie. 2005. "Fashioning Protection: A Note on the Protection of Fashion Designs in the United States." *Lewis and Clark Law Review* 9 (2): 447–468.
Tsing, Anna Lowenhaupt. 2000. "The Global Situation." *Cultural Anthropology* 15 (3): 327–60.
———. 2005. *Friction: An Ethnography of Global Connection.* Princeton, NJ: Princeton University Press.
———. 2012. "On Nonscalability: The Living World Is Not Amenable to Precision-Nested Scales." *Common Knowledge* 18 (3): 505–524.
———. 2015. *The Mushroom at the End of the World: On the Possibility of Life in Capitalist Ruins.* Princeton, NJ: Princeton University Press.
Tu, Kevin. 2010. "Counterfeit Fashion: The Interplay between Copyright and Trademark Law in Original Fashion Designs and Designer Knockoffs." *Texas Intellectual Property Law Journal* 18 (3): 419–449.
Tushnet, Rebecca. 2012. "Second Circuit Tries Again on 'Use as a Mark,'" Rebecca Tushnet's 43(B)log. September 5, 2012. http://tushnet.blogspot.com/2012/09/second-circuit-tries-again-on-use-as.html.

Urban, Greg. 1990. "Ceremonial Dialogues in South America." In *The Interpretation of Dialogue*, edited by Tullio Maranhão, 99–119. Chicago: University of Chicago Press.

———. 1991. *A Discourse-Centered Approach to Culture: Native South American Myths and Rituals*. Texas Linguistics Series. Austin: University of Texas Press.

Walsh, Michael. 2005. "Will Indigenous Languages Survive?" *Annual Review of Anthropology* 34:293–315.

Weber, Max. 1951. *The Religion of China: Confucianism and Taoism*. Glencoe, IL: Free Press.

Webster, Anthony K. 2011. "'Please Read Loose': Intimate Grammars and Unexpected Languages in Contemporary Navajo Literature." *American Indian Culture and Research Journal* 35 (2): 61–86.

Weikart, Maurice A. 1944. "Design Piracy." *Indiana Law Journal* 19 (3): 235–257.

Whicher, George F. 1953. *William Jennings Bryan and the Campaign of 1896*. Boston: D. C. Heath.

Whitington, Jerome. 2010. "Book Review: 'Alien Ocean: Anthropological Voyages in Microbial Seas' by Stefan Helmreich." *Cultural Anthropology* 25:165–169.

Williams, R. Hal. 2010. *Realigning America: McKinley, Bryan, and the Remarkable Election of 1896*. Lawrence: University Press of Kansas.

Williams, Raymond. 1983. *Keywords: A Vocabulary of Culture and Society*. New York: Oxford University Press.

Willis, Paul. 1977. *Learning to Labour: How Working-Class Kids Get Working-Class Jobs*. New York: Columbia University Press.

———. 1981. "Cultural Production Is Different from Cultural Reproduction Is Different from Social Reproduction Is Different from Reproduction." *Interchange* 12 (2–3): 48–67.

———. 1983. "Cultural Production and Theories of Reproduction." In *Race, Class and Education*, edited by Len Barton and Stephanie Walker, 107–138. London: Croom Helm.

Wirtz, Kristina. 2014. *Performing Afro-Cuba: Image, Voice, Spectacle in the Making of Race and History*. Chicago: University of Chicago Press.

Wong, Mitchell. 1998. "The Aesthetic Functionality Doctrine and the Law of Trade-Dress Protection." *Cornell Law Review* 83 (4): 1116–1167.

Wortham, Stanton. 2001. *Narratives in Action*. New York: Teacher's College Press.

———. 2006. *Learning Identity*. Cambridge: Cambridge University Press.

———. 2012. "Special Issue: Beyond Macro and Micro in the Linguistic Anthropology of Education." *Anthropology and Education Quarterly* 43.

Yaneva, Albena. 2005. "Scaling Up and Down: Extraction Trials in Architectural Design." *Social Studies of Science* 35 (6): 867–894.

Zuckermann, Ghil'ad, and Michael Walsh. 2011. "Stop, Revive, Survive: Lessons from the Hebrew Revival Applicable to the Reclamation, Maintenance and Empowerment of Aboriginal Languages and Cultures." *Australian Journal of Linguistics* 31 (1): 111–127.

CONTRIBUTORS

RICHARD BAUMAN is Distinguished Professor Emeritus of Anthropology and Folklore at Indiana University, Bloomington. The principal foci of his research include narrative, oral poetics, performance, genre, and language ideologies. He has done fieldwork in Scotland, Nova Scotia, Texas, and Mexico, historical research on early Quakers and medieval Iceland, and is currently engaged in research on the metapragmatics of early commercial sound recordings. Among his publications are *Verbal Art as Performance* (1977), *Let Your Words Be Few* (1983), *Story, Performance, and Event* (1986), *Voices of Modernity* (with Charles L. Briggs, 2003; 2006 Edward Sapir Prize), and *A World of Others' Words* (2004).

E. SUMMERSON CARR is Associate Professor in the School of Social Service Administration at the University of Chicago, where she is also an affiliate of the Department of Anthropology, the Department of Comparative Human Development, and the Center for Gender Studies. She is author of *Scripting Addiction: The Politics of Therapeutic Talk and American Sobriety* (Princeton University Press, 2011; 2012 Edward Sapir Prize), and is currently writing a second monograph—titled *Motivating Apprentices: Science, Spirit, and the Institution of American Expertise*—based on her research on the dramatic spread of an American behavioral therapy called motivational interviewing.

BROOKE FISHER holds a BA from Duke University and an AM in Social Service Administration from the University of Chicago. Interested in social welfare interventions in times of disasters and "mega-events," she has previously published work on the intersections between social welfare and crime control policy in Rio de Janeiro's favelas, before the 2014 World Cup and 2016 Olympic Games. Currently researching and cowriting a book on the ambiguities of structural, state, and interpersonal violence in the United States, she plans to initiate doctoral studies so as to pursue her interests in the culture and ethics of social welfare interventions.

SUSAN GAL is Mae and Sidney G. Metzl Distinguished Service Professor in the Departments of Anthropology and Linguistics at the University of Chicago. She is the author of *Language Shift* and coauthor of *The Politics of Gender after Socialism*. As coeditor of *Languages and Publics: The Making of Authority*, and in numerous articles, she has written about the political economy of language and the semiotics of linguistic differentiation. Her continuing ethnographic work in eastern Europe explores the relationship between linguistic practices, power relations, and the construction of social life.

JUDITH T. IRVINE is Edward Sapir Professor of Linguistic Anthropology at the University of Michigan. Her research has focused on language and communication in social, cultural, and historical context, with particular attention to how communicative practices both shape and reflect ideology and social hierarchy. She has done ethnographic, linguistic, and sociolinguistic fieldwork in Africa, mainly in Senegal but also other parts of the continent. In addition to publications resulting from those research efforts, and theoretically oriented works on ideologies of language (especially in conversation with Susan Gal), she is the author of many articles on the colonial history of African linguistics.

MICHAEL LEMPERT is Associate Professor of Anthropology at the University of Michigan in Ann Arbor and Fellow at the Center for Advanced Study in the Behavioral Sciences at Stanford University. He was formerly Assistant Professor of Linguistics at Georgetown University and visiting professor at l'École des hautes études en sciences sociales (EHESS) in Paris. He is author of *Discipline and Debate: The Language of Violence in a Tibetan Buddhist Monastery* (University of California Press, 2012; 2013 Clifford Geertz Prize) and coauthor (with Michael Silverstein) of *Creatures of Politics: Media, Message, and the American Presidency* (Indiana University Press, 2012). He is currently working on a genealogy of face-to-face interaction, tracing how interaction became an object of knowledge in twentieth-century social science.

BARBRA MEEK is Associate Professor of Anthropology and Linguistics at the University of Michigan in Ann Arbor, where she is also an affiliate of Native American Studies. She is author of *We Are Our Language: An Ethnography of Language Revitalization in a Northern Athabaskan Community* (Arizona Press, 2010). Her current research and teaching focuses on representations and performances of linguistic difference in the management of social inequality. She also continues to work on projects in the Yukon Territory in collaboration with colleagues at the University of British Columbia, teachers and administrators at the Department of Education (Yukon), and Dene First Nations.

CONSTANTINE V. NAKASSIS is Assistant Professor of Anthropology at the University of Chicago. His ethnographic research, conducted in south India, has focused on youth culture and mass media. This research is the subject of his book, *Doing Style: Youth and Mass Mediation in South India* (University of Chicago Press, 2016), as well as a number of articles published in *Current Anthropology, Cultural Anthropology, American Anthropologist, Journal of Linguistic Anthropology, Anthropological Quarterly*, and *Contributions to Indian Society*, among other journals. He is currently working on a second research project on the ontology and performativity of the film image in commercial Tamil cinema.

SUSAN U. PHILIPS is Professor Emerita of Anthropology at the University of Arizona. She is author of *The Invisible Culture: Communication in Classroom and Community on the

Warm Springs Indian Reservation, and *Ideology in the Language of Judges: How Judges Practice Law, Politics and Courtroom Control*. Her ongoing research interests include Tongan language use in and out of courts in public settings in the Kingdom of Tonga, with a current focus on Tongan chiefly speech, a lexical honorific speech register.

MICHAEL SILVERSTEIN, on the faculty of the University of Chicago since 1970, is Charles F. Grey Distinguished Service Professor of Anthropology, Linguistics, and Psychology, and Director of the Center for the Study of Communication and Society. He has done linguistic and ethnographic fieldwork with Native North Americans in the Pacific Northwest of the United States and among Wororas and related Northern Kimberley groups in Western Australia. Silverstein's recent work has addressed the transformation of local speech communities by forces of globalization, nationalism, and mass-mediatization, powerful social institutions shaping—and shaped by—language and its use in our own society's discursive universe.

INDEX

Aboriginal Language Services [ALS] (Yukon Territory), 70, 73–74, 75; disbanding of, 88n2; funding of, 79, 88n1; *A Profile of the Aboriginal Languages of the Yukon*, 76
Actor Network Theory, 4
advertising: semiosis of, 209–10; visual codes of, 204
affordances, 43, 188, 210n2
Africa, 16, 217–18
Agate Beach, Oregon, 15, 138, 139, 143
aggregation, 11
Alien Oceans (Helmreich, 2009), 5, 146, 155n31
analogy, 3, 18, 94, 103, 110
anchor categories, 96
anthropology, 5, 8; linguistic, 6, 62, 68, 162; ontological turn in, 145; semiotic, 62
Appadurai, Arjun, 5
Argonauts of the Western Pacific (Malinowski), 213–15, 222, 230n1
Aristotle, 58
Armstrong, Robert Plant, 34, 35
aura: Bryan's campaign oratory and, 34–39; recorded oratory and auratic presence, 44–48
Austin Lounge Lizards, 228–29
Au-Tomotive Gold v. Volkswagen et al. (2006), 175–78, 176, 183n27

Bakhtin, Mikhail, 6, 210n1, 228
balance scale, 17

Bauman, Richard, 11
bending, 4, 19
Benjamin, Walter, 34, 208
Bible, 32, 220
biodiversity, 86
blockage, 101, 104
Blommaert, Jan, 7, 87
Boehlert, George, 149
Bóly (Hungary), town of, 15, 99; "farmer" and "artisan" as person-types in, 96–97, 98; liberal intellectuals in Budapest and, 106, 107; rural capitalism in, 105–6
boundary-making, 54
Bourdieu, Pierre, 18, 69n3, 188, 209
brand identity, 162, 170, 172, 173
brand image, 165, 180n6
bridging, 19
Broadbent, Sir Michael, 189, 190, 191, 192, 194, 198
Broffenbrenner, Urie, 13
Brown, Kate, 147–48
Bryan, Mary, 26–27, 31
Bryan, William Jennings, 10, 11, 27, 48–49; aura and oratory on campaign trail, 34–39; "Bryan Windows," 45; "Cross of Gold" speech, 28, 29, 31; as orator, 26–29; phonographic scaling in presidential campaign (1908), 40–44, 41; recorded oratory and auratic presence, 44–48; at Scopes trial, 26; whistle-stop presidential campaign (1896), 29–34, 31, 34, 43, 49

255

Buddhism, Tibetan, 55, 66; as religion of "reason," 65; "textbook" (*yig cha*) literature, 58, 59–60. *See also* debate (*rstod pa*); Geluk sect
built environment, 10, 14, 62
bureaucracies, 75, 114, 143
Burke, Robert, 166
Burnaby, Barbara, 73

Cabranes, Judge José A., 173
Callon, Michel, 4, 5
Canadian Multiculturalism Act (1988), 73
capitalism, 8, 94, 187; Cold War and, 107, 108; consumptive class in late capitalism, 208; in Hungary during Cold War, 105–106, 109; ideologized "view from nowhere" and, 96
Carr, Summerson, 14, 15, 16, 168
cartographies, 5
celebrative events, 33
celebrity, 35, 36, 39, 48
census-taking, 216–17, 221, 230n4
centrality, 3
Chapman, John, 140–42, 144
charisma, 35, 36
Chesterton, G. K., 171
Choy, Timothy, 6
Christian Louboutin v. Yves Saint Laurent [CL v. YSL] (2012), 159, 167–170, 180n1; appellate (Second Circuit) court's decision, 173–75, 178, 183n26, 184n32; as clash of scalar arguments, 170, 174; Whitman invoked in Judge Marrero's decision, 171–73, 180
Christian Louboutin v. Zara, 170
chronotopes, 186–87, 188, 198–203, 210n1
class, 11, 29, 208, 209
coffee, "vinification" of, 204–207, 205, 212n15
Cold War, 93, 106, 107, 108, 154n9
Coletta, Paolo E., 31–32
Collins, Lauren, 159
commodities, 10, 107, 125; capitalist/communist distinction and, 107, 110; commodity fetishism, 208; consumable, 185; lifestyle, 198–99; status, 20; trademarks and, 162–66, 181n7
communism, 106, 107, 108, 110
community, 19, 38, 196, 221, 225; autonomy of, 106; Canadian aboriginal, 75, 81; celebrative events and, 33; of endangered language, 87; imagined community, 13; of practice, 197; registers in, 212n11; scientific, 141; Tibetan Buddhist exile community in India, 67; Tongan courts and, 121, 125
connoisseurship, 185, 186, 188, 189, 191, 197, 198; applied science and, 201; commodity fetishism and, 208
conspiracy narratives, 7
contextualization and recontextualization, 44, 45, 46, 49, 206; of experience, 92; fractal distinctions and, 105
copresence, 30, 33, 47, 49; bodily, 186; ecology of, 25
copyright, 163, 164, 165, 181n10; fashion design excluded from, 166, 169; legal doctrine of "separability" and, 181n8
Cultural Anthropology (journal), 6

Dalai Lama, 12, 56, 64, 65, 66, 69n9
debate (*rtsod pa*), in Tibetan Buddhism: challenger and defendant roles, 57–58, 63; dimensions of, 55–56; redistributed off the courtyard, 59–61; rescaled as diasporic pedagogy, 64–67; as rite of institution, 61, 69n3; scalar assemblages and, 62–64
de-escalation, 15, 135, 136, 146–47, 152, 154n9
deictics, 37, 39, 44, 50n12, 101
De Jong, Ferdinand, 226
democracy, 11
Dewey, John, 9
dialectic, 19, 53, 64, 197–98, *197*
differentiation, 111n6, 196, 231n17; of commodities, 181n7; farmer-artisan divide, 101; fractal recursivity and, 96, 97; linguistic, 222, 223; register, 230n1; semiotics of, 92; of Tongan courts, 114
Distinction (Bourdieu, 1984), 188
Drayton, Michael, 32
Dreyfus, Georges, 59, 61
Durkheim, Émile, 57, 62, 63

earthquakes, 133, 135, 154n7
ecologies, 10, 134, 199
Edison, Thomas A., 40
elevation, 3
embedding, 54
encompassment, 91, 92, 223; fractal recursivity and, 98, 223; ideology and, 223, 224; relative, 104; rescaling of indigenous languages and, 71; token/type relation and, 16, 222; vertical, 17
Enlightenmet, European, 12, 209

enregisterment, 196, 207; semiotics of, 188; verbal, 187, 208; wine talk (oinoglossia) and, 198, 199, 202. *See also* register
Ethnologue catalogue, 220
event boundaries, 6, 9

Fanon, Franz, 104, 110
Farley, Mark, 152
farmer–artisan divide, 15, 96–97, 99–100; "authenticity" and, 98, 100, 101; categories of identity and, 101–102; farmer language and artisan language, 97, 98, 102; nationalism and, 104; stereotypes and, 97, 98, 101, 103, 106; story-telling and, 105
Fear of Small Numbers (Appadurai, 2006), 5
feminism, 4
Ferguson, James, 5
First Nations, of Canada, 70, 71, 74, 86; dependent relationship upon nation, 82; devolution process and, 71, 75, 78, 80, 87, 88n2; self-determination of, 75, 78
Fisher, Brooke, 14, 15
Fleischer Studios v. A.V.E.L.A. (2011), 175
Foucault, Michel, 19
fractal recursivity, 63, 93, 94, 95; analogies and, 94, 110; blockage of, 101; Hungarian economy and, 108; ideological construction of, 96–98; perspectival (point-of-view) features of, 92, 98; scale-making as, 222; standard metrics and, 98–101
French language and dialects, 221–22, 230n9
Friction (Tsing, 2008), 5
functionality, trademarks and, 163, 164–66, 169, 170, 180n3; aesthetic function as unavoidable, 175–78, *176*; avoidance of aesthetic functionality, 173–75; interscalarity and, 179

Gábor, István R., 109
Gal, Susan, 15, 222
Galasi, Péter, 109
Geluk sect, 12, 56, 58, 59, 65, 66, 68n2. *See also* Buddhism, Tibetan; debate (*rstod pa*)
gender, 4, 11, 202–203
genre, 120, 207; Bryan's oratory and, 36, 37, 43, 49; bureaucratic, 82; corporate-specific formulas, 206; speech genres, 117, 118, 123; wine talk (oinoglossia) and, 187, 188, 192, 198, 201, 204
geography, 4, 21, 156
German language, 15, 16, 99, 102; "artisan" and "farmer" registers of, 97, 101; as mother tongue, 99, 111n9

globalization, 5, 6
Gluckman, Max, 61
Goffman, Erving, 26, 32, 33, 52, 53, 67–68
Great Britain, 115, 117, 129
Great East Japan Earthquake and Tsunami (March 2011), 133, 147
Grégoire, Abbé, 221
Guyer, Jane, 17

Habermas, Jürgen, 49–50
Hans Rausing Endangered Languages Project, 76
Haraway, Donna, 145, 146
Hatfield Marine Science Center (HMSC), 140, 145, 154n12; Misawa dock exhibition at, 138, 149, *150–51*, 151–52; scaling by synecdoche and, 135
Havel, Chris, 133–34, 136, 149, 152
Hearst, William Randolph, 40, 42
Helmreich, Stefan, 5, 6, 146, 147, 155n31
hierarchies, 3, 10, 113, 231n12
Hill, Jane H., 76
Hobbes, Thomas, 22
homology, 61
Hughes, Charles Evans, 42
Hungarian language, 15, 16, 97, 99, 102
Hungary, 106, 107–10
Hynek, J. Allen, 142, 155n39

Ibibio language, 219, 220, 230n5
"Ideal Republic, An" (Bryan speech, 1900), 40, 43
identity, 53, 75
ideology, 91, 92, 217, 227, 230; encompassment and, 223; as interpretive practice, 214; languages and, 95, 111n5, 220, 223, 225, 229; "textual ideology," 60–61; token/type relationships and, 222; as "view from nowhere," 92, 96
Igbo language, 219, 220, 230nn6–7
immediacy, 25, 46, 48
"Immortality" (Bryan speech), 40, 43
indexical relation, 35, 94, 165, 180n5, 203, 211n5; linguistic folk consciousness and, 195; "second order," 187–88, 208–209, 210; source-indexicality, 159, 163, 175, 178, 179; tiered and dialectical, 197–98, *197*
infrastructures, semiotic, 95, 111n4
institutions, 3, 4, 17, 58, 112, 119, 203; anthropology and, 5; bigness associated with, 216; connoisseurship and, 188, 198; enregisterment and, 199; European colonial imposition of, 114; hierarchical scaling

of, 113; ideology and, 216; interscaling and, 12–16, 112, 127, 131; legitimacy of, 61; presence and, 26; rescaling and, 20; rite of institution, 55, 61, 63, 64, 69n3; scalability and power of, 131; scalar logics and, 16, 153; as systems of interaction, 131n1; in Tonga, 126; transnational, 114, 129, 130

intellectual property, 162, 163–64, 165, 181n9, 181n11

interaction, 53–54; (re)scaling of, 55, 67–68; face-to-face, 52, 53, 64

interaction order, 25, 55, 68; Bryan's oratory and, 31, 36, 39; defined, 26; face-to-face encounters and, 52, 53

International Trademark Association, 173

interscaling, 12–16, 112–13, 122–25, 131; defined, 134; Misawa dock and, 136–39, 147

intertextuality, 6, 44, 68, 69n5

Irvine, Judith T., 16, 92

Italian language and dialects, 221, 223–24, 231n11

jaam (Wolof: "slave"/"cross-cousin"), 224–27, 231n12, 231n14, 231n16

James, William, 9

Jameson, Fredric, 7

Jensen, Richard, 49

Job, Book of, 20, 21

jumping, 4, 7, 19, 54

Kaska language group, 12–13, 77, 78, 80; Athabaskan/Dene, 82, 83; generations of speakers, 87; as "mother tongue," 81; scaling of fluency in, 84–85, 85; sociolinguistic situation of, 82

Kazin, Michael, 35, 39

Kohn, Eduardo, 146

Krugman, Paul, 94–95

Kubrick, Stanley, 141, 145

Labov, William, 196, 231n11

language, 3, 21n2, 52, 61, 189; bilingual court procedures in Tonga, 14, 113, 118, 121, 131nn3–4; census-taking and, 217–18; ethnicity and language in Nigeria, 218–220; globalization and, 6–7; ideology and, 95, 111n5; indexical variability and, 195; linguistic nationalism, 104; multilingualism, 218, 230n1, 231n16; origin of, 8; registers and, 186, 187, 195–98, 210–11n3, 211n10, 212n11; scalar issues in lexical denotation, 224–28; scaled language use in Tongan courts, 118–19; standards and dialects, 220–24; taxonomies of, 95

languages, indigenous, 13, 70–71, 80–85; charting fluency in, 76–80, 77, 84–85; child speakers of, 79; community and, 20; endangered status of, 70, 71–73, 86; "mother tongue," 72, 81; recognition of "aboriginal languages," 73–75

Lanham Act (1946), 162, 181n13

Latour, Bruno, 4, 5, 53–54, 216; flat imaginary of, 111n2; on "flatness," 163

Lempert, Michael, 12

Likert scales, 12

linguistics, 10, 52

linking, 19

logbooks, nautical, 143, 156n41

longue durée, 4

Louboutin, Christian, 159, 167; brand identity of, 162, 170, 172, 173; injunction filed against YSL, 160, 162, 168; "lacquered red sole" mark of, 159, 160, 172, 178, 182n18; popularity of Louboutin's red shoes, 167–68

Louis Vuitton v. Dooney & Bourke (2008), 175

Magistrate's Courts, of Tonga, 113, 119, 125, 132n7; "bush lawyers" and licensed lawyers in, 117, 131n6; constitution of Tonga and, 114; interscaling of seriousness in, 122–24; jurisdictional areas for, 120–21; lawyers in, 128; police prosecutor in, 115

Magritte, René, 192

Malinowski, Bronislaw, 16, 213–15, 222, 229, 230n1

Manning, Paul, 206

Mantini-Briggs, Charles and Clara, 7

maps, 3, 93–94

Marrero, Judge Victor, 171–73, 174, 175, 180, 182n19, 183n26

Marx, Karl, 208

Mauss, Marcel, 57, 62, 63

McConnell, Mark, 149, 151–52

McKinley, William, 37

measurement, 19

Meek, Barbara, 12, 13, 118

Meek, C. M., 218–19

Melville, Herman, 1, 3, 20, 168

memes, 192

mensural scales, 12–13

micro-macro distinction, 4, 8–9, 10, 19, 111n1, 215; ideology and, 216; linguistic topics and, 229; "meso"-level distinctions and, 53; "nested," 13

INDEX

Misawa (Japan), town of, 15, 133
Misawa dock, washed ashore in Oregon, 15, 133–35, 152–53; de-escalation of, 146–47, 152; dimensions of, 136–37; HMSC exhibition of, 149, *150–51*, 151–52; media coverage of, 136–37, *137*, 145, 154n12; official management of awe and logging of, 143–45; production of awe in metaphoric scaling of, 140–42; sea creatures attached to, 134, 135, 138–39, 140, 144; as tourist attraction, 137–38, 143
Moby-Dick (Melville), 1–3
models, 93–96, 111nn2–3
Moore, Robert, 87, 88n4
Morgan, Mary S., 111n3
Morrison, Margaret, 111n3
Mukerji, Chandra, 146
Murabayashi, Hirofumi, 149

Nakassis, Constantine, 17
nation-states, 5, 71, 80, 163; communities and, 3; European colonizers' constitution of, 114; indigenous languages and, 70, 86; multilingual, 7; official languages of, 74; transnational cases in Tongan courts and, 125, 128, 130
New Zealand, 115, 117, 118
Nigeria, 218–221, 230nn4–7

object status, 20
Occupy Movement, 6
oratory, 26–29, 48; aura and oratory on Bryan campaign trail, 34–39; live oratory interrupted by applause, 47; recorded oratory and auratic presence, 44–48
Oregon Parks and Recreation Department (OPRD), 143–45, 146, 149

panorama, scalar model as, 72, 78
Parker, Robert, 194, 198, 209
Parmentier, Richard, 210
parody, 228–230
part-whole scale, 13
patent, 163, 164, 165, 166, 169
Patrick, Donna, 86
Peirce, Charles Sanders, 9, 62, 94, 142, 190; on affective interpretant, 208; on indexical relations, 180n5
performance, 25, 33, 48; auratic, 34, 36, *37*, 49; technologically mediated, 47
performativity, 66–67, 178; debate as rite of institution, 61; interscalar, 55, 62; scalar, 163–64

perspective (point of view), 3, 20, 104, 228; fractal recursivity and, 96, 98, 110; ideology and, 92–93, 105, 214, 227, 230; parody and, 228–230; perspectival nature of scale, 15
Philips, Susan, 14
phonograph, 11, 46–49; phonographic scaling in Bryan campaign (1908), 40–44, *41*; as technology of home entertainment, 45
placement, 62, 63, 67, 68
Planck, Max, 96
platform events, 25, 32
political economy, 8, 38
posthumanism, 145–46, 147, 149, 151, 152
Power, Cormac, 34
Prentice, Michael, 76
presence, 34, 42; auratic, 34, 44–48; metaphysics of, 25
Primitive Classification (Durkheim and Mauss, 1963), 61, 62
"Prince of Peace, The" (Bryan lecture), 40

qualia, 189, 192, 194, 204, 208; advertising semiosis and, 210; applied science and, 209; defined, 187
Qualitex v. Jacobson, 167, 171, 181n11

race, 11
railroads, Bryan presidential candidacy and, 30, *31*, 43, 49
Rampton, Ben, 87
register, 186, 207, 222, 230n1; community and, 212n11; language and, 186, 187, 195–98, 210–11n3, 211n10; speech registers, 101, 118. *See also* enregisterment
rescaling, 18, 55, 66, 94; of indigenous languages, 71; indigenous languages and, 83
risk management, 15
ritual, 10, 19, 55, 62, 111n3; Buddhist debate as rite of institution, 61, 63; Buddhist debate as ritual site, 61; cross-scalar work of, 64; interactional, 54; rite of institution, 69n3; ritual authority, 4; rituals of rebellion, 61

Saint Laurent, Yves, 160
Saussure, Ferdinand de, 52
scale, 42, 48, 64; definition of, 9; ethnography of, 7; ideology and, 16, 91, 92; institutionalized, 3–4, 17; of interaction, 54; logistics of, 33; metric and, 215, 230n2; perspective and, 15, 214; problems of, 4–7, 25; qualitative contrasts and, 104; quality of, 163–64;

scale-making as encompassment, 222; semiotic processes and, 91, 93; temporal, 20; wine culture and, 194
scale, pragmatics of, 9–11, 12, 15, 17, 19; communicative labor and, 55; communicative practices and, 110; mediation of Misawa dock and, 135, 136; metapragmatics of scale, 162–63, 172, 179, 182n22; Misawa dock and, 143, 149; perspective and, 14; superordinate analysis and, 20; trademark law and, 162; unintended, 85–87
scaling, 15, 54, 94; color as mark, 166–171; comparison as basis of, 110; dimensions of scaling in Tongan courts, 116–122; interaction order and, 52; oratorical scaling in Bryan presidential campaign, 29–34; perspective (point of view) and, 3, 91, 146, 153; phonographic scaling in Bryan campaign (1908), 40–44, *41*; predatory, 16–17; of quality, 163–64, 170; spatial, 120, 121, 130; spatiotemporal relations and, 2. *See also* rescaling
Schotte, Margaret, 156n41
Schulz, Kathryn, 135, 154n7
science studies, 4
Scopes trial (1925), 26
semiotics/semiosis, 8, 147, 198, 203; of differentiation, 92; ideology and, 214; judgments of taste and, 186–88; models as diagrammatic icons, 93; of register, 188; trademarks as semiotic types, 183n28. *See also* signs
Sera monastery (India), 55–56, 59, 61, 63, 67, 68n2
Serer ethnic group, 224–27
Shakespeare, William, 32
signs, 10, 62, 94, 203–204; fixation of, 182n20; metasigns and, 179; micro-macro distinction and, 8–9. *See also* semiotics
Silverstein, Michael, 17–18
Smith, Etienne P., 226
Smith, Neil, 4
social actors, 3, 4, 9, 13, 107; contextual boundaries and, 10; interscalability and, 14; language endangerment/rehabilitation and, 86, 87; orienting of, 19, 20, 187; a-perspectival models and, 93; scalar projects and, 11
sociolinguistics, 6, 21n2, 222; indigenous languages and, 70–71, 73, 74, 76, 81, 82; semiotics of consumptive class and, 208; verbal registers and, 195
sociology, 4, 52, 145, 208

source-indexing, 159, 163, 175, 178, 179
Soviet Union, 107
specificity, 6
"speech event," 6, 56, 57
speech genres, in Tongan courts, 117, 123
Strathern, Marilyn, 5
Stupid Texas Song (Austin Lounge Lizards, 1998), 228–29
Supreme Court, of Tonga, 113, 116, 120–21, 126; bilingual procedures in, 113, 118, 121; British judges, 116–17; Crown prosecutor in, 115; interscaling of cases in, 124–25, 132n9; lawyers in, 119
Supreme Court, U.S., 167, 210
Swyngedouw, Erik, 4
synechdoche, scaling by, 134–35, 138, 147, 152

Talbot, P. Amaury, 218–19, 230n4
Tanzer, Stephen, 192, 193, 198
Tāufaʻāhau, chief of Tonga, 114
taxonomies, 96, 101, 104, 191; of categories, 98; of the Cold War, 93; linguistic, 15; of wine aroma terminology, 199, *200*
texuality, 60, 61
Thurber, James, 192, 198
Tobias, Lori, 133
token/type relation, 16, 94, 214, 222
Tonga, trial courts in, 14, 18, 20, 113–14, 129–131; interscaling of higher and lower courts, 112; overview of, 114–16; scaled hierarchical dimensions of, 116–122; seriousness scaled in, 119, 122–25, 128–29; "transnational" discourses and, 125–29, 130. *See also* Magistrate's Courts; Supreme Court, of Tonga
trademark law, 162–63, 180n6; colors and, 166–171; design not protected by, 166; fair use doctrine, 169, 182n15; functionality and, 163, 164–66; interscalarities and, 164, 179; "secondary meaning" and, 167, 181n12, 183n25; trademark as pure index, 175
Trahison des images, La (Magritte painting, 1928–29), 192
"Trust Question, The" (Bryan, recorded speech), 44, 47
Tsing, Anna, 5, 19
Tsongkhapa, 59, 60, 63
Tsunami Evacuation Interpretive Trail (Oregon), 151, *151*
Tushnet, Rebecca, 174, 182n24, 183n26, 183n28
2001: A Space Odyssey (film, 1968, Kubrick), 141–42, *141*, 145, 156n43

UFOs (unidentified flying objects), 142, 155n39
uniform scaling, 13
United States, 16, 50, 118; census in, 216–17; Cold War and, 107; legal system of, 115, 116, 126; linguistic differentiation in, 223, 231n11; popularity of Louboutin's red shoes in, 167–68; trademark and intellectual property law in, 164, 167; wine marketing in, 202; xenophobia and migration in history of, 139
use-values, 185
U.S. Patent and Trademark Office (USPTO), 167, 169, 174, 182n20

Venezuela, cholera epidemics in, 7
vinification, 18, 186, 188, 191, 199, 206. *See also* wine talk (oinoglossia)

Weber, Max, 114
Whitman, Walt, 171, 173, 180
wine culture, 17–18, 185–86
wine talk (oinoglossia), 18, 187, 188, 209; aesthetics of, 188–194, 201; dialectical indexical orders and, 196–97, *197*; intersecting chronotopes and, 198–203; prestige of wine as influence on other comestibles, 202, 203–10, *205*
Wolof people/language, 224–27, 231n12
"Work of Art in the Age of Mechanical Reproduction, The" (Benjamin), 34
world-system theory, 6, 8

Yiddish language, 223
Yukon Territory (Canada), 12–13, 71, 86; aboriginal self-determination in, 75; Umbrella Final Agreement, 75, 79, 80; Yukon Languages Act, 73, 74. *See also* Aboriginal Language Services [ALS]
Yves Saint Laurent (YSL): Cruise collection, 159–160, *161*; lawyers' defense strategy against Louboutin, 168–170, 182n14; monochromatic red shoe of, 160, 168, 174

zooming, 54